Racist Culture

B

For A., who so often saved me from myself;
and for G., that he may recognize and resist.

Racist Culture

Philosophy and the Politics of Meaning

David Theo Goldberg

BLACKWELL
Oxford UK & Cambridge USA

First published 1993

Blackwell Publishers
238 Main Street, Suite 501
Cambridge, Massachusetts 02142
USA

108 Cowley Road
Oxford OX4 1JF
UK

Library of Congress Cataloging in Publication Data

Goldberg, David Theo.
    Racist culture : philosophy and the politics of meaning / David Theo Goldberg.
      p. cm.
    Includes bibliographical references and index.
    ISBN 0–631–18077–X. — ISBN 0–631–18078–8 (pbk.)
    1. Racism. I. Title.
HT1521.G55 1993
305.8—dc20   92–36107
                                                  CIP

British Library Cataloguing in Publication Data

A CIP catalogue record for this book is available from the British Library.

Typeset in 10 on 12 pt. Times Roman by Publication Assistance Center, College of Public Programs, Arizona State University

Printed in Great Britain by Biddles Ltd, Guildford, Surrey.

This book is printed on acid-free paper

Contents

Preface

The prevailing view concerning contemporary racism is that it is something that belongs to the past. Where it is taken to occur at all, it is considered as socially anomalous, as *un*usual, an individual aberration or institutional hangover placed in check as soon as its occurrence is noticed. Anyone extending to racist expression a greater place in contemporary culture than this picture warrants is bound to be considered paranoid—or (as the current charge would have it) politically correct. It is the aim of this book to challenge directly and vigorously this prevailing picture of the place of race, of the role of racist expressions in our culture, and by extension to resist the assumptions on which this view rests.

Any book about race and racism runs the risk of using categories that have long carried objectionable connotations. It is, for example, very difficult to talk in any meaningful way about issues of race in South Africa without using—not just mentioning—the categories in virtue of which *apartheid* expresses itself. Where I find myself having to use these terms, I have tried to be sensitive to the concerns of those objectified by them, and attempting always to place the categories they turn on in question. In this respect, I have largely used 'black' throughout; and where the context makes it especially sensitive I have used 'black' as an adjective qualifying persons. I have used 'African-American' only sparingly, not for ideological reasons or to deny the ongoing dialectic of racial self-identification. The book is about racist expression wherever it manifests, about the conditions for its emergence, expression, and transformation, and not only, sometimes not even primarily about the United States. Like 'white', then, 'black' is employed to reflect (upon) the racializing of referential schema and to draw attention to the discursive interconnections and differences between people so defined and referenced at different times and places.

Many people, some who may not even know it, have helped me to and through the arguments in this book. To all, my deepest gratitude. I read various parts of this work in various fora. I am grateful to the institutions that made this possible, and especially to my hosts on each occasion. Nahum Chandler and Tom Hill hosted an especially helpful session on chapter 7 for the Workshop on the Politics of Race and the Reproduction of Racial Ideologies at the University of Chicago. The gracious invitation of Bob Gooding-Williams, Austin Sarat, and Kristin Bumiller enabled me to benefit from a reading of chapter 8 for the Charles Hamilton Houston Forum, Amherst College. Various portions of the book were improved as a result of readings arranged by Mala Singh and the Philosophy Department at the University of Durban–Westville, Rafael de Kadt and the

Department of Politics at the University of Natal, and Vincent Maphai and the Department of Politics at the University of Western Cape. The conclusion was greatly facilitated by Lou Outlaw and the Committee on Blacks in Philosophy that enabled an exchange with Patricia Williams, Gerald Torres, and Leonard Harris on Critical Race Theory in Law and Philosophy at the American Philosophical Association Meetings, New York, December 1991. Anne Schneider, dean of the College of Public Programs, Arizona State University, kindly funded the research in South Africa that forms chapters 7 and 8. Barbara Lammi, Yang Zhang, and Lance (Chris) Miller graciously produced all the bibliographical references thrust sometimes all too summarily and ungraciously before them. Pietro Toggia was helpful in compiling the index. A close and insightful reading of the concluding chapter by Werner Ernst provoked me into revising it substantially, though I fear insufficiently to meet all of his cogent criticisms. Laurence Thomas, Tommy Lott, Nahum Chandler, and Howard McGary showed me how vigorous criticism can be without compromising much-valued friendship. Pat Lauderdale, my close colleague, collaborator, and critic par excellence, read the entire manuscript, insisting that every idea be clear, every criticism justified, every chapter as rigorous as I had tried to make it vigorous. The book would not have been nearly the same without his sharp eye. Peter Fitzpatrick and Maxim Silverman graciously reviewed the manuscript for the publisher and pushed me to clarify much that I had taken for granted. Peter's incisive critique and suggestions were softened by a guided cycling tour through the Kentish countryside that included a strenuous climb of 'Habermas Hill'.

I take this opportunity also to thank Janet Soper of the Publication Assistance Center, College of Public Programs, Arizona State University, for so rigorously copyediting the manuscript and producing the camera ready copy. Stephan Chambers, my editor at Blackwell's, eased me graciously through the process of producing the book.

Where there are oversights or errors in the text, it is simply because I didn't listen, or heard only what I wished to. Every writer deserves such readers.

Alena and Gabriel suffered my absences and flights of inattention with characteristic comprehension. While it would be untrue to say the book was written only for them, it clearly is true that it would not have been the same without their support. Gabriel's gratifying desire to write books upon growing up rather than be a soldier is perhaps further evidence that the pen is sometimes mightier than the sword.

A Note on Terminological Use

I have followed philosophical convention in italicizing reference to the concept of *race* and in placing between single quotation marks the word 'race' when mentioning (referring to) it.

When I use race in the course of ordinary analysis, I neither italicize it nor place it between single quotation marks. Thus, the word 'race' has been used from the sixteenth century even though the concept of *race* may have predated it, and this book is in part about whether and how races form.

1

Introduction: Racial Subjects

'Individuals may well come and go; it seems that philosophy travels nowhere.' [1]

The subject of social analysis is increasingly being conceived in racial terms. The ambiguities inhering here in the subject of address reflect both what this book is broadly about, its primary subject matter, and what I principally set out to argue. The book focuses on race, both on the variety of its social expressions and implications and on the prevailing understanding of these expressions in contemporary social analysis. My principal argumentative focus is that we have come, if often only silently, to conceive of social subjects foremost in racial terms. The primary definition of social subjectivity has not always been racialized, and where it has, the dominant mode of racialization has not remained constant. Thus, I will argue that racial definition and its attendant forms of racist articulation emerge only with the institution of modernity, and they transform in relation to the principal formative developments in modernity's self-understanding and expression.

Racial thinking and racist articulation have become increasingly normalized and naturalized throughout modernity, but in ways *not simply* determined (as dependent variables) by social conditions at specified times. Conceptual and material logics internal to the emerging (trans)formation(s) of racialized discourse define self-determinants, directing its discursive expressions and implications *in intersection* with the broader sweep of sociohistorical conditions and other sociodiscursive formations. Liberalism plays a foundational part in this process of normalizing and naturalizing racial dynamics and racist exclusions. As modernity's definitive doctrine of self and society, of morality and politics, liberalism serves to legitimate ideologically and to rationalize politico-economically prevailing sets of racialized conditions and racist exclusions. It is thus key in establishing racialized reasoning and its racist implications as central to modernity's common moral and sociopolitical sense. Hence, also, we must acknowledge the role of philosophical discipline in establishing racialized discourse and the culture of racisms, as well as the importance of philosophical analysis in any comprehensive commitment to their disarticulation.

By 'race' and 'racial' I will refer throughout to the various designations of group differentiation invoked in the name of race throughout modernity. The appearance of circularity here, I will argue in chapter 4, is avoidable only in one of two problematic ways: either by wrongfully assuming racial reality or by admitting racial fabrication. I will use 'racialized' to include any and all significance extended both explicitly and silently by racial reference over discursive expression and practice. Further, 'racist' will always be made to invoke those exclusions prompted or promoted by racial reference or racialized significance, whether such exclusions are actual or intended, effects or affects of racial and racialized expression.

The intertwining of personal and social identity is fashioned in terms of the historically prevailing conceptual order. How we comprehend others and conceive our social relations and how we come thus dialectically to some sort of self-understanding are molded by concepts central to the dominant sociodiscursive scheme. The social formation of the subject involves in large part thinking (of) oneself in terms of—literally *as*—the image projected in prevailing concepts of the discursive order. These concepts incorporate disciplinary norms of behavior, rules of interaction, and principles of social organization. The values inherent in these disciplines exercise themselves upon individual and social being as they are assumed, molded, and sometimes transformed in their individual and social articulation. So the social (self-)conception, the identity of the subject, is mediated, if not quite cemented by the set of discursive practices and the values embedded in them.

Commentators usually identify a small set of very fundamental changes of discourse, of worldview and self-image, in the tradition that is commonly considered 'Western': from classical to Christian; from the doctrinal philosophy of an agrarian age—the closed world—to the 'evidence-revering epistemology' of the scientific—the infinite universe;[2] from the industrial and utilitarian nineteenth century to the atomic and electronic twentieth. Each of these shifts involved a range of complex relations. They did not come all of a piece but staggered, a bit at a time. The change from a predominantly bodily form of discipline, for example, from overt violence and brutality to technologies of surveillance and internalized constraint ('the anguish of responsibility') identified so dramatically by Foucault was made possible (as he says) by the emergence of the gaze of scientific epistemology. Yet, this shift is at once a cornerstone of the modern bureaucratic *Weltanschauung*.[3] Slightly more local shifts within these discursive orders respectively include those from early to late medievalism, from the age of doubt to egalitarian enlightenment and emancipatory revolution, and from the certitude of Newtonian mechanics to the relativity of Einstein's general theory and the randomness of quantum. These more finite discursive expressions may themselves constitute smaller discursive fields, in much the way that a large transportation system is divided into zones.

The sum total of these intradiscursive shifts could add up to or prompt transdiscursive alterations. By contrast, very general concepts can stretch across any number of discursive orders, acquiring new interpretations as they assume the values inherent within each, waxing and waning in strength across the stretch of time. This makes sense, for instance, of the 'great chain of being'.[4] The more general the expression, the more ahistorical it pretends to be; so the more malleable and pliant it tends to become, and the more susceptible to theoretical if not practical vacuity. Indeed, the more theoretically fluid the expression, the more will its currency tend to turn on assuming the significance of legitimate and established discursive practices and expressions. These 'chameleonic' concepts are especially dangerous, for they hide their discriminatory or exclusionary significance behind more readily acceptable conceptual schemata.[5] This captures a central feature of the concept of race in modernity. To show just this underlies the general task I have set myself here in mapping racist culture.

Race is one of the central conceptual inventions of modernity. As I suggested above, the concept assumes specificity as modernity defines itself, refining modernity's landscape of social relations as its own conceptual contours are mapped out. The significance of race transforms theoretically and materially as modernity is renewed, refined, and redefined.

By *modernity,* I will mean throughout that general period emerging from the sixteenth century in the historical formation of what only relatively recently has come to be called 'the West'. This general self-understanding becomes self-conscious in the seventeenth century, reaching intellectual and material maturity in the Enlightenment, and solidifies as Western world hegemony the following century. In our own time, what Zygmunt Bauman properly identifies as the ambivalence at the heart of the modern project intensifies to the point of social and intellectual implosion: In searching the frontiers of its own limits, modernity at once erases the conditions of its own possibility as it seeks to pass beyond itself.

The modern project accordingly emerges as and in terms of a broad sweep of sociointellectual conditions. These include the commodification and capital accumulation of market-based society, the legal formation of private property and systems of contract, the moral and political conception of rational self-interested subjects, and the increasing replacement of God and religious doctrine by Reason and Nature as the final arbiters of justificatory appeal in epistemology, metaphysics, and science, as well as in morality, legality, and politics. As Bauman stresses, at the heart of modernity lies the concern with order. This concern is expressed through the domination of Nature by Reason; through the transparency of Nature to Reason in the Laws of Nature; through the classification of Nature in rational systems of thought; and through the mastery of Nature, physical and human, by way of 'design, manipulation, management, engineering'. Modernity manifests itself in the fixing of the social in terms of bureaucracy, of the political in terms of the law, and of the economic in terms of the laws of the market, the hidden hand of Reason. Opacity and obscurity are supposed to give way to the light of rational transparency and precision, the chaotic limits of indeterminacy and ambiguity to the perspicuity of definition, irrationality to the intelligibility of logical regularity, and the contingency of inclination to the absolute certainty of rational (self-)determination. Thus, the spirit of modernity is to be found most centrally in its commitment to continuous progress: to material, moral, physical, and political improvement and to the promotion and development of civilization, the general standards for which the West took to be its own values universalized.[6]

Basic to modernity's self-conception, then, is a notion not of social subjects but of a Subject that is abstract and atomistic, general and universal, divorced from the contingencies of historicity as it is from the particularities of social and political relations and identities. This abstracted, universal Subject commanded only by Reason, precisely because of its purported impartiality, is supposed to mediate the differences and tensions between particular social subjects in the domains of market and morality, polity and legality.

Enter race. It pretends to universality in undertaking to draw otherwise disparate social subjects together into a cohesive unit in terms of which common interests are either found or fabricated. Nevertheless, race undertakes at once to furnish specific identity to otherwise abstract and alienated subjectivities. Sufficiently broad, indeed, almost conceptually empty, race offers itself as a category capable of providing a semblance of social cohesion, of historical particularity, of *given* meanings and motivations to agents otherwise mechanically conceived as conduits for market forces and moral laws. Like the conception of *nation* that emerges more or less coterminously, race proceeds at its inception by arming social subjects with a cohesive identity. It is an identity that proves capable of being stretched across time and space, that itself assumes transforming specificity and legitimacy by taking on as its own the connotations of prevailing scientific and social discourses. In colonizing these prevailing connotations, race in turn has been able to set scientific and political agendas, to contain the content and applicability of Reason, to define who may be excluded and to confine the terms of social inclusion and cohesion.[7]

This is a central paradox, *the* irony perhaps, of modernity: The more explicitly universal modernity's commitments, the more open it is to and the more determined it is by the likes of racial specificity and racist exclusivity. Liberalism, I suggested at the outset, has become the defining doctrine of self and society for modernity. The way in which racial characterizations are articulated in and through, and so come in part to define liberalism, will thus serve to locate this paradox at the center of the modern project.

Philosophical liberalism stretches from identification of some of its conceptual sources by Hobbes and its more self-conscious expression by Locke, through its Enlightenment maturation at the hands of Rousseau and especially Kant, its utilitarian and welfarist formulation in the nineteenth century work of Bentham,

James and John Stuart Mill, to its twentieth century libertarianism in the likes of Von Hayek and Nozick, and its contractarianism in Rawls. There are, of course, deep philosophical differences between social contract theory and libertarianism, deontology and utilitarianism, rights-based and welfarist accounts. Differences notwithstanding, there is a core set of central ideas common in varying degrees to these thinkers and others like them, whether more or less radical or conservative, that identifies them as liberals and marks their modernity. Other cultural strains and ideological expressions were spawned by and matured with modernity. One thinks here of fascism, marxism, and anarchism, to name the most readily recuperable, or futurism, dadaism, and surrealism to recall something like their aesthetic analogues. To the extent that these were at the time of their emergence and height of popularity all marginalized as extreme movements by a self-professed rational and liberal center, movements at the limits of liberal tolerance and sometimes beyond, their possibility reflects the relative hegemony, pervasiveness, and self-confidence of that center's liberalism.

What unites liberals in spite of their deep differences, then, is the core set of general ideas, indeed, of ideas taken at once as basic presuppositions and as ideals. Liberalism is committed to *individualism* for it takes as basic the moral, political, and legal claims of the individual over and against those of the collective. It seeks *foundations* in *universal* principles applicable to all human beings or rational agents in virtue of their humanity or rationality. In this, liberalism seeks to transcend particular historical, social, and cultural differences: It is concerned with broad identities which it insists unite persons on moral grounds, rather than with those identities which divide politically, culturally, geographically, or temporally. The philosophical basis of this broad human identity, of an essentially human nature, is taken to lie in a common rational core within each individual, in the (potential) capacity to be moved by Reason. In keeping with this commitment to the force of reason, liberalism presupposes that all social arrangements may be ameliorated by rational *reform.* Moral, political, economic, and cultural *progress* is to be brought about by and reflected in carefully planned institutional improvement. The mark of progress is measured for liberals by the extent to which institutional improvement serves to extend people's liberty, to open up or extend spaces for free expression. Finally, and for the concern at hand perhaps most significantly, liberalism takes itself to be committed to *equality.* This commitment is open to a wide range of liberal interpretations the particular nature of which distinguishes one form of liberalism from another. Nevertheless, the egalitarian core on which all liberals agree consists in the recognition of a common moral standing, no matter individual differences. From the liberal point of view, particular differences between individuals have no bearing on their moral value, and by extension should make no difference concerning the political or legal status of individuals.[8]

In keeping with these commitments, contemporary moral theorists in the liberal tradition traced back to Hobbes, Locke, and Kant have come to insist that *race* is 'a morally irrelevant category'. A morally irrelevant difference between persons is one they cannot help, for which they thus cannot be held responsible. To count as relevant, the persons in question must have had 'a fair opportunity to acquire or avoid [the property or capacity]'.[9] The property or capacity, in other words, must have been earned. Accordingly, it is basic to the dominant portrait of social identity in modernity that moral subjects must avoid choices that appeal to 'those contingencies [like race] which set men at odds and allow them to be guided by their prejudices'.[10] So widespread is this view, this commitment to the principle of color blindness, that it unites under the liberal banner those as seemingly different as Dinesh D'Souza, on one hand, and Ronald Dworkin, on the other.

Liberalism is self-conscious in its idealization of acceptable social conditions, and no more so than in its consideration of matters racial. By contrast, the historical record of moral appeals to race by many of the greatest intellectual and political figures in the liberal tradition is overwhelming. A few examples will suffice. Kant, citing with approval David Hume's likening of learning by 'negroes' to that of parrots, insisted upon the natural stupidity of blacks. John Stuart Mill, like his father, presupposed nonwhite nations to be uncivilized and so historically incapable of self-government. Benjamin Disraeli captured the sensibility of the mid-nineteenth century by declaring the only truth to be that 'all is race'. The basic human condition—and so economic, political, scientific, and cultural positions—was taken naturally to be race determined. By the turn of the century, Cromer and Balfour, the most important—some would say the greatest—British colonial administrators, took it as a matter of course that Europeans (and the British in particular) were the master race, all others were 'subject races'. More recently, we have come to witness the expression of racism by other means, in terms of seemingly acceptable socioscientific discourses like sociobiology or genetic differences in dispositions to crime or capacity for intelligence, or in terms of overtly neutral political concerns about immigration, welfare, unemployment, and work habits by Tory and Labour politicians, by Republicans and occasionally by Democrats, by Christian Democrats and Socialists in Europe, and by Liberal Democrats in Japan. This deep disjunction between moral idealization and actual racial appeal, between color blindness and racial consciousness, must imply either that morality is irrelevant, that in the case of race it has no force or that liberalism's relative silence concerning racial considerations masks a much more complex set of ideas and experiences than commonly acknowledged.

So the irony of modernity, the liberal paradox comes down to this: As modernity commits itself progressively to idealized principles of liberty, equality, and fraternity, as it increasingly insists upon the moral irrelevance of race, there is a multiplication of racial identities and the sets of exclusions they prompt and rationalize, enable and sustain. Race is irrelevant, but all is race. The more abstract modernity's universal identity, the more it has to be insisted upon, the more it needs to be *imposed*. The more ideologically hegemonic liberal values seem and the more open to difference liberal modernity declares itself, the more dismissive of difference it becomes and the more closed it seeks to make the circle of acceptability.

One would have to be chained permanently behind Rawls's veil of ignorance to fail to notice the dilemma and the social conditions it marks. Nevertheless, liberal modernity seems prepared to respond in only one of two problematic forms. The first is to deny otherness, the otherness it has been instrumental in creating, or at least to deny its relevance. The second seems less extreme, but the effect is identical. Liberals may admit the other's difference, may be moved to *tolerate* it. Yet tolerance, as Susan Mendus makes clear, presupposes that its object is morally repugnant, that it really needs to be reformed, that is, altered.[11] Thus, liberals are moved to overcome the racial differences they tolerate and have been so instrumental in fabricating by diluting them, by bleaching them out through assimilation or integration. The liberal would assume away the difference in otherness, maintaining thereby the dominance of a presumed sameness, the universally imposed similarity in identity. The paradox is perpetuated: The commitment to tolerance turns only on modernity's 'natural inclination' to *in*tolerance; acceptance of otherness presupposes as it at once necessitates 'delegitimation of the other'.[12]

Liberal modernity's response to racism is of a piece with its failing to take race seriously. Racist expressions are generally reduced to personal prejudices of individuals, to irrational appeals to irrelevant categories, to distinctions that delimit universal liberal ideals. This, too, is the paradigm that has prevailed in social science analysis of racism since its inception in the 1930s. Racism is deemed a singular phenomenon, its wrongness to consist merely in individual invocation of the category of race to differentiate between people for distributing goods and power and social status. Racism is considered a premodern prejudice, one that enlightened modern meliorism takes itself to be overcoming through the force of reason. Liberal social scientists may thus admit race as a given, a natural social identity, one that works its way into and between social identities before rationality, before the Age of Reason takes its hold. The concern then shifts to managing 'race relations'. Liberal social science consequently undertakes to identify the individual and intentional causes of racial conflict and the means for its alleviation. One finds this paradigm reflected in the contemporary popular and academic reduction of racial concerns to the irrational prejudices of 'hate crimes' and 'hate offenses', 'white rights' and 'free speech'.

Liberal modernity denies its racialized history and the attendant histories of racist exclusions, hiding them behind some idealized, self-promoting, yet practically ineffectual, dismissal of *race* as a morally irrelevant category. By contrast, indeed, in resistance we might better confront just what it is about the notion of race that since the sixteenth century has both constituted its hold on social relations and prompted thinkers silently to frame their conceptions of morality, polity, and legality in its terms. Liberal meliorism takes it that we have largely progressed beyond these racist social formations of the past. Most contemporary constitutional systems explicitly exclude institutional and public race-based discrimination. Even *apartheid*—for some, 'racism's last word'—appears now to be little more than a dying gasp. Nevertheless, past kinds of racist expression need not exhaust the sorts of exclusions capable of being expressed in the name of race. To assume definitively that there is a racism that has spoken its last word may simply, though perhaps inadvertently, cover for some racism having the last word. The possibility of a new racism, a more subtle and silently sophisticated racism, is assumed away as it orders social formations anew.[13] It is denied just as it maps the contours internal to and bordering the postcolonial, postcommunist, postmodern, post*apartheid,* and increasingly transnational era. It is contradictorily celebrated as multicultural diversity just as it rationalizes hegemonic control of difference, access, and prevailing power. In short, liberal meliorism—whether that of modernity or postmodernity—blinds itself to the transformations in racist expressions, in racist culture. It runs from the alterations in the varying forms of racisms, in the contents of their representations, in the modes and implications of their significations, and in their functions and outcomes.

In contrast to the prevailing picture of a singular and passing racism, I will be developing a conception of transforming racisms bound conceptually in terms of and sustained by an underlying culture. Like all cultures, that which I identify as racist grows and ebbs. My undertaking is to account for the emergence, transformation, and extension, in a word, the (continuing re-) invention of racist culture, and for the varying kinds of discursive expression that it prompts and supports. The significance of any prevailing racist expression and of social relations and institutions in a racialized formation must be read against this cultural background.

Included in racist culture, as in culture generally, are ideas, attitudes and dispositions, norms and rules, linguistic, literary, and artistic expressions, architectural forms and media representations, practices and institutions. These cultural expressions and objects embed meanings and values that frame articulations, undertakings, and projects, that constitute a way of life. In this sense, a culture is both, and interrelatedly, a signifying system and system of material production. In commanding the culture, social subjects are uniquely situated to assert power. Where the cultural invention is given over to cultivating order, to rendering the strange familiar so as to control it, and to defining exclusion and inclusion, the violence of power and the power of violence will be central to it. Culture in the sense intended here consists in knowing and doing. It is made up by the totality of created knowledge—in this case, concerning race(s)—and it involves a set of rules or conventions, a logic or grammar of their relation, and a vocabulary of expression and expressibility. It extends over the various ways of acting in racial terms, over the shared meanings through which these actions are rendered more or less significant, and over the conditions of their perpetuation and transformation.

Racist culture has been one of the central ways modern social subjects make sense of and express themselves about the world they inhabit and invent; it has been key in their responding to that world they conjointly make. In this sense, culture not only informs and locates social subjectivities but also makes possible the conditions and materials for resisting subjection and (dis)location.[14] This book will be concerned with delineating the contours and details of this culture of racialized exclusion and the conditions of possibility for resisting and responding to it. I will be concerned in these pages to map the overlapping terrains of racialized expression, their means and modes of discursive articulation, and the exclusions they license with the view to contending and countering them.

It is not just that the fact of discourse defines our species as meaning making, as both producer and product of these meanings and their embedded values. Particular conceptual systems signify in specific ways, encode values that shape thought in giving voice, even silently, to their speakers. Dominant discourses—those that in the social relations of power at some moment come to assume authority and confer status—reflect the material relations that render them dominant. More significantly, they articulate these relations, conceptualize them, give them form, express their otherwise unarticulated and yet inarticulate values. It is this capacity—to name the condition, to define it, to render it not merely meaningful but actually conceivable and comprehensible—that at once constitutes power over it, to determine after all what it is (or is not), to define its limits. To control the conceptual scheme is thus to command one's world.

If language is now widely taken as the primary vehicle of conception,[15] then discourse is the mode of communicative practice that enables its effectivity. Though dominant discursive practices will obviously be most effective in defining expressive possibilities (the turnpikes, so to speak), they need not always determine the entire social formation. For if they did there could be no space, conceptually speaking, for resistance (a neighborhood without local routes ceases to have identity, ceases to be a neighborhood). Conceptual command can never be exhaustive; what Bourdieu refers to as the hegemony of symbolic violence is seldom complete.[16] Conceptual hegemony turns not only upon the totally imposed order of terms in defining the social subject, but upon the subject's acceptance of the terms as his or her own in self-definition and conception. In the shift from imposition to self-interpretation, received terms are rarely if ever entirely synonymous with self-assumed ones. What is traditionally marked as resistance is probably impossible—it will likely be inconceivable—absent discursive counteraction. Conceptual contention is necessary at the very least to conceiving the ordered imposition of the terms of social subjectivity as symbolic violence, necessary to *seeing* the established conditions of subjectivity as domination, as subjectification. To command change of one's world one needs first, of course, to understand it, basically to apprehend that change is needed.

Discursive counteraction may assume various forms. In general, we can distinguish between changes *within* a discourse and changes *of* a discourse. The former involves more local changes in some constitutive feature or element of the discourse, the latter shifts from one discourse or discursive formation to another. Countering elements within a discourse may involve substituting a new term for some standard one local to the discourse, or assigning new meaning to some established term. But it may also involve conscious disavowal of grammatical or phonetic or conversational conventions, flying in the face of communicative fashion. One may choose to use the singular form of the verb with a plural pronoun as a pointed instance of resistant solidarity, to accent some basic term so as to take distance from received usage, to speak simply or elliptically or loudly or casually where convention would have one do otherwise.[17] To change a discourse obviously requires much more fundamental shifts, shifts in whole ways of world making. The former might add up to basic changes, though predicting such transformations is risky business. Switches in one strand might well prompt changes in other strands of the web of belief. Such domino changes may be prompted by a concern to preserve conceptual consistency, or by functionalist considerations where systemic changes will enable things to work better. For example, a discursive shift from communism to capitalism as a legitimating economic doctrine (it was not so long ago that many took the reverse shift for granted) will prompt both conceptual and material changes at the social, political, legal, and cultural levels, just as changes in the latter terms will affect the former. The combined effects of this nexus of alterations will simultaneously prompt and turn upon transformations in the ways agents are conceived subject to the new discursive order, and how they come to see themselves.[18] Such changes will not alone necessarily erase racist expression, though if sufficiently deep they may. It is more likely that racist expressions will be configured anew, and thus reordered. Similarly, such a renewed racism is likely to reorient itself as it redirects the social order it serves in part to chart. Or so I will argue.

I show in chapter 2, then, how race emerged with and has served to define modernity by insinuating itself in various fashions into modernity's prevailing conceptions of moral personhood and subjectivity. By working itself into the threads of liberalism's cloth just as that cloth was being woven, race and the various exclusions it licensed became naturalized in the Eurocentered vision of itself and its self-defined others, in its sense of Reason and rational direction. Racial divisions and racist dominations came to be normalized in the Western sociophilosophical tradition. So chapter 2 documents the racializing paradox at liberalism's heart. The wide variety of racialized expressions and their attendant racist exclusions, as well as their transformations from one period and social formation to another, necessitates an account of both race and racism capable of holding together these expressive differences and similarities and of accounting for their internal changes and developments. In chapter 3, accordingly, I lay out a general conception of racialized discourse elaborated in terms not of necessary and sufficient conditions but of the variety of its historical expressions. The unity of the discourse, what holds it together and characterizes it as racialized, is a set of conceptual primitives that began to be articulated in the sixteenth century and became embedded since in and through popular social, scientific, and political discourses. The account in chapter 3 offers a framework for elaborating these conceptual primitives, for revealing the historical transformations occurring between them in their discursive domination, and for reflecting their sometimes only silent manifestation in those social or scientific expressions considered more legitimate. I begin here also two lines of extended argument to which I return throughout the text: first, a critique of class reductionism; and second, the implication of social science in extending racialized expression and race-defined exclusions.

The discursive account developed here suggests a distinction between racialized expression and racist exclusion, between more or less acceptable, even celebrated identities and identifications and those that are oppressive and exclusionary. In chapter 4, a general, nonessential conception of race is explicated, one that accords with the wide variety of its prevailing historical usages and meanings. The tension between earlier biologically based and more recent socially centered conceptions of race is traced out. This tension reveals that racial reference need have no recourse, implicitly or explicitly, to biological reference, nor is it reducible simply to ethnic articulation. I elaborate the sorts of socioconceptual conditions under which racial reference may assume ethnic articulation and in terms of which ethnicity tends to be racialized. Another thread woven throughout the extended argument of the book is introduced here, namely, the role of the State in articulating, legitimating, elaborating, and transforming racialized expression and racist exclusion, in rendering them rationally acceptable. In chapter 5, then, I stipulate and defend a definition of racisms as the set of racialized exclusions, and I argue that its determinants—and therefore the explanations that need to be offered for them—are manifold and situationally specific. Just as the State, for example, is deeply implicated in formulating divisive racial definition, so too is it central in extending racist exclusions, though it must be added that the modes of State racializing are various and that racialization and racist restriction and elevation are not simply State bound. This complex picture is contrasted with prevailing conceptions of racism, of racism's singularity and univocity, as well as with prevailing explanatory accounts in the social sciences. A typology of racisms and their periodization is developed, and their predominant explanations and modes of rationalization are both discussed.

Underlying received wisdom concerning race and racism, by extension, is the widespread presumption of racism's inherent irrationality. I show in chapter 6 that this presumption is mistaken and that therefore the general rationalistic grounds of the liberal moral and political condemnation needs to be rethought. Racist exclusions throughout modernity can and have been rationally ordered and legitimated. The analysis of racisms' rationalities and of the poverty of presuming that racism is in its singularity necessarily irrational is embedded in a discussion of modernity's prevailing conception of the 'Western Man of Reason' and of the values upon which this conception turns. This account thus highlights the ways in which the social sciences—particularly sociology, social psychology, and economics—are deeply implicated in perpetuating racializing expressions and their exclusionary implications. Chapter 7 accordingly demonstrates how contemporary social sciences in the prevailing liberal tradition—here, primarily anthropology, art history, political science and economy, sociology and urban studies—extend the conceptual prism of racialized social orders and encourage continued or renewed racist exclusions. In this sense, the social sciences and humanistic disciplines are shown to be deeply implicated in the reproduction of racializing culture and racisms as common sense. Though I illustrate State direction of racialized social science in the case of South Africa, I argue that *apartheid* social science is a logical, if extreme, extension of prevailing socioscientific assumptions and dispositions.

In keeping with this line of analysis, I show in chapter 8 how the reconceived model of racisms offered here may be applied to illuminate the racialized and racially exclusionary definition of spatial location throughout South Africa and 'the West'. This spatial analysis turns on an extended demonstration of the intersection of conceptual and social histories. The central thesis here is that just as racial location of the socially marginalized throughout the West reflects the idealization of the *apartheid* polis, so post*apartheid* space in South Africa is being representationally (re)constructed to reflect the racialized space in the West. This analysis serves to illustrate both the racial normalization that takes place throughout the West as well as its spheres of influence, highlighting State implication in the processes. It demonstrates the deep and abiding effectivity—precisely at the level of the political economy of spatial configuration—extended by racialized common sense. I conclude in chapter 9 by conceptualizing the theoretical conditions of possibility for resisting these socioconceptual configurations and for the emergence of effective antiracist practices. A conception of praxis as principled pragmatism is articulated, and the commitment to pragmatic antiracisms is contrasted with liberalism's policy of nonracialism. This distinction between the multiplicity of antiracisms and the reductive singularity of nonracialism is illustrated finally in terms of some pressing contemporary policy issues pertaining to matters racial.

A cautionary word concerning methodology requires emphasis. I am engaging primarily in a set of theoretical analyses and philosophical reflections, not first and foremost in empirical detailing and historical accounting. In this sense, the study will be more like mapping new routes in already charted and chartered terrain than like the treasure hunting of traditional social science or the digging of archaeology. This map making and remaking will be replete with intersections, parallel routes, flyovers, tunnels, dual lanes, and perhaps even dead ends. Here, instances and particulars and details—roughly what falls under the empirical—will be invoked as signposts and mileposts, checkpoints and mileage markers to elucidate the argument and to establish where the arguments are coming from and taking us, to assure that the route at hand is one we would want to take. And as with mapping terrain, routes to a chosen destination may be direct or circuitous, speedy or scenic, rough or smooth, short or long. The destination to which all my maps' routes will lead, nonetheless, are not so much final as they are plateaus of sorts, points or sets of intersecting points from which to launch more or less spatiotemporally specific and effective antiracist practices and interventions. In this sense, cartography is designed not simply to reflect, to represent by 'capturing' the geography of racialized power.[19] It is meant rather to re-present, to intervene in these racialized relations so as to initiate possibilities of resistance and response.

2

Modernity, Race, and Morality

Moral notions tend to be basic to each sociodiscursive order, for they are key in defining the interactive ways social subjects see others and conceive (of) themselves. Social relations are constitutive of personal and social identity, and a central part of the order of such relations is the perceived need, the requirement for subjects to give an account of their actions. These accounts may assume the bare form of explanation, but they usually tend more imperatively to legitimate or to justify acts (to ourselves or others). Morality is the scene of this legitimation and justification. So to comprehend the various ways in which race has defined social subjectivity and relations throughout modernity, it is imperative that we get clear about the distinction between premodern and modern moral conceptions. We need also concern ourselves here with a second and related consideration, namely, the conditions under which race may find expression in terms of the prevailing moral conceptions of modernity.

Philosophical reflections on the ethical have sought to reconstruct the principles underlying popular moral conceptions while at once furnishing idealized rational principles to guide individual behavior and social relations. In this, moral theory has served as both mirror and counsel. Persons embodying their respective historical conjunctures are fleshed out, given content and by extension value in terms of these moral concepts. The preeminent examples in the Western philosophical tradition have been well documented: *virtue* as central to classical social identity; *evil* or *sin* as basic to medieval Christianity; *autonomy* and *obligation* as defining morality in the Enlightenment shift from Christian to secular ethics; *utility* as the primary concern of the emerging nineteenth-century bureaucratic technocracy; and *rights* as definitive of the contemporary insistence upon the autonomous and atomic individual.[1] We turn now to consider the way moral conceptions serve to distinguish the modern from the premodern, and how race is normalized in terms of modern moral reason.

Morality and Subjectivity

The doctrine of virtue articulated so clearly by Aristotle was a fundamental part of the moral (self-)conception of classical Greece. Aristotle's concern focused not upon rules for establishing what acts one ought to be doing but in the first instance upon spelling out the conditions for a life worth living. The human virtues were considered as cultivated habits or states of character that dispose their bearers to act excellently in the circumstances at hand, that is, to act as reason directs. Acting well was considered a function of what is conducive to the human well-being ('flourishing' or 'excellence') of citizens in a well-ordered state. Virtues included temperance or self-restraint, generosity, courage, justice (lawfulness or fairness), and mildness; while their related vices were intemperance, stinginess or wastefulness, cowardice or rashness, injustice (unlawfulness or unfairness), and irascibility or slavishness. Acting virtuously in any instance—literally being virtuous—consisted in being moved by the right things, towards the right people, at the right time, in the right way, and with the right end in view. The virtuous condition thus required action to be informed by perception and judgment. As such, it could not be fully determined by a fixed set of rational rules, for rules by their nature are insensitive to the shades of situational difference. Being virtuous, then, was not simply a function of learning and following a rule; one had to acquire the experience and habits by following the example of virtuous citizens and, above all, by practice.[2]

In this view, virtues could be fulfilled only in terms of citizenship in the city-state. To be a virtuous subject meant nothing less than being a good citizen. One could not think of oneself outside the context of one's social roles: The catalog of virtues specified for citizens what actions and attitudes would merit social standing in the shared political project of the polis.[3] A subject's image, given or received, was always as a citizen of the polis or, by contrast, as lacking citizenship, as stateless.

The concept of *virtue* was of great importance also to human self-conception for medieval Christianity from Augustine to Aquinas. However, it was not the basic moral concept. *Virtue,* and so the primary Christian virtues of faith, charity, and hope, were in conceptual service to the more fundamental notion of preventing sin or the production of evil. Sin, on this account, is the transgression of divine law. Divine law specifies the nature of the good, the good for each thing in its hierarchically ordered proper place, and as such it establishes the properly human good. The human good was conceived in terms of the social roles each human being is naturally considered to play in the community. Evil accordingly is not something that exists in and of itself; it is, as Augustine emphasized, a privation of good, a perversion or corruption of it, a withholding of good by subjects with a will free to command and so be responsible for it. Thus, human evil or sin is the product of corruption by a free human will of the divine and inherently good order of things.

By the thirteenth century, the proper performance of each thing established by the divine law in this way was taken by medieval Christianity to be its natural state. Human nature, for Aquinas, consisted in those characteristics essential to humans as a kind, and that differentiated them from other kinds of things. All bodies and creatures below human and rational beings on the hierarchical scale cannot act otherwise than they do; they are not free to act contrary to the laws of their own nature. Human beings, however, are free to follow or disobey the dictates of practical reason, free that is to establish the rational principles of morality and to choose (not) to follow them. But because the Natural Law of morality was considered nothing else than the Eternal Law applied to human beings, creating moral principles was deemed nothing more than recognizing God's law. (As MacIntyre makes abundantly clear, our contemporary bifurcation of law and morality knows no place here.) Following God's law—actually being a moral subject—in this view turns on an assertion of free human will. In this psychological interiorization of moral space that came to define medieval Christian subjectivity, the virtues are those qualities of character that daily enable the self to stave off sin, to guard against self-corrupting evil, to sustain the lawful order of things.[4]

It will be important in pulling together shortly the threads of this argument about moral (self-)conception to remember that under Natural Law theory membership in the human community does not simply turn on being seen to follow the law, for if this were all it would be enforceable where found lacking. Humanity is also a matter of the conceived capacity to follow the law, of perceived place in the hierarchical order. Exclusions and their associated moral treatment were a matter not just of violating law and order but also of inherent capacity to be ruled by reason. The material force of this conceptual scheme was made possible by the emergence in the medieval Catholic Church of a centralized and literate clerisy able to exercise authority over moral culture.[5]

Before turning to the forms these exclusions could assume and the role of the moral in effecting them, we must first consider the moral concepts central to the self-image of modernity. The forms exclusions could assume under modernity, indeed, morally sanctioned exclusions, altered dramatically from those encouraged under medieval Christianity.

If the modern period is primarily marked by the dominant rise of secular culture, then the Enlightenment is clearly a key bridge in the shift from the scholastic to the civil. Basic to this cultural shift, at least in Europe but increasingly throughout the spread of what I'll loosely call the European cultural empire, is the expansion of literacy. This was prompted by technological developments in printing and the increasing importance of vernaculars as forms of communication and learning. In turn, this generated a widening attraction to egalitarianism in both religious and secular domains. This is perhaps reflected in the two central moral principles that emerged in the Enlightenment to define self-conception: *autonomy* and *obligation.* The force of a self-sufficient Reason replaced the authority of God and defined a human nature free, at least in part, from external constraint and thus autonomous in the sense of self-commanding. While the relative political and cultural freedoms of the Enlightenment both encouraged and reflected independent voices of philosophical skepticism, notably Hume, Diderot, and Voltaire, the definitive political and moral framework was best articulated by Rousseau and Kant.[6]

Rousseau was concerned to specify the political and moral conditions under which self-protection, self-expression, and freedom would be maximized for all. Each citizen would accept the law established by the general or collective will. As the product of the social contract, the law was supposed to be autonomously chosen by each individual subject. The rule of the general will for Rousseau is the rule of each individual will: in prescribing the law for all, each individual prescribes it for him- or herself. This equality and autonomy turns on the underlying assumption that rational subjects recognize common interests. Such recognition would be produced in practice by a democratic state that in its socialization of citizens would engender a conception of the general rational will, of moral and political right. Thus, subjects would recognize that what it takes to be a moral person is what is required of a good citizen.

Where autonomy and equality were central for Rousseau, Kant aimed to show that these concepts entail the (self-)imposition of moral obligation. Like Rousseau, Kant was concerned with a notion of morality possible on its own terms, that is, without justifying appeal to God or self-interest, human benevolence or happiness. As Rousseau had recognized, this entailed that self-interest must be governed by moral reason. And this required demonstrating that practical reason is necessarily self-motivating: Moral reason must be independent of self-interest but also of any such Humean moral sentiment as benevolence or sympathy. Kant set out to establish what conditions must hold for subjects if moral reason is to provide them with its own motive to act. The shift from religious to secular morality is reflected in the fact that Kant began by assuming that ordinary moral judgments in the Judeo-Christian tradition may legitimately be claimed to be true. The difference between the religious and the secular, then, is in the conditions appealed to in justifying the claims as true. Thus, Kant represented his undertaking as moving from 'common sense morality' to 'philosophical morality'. Reason is represented in its application to practical affairs by a single, unchanging principle of right conduct, a principle freely chosen by subjects themselves and so for which they turn out to be fully responsible. The circumstantial application of this single moral law commands rational agents and imposes upon them an obligation to undertake impartial action, to act as any rational agent would who faces suitably similar options. Though constrained, actions done from duty are nevertheless free or autonomously chosen because the principles of duty are self-legislated: They are consistent universalizations of the subject's own motives. Rational agents are accordingly seen to be free and self-determined. In legislating rationally for themselves, subjects legislate for all other rational agents. The impartiality and practicality of Rousseau's dictum of rational self-determination, interpreted from the standpoint of the individual subject rather than the body politic, echoes through Kant's conception of the moral self: 'each one uniting with all obeys only himself and remains as free as before'.[7]

The voices of Rousseau and Kant reverberate not just through the Enlightenment but across the moral domain of modernity. Self-commanding reason, autonomous and egalitarian, but also legislative and rule-making, defines in large part modernity's conception of the self. Given these very different terms in virtue of which the subject is constituted, we can expect to find altogether-changed (and perhaps changing) forms of exclusion throughout modernity, and indeed altered forms of legitimation for the exclusions that do take place. One of the ways this has worked out, as we will come to see, is in terms of the social subject split between a conception singularly self-interested and free, on one hand, and altruistic and egalitarian, on the other. This way of grounding the moral self, indeed, of taking the moral self as central to the specification of the moral, was rejected by another major moral strain that has come to define modernity, namely, the nineteenth-century utilitarian drive to make morality practical.

Bentham inverted the Kantian line of thought that the institution of morality depends upon the imposition of moral principles on an otherwise recalcitrant self, the molding of delinquent human nature by moral reason. The basic premise of classical utilitarianism, rather, is that moral consideration is, and can only be, an implication of individual psychology. Humans, insisted Bentham, are by nature psychologically motivated to do whatever produces pleasure or pain; these empirically are the sole motives there are for human action. It follows, as Bentham quickly noted, that the only acceptable ground for moral action, acceptable because practicable, is the principle of utility: Act to produce the greatest happy consequences (interpreted strictly as pleasure) for the greatest number, or failing which to minimize unhappiness (pain). Morality is thus deemed derivative from and shaped by empirical psychology.

So those acts, rules, policies, or institutions (in a word, expressions) would be required that tend to increase the happiness of all subjects likely to be affected by them more than by any other viable alternative, or failing this, that would tend to diminish unhappiness more. In this moral calculus each individual is to be considered equal. Here, utilitarianism walks a narrow neutral line between egoism and altruism: Whether I pursue my or another's interest will be determined impartially by which maximizes utility. The single consideration at stake is the balance in quantity of pleasure or pain (to be) experienced: No consequence is considered superior in kind to any other.[8]

Subjects' motives, as John Stuart Mill recognized, are irrelevant in this view to establishing the morality of expressions, pertinent though intentions are to a judgment of a subject's character. More recent commentaries have pointed out that character of a certain kind may be conducive to maximizing utility, that the principle of utility may therefore require character dispositions of a particular sort on pragmatic grounds. Mill, himself, seems implicitly to advance something like this view in recommending (ironically in *On Liberty*) that it is in the utilitarian interests of subjects not-yet-civilized ('races [which] may be considered as yet in their nonage') to be governed by the civilized until the former are sufficiently developed to assume self-direction.[9] It may be objected that Mill was here contradicting his warning in the earlier *Principles of Political Economy* (1848) that explanations in terms of 'inherent natural differences' are vulgar. Yet, his remark about 'races ... as yet in their nonage' is intended not so much as a claim about *inherent* racial capacity as a historical observation about the state of certain people. While Mill could thus insist on sustaining the empirical foundations of his value claims, this was clearly possible only by imputing value laden suppositions to his empirical claims.

This makes explicit what should already be theoretically obvious: in the eyes of classical utilitarian beholders, autonomy could be sacrificed to utility and, by extension, the self-governance of some in the nineteenth century to the imperial direction of others. This was an implication of great import given the key contribution of utilitarian methodology to bureaucratic decision making, both locally and colonially. It is not just that the principle of utilitarian impartiality may well have partial effects; it may also be partially applied.

It has been the reticence of living with, and under, this utilitarian implication that has made the appeal to rights increasingly attractive to many. Already recognized by Hobbes and Locke in the seventeenth century, though perhaps in different ways, as fundamental to the self-conception of the emergent possessive individualism of bourgeois culture, the concept of *rights* has come to assume central importance in moral, political, and legal vocabulary. Rights, as Mackie has noted, are now legislated, enacted by government executives, ruled upon judicially, and demanded politically. Rights are more popular than duties, for subjects want them for their own sakes whereas obligations are impositions tolerated to secure and sustain morality and freedom. We have come this century to conceive all human beings as bearing the inalienable—the natural or human—right to choose individually and equally how to lead their own atomic lives without disadvantaging anyone else (and so violating their rights). A right, then, is understood minimally as the conjunction of the *freedom* to do whatever one chooses and the *claim* to be protected from interference by others (whether individual, group, or state) in so doing. Each individual is taken equally as occupying a domain of sovereign autonomy free from trespass or transgression by others. Respect for individual subjects may be considered simply as respect for their rights, as recognizing their capacity to assert claims.[10] Sometimes the notion is extended to include not only a freedom but an *interest* so to choose, not simply a claim but a *power* subjects should have both to undertake the act and to prevent interference.[11] It is in this more positive sense that the right to food and shelter, or education, or employment are to be understood.

Dominant conceptions of the scope of rights now seem more readily committed to the minimal view of social subjects as properly entitled to equal opportunity (to compete) and to equal treatment (before the law, say)—in general, as freedom from constraint—than to the equality of result that a more robust egalitarianism may entail. On the minimal view, deeply skewed and group-patterned differential outcomes will be considered justified if no opportunity and treatment rights are violated. This highlights a disturbing feature of the principle that rights are to be considered exhaustively in terms of fair treatment and opportunity, namely, that this effectively excludes only explicit and intentional discrimination. It fails to recognize structural forms of discrimination or (unintended) patterns of exclusion, fails to recognize them, that is, as discrimination or unjustifiable exclusion at all. I do not mean thus to deny that important political and personal freedoms, in particular those concerning considerations of race, have been won and defended in the name of rights, especially in the second half of the twentieth century. Nevertheless, the peculiar failure of the narrow but dominant commitment to the contemporary rights-conception of the subject suggests a curious corollary: Where exclusions and domination persist, they may be obscured or legitimated (if not quite justified) by the dominance of rights-talk, and this in either of two ways. First, the inviolable rights of those included may be stressed to the exclusion or irrelevance of the rights of the nonincluded. And second, assuming the necessity in a moral economy of scarce resources to balance between rights claims, assertion of the rights of some may imply (in a sort of zero-sum game) the denial of another's rights. Denial, of course, may mean not simply the refusal to act on a recognized though recognizably weaker right-claim but also the repudiation of the right-claim, the refusal to recognize its existence. The right of each to inviolate self-direction and self-rule implies in practice, if not principle, the clash of directions and rules as each subject undertakes to assert and impose the inviolability of individual right.[12] The rights of each becomes a matter of the power of and over the means of representation.

Thus, moral discourse has both reflected and refined social relations, centrally defining changed images of social subjectivity across time and place. Indeed, the differences between these images are suggested by the syntax of their basic terms: We are virtuous; we sin; we have obligations; we bring about or effect utility; we are the bearers of rights.[13] I have indicated initial ways in which historically dominant pictures of moral nature have been key in forming both social self-conception and the figure of the Other: what each agent at some conjuncture could be, expect, and achieve. And the forms of exclusion each enables are perfectly general. In so far as they exclude at all, they may do so in terms of varying forms of related group membership: class, ethnicity, gender, national or religious affiliation. The form I am centrally interested in here is racial. My concern is to see how, in fact, racial exclusions have been effected, what their relations are to these other forms of exclusion, how they have been legitimated and may disturbingly be justified in terms of the historically prevailing conception of moral subjectivity.

Race, Morality, and Subjectivity

The first thing to notice is that race *is* a morally irrelevant category in the Greek social formation, but on empirical grounds not normative ones. There are no exactly *racial* exclusions in the classical Greek social formation, for there is no racial conception of the social subject. While things were more complex at a later time, I want to suggest that this is also the case for the medieval experience. The word 'race' is sometimes used in translation of classical and medieval texts, but the term translated is almost invariably 'species,' and what is intended conceptually is not *race* but *peoples* or *man* generically.[14] I do not mean to deny that discriminatory exclusions were both common and commonly rationalized in various ways in Greek and medieval society, only that these exclusions and their various rationalizations did not assume racialized form. The concept of *race* enters European social consciousness more or less explicitly in the fifteenth century. Indeed, the first recorded reference to the sense of Europe as a collective 'we' is in papal letters of the mid-fifteenth century, the first recorded usage of 'race' shortly after that. It is only from this point on that social differentiation begins increasingly to take on a specifically racial sense. Not only did the Greeks have no concept for racial identification, strictly speaking they had no conception of race. There is considerable evidence of ethnocentric and xenophobic discrimination in Greek texts, of claims to *cultural* superiority, yet little evidence that these claimed inequalities were generally considered to be biologically determined.[15] In the absence of both the term and the conception, the social sense of self and other can hardly be said to be racially conceived nor the social formation to be one properly considered racist.

The primary objects of Greek discrimination and exclusion were slaves and barbarians, indeed, relatedly so. (Significantly, women were conceived in representational terms not dissimilar to slaves and barbarians.) As a general category of discriminatory sociolegal exclusion, barbarianism was the invention of fifth-century Hellenism. A barbarian was one of emphatically different, even strange, language, conduct, and culture and lacking the cardinal virtues of wisdom, courage, temperance, and justice. The principle distinction was political. Hellenic democracy was contrasted with barbarian despotism and tyranny. The democratic state alone was deemed a free one, the state where political relationships—and so the distinctly human virtues—could flourish. The polis, as the embodiment of democracy, was the state where citizens ruled themselves. It was, in other words, properly a political state, and so one in which the state of subjection was ruled out. So, stripped of self-determination, barbarianism was close to statelessness.

The freedom of Hellenic citizenship was thus sharply contrasted with barbarian servility: Virtually all slaves of the Athenian polis were barbarian.[16] The distance from the increasingly racialized post-Renaissance political space and relations is most succinctly reflected in the fact that slaves in Greek society could be virtuous—not the virtue of citizens, of course, but of those defining service. As Aristotle noted in *Politics,* slaves are slaves by nature, but also human. *Qua* barbarian, slaves perhaps are virtueless; however, the role of slave entails virtues defining excellence in that role. This role and its associated virtues may be given by the order of things, either by its place in the cosmic order or in terms of the legally enforced political order.[17] Accordingly, though barbarians were held to be inferior, this was for the most part politically and culturally conceived rather than biologically or in terms of origins. Nevertheless, this condition expresses the onset of the more general consideration that I wish to emphasize, namely, that discriminatory exclusions were principally effected in terms of prevailing moral discourse, here in terms of the virtues. In short, these exclusions were authorized in the very name of the moral.

In medieval thought, by contrast, individuals and groups were conceived as the subjects of theological categories, and discriminatory characterization and exclusion came to serve a different order. There appear in medieval literature and art representations of a range of strange, exotic beings, often falling between the human and the animal. These representations in part refer to and are influenced by mythological figures in early Western literature and art. Nevertheless, they were also tenuously imagined and invented on the preconceived basis of observing those dramatically different both among themselves (for example, deformed births) and elsewhere. In the first century A.D., Pliny the Elder (who is thought to have died of asphyxiation in the volcanic destruction of Pompeii) constructed a catalog of these human and quasi-human figures that remained influential throughout the medieval period.[18] The more extreme mythological and fabulous figures listed by Pliny include the Amyctyrae or 'unsociable' who have lips protruding so far as to serve as sun umbrellas; Amazons, or women who cut off their right breasts so as to shoot arrows more accurately; the Blemmyae, or men in the deserts of Libya whose heads are literally on their chests; giants; Hippopodes or 'horse-footed' men; horned men, and so on. Pliny also listed those peoples whose identities were established on geographical or physical or cultural grounds. They included Albanians, Ethiopians, and pygmies but also speechless, gesturing men, many types of hairy men and women, troglodytes or cave dwellers, ichthiophagi or fish-eaters, 'wife-givers', and so on. Clearly, peoples were often constructed on the basis of some combination of these various categories.[19]

In general, the exotic peoples of the Middle Ages were referred to as *monstra* (monstrous). As the duality in Pliny's catalog suggests, the category of *monstrum* was subject to two interpretations: on one hand, the prophetic but awful births of defective individuals, and on the other, strange and usually mythological people. Defective births were deemed an ominous sign of the destruction of celestial and earthly order. Observers were thus overcome by awe, repulsion, and fear of the implied threat to spiritual life and the political state. This concern translated into vigorous debates about the proper treatment of strangers, both in religious terms (could they be baptized and so saved as rational creatures having a soul) and in political terms (how were they to be treated juridically). Some insisted that human form is the mark of rationality and by extension of civil liberty, of the capacity to follow the law. Pygmies, for example, were deemed to represent a stage in the development of man, a step below humanity in the great chain of being, higher than apes but lacking true reason. True reason was thought to consist in the Aristotelian ability to formulate syllogisms and derive conclusions from universals. Pygmies were considered capable only of speaking instinctively, from the perception of particulars and not from universals. They thus lacked the discipline of rationally controlling instinct and imagination. By contrast, others claimed that social custom is the mark of man, that both ordinary and deviant humans could originate from the same parents and so share a common humanity. Humanity might be taken more inclusively in this view, though here, too, God's word would be imposed upon the unobliging seemingly against their will.[20]

This defining of humanity in relation to rationality clearly prefaces modernity's emphasis on rational capacity as a crucial differentia of racial groups. The concern in medieval thought with rationally defined categories of inclusion and exclusion seems to mirror later racial categorizations. However, while the medieval experience furnished models that modern racism would assume and transform according to its own lights, we need to proceed with care in labeling this medieval *racism*. As we have seen, there was no explicit category of race or of racial differentiation—no thinking, that is, of the subject in explicitly racial terms. More fundamentally, the place such exclusions occupy in medieval thought is very different than the space of racial thought in modernity. Late medieval experience was marked by increasing contact with peoples geographically, culturally, and, seemingly, physically different from people of familiar form. Over time, then, the Plinian categories grew increasingly empty. The folk monster of the earlier period was replaced by a new category, the *Savage Man*. This figure was usually pictured as naked, very hairy though without facial or feet fur, apelike but not an ape, carrying a large club or tree trunk (a version, perhaps, of what later would become modernity's cartoon characterization of the caveman dragging off 'his' woman by her hair).[21]

The generic image of the savage represented violence, sexual license, a lack of civility and civilization, an absence of morality or any sense of it. Thus, with the psychological interiorizing of the moral space in late medieval thinking, the savage man came to represent the wild man within—sin or lack of reason, the absence of discipline, culture, civilization, in a word, morality—that confronts each human being. The Other that requires repression, denial, and disciplinary constraint was taken first and foremost to be the irrational other in us, and only by extension did it come to refer to those not ruled over (or lacking the capacity to be so ruled) by the voice of Reason, the purveyor of the Natural Law. It follows that the primary forms of discrimination were against non-Christians, or infidels: Those subjects who were seen to fail in constraining themselves appropriately would either have discipline imposed upon them or be excluded from God's city. For example, the primary objection of medieval Christians to Islam was stated in theological terms—that is, in terms first of the absence of miracles from Muhammad's experience in contrast with Christ's, and second in terms of the emphasis on the Trinity as basic to Christian theology and its denial in the Islamic.[22] Similar sorts of distinction were seen to define the differences between Christian and Jew. These doctrinal differences, in turn, were taken by medieval Christianity as signs of the cultural (or moral) incapacity of others to reap the fruits of salvation. In short, medieval exclusion and discrimination were religious at root, not racial.

If premodernity lacked any conceiving of the differences between human beings as racial differences, modernity comes increasingly to be defined by and through race. The shift from medieval premodernity to modernity is in part the shift from a religiously defined to a racially defined discourse of human identity and personhood. Medieval discourse had no catalog of racial groupings, no identification of individuals or groups (or animals for that matter) in terms of racial membership; by the mid-nineteenth century, on the other hand, Disraeli could declare without fanfare in *Tancred* that 'all is race'. In three and a half centuries the world had of course become dramatically different, and a central strand of that difference was the growing impression of race upon human self-identity and upon identification, human and animal.

The influential classical ethnographers Pliny and Strabo had both thought the equatorial regions unfit for human habitation. This view crumbled in the late fifteenth century, first as West Africa was explored, conquered, and its peoples enslaved by the Spanish and Portuguese, and then as the New World was created, subjugated, and plundered. The sixteenth century thus marks the divide in the rise of race consciousness. Not only does the concept of race become explicitly and consciously applied but also one begins to see racial characterization emerging in art as much as in politico-philosophical and economic debates. Hieronymous Bosch's provocative *Garden of Earthly Delights* (1500) ambivalently reflects the shift from religiously to racially conceived identity in his pictorial allusions to black devils. The eye lines of the numerous black figures throughout the three panels of the triptych are directed at no particular objects depicted within the work; the various groupings of white figures, by contrast, gaze explicitly, even quizzically, at the respective black figures, curious about 'objects' seemingly so different yet at once enchanting and enticing. (It should be noted that the signification in Western metaphysics of evil as black and good as white is as old at least as Pythagoras, but the identification of this color symbolism with racial groupings is a mode only of modernity.) In 1492, the European year of discoveries (not only had the Americas been reached by then but also the southern tip of Africa, the Cape of Good Hope), Antonio de Nebrija armed Isabella of Spain with the first grammar of a modern European language, expressly as an 'instrument of empire', the very mark of civilization.[23] The imperial force of language—colonizing minds not just bodies and territory—was quickly realized. But the shift is most clearly captured in the unfolding debate in Spain over how properly to manage the spreading empire, a debate that assumed moral dimensions as much as it did economic, political, and legal ones.

The issue was defined almost at the outset of the drive to empire in terms of the conditions for a just war. In 1510, Aristotle's doctrine of natural slavery in *Politics* was first suggested as a justification for applying force in Christianizing the American Indians. The following year a Dominican priest registered the first major public protest against Spanish treatment of the American Indians. The seriousness with which the Spanish took their imperial mission in the Americas is revealed by the fact that this protest led almost immediately to the Laws of Burgos (1512), which regulated the conditions of American Indian Christianization, labor, daily treatment (no beating or whipping) and reference (no names other than their proper ones, and explicitly not to be called 'dog'). The signs of civil treatment were marked as much by the bounds of polite language as by limits on physical force. The contrasting positions with respect to American Indian treatment and the vested interests they reflected were most clearly articulated in the remarkable debate of 1550 at Valladolid between Sepulveda and Las Casas over the justice of methods in extending empire.[24]

Sepulveda, a noted Aristotelian scholar and translator of *Politics,* represented the interests of commerce and the conquistadors. New World Indians were widely portrayed, even by renowned Spanish humanists of the day, as a stupid and impoverished race, lacking culture, kindness, and most of all incapable of Christianity. For the Aristotelian in the sixteenth century, hierarchy was the definitive feature of the universe: Domination of inferior by superior was considered a natural condition, and so of slaves by masters, of American Indians—like monkeys—by men. American Indians were portrayed as cannibalistic, as slavish in their habits, as barbaric—not just barbarian. Wars against American Indians and their subsequent enslavement were taken to be justified, therefore, because of their slavish disposition to obey, to prevent their barbarism, and so to save their innocent victims from harm. But above all they were justified to enable the spread of the Christian gospel. The 'natural' European drive to conquer and enslave the racial Other assumed accordingly the force of a moral imperative. However, in so far as this imperative was still religiously defined and so required the annihilation of vast numbers for the sake of principle (to save but a single soul), Sepulveda's view can be said in this sense quite properly to represent the dying Aristotelian order of the Middle Ages.

Las Casas, the Dominican missionary, by contrast and perhaps ironically, signaled the beginning of a shift of discourse from the insistence upon religious principle to the modernist value of individual equality. The life of a single human being, one even of a different race, was more important than his or any other's salvation. Equality not hierarchy defined humanity: All—Christian as well as non-Christian, European as well as non-European, whatever their color or culture—were ruled, in the words of Las Casas, by the common 'natural laws and rules of men'. This equality is ultimately the equality of each to become Christian. Monogenic biological equality is reflected in a univocal culturalism defined and represented by Christianity. The egalitarian conclusion is that American Indians could not be enslaved. It must be stressed that this is the onset not the high point of modernity, for it is the capacity to be Christianized that constitutes the egalitarian principle here, and the inherent resistance of peoples of Islam to Christianization was considered to justify their condemnation by Las Casas 'as the veritable barbarian outcasts of all nations'.[25]

This debate marks the watershed in my periodization of modernity in another, perhaps more instructive sense, for both the participants premised their positions upon the unquestioned *racial* difference between European, American Indian, and Negro. Different 'breeds' or 'stocks' were taken to determine and were characterized by differing traits, capacities, and dispositions. In this sense, the debate signals the onset of that peculiar configuration of social and natural qualities that is a mark of much racial thinking. However, the *humanism* of Las Casas's incipient egalitarianism was perhaps still less racial than it was religious, for it consisted in the capacity of the American Indians to be Christianized even as Las Casas celebrated their racial difference.

By the seventeenth century, whatever tensions might have existed between the racial and the religious as modes of identity and identification had largely been resolved in favor of the former. Imperatives of European empire and expansion entailed territorial penetration, population regulation, and labor exploitation. The institution of racialized slave labor in spite of, indeed, in the name of Las Casas's Christian humanism seemed necessary for exploiting the natural resources offered by the new territories. Nevertheless, it is important to notice that slavery turned also and fundamentally on the conception of indigenous peoples as a natural resource, as part of the spoils acquired in the victorious but 'just wars' of colonial expansion. Witness Velasquez's haunting painting, *The Servant* (1618–22), and the gigantic black marble statues of four Moor slaves, a monument to the Doge Giovanni Pesaro, that stand guard over the side door of the Church of Santa Maria dei Frati in Venice. So though it is in part true that '[r]acial terms mirror the political process by which populations of whole continents were turned into providers of coerced surplus labor,'[26] any reductive account of racial categorization and subjugation should be rejected. For while slavery may be explained largely (though not nearly exhaustively) in economic terms, one must insist in asking why it was at this time that racial difference came to define fitness for enslavement and why some kinds of racial difference rather than others. After all, strictly economic determinations should be indiscriminate in exploiting anyone capable of work. Racial definition and discourse, I am suggesting, have from their outset followed an independent set of logics, related to and intersecting with economic, political, legal, and cultural considerations, to be sure, but with assumptions, concerns, projects, and goals that can properly be identified as their own. Emergence of racial difference on its own terms as a significant feature of social definition could then be invoked as the rationalized grounds for enslavement. The peculiarities of this claimed difference—their brutishness and barbarism—delivered those so racialized up to enslavement.

Consider here John Locke's philosophical reflections on race, slavery, property, the just war, and their influence on the emerging Enlightenment. The opening sentence of Locke's justly famous *First Treatise on Government* (published in 1689 but probably written in the early years of that decade) unmistakably rejects slavery or property in other persons as a justifiable state of civil society, rejects it interestingly as un-English and ungentlemanly. Human beings are free, and equally so, in virtue of equal endowment in and command by rationality. Many commentators have pointed out that Locke seems to contradict this repudiation of slavery in the name of liberty, equality, and rationality both in his comments on slavery in the *Second Treatise* and in his practice as a colonial administrator. In the *Second Treatise,* Locke specifies the conditions under which he considers slavery justifiable, namely, for persons otherwise facing death, as in a just war when the captor may choose to delay the death of the captured by enslaving them. As secretary to the Carolina Proprietors (South Carolina), Locke played a key role in drafting both that colony's Fundamental Constitution of 1669 and the Instructions to Governor Nicholson of Virginia. The former considered citizens to 'have absolute power over [their] negro slaves', and the latter considered the enslavement of negroes justifiable because prisoners of a just war who had 'forfeited [their] own Life ... by some Act that deserves Death'. Locke considered the slave expeditions of the Royal Africa Company to be just wars in which the 'negroes' captured had forfeited their claim to life.[27]

Locke committed no inconsistency here. Moreover, his view on this point actually reflected widely held European presuppositions about the nature of racial others, and by extension about human subjectivity. First, it is a basic implication of Locke's account that anyone behaving irrationally is to that degree a brute and should be treated as an animal or machine. Hence, rationality is a mark of human subjectivity and so a condition of the necessity to be extended full moral treatment.[28] Rational capacity, in other words, sets the limit upon the natural equality of all those beings ordinarily taken to be human. To see that this really was Locke's view, we need turn no further than to his epistemological essay (which was published in the same year as the *Two Treatises on Government*).

Locke's empiricist antiessentialism led him to reject the notion of properties essential to the constitution of any object. Locke substitutes the notion of a 'nominally essential property', that is, any contingent property of an object conventionally designated by speakers of a language to be essential, for essences. Any property in this sense can be so nominated; and choices are a function of the speakers' interests. For seventeenth-century English speakers, and for speakers of European languages in general, color was considered such a property of human beings, and it was considered such in Locke's view because it was taken on grounds of empirical observation to be correlated with rational capacity. Thus, Locke could conclude that in formulating a concept of *man* for himself, an English boy would rationally fail to include Negroes.[29] It follows not only that Negroes could be held as chattel property; in their enslavement they could justifiably be treated as brutes and animals. Anthony van Dyck's *Henrietta of Lorraine* (1634) portrays a young black and garishly dressed slave boy gazing adoringly up at his tall, elegant, ghost white mistress. Her mannered hand on his shoulder keeps him firmly in his place: behind, inferior, subservient—the paradigm of European 'Mother Country and [Negro] Child Colony'.[30]

Thus, Chomsky and Bracken are on firm ground in concluding that classical empiricism could offer no conceptual barrier to the rise of racism, that historically it 'facilitated the articulation of racism'.[31] Yet, because their concern is with criticizing empiricism in the name of rationalism, they, too, fail to notice an enduring and significant feature of the nature of race: The concept of race has served, and silently continues to serve, as a boundary constraint upon the applicability of moral principle. Once this is acknowledged, the critical concerns of Chomsky and Bracken can be seen to be too narrowly cast, for it is not only empiricism that has failed to furnish a 'modest conceptual barrier' to the articulation of racism. The criticism tugs at the very heart of the Enlightenment's rational spirit. The rational, hence autonomous and equal subjects of the Enlightenment project turn out, perhaps unsurprisingly, to be exclusively white, male, European, and bourgeois.

Locke is representative of the late seventeenth century, and not just of English empiricists at the time, in holding this set of assumptions about race. Locke's influence upon the Enlightenment is pervasive, not just on empiricists like Hume. Emphasis upon the autonomy and equality of rational subjects is a constitutive feature of eighteenth-century thought, though qualified by the sorts of racial limits on its extension that we have identified as a condition of Locke's conception. This is not to endorse the error that empiricism is solely responsible for Enlightenment racial exclusion. The contemporaneous innatism of Leibniz's rationalism, for example, is clearly reflected in his remark that 'the greater and better part of humanity gives testimony to these instincts [of conscience] ... one would have to be as brutish as the American savages to approve their customs which are more cruel than those of wild animals.'[32] This should give pause to anyone accepting Bracken and Chomsky's further claim that rationalism offers 'a modest conceptual barrier to racism'. Empiricism encouraged the tabulation of perceivable differences between peoples and from this it deduced their natural differences. Rationalism proposed initial innate distinctions (especially mental ones) to explain the perceived behavioral disparities. This contrast between Lockean empiricism and Leibnizean rationalism on the nature of racialized subjectivity and the implications for the domain of the moral stand as prototype of the contrast between two great philosophical representatives of the Enlightenment, Hume and Kant, half a century later.

Subjugation perhaps properly defines the order of the Enlightenment: subjugation of nature by human intellect, colonial control through physical and cultural domination, and economic superiority through mastery of the laws of the market. The confidence with which the culture of the West approached the world to appropriate it is reflected in the constructs of science, industry, and empire that principally represent the wealth of the period. This 'recovery of nerve', as Gay aptly calls it, was partly a product of the disintegration of customary social hierarchies and their replacement by egalitarian sentiment, as much as it was accompanied by them. This recovered confidence was both expressed in and a consequence of the epistemological drive to name the emergent set of conditions, to analyze, to catalog, and to map them.[33] The scientific catalog of racial otherness, the variety of racial alien, was a principal product of this period.

The emergence of independent scientific domains of anthropology and biology in the Enlightenment defined a classificatory order of racial groupings—subspecies of Homo sapiens—along correlated physical and cultural matrices. Enlightenment thinkers were concerned to map the physical and cultural transformations from prehistorical savagery in the state of nature to their present state of civilization of which they took themselves to be the highest representatives. Assuming common origin, biology set out in part to delineate the natural causes of human difference in terms primarily of climatic variation. Anthropology was initially concerned to catalog the otherness of cultural practices. However, as it became increasingly identified as 'the science of peoples without history', anthropology turned primarily to establishing the physical grounds of racial difference.

Thus, general categories like 'exotic', 'oriental', and 'East' emerged, but also more specific ones like 'Negro', 'Indian', and 'Jew' (as racial and not merely religious other), and modes of being like 'negritude', along with epistemological subdisciplines like 'sinology'. Where the exotic of the medieval order had been placed in times past or future, the exotic of the Enlightenment occupied another geography, namely, the East or South, places indicative of times gone. Indeed, these spatial distinctions defined differences within the order of the exotic. Those of the East were acknowledged to have civilization, language, and culture. But, generically, the East was a place of violence and lascivious sensuality, the rape of which was thus invited literally as much as it was metaphorically. Africa to the south, by contrast, was the Old World of prehistory: Supposedly lacking language and culture, the Negro was increasingly taken to occupy a rung apart on the ladder of being, a rung that as the eighteenth century progressed was thought to predate humankind. In cataloging the variety of racial aliens, however, Enlightenment science simultaneously extended racial self-definition to the West: Western Europeans were similarly classified on the hierarchical scale moving upward from dark-skinned and passionate Southern Europeans to fair-skinned and rational Northerners. The catalog of national characters emerged in lock step with the classification of races. Racial and national identities, it could be said, are identities of anonymity, identities of distance and alienation, at once prelude to and expression of the drive to marginalize and exclude, to dominate, and to exploit.[34]

Now the Enlightenment consolidation of racialized discourse in terms of the scientific and philosophical was also effected on the basis of the eighteenth-century resurrection of classical values of beauty[35] and their similitude with the criteria of value in the classical economic tradition. Equilibrium and utility functioned in classical economic theory in ways analogous to proportion, symmetry, and refinement for classical aesthetics. Both sets of criteria determined an order of balance and harmony established on the basis of the geometric model. Beauty, for classical aesthetics, was a property possession of which determined subjects' ontological value, just as possession of economic goods for classical economics created utility. Possession of property was a sign of wealth, a measure of what the agent was capable of appropriating in the face of competition.[36] To lack the 'natural' qualities of classical beauty was to be poor; and as with laissez faire economic theory, this was considered the subject's own responsibility. By the late eighteenth century, beauty was established in terms of racial properties: fair skin, straight hair, orgnathous jaw, skull shape and size, well-composed bodily proportions, and so on. To fail to possess these traits was considered a fault of inheritance, much as heirs were identified to maintain wealth within the confines of the family bloodline. So, following Locke's lead, as economic poverty (lack of property ownership or the means of production) inevitably led subjects to work for pittances in factories and mines, 'racial poverty' was taken to justify property in persons.

Thus, natural qualities of beauty and perfection were supposed to be established on a priori grounds of racial membership. Aesthetic value solidified into natural law, which in the eighteenth century was considered as compelling as the laws of nature, economics, and morality precisely because they were all deemed to derive from the same rational basis. It is for this reason that many natural historians, biologists, and anthropologists at the time classified humankind not simply on grounds of physical criteria like size and shape, climate, or environment but according to the aesthetic values of beauty or deformity.[37] These aesthetic values of bodily beauty were established as the mode of determining the individual's place in the racial, and therefore social, hierarchy; and perceived intellectual ability or its lack were considered to reveal inherent racial differences in mental capacity. Blacks were quite frequently represented in eighteenth-century European portrait painting and, as with Joseph Wright's *Two Girls and a Negro Servant* (c. 1769–70), most often in subservient and demeaning fashion. Paintings like John Wootton's *The Racehorse Lamprey* or Bartholomew Dandridge's *Young Girl with Dog and Negro Boy* represent childish and so mentally immature black slaves in positions explicitly or implicitly analogous to the master's or mistress's horse or dog. The racialized relations of social power are reflected in and reproduced by the aesthetics of popular portraiture at the time.[38]

Those critics committed to the moral irrelevance of race tend to assume that racists inevitably combine these two strains, aesthetic values and natural qualities, into a spurious causal principle. If racists are inherently committed to such spurious causal presuppositions, sophisticated Enlightenment philosophers must have claimed that racial membership defines both one's degree of beauty and one's intellectual capacity. It would follow that where an observer knows either one's intellectual or aesthetic standing, the other may be deduced. Nevertheless, this fails to recognize that more careful racial theorists have sometimes expressed other forms of racial thinking.

David Hume, for example, had begun to think of mind and nature as merely *correlated* in various ways. Hume distinguished between the moral and physical determinants of national character. The latter are those physical elements like climate and air that eighteenth century monogenists so readily supposed to be the sole determinants of perceived human difference. By moral causes, Hume meant social.considerations like custom, government, economic conditions, and foreign relations that influence the mind and manners of a people. Hume insisted that national characters are a function almost completely of moral causes. Thus, Jews in general were 'fraudulent' (Hume was careful enough to emphasize that what we now call stereotypes admit to exceptions); Arabs 'uncouth and disagreeable'; modern Greeks 'deceitful, stupid, and cowardly' in contrast with both the 'ingenuity, industry, and activity' of their ancestors and the 'integrity, gravity, and bravery' of their Turkish neighbors. Superior to all others were the English, in large part because they benefited from their governmental mixture of monarchy, aristocracy, and bourgeois democracy. In general, Hume agreed with the earlier judgments of Bacon and Berkeley that inhabitants of the far north and of the tropics were inferior to inhabitants of more temperate regions (mainly Central Europe) owing in large part, however, not to physical causes but to matters of habit like industry and sexual moderation.

While *national* differences for Hume were social, *racial* differences were inherent. All '*species* of men' other than whites (and especially the 'Negro') were '*naturally* inferior to the whites'. Hume's justification of this footnoted claim was empirical: Only whites had produced anything notable and ingenious in the arts or sciences, and even the most lowly of white peoples (ancient Germans, present Tartars) he thought had something to commend them. 'Negroes', even those living in Europe, had no accomplishments they could cite. Like Locke, the only probable explanation of this 'fact' Hume could find was an original natural difference between 'the breeds'. Thus, Hume concluded, 'In Jamaica they talk of one negroe as a man of parts and learning; but tis likely he is admired for very slender accomplishments, like a parrot, who speaks few words plainly.'[39] Inherent nature admits of no exceptions.

Like Hume, Kant proceeded from a catalog of national characters to a characterization of racial difference.[40] Where Hume had identified the English as superior among all national characters, Kant predictably elevated Germans above all others, finding in them a synthesis of the English intuition for the sublime and the French feeling for the beautiful; Germans were thus thought to avoid the excesses of either extreme. Of the peoples of the Orient (what Kant elsewhere calls the Mongolian race[41]), the Arabs were deemed most noble ('hospitable, generous, and truthful' but troubled by an 'inflamed imagination' that tends to distort), followed by the Persians (good poets, courteous, with fine taste), and the Japanese (resolute but stubborn). Indians and Chinese, by contrast, were dominated in their taste by the grotesque and monstrous, with the former committed to the 'despotic excess' of *sati*.

Nevertheless, compared to Negroes, Oriental races fared relatively well in Kant's scheme.[42] Kant's remarks about 'Negroes' and their position in relation to his moral theory need to be read against the general discourse of racialized subjects that defined the Enlightenment. 'Savages' are wanting in 'moral understanding', and 'Negroes' in Kant's view are the most lacking of all 'savages'. (American Indians—'honorable, truthful, and honest'—were considered the least lacking of 'savages'.)[43] As a moral rationalist Kant turned Hume's empiricist endorsement of racial subordination into an a priori principle:

> So fundamental is the difference between [the Negro and White] races of man, and it appears to be as great in regard to mental capacities as in color.... The blacks are vain in the Negro way, and so talkative that they must be driven apart from each other by thrashings.[44]

Hume's correlation of race and nature was reworked by Kant back into a strictly causal relation. This enabled him to conclude logically that 'the fellow was quite black from head to foot, *a clear proof* that what he said was stupid'.[45] Kant could therefore consider himself to have derived a 'Negro's stupidity' from the fact of his blackness.

This outcome of Kant's reckoning is perhaps less surprising if we recall that he had set out assuming the acceptability of 'common sense morality' in the Judeo-Christian tradition, and as we have seen racial differentiation and subordination were basic to it at the time. So in establishing the justificatory conditions for commonsense moral value, Kant would also be justifying racially defined discrimination. One way for Enlightenment philosophers committed to moral notions of equality and autonomy to avoid inconsistency on the question of racialized subordination was to deny the rational capacity of blacks, to deny the very condition of their humanity. This implication is borne out even if we interpret in generous ways the Enlightenment commitment to universalistic moral principles. It is true that vigorous movements emerged at the time opposing race-based slavery, movements that justified their opposition precisely in the name of universalist Enlightenment ideals.[46] We should recognize, though, that this resistance, valuable as it may have been at the time, presupposed and reproduced recognition of racial difference. And the standard by which any measure of equality was set remained uniform and unchanged: It was, namely, European and Western. Local values became fixed as universal; in issuing moral commands autonomous agents may impose upon others their own principles and impose them in the name of universality and objectivity. Cloaking themselves in the name of the natural, the certain, and the timeless, racial discrimination and exclusion imprinted themselves as naturally given and so as inoffensive and tolerable.

If there is any content to the charge of cultural chauvinism, it does not lie simply in the refusal to recognize the values of other (in this case non-European and non-Western) cultures; it lies also in the refusal to acknowledge influences of other cultures on one's own while insisting on one's own as representing the standards of civilization and moral progress. This became the nineteenth-century modernist legacy of the Enlightenment project, and it was in the name of the principle of utility emerging from the Enlightenment that this was carried forward.

The principle of utility, that morality is a matter of producing 'the greatest happiness of the greatest number', furnishes no principled restriction of racially discriminatory, exclusionary, or violent acts, policies, or institutions. In weighing up utility, the theory insists on treating each social subject affected equally and impartially, and it therefore rejects paternalistic expressions. Subjects are considered the best judges of their own happiness, of the goals they set themselves, and of what they take their happiness to consist in. Utilitarianism, for example, does not exclude anyone as a proper object of obligatory aid: On the face of it, strangers and aliens have as much claim to aid as those at hand.[47]

There are severe limits to utilitarian benevolence and self-determination. First, we mostly find ourselves better able to aid those we know, whose needs we are more readily able to identify, empathize with, and satisfy. So utilitarian considerations are strongly likely to have us aid those in close proximity to us, spatially and culturally. But there are more straightforwardly racial delimitations on the principle's applicability. In the eighteenth and nineteenth centuries, the natives of India and Africa were increasingly characterized as less than fully human, or prehuman. Already in 1734, Voltaire, Europe's voice of equality, declared himself against the prevailing monogenist explanation of racial differences in terms of environmental factors and that 'bearded whites, fuzzy Negroes, the long-maned yellow races and beardless men are not descended from the same man.... [Whites] are superior to these Negroes, as the Negroes are to apes and the apes to oysters.' Twenty years later he added that 'only a blind man is permitted to doubt that Whites, Negroes and Albinoes ... are totally different races.'[48] By the end of the century this sort of polygenic presupposition had become the prevailing scientific paradigm, and it dominated natural history, biology, and anthropology until Darwin rendered it obsolete. Bentham and his friends, James and John Stuart Mill, to their credit firmly rejected the polygenic presupposition, and in the name of the principle of utility asserted: 'It may come one day to be recognized, that the number of legs, the villosity of the skin, or the termination of the *os sacrum,* are reasons equally insufficient for abandoning a sensitive being to the same fate.' The underlying reason for this is that sensitive beings are those capable of *suffering!* Nevertheless, though rejecting the polygenist conception of races, Bentham and his followers admitted racial difference as having at least secondary influence on utility. 'Race' or 'lineage' was treated in Humean fashion not as climatically determined but as 'operating chiefly through the medium of moral, religious, sympathetic and antipathetic biases'.[49] This interpretation exercised great influence on British colonial bureaucracy, indeed, through the direct hand of James and John Stuart Mill.

It has often been pointed out that were the calculus of pleasure and pain to establish it, slavery and severe racist treatment of a minority by a majority would be obliged by utilitarian consideration. The acceptability of slavery and racism turn for utilitarianism on the number of beneficiaries and the extent of their benefits from such practices and institutions. A utilitarian might argue that the disutility from enslavement and racism would always likely be so severe as to outweigh any utility they might generate. As a matter of empirical fact this is questionable, and as Bernard Williams insists, the rejection of such practices should not be made at all to turn on contingent factors of this sort. Moreover, any attempt to exclude antisocial or fanatical desires or interests from the calculus can only succeed as unmotivated exclusions of anti-utilitarian preferences.[50] More damaging still to the utilitarian position is John Stuart Mill's justification of past slavery as historically the only means of enabling sufficient economic development to bring about broad human progress and benefit. Slavery in his view ceases to be acceptable with advance in civilization. While Mill thought that social subjects in the early nineteenth century should be committed to abolition, he insisted that slave owners ought to be compensated for their lost investment: Slaves were considered to be like property appropriated by the government for public benefit.[51]

The same paternalistic logic was used by both James and John Stuart Mill and their administrative followers to justify colonial rule, namely, the general civilizing and utilitarian benefits of capitalist development for the sake of the colonized so as to broaden the scope of the latter's liberty. James Mill entered service with the East Indies Company first as Assistant Examiner (from 1819) and eleven years later as Examiner in the chief executive office. As such, he effectively became the most powerful Indian administrator of his day. In these capacities he was able to institute the principles of administration for India that he had insisted on in his celebrated *History of British India.* Here, Mill attacked the 'hideous state' of 'Hindu and Muslim civilization' that prevailed in India. Like the Chinese, Indians were found to be 'tainted with the vices of insincerity, dissembling, treacherous ... disposed to excessive exaggeration ... cowardly and unfeeling ... in the highest degree conceited ... and full of affected contempt for others. Both

are, in the physical sense, disgustingly unclean in their persons and houses.'
Indians and Chinese, in short, were found completely lacking in morality. This
state of affairs Mill ascribed to underlying political causes, namely, the
shortcomings of 'oriental despotism'. Incapable of representative democracy, Mill
recommended that the Indian government should thus submit to the benevolent
direction of the British Parliament.[52]

John Stuart Mill followed his father into colonial service in 1823, conducting
the correspondence with India in the Department of Native States, one of the
Company's important divisions. He later succeeded the older Mill as Examiner,
remaining with the Company until its abolition shortly after the Indian Rebellion
of 1857–58. Echoing his father, John Stuart insisted that India required direction
by colonial government—recall that he deemed the principles of *On Liberty*
applicable only where civilized conditions ensured the settling of disputes by
rational discussion. Like his appeal to those who have experienced both sorts of
pleasure in proving the qualitative superiority of the 'higher' kind over the 'lower',
the younger Mill's distinction between civilized and uncivilized peoples implicitly
invoked the standard of the white European. Unlike his father, Mill
acknowledged—in principle, if not in fact—that India should exercise
self-government once it had assumed civilized forms of social life, and he saw
nothing in the nature of its people to prevent it from developing in this direction.[53]

Both James and John Stuart Mill thus viewed natives as children or childlike,
to be directed in their development by rational, mature administrators concerned
with maximizing the well-being of all. Natives ought not to be brutalized, to be
sure, nor enslaved but directed—administratively, legislatively, pedagogically,
and socially. Paternalistic colonial administration was required in their view until
the governed sufficiently mature and throw off the shackles of their feudal
condition and thinking and are then to assume the civilized model of reasoned
self-government. It was therefore in the name of the natives' own happiness, their
future good defined in utilitarian terms, that they should have been willing to
accept this state of affairs. This conclusion is established, in Taylor's fitting phrase,
by utilitarianism's 'homogeneous universe of rational calculation'.[54] Though each
sentient subject is in principle equal, 'civilized' subjects furnish the criterion of
calculation and hence control the outcome. Application of the utilitarian method
facilitates the drive for power and control, the subjugative drive of/over physical
and human nature that is central to the modernist legacy of the Enlightenment.

For utilitarians, accordingly, nothing in principle save a subject's good intention
stands in the way of racially discriminatory or exclusionary undertakings. And as
I noted earlier, though intentions are on John Stuart Mill's own admission relevant
to judgments of character, they are irrelevant to establishing the rightness or
wrongness of any act. Indeed, even judgments of intention and character are a
matter of racial definition in a social milieu in which the bishop of Kentucky could
unself-consciously declare that 'instinct and reason, history and philosophy,
science and revolution alike cry out against the degradation of the race by the

commingling of the tribe which is the highest [whites] with that which is the lowest [blacks] in the scale of development' (1883).[55] Not only does the principle of utility offer no effective delimitation of discriminatory exclusion; we have seen how such exclusion was mandated by its staunchest proponents in the name of the principle itself. Utilitarianism rationalized nineteenth-century racial rule in two related senses, then: It laid claim to a justification of racialized colonialism, and it systematized its institution.

Where utility fails the application of 'rights', as I mentioned, has been thought to succeed. Articulation of the concept in various important ways can be traced back to the seventeenth century, and the contemporary emphasis upon legal and moral rights needs to be understood in light of this tradition. The American and French revolutions, torchbearers of the Enlightenment, both licensed influential doctrines of rights.[56] Nevertheless, the great popular authority the concept of *rights* has come to exercise in defining the space of social subjectivity and especially the effectivity it has enjoyed in combatting racial discourse both followed World War II. The (self-)conception of the social subject predominantly as the bearer of rights—that is, in the name of those rights vested in and borne by the subject—has only come to prevail in the latter half of the twentieth century. It is pertinent, then, that the contemporaneous critical attack on racial discourse and definition has been authorized in terms of rights: witness, most notably, the United Nations Declaration on Human Rights, the Civil Rights movement in the United States, and the various United Nations statements on race.

In recent history, insistence on rights has served as a rallying point for the oppressed and given pause to oppressors. By contrast, oppression has been carried out not in virtue of a commitment to rights but under the banner of their denial. This suggests the semantic relation between 'rights' and 'justice' that is attributable to their common derivation from the Latin *jus:* A right is what is (considered) at least in the context just. Even where justice and so rights are naturalized, as in the history of their initial co(e)mergence ('natural rights', the 'rights of man', 'human rights'), there were considered to be limitations on their referential range, a range which by extension was also naturalized. Slaves, as we have seen, fell outside this scope, and the criteria of enslavability and rights-applicability were racialized.

So rights are in their very formulation relative to their *social* recognition and institution. In this sense, they are never absolute or universal: Rights exist and empower, if at all and even where they claim universality, only on the basis of some socially constructed and civil system already established by a specific process of politics and law.[57] It follows that even where a discourse of rights purports to include and embrace, in its application and range of reference it is open to circumscription and constriction. The reformulation of moral space in the twentieth century in terms of radically atomized and isolated individuals vested with rights on the basis only of their contractual relations has made conflicts of rights and dispute resolution central to moral and legal (self-)conception. In this culture of bureaucratic individualism, utility defines the bureaucratic rationality, and rights service the social invention of the autonomous moral individual.[58] Racialized and national identifications have served as modernist compensations for the merely 'agglomerative' and instrumental social identities that this radically individualist and atomistic order entails.[59] Rights-assertion, accordingly, has come to refract these social identities, 'delimiting certain others as "extrinsic" to rights entitlement'. The objects of the contractual arrangement, those excluded from this contract or from contracting as such, have no rights.[60]

Subjects assume value, then, only in so far as they are bearers of rights; and they are properly vested with rights only in so far as they are imbued with value. The rights others as a matter of course enjoy are yet denied people of color because black, brown, red, and yellow subjectivities continue to be disvalued; and the devaluation of these subjectivities delimits at least the applicability of rights or restricts their scope of application that people of color might otherwise properly claim. 'Where one's experience is rooted not just in a "sense" of illegitimacy but in *being* illegitimate',[61] in literally being outside the law, the rights to which one might appeal are erased. The space in which a subject might construct rights and their conceivable range of possibility are severely circumscribed.

Part of the difficulty with rights-application is the conflict it not only implicitly presupposes but also that it serves in part to generate. This conflict may assume either conceptual or substantive form. Conceptually, by a right one subject may intend a liberty, another a claim, or entitlement, or power. Substantively, one person's liberty may conflict with another's, or one's liberty or claim with another's entitlement or power, and so on. Where these conflicts are racialized, whatever gains and losses or inclusions and exclusions there are will be exacerbated, magnified, emphasized, and accentuated. We have already seen an example of this in terms of property rights and slavery. For those influenced by Locke, the right to property is as basic as the rights to life and liberty, and the former right was taken to entail under certain constraining conditions a right to property in another. Slavery, recall, was deemed justifiable by Locke in case slaves, in losing a just war, had alienated their own rights to liberty and property (and in the extreme to life also). Where racial grounds characterized subjects as lacking full social rights, slavery was still more readily legitimated.

Long and bitter struggles have undermined both the nonracial and the racialized conditions for the justification of property rights in human beings. Nevertheless, there continue to be conflicts between subjects' interpretations and assertion of rights, conflicts deepened in assuming racialized form. The U.S. Civil Rights Act of 1964 promoted preferential treatment programs for those suffering racial discrimination. The claim to be treated preferentially, subject to qualifying conditions, and the entitlement to be admitted to colleges or hired preferentially generated the counterclaim a decade later of reverse discrimination suffered as a result by whites. Preferential treatment programs, it was charged, violate the right of all to equal opportunity: entitlement right of one subject conflicting with entitlement or claim right of another, each in the context assuming racial definition. Similarly, the right of all to protected speech may be taken to entail the right (liberty) of racist expression, at least in the nonpublic domain, but not the (claim or entitlement) right or empowerment to be shielded from such expression. As I will argue in the conclusion, this turns on the standard but questionable interpretation of racist expression as merely offensive, never harmful.

For reasons of this sort MacIntyre condemns rights, like utility, as a moral fiction. Moral fictions purport to furnish us with an objective and impersonal criterion of morality but in practice do not.[62] I have argued that the primary concepts in terms of which social subjectivity has been set in our moral tradition are fictive in this way. That they are open to abusive interpretation and application is a function of their inherently social character. Postmodern accounts of ethics emphasize this latter point, but largely as an instrument in criticizing the hegemonic authority of the prevailing moral order.[63] Postmodern thinkers have for the most part been notably silent about a positive ethic, in large to avoid repeating the errors committed by the disciplinary reason of moral modernity in issuing its categorical commands. Postmodern attempts to develop accounts of the ethical have mostly appealed to communitarian rather than atomistic considerations. MacIntyre's account is probably the most coherent, for he spells it out in terms of a tradition alternative to the one that culminated in modernity's prevailing conception of subjectivity. He identifies a core structure to the notion of the virtues across five accounts: Homer's, Aristotle's, Christianity's, Jane Austen's, and Benjamin Franklin's. This common structure is supposed to furnish the basis for identifying standards of social excellence. MacIntyre, however, admits that exclusion is central to every one of the five accounts: 'Every one of these accounts claims not only theoretical, but also an institutional hegemony.'[64] It follows that MacIntyre can find no principled barrier, theoretical or institutional, to racialized exclusions. This is borne out by the definition MacIntyre offers of 'a practice': 'a coherent and complex form of socially established cooperative human activity' which is 'fundamental to achieving standards of excellence'.[65] If racially defined exclusion is established as (a set of) practices necessary at a stage of a community's history for it to achieve excellence, on MacIntyre's account it must be virtuous at that stage.

The centrality of moral notions to social and self-conception enables and constrains actions of certain kinds. It also makes possible those basic categories of distinction between self and other that promote and sustain thinking in the terms of exclusionary discrimination. In this sense, *formal* moral notions of any kind are perniciously fictive in respect to racial and racializing discourse (whatever their redeeming value in authorizing or constraining some kinds of expression and disciplining subjects). This fictive character has to do with the nature of the moral concepts themselves, and with their role in fixing social subjectivity. They serve to naturalize the concept of race, to render it basic to modernity's (and so far, at least in transformed form, to postmodernity's) common sense.

As Hobbes noted, a moral order permits those expressions it does not explicitly prohibit. In the case of discriminatory exclusions it can be concluded more strongly that what the moral order fails explicitly to exclude it implicitly authorizes. The moral formalism of modernity establishes itself as the practical application of rationality, as 'the rational language and the language of rationality'[66] in its practical application. Modernist moralism is concerned principally with a complete, rationally derived system of self-justifying moral reasons logically constructed from a single basic principle. But in ignoring the social fabric and concrete identities in virtue of which moral judgment and reason are individually effective, in terms of which the very content of the moral categories acquires its sense and force, moral modernity fails to recognize the series of exclusions upon which the state of modernity is constituted.[67] So though the formal principles of moral modernity condemn and discourage some racist expressions, they fail, and fail necessarily, to condemn and discourage such expressions exhaustively. Indeed, where they fail in this way, they extend discriminatory racialized expression either indirectly and inadvertently by seeming to condone and approve what they do not explicitly disapprove, or directly by enabling racialized expression and effectively authorizing discriminatory racial exclusions on the basis of the principle of moral reason itself.

This colonizing of the moral reason of modernity by racialized categories has been effected for the most part by constituting racial others outside the scope of morality. This has been done not by denying the social and so moral relevance of racial identity but by taking race as a central expression of the language of 'thick description'. This is the culturally developed and articulated language of everyday and intellectual life in terms of which morality is lived out, the thick description in terms of which the moral notions apply or fail to apply, and in terms of which discriminations are made and acquire legitimacy.[68]

I have stressed that the primary principles of our moral tradition—virtue, sin, autonomy and equality, utility, and rights—are delimited in various ways by the concept of *race*. It should be clear that one could make out the same argument for moral method, that is, whether the moral principles are produced out of and so justified by appeal to social contract, or pure reason in its practical application, or to the appeal to consequences, or to the standards of a community tradition. In each case, race is conceptually able to insinuate itself into the terms of the moral analysis, thereby delimiting by definition the scope of the moral. Thus, the racializing paradox of liberal modernity is firmly established: Liberalism's commitment to principles of universality is practically sustained only by the reinvented and rationalized exclusions of racial particularity.

It should also be evident that there is considerable historical variation both in the conception of races and in the kinds of social expression we seem ready to characterize as racist. Indeed, it is upon just this contextual particularity that the renewable racializing paradox of liberalism turns. Accordingly, we require a general covering account that would make sense of these differences in racial conception and of the variety of racist exclusions they enable. The possibility and contours of such a covering account form the focus of the following chapter. This, in turn, will furnish the conceptual map against the background of which we can draw the central definitions of race and racism (chapters 4 and 5 respectively), as well as trace reason's silent role in normalizing racial thinking and racist exclusions (chapter 6).

3

Racialized Discourse

Paul Gilroy has argued that because racisms vary so widely and are by nature historically specific, no general theory of *'race relations* and race and politics' can be sustained.[1] Gilroy's criticism is primarily directed at a specific tradition that has prevailed in social theorizing about race and racism, namely, the race relations industry, though the criticism potentially applies to any attempted analysis of racial phenomena. One direction to explore in responding to Gilroy's challenge, then, and in accounting for the ways in which racisms become normalized involves developing a general but open-ended theory concerning race and racism. The theory would have to account for historical alterations and discontinuities in the modes of racial formation, in the disparate phenomena commonly expressed in racialized terms, as well as in those expressions properly considered racist. It must also enable and encourage opposition to racist expression, for ultimately the efficacy of a theory about race and racism is to be assessed in terms of the ways in which it renders possible resistance to racisms. Moreover, architectural safeguards against the theoretical imperative to closure must be built into this framework so that it will be open to identifying and theorizing continuities or new additions to transforming racialized discourse, as well as discontinuities and aberrant expressions.

The Discourse of Race and Racism

I hinted in the introduction at conceiving *racialized* expressions in terms of a *field of discourse*. I have argued elsewhere that racism itself is a discourse; here I am widening that claim, taking the broader position that the field of discourse at issue is made up of all racialized expressions.[2] As a theoretical construct, the discursive field is sufficiently broad to incorporate the various expressions constitutive of racialized discourse. These expressions include beliefs and verbal outbursts (epithets, slurs, etc.), acts and their consequences, and the principles upon which racialized institutions are based. In addition, the 'field of racialized discourse' is a designation wide enough to include the racialized expressions that arise in analyzing and explaining the historical formations and logics of racial thinking and reference, as well as of racisms. The field of racialized discourse accordingly consists of all the expressions that make up the discourse, that are and can be expressions of this discursive formation. It is the (open-ended) theoretical space in which the discourse emerges and transforms in and through its expression(s).

What is established in this emergence of discourse is a set of *discursive* or *expressive objects*. Rules of implication (implicatures) constituted in the establishment and formulation of the discourse define the object(s) of discursive expression. Racism turns out to be one such object among possible others in the emergence and elaboration of racialized discourse. As the formative rules are historically specific and thus subject to change, so, too, is the discursive object in question. Racism is not a singular transhistorical expression but transforms in relation to significant changes in the field of discourse.

Analytic accounts of both race and racism may constitute another object of racialized discourse, an object by extension open at least metadiscursively to critical discussion. So, at the most general level of description, the domain or field of racialized discourse is populated by two sets of texts: the enunciative and the analytic. Racism as a discursive object has been variously analyzed as rationalizations for psychosexual fear; for economic or social disparities; for cultural exclusions; or for political entitlements. Racist expressions, whether practices in the traditional sense or texts, are informed by beliefs. They involve enunciations of racist principles, supposed justifications of differences, advantages, claims to superiority (whether considered 'natural' or 'developed'), and legitimations of racist practices and institutions. The enunciative expressions at issue here have assumed widely divergent forms: scientific, linguistic, economic, bureaucratic, legal, philosophical, religious, and so forth. These racisms may be contrasted conceptually with, while they are naturally tied both conceptually and materially to racialized expressions, to those expressions indicating ascribed or self-assumed social identities predicated on racialized group membership. It follows that *race* is a discursive object of racialized discourse that differs from *racism. Race,* nevertheless, creates the conceptual conditions of possibility, in some conjunctural conditions, for racist expression to be formulated.

Interpreting racism as the dominant object of the field of racialized discourse can be used to organize the resemblances among the apparently disparate data of racism. Nevertheless, the concepts of *racialized discourse* and *racist expression* will also be used below as explanatory devices. Distinguishing analytically between racialized discourse and racism as (one of) its expressive objects will enable elaboration of subtle points otherwise often overlooked. For example, we will come to see that the law, moral discourse, and the social sciences can thus silently incorporate racialized language, or what I will shortly identify as the preconceptual elements of racialized discourse, while claiming to be *anti*racist.

So a number of interrelated and general puzzles emerge here: How have the forms of racialized expression changed over time, and why? How have these discursive changes in racial expression affected the forms of racist expression? Mapping the field of racialized discourse will inevitably involve addressing these questions.

Three general factors make up the methodological terrain of sociodiscursive fields: sociohistorical conjuncture; formal (grammatical) components and relations constitutive of the discourse; and the subjective expression or internalization and use of the discourse by social subjects. My concern is to account critically for the success of racialized discourse and racist expression in pervading social formations and cultures. I will have something to say accordingly about each of these discursive constituents. However, I will focus primarily upon the second, namely, the emergence and elaboration of the discourse's formal structures in relation to economic, political, legal, and cultural demands in specific conjunctures.

Casting the analysis in this way also enables differentiation of racialized discourse from other social discourses like class, nation, and gender. Briefly, *nationalism* emerges as a primary, though not necessarily the exclusive, expressive object of the discourse of nation. Similarly, *sexism* is a dominant discursive object emerging in the discourse of gender. In chapter 5, I argue that *exploitation* is the primary expressive object that emerges out of the discourse of class. I turn now to discuss the social conditions out of which racialized discourse arises.

The Social Conjuncture of Racialized Discourse

The sociohistorical conjuncture that facilitates development of a discourse generally consists in the confluence of material and conceptual conditions over a period of time from which arises the definition of the discursive object and articulation of the field of discourse. Once the discursive field is constituted, variations and transformations in these sociohistorically specific conditions may stimulate discursive modification, development, even dissolution.

It may help here to distinguish racisms in their historical specificity from the general conditions of possibility for the emergence of racialized discourse as such and of racism as (one of) its expressive objects. I argued in the preceding chapter that racialized discourse emerges with modernity and comes to colonize modernity's continually reinvented common sense. Changes within racialized discourse and transformations from one form of racism to another, that is, from one set of social expressions constituted as racist to another, are intimately tied to discursive developments internal to modernity. Here, I am simply concerned to stress the macrosocial conditions that enabled racialized expression to emerge so forcefully, that enabled it increasingly to pervade the terms of social and personal identity throughout the course of modernity. What then are the material and conceptual conditions of emergence for racialized discourse?

The voyages of discovery from the late fifteenth century on reported vast areas of 'unconquered' land with inestimable mineral wealth and natural resources but cautioned that these lands were peopled by 'strange', often 'hostile' beings. These forays into the unknown challenged the prevailing European conceptions of the possible forms of life, just as they helped to undermine *stasis* as the central epistemic strand of the dying Aristotelian order, replacing it with motion. Nascent capitalist industrialization, fueled by this emergent (self-)definition of mobile atomistic and anonymous individualism and an ever-expanding appetite for profit and accompanied by increasing and increasingly refined specialization, led quickly but variously to demands for cheap labor and raw materials, slavery, and the denuding of natural resources. Increasingly, science displaced religion as the grounds of intellectual authority and truth claims; the multiplicity of vernacular languages edged out the primacy of a singular 'sacred' language as the medium of epistemological veracity and cultural authenticity; and literacy expanded as print capitalism, in its drive to expand markets, made books and newspapers more readily available.[3] Thus, anonymous individualism came to be circumscribed by the cultural homogeneity and commonality of popular textual (and more lately electronic) consumption; and the increasing hegemony of racialized identity and identification in popular and intellectual culture assumed through the eighteenth and nineteenth centuries the authoritative endorsement of biological science, natural history, anthropology, and psychology.

It is against this scientific background that we must assess the call for, and then the reality of colonial spread in the early nineteenth century as a response to rapid population increase and urbanization in Europe and the accompanying drive for market expansion to satisfy the desire to maximize profit.[4] The nineteenth-century 'economic miracle', accompanied by ideological commitment to the bureaucratic rationality of orderliness and economic efficiency, brought with it political solidification of the state. The forces of state were no longer directed just at the native barriers to colonial extension but were quickly employed to promote division and exclusion, domination and violence internally, within the structures of the colonizing societies. By the turn of the nineteenth century, utilizing scientific and technological developments, the metropoles had internalized some of the dynamics of colonialism to institute and maintain the intersection of clear class lines and racialized metropolitan ghettoes.[5]

It may seem that this broad overview of the sociohistorical grounds that have nourished racialized discourse but which the discourse has served coterminously in part to define is consistent with a class-reductionistic account of race formation and discrimination. Any attempt at such reductionism is mitigated by two fundamental and related considerations. First, the formation and logics of racialized discourse have a history and dynamic comprehensible in the last analysis in their own right. Class plays a part in the explanation, but not nearly the whole and often not even the fundamental part. Second, just as the history of the emergence of racialized discourse cannot properly be accounted for without specifying its class dimension, so any account of class formation in modernity (or postmodernity) that excludes its racialized delimitation is radically incomplete.

Analytic relations between race and class are considerably more complex than reductionistic accounts acknowledge. This complexity is reflected in the systems of value and appropriation informing the emergence and maturing of modernity. The paradigmatic articulation of racialized discourse (including racism) was made possible in terms of a remarkable confluence of the modes of economic and aesthetic valorization and appropriation. It was enabled, in other words, in terms of the general criteria according to which things are imbued with value and how such objects are made our own. These criteria include some noneconomic dimensions molding racialized discourse that further negate the reductionism of economistic accounts.

First, the criteria of value for classical aesthetics, as for classical economics, are thoroughly intellectualist. Beauty was considered a property, present as an ideal essence to the intellect and characterized, thus, by its clarity and knowability.[6] Though *utility* in the classical economic tradition appears to be defined in terms of 'satisfaction of desire', the market mechanisms in virtue of which the classical model 'tends to equilibrium' are equally intellectualist.[7] This intellectualism is supported by a very strong naturalism. Objects were deemed beautiful in so far as they tend to or mirror the order of things, just as they were supposed to tend to their true or natural value (price) to the degree that they approach their natural equilibrium as demand and supply 'mirror' each other.[8] This common intellectualism and naturalism pervade the foundations of modern philosophic discourse. Both the rationalist and empiricist traditions rest ultimately upon common assumptions: truth as the correspondence of idea to reality, knowledge as mind mirroring nature.[9] This supports the conclusion drawn in chapter 2 that rationalism and empiricism are in their own ways equally open to racist conjecture, and served historically to authorize racist exclusions.

Racialized discourse accordingly emerged only with the displacement of the premodern discursive order and the accompanying epistemic transformations. It developed and matured with the social and intellectual formation of modernity. Indeed, it increasingly came to give definition to the sociocultural order of modernity, furnishing in large measure a central strand of the novel means of tying people, power, and history together.[10] This highlights two reasons why an account of the rise of racialized discourse in conventionally material terms is inadequate. First, roughly the same general social conditions underlie the emergence of *nation* and its discursive object(s) as those that ground racialized discourse. (In various specific contexts, 'race' and 'nation' have been used synonymously.) So commonly construed 'material' or class determination cannot be all that uniquely individuates their respective emergence. Second, and perhaps more fundamentally, race in its various articulations has served not only to rationalize already established social relations but to order them. In insisting on the material determination of the 'ideology of racial inferiority', Barbara Fields credits only one side of the equation: 'People are more readily perceived as inferior by nature,' she writes, 'when they are already *seen* as oppressed,' and she explicitly contrasts this with the more commonly held reverse charge.[11] Fields properly recognizes that the fact of oppression and the perception of it can be held analytically and historically apart. But she privileges what is commonly considered material determination over ideological influence.

By contrast, the concept of 'racialized discourse' is designed to show how, methodologically, socioeconomic materiality and ideological conception are mutually interactive or codetermining. The social conditions that have made possible the expressibility of racialized discourse, in general, and racism, in particular, are various. Changes in these conditions may render racialized discourse inexpressible, or literally unthinkable. Yet once the general boundary conditions for the discourse are set, transformations in these background conditions will likely provoke only local alterations in particular expressive forms of the discourse. For example, the manifestations of racialized discourse that were a central part of plantation slavery and served to make it so effective necessarily differed from those discursive articulations like segregation that emerged in the wake of abolition. Those who hold that intradiscursive formations and transformations local to a discourse or to its expressive object are exclusively 'a *byproduct* of the day-to-day ... existence, through which people make rough sense of the social reality that they live and create from day to day'[12] fail to give any determinative credit to the self-transforming elements of the discursive formation in their interaction with the material experience of daily life. No explanation in traditionally material terms will adequately account for the shift in racialized expression from monogenism to polygenism, say, or from the latter to Social Darwinism and of their implications for ordering experience and expression. To see this more fully, the analytic formation and logic of racialized discourse in its own terms must be specified.

The Grammar of Racialized Discourse

In a field of discourse like the racial what is generally circulated and exchanged is not simply truth but truth-claims or representations. These representations draw their efficacy from traditions, conventions, institutions, and tacit modes of mutual comprehension.[13] The line of analysis I have adopted faces two sorts of basic questions here: The first concerns the objects to which the discursive representations refer and the styles of reference to be found in the figures of speech and metaphors as well as in the categories and expressions of the discursive field. The second involves a more abstract concern, for in the relations between the expressions lies a *grammar,* and underlying the categories representing the objects is a *preconceptual plane* or set of *primitive terms.* Analysis of the structures of racialized discourse must seek to uncover this grammar and the preconceptual primitives.

The close relation between the two sorts of questions is revealed in posing fundamental puzzles: whether a unified grammar of racialized discourse can be identified, and how this grammar orders racist expression. If a unifying grammar cannot be specified, if the unity of racialized discourse seems chimerical, more than simply its existence is thrown in doubt. Skeptics may gather strength in claiming that the public expression of racism has been much less pronounced than its critics charge. The implications for public policy and for moral judgments of individual behavior are thus considerable.

Contrary to Cornel West's claim, discursive unity is not a product of figures of speech (including metaphors). Discourse is only expressed by such means, and partially so. The metaphors of racialized discourse, and more particularly of racist expression, are not reducible to a single form: 'Nigger dogs' or 'Blacks (or Red Indians) are savages'[14] differ in form, substance, and probably in the specificity of their purposes from 'the Jewish conspiracy' or Chamberlain's 'Aryan race-soul' but also from 'Sambo, the typical plantation slave [as] docile but irresponsible, loyal but lazy, humble but ... lying and stealing.'[15] It is not simply that color racism and anti-Semitism differ in virtue of the fact that blacks are referred to as animals and Jews only in the context of some abstruse mythology. Jews are often described in terms of animal imagery;[16] and a color racism relying upon character-trait stereotyping need have no recourse to animal metaphors.[17]

It is equally misleading to consider discursive unity of racist expression and racialized discourse a function either of a prevailing corpus of norms or of a prevailing style. Such norms are supposed to be established in terms of a series of descriptive statements about others that delimit the way we perceive them. Style, in turn, is the dominant mode of discursive expression. Prevailing norms and style are inadequate to the task of unifying racist expression and, by extension, racialized discourse. The underlying point here is that racialized discourse does not consist simply in descriptive representations of others. It includes a set of hypothetical premises about human kinds (e.g., the 'great chain of being,' classificatory hierarchies, etc.) and about the differences between them (both mental and physical). It involves a class of ethical choices (e.g., domination and subjugation, entitlement and restriction, disrespect and abuse). And it incorporates a set of institutional regulations, directions, and pedagogic models (e.g., *apartheid*, separate development, educational institutions, choice of educational and bureaucratic language, etc.).[18] Norms or prescriptions for behavior are contextually circumscribed by specific hypotheses, ethical choices, regulations, and models. Yet no unidirectional norms are basic to racialized discourse: A decision that one race is intellectually inferior to another may be taken as grounds for a norm of exclusion from educational institutions or of the concentration of special resources.

Similarly, the mode of racist expression—its style—may be interpreted variously as aversive, academic or scientific, legalistic, bureaucratic, economic, cultural, linguistic, religious, mythical, or ideological. Racialized descriptions, hypotheses, choices, and modes and rules of discourse have altered over time. This precludes the possibility of establishing a singular transhistorical stylistic or normative pattern.

A complementary criticism can be launched against attempts to establish discursive unity on the basis of common objects referred to, or common themes developed and spoken about in the discourse of and concerning race. Anti-Semitic statements pick out objects different from those racist statements that objectify black persons. The theme of an anti-Semitic slur (e.g., 'Communist conspirators!' or 'Red kikes' as grounds for excluding Jews from trade unions or political office)[19] differs largely from that of black ones ('Dumb nigger!' as the ground for restricting blacks to manual labor or slavery). Various objects are named, described, analyzed, and judged—in a word, emerge—*in* the discourse; just as themes are chosen, delineated, and developed *in* speaking. Determined by the discursive field, these objects and themes cannot be all that differentiates the discourse of race from other discourses.

Themes and objects emerge only *in* discourse, delineated by the set of norms, principles, hypotheses, and choices, and articulated in figures of speech and styles. The grammar of racialized discourse assumes coherence and uniqueness only when compared from the vantage point of the discourse as a whole with other discursive fields like those of nation or class or gender. If discursive unity is to be achieved, it can only be a product of those underlying factors which directly generate the discursive field. Foucault calls this set of factors the *preconceptual* level.[20] These factors may be likened to 'primitive terms' in an artificial language. Grammatical changes in descriptions, hypotheses, rules, models, norms, and styles are reflected in transformations in the preconceptual grounds of racialized discourse. Accordingly, the structural unity of the discourse must be sought in a transformational schema of its preconceptual set and in the implicative 'interplay between their location, arrangement and displacement'.[21]

The Preconceptual Elements of Racialized Discourse

The preconceptual set for racialized discourse consists of those factors both reflective and constitutive of power, including dominant values, that directly enable the expression of racialized discourse. These conceptual primitives are not abstract a priori essences; they do not constitute an ideal foundation of the racialized discursive formation. Nor are they to be confused with the actual, explicit concepts and terms by which racialized discourse is usually expressed. The primitive terms are manifestations of power relations vested in and between historically located subjects, and they are effects of a determinate social history. These factors of power effect 'implicatures' that circumscribe the transformations, inferences, and references for the field of discourse. They generate the concepts and categories in terms of which racism is actually expressed and comprehended. Thus, these preconceptual factors define in a general way the expression of those agents, and only those, who speak and act in terms of racialized discourse and racist expression.

It follows that the unity of racialized discourse is not given in any purportedly ahistorical durability of race or racism. The discourse of race transforms—arises, alters, and perhaps will eventually disintegrate—both with actual social conditions and with conceptual reformulations, with implicative redirection. The overall coherence of racialized expression and the racist project, rather, turns on the preconceptual elements structuring dispositions and the drawing of implications. These elements include classification, order, value, and hierarchy; differentiation and identity, discrimination and identification; exclusion, domination, subjection, and subjugation; as well as entitlement and restriction.

The relations of power expressed in terms of and by these conceptual primitives inscribe social conditions of racialized violation and violence. In turn, the preconceptual elements or primitives of racialized discourse and of the conditions, implications, and practices that they inform are embedded in social discourses central to and legitimized by practices and relations constitutive of modernity. Normalization of racialized expression and racist exclusion turns on the embedding of their conditions of possibility deep in modernity's formative sociodiscursive structures and scientific vision. It is from this broad social context that these primitives are to be derived.

Classification is basically the scientific extension of the epistemological drive to place phenomena under categories. The impulse to classify data goes back at least to Aristotle. However, it is only with the *'esprits simplistes'* of the seventeenth century and the Enlightenment that classification is established as a fundament of scientific methodology.[22] With its catalogues, indices, and inventories, classification establishes an ordering of data; it thereby systemizes observation.[23] But it also claims to reflect the natural order of things. This ordering of representations accordingly always presupposes value: Nature ought to be as it is; it cannot be otherwise.[24] So the seemingly naked body of pure facts is veiled in value.

In the eighteenth century, the data that lent themselves most readily to systematic seeing, to representations by rules, were those of biology and of natural history. Extended to human affairs, the pervasive spirit of simplicity sought to reproduce for social relations the sort of simple order thought to inhere in nature.[25] Hence the application of categories of speciation (e.g., racial classification) to human groupings on the basis of natural characteristics. Unsurprisingly, a major assumption underlying anthropological classification at the time turns out to be that identification of races in terms of their differentia is adequate to establish the laws of behavior for their members.

So classification is central to scientific methodology, and scientific method has long been taken as the ideal model of rationality. The capacity for rationality, in turn, was considered the mark of humanity. It seemed obviously to follow that the anthropological ordering into a system of races in terms of rational capacity would establish a *hierarchy* of humankind. The race represented by the classifiers was assumed as a matter of course to stand at the hierarchical apex. Racial ordering accordingly implied a racial hierarchy and a behavioral expectation. The rational hierarchy was thought to be revealed through its physical, its natural, correlates: skin color, head shape, body size, smell, hair texture, and the like. This engendered a metaphysical pathos, an aesthetic empathy or aversion. Because so 'obviously' natural, this pathos was assumed unquestioningly to be rational.[26]

Thus, racial classification—the ordering of human groups on the basis of putatively natural (inherited or environmental) differences—implied a racial hierarchy of races. The derivation of hierarchy from classification rested upon the long-standing assumption that the universe is perfectly intelligible to reason and on the *principle of gradation* inherent in this. Formulated initially as Aristotle's 'hierarchy of being', this principle was adopted later as a fundament of Christian thought. It evolved systematically 'from a less to a greater degree of fullness and excellence'.[27] The neutrality and objectifying distantiation of the rational scientist created the theoretical space for a view to develop of subjectless bodies. Once objectified, these bodies could be analyzed, categorized, classified, and ordered with the cold gaze of scientific distance.

So the principle of gradation was employed to ground racial classification. Classification could then claim to provide an objective ordering. The subjectivity of aesthetic taste and judgment, of empathy and aversion, was applied to this objectification of human subjects. The full weight of eighteenth century science and rationality, philosophy, aesthetics, and religion thus merged to circumscribe European representations of others. This reduction of human subjects to abstract bodies had the implication of enabling their subjection to the cold scientific stare and economic exploitation of Europeans and their descendants. Subjectless bodies were thus dramatically transformed into bodies of subjection.

The principle of gradation also carried a moral implication: Higher beings were extended greater worth than lower ones.[28] The chain of elements—classification, order, value, hierarchy—was supposed to delineate the realm of possibilities at each level of existence. If 'ought implies can', the range of moral imperatives was thereby delineated, and a ladder of command was accordingly authorized. The ladder of command consisted in a hierarchy of imperatives and injunctions which simultaneously reflected and cemented the putative racial order. This hierarchy of command was promoted by a complex configuration of power relations and its representations. Nevertheless, the structure of commands has also served to perpetuate established relations of power. For example, various interpretations of the principle of gradation considered it justifiable to treat 'lower racial orders' as animals, subjecting their members to forms of labor and living conditions otherwise reserved for animals.[29] Polygenists like Edward Long reasoned that because 'Negroes' and whites are incapable of forming properly fertile hybrids ('mulattoes'), they must constitute different species. Long held that 'Negroes' are not properly human and ought not to be treated as such.[30] A century later, leading scientists and social theorists in Europe and the United States encouraged inferences to the same conclusion though from different presuppositions. Cutting across different theoretical formations, the principle of gradation, it could be said, is at once a principle of degradation.

Classification, order, and value are fundamental to the forms of rationality we have inherited. Socially, it is evident that we labor still under the constraints of this rationalized authority; we order our relations with others in its light. The principle of racial hierarchy, by contrast, is now widely considered obsolete. This has motivated various responses to racist thinking and racialized discourse. The most widespread is that the concepts of *inferiority* and *superiority* implicit in *racial hierarchy* are part of a buried social setting and scientific paradigm. The ladder of command they authorize is thought to have no scientific or rational legitimacy. At best, *'the* theory of racism' is likened to the phlogiston theory of gases in the Enlightenment: Despite empirical discoveries and new scientific paradigms, the phlogiston theory persisted to the turn of the nineteenth century.[31] At worst, racism is dismissed as a crude rationalization for the domination and subjugation of others. A more sophistic response has been the denial that racist principles exist any longer: If the principle of natural hierarchy has now been abandoned, there can be no concept of racial superiority commanding acts or authorizing differential distributions.[32]

In abandoning appeals to superiority connoted by hierarchical classification, racists are committed neither to irrationality and rationalization nor to extinction. History for the moment aside, though hierarchy may not be conceptually implicit in the concept of 'racial classification', *difference* surely is. This is borne out by the synonym *racial differentiation. Difference* and *identity* inhere in the concept of race, furnishing whatever grounds can be claimed for racial classification. Domination of a particular race is established in respect to a series of differences from other individuals or groups and by virtue of a series of identities between those considered alike. The choice of what is to count as a relevant difference or identity is not straightforwardly determined by the prevailing discursive primitives outlined earlier. The choice is overdetermined, for it is circumscribed by various assumptions effective in social or scientific discourse at the time.[33] This commits us conceptually not to a single racism—*the* theory—but to a set of transforming expressions, including theoretical expressions, that fall properly under the sign 'racist'.

Racial differentiation—the mere discrimination *between* races and their purported members—is not as such necessarily racist. I will begin to address the set of issues this raises in the next chapter. Suffice it to say here that racial identity, even when externally ascribed, implies unity—at least conceptually. When this identity is internalized it prompts identification, a social sense of belonging together.[34] It is then that racial differentiation begins to define otherness, and discrimination *against* the racially defined other becomes at once *exclusion* of the different. Since the seventeenth century elaboration of racial differences and identities has served as a leading mode of promoting exclusions and inclusions. It has recently allowed racists to applaud the debunking of social hierarchies, serving in the same breath to establish basic conceptual unity for modern racialized discourse and racist exclusions.

Exclusion on the basis of racialized difference furnishes common ground for the transformational schema generated by classification. *Differential exclusion* is the most basic primitive term of the deep structure underlying racist expression. As the basic propositional content of racist desires, dispositions, beliefs, hypotheses, and assertions (including acts, laws, and institutions), racialized exclusion conceptually grounds the entire superstructure of racist expression. Most notably, racial exclusion establishes the pertinent mark of entitlement and restriction, endowment and appropriation. Here, racial exclusion serves in at least two general ways. It is most usually taken as a *presumption* in the service of which rules or rationalizations may then be formulated or offered. But what is seldom acknowledged, by legislators and social scientists alike, is that racist exclusion may often be the *outcome,* implicitly or explicitly, of practical deliberation in some domain—in economics, say, or pedagogy, or legislation.

To summarize: Classification enabled racial differentiation, whereas the historically grounded derivation of order, value, and hierarchy authorized the various forms of located racial exclusions in the name of difference. It remains to be seen how the normalization of racist articulation licenses individual subjective expression in its terms.

Discursive Power and the Body of Racist Expression

Each *episteme* is characterized by a 'regime of rationality'. This consists not simply in a collection of objective truths to be discovered and affirmed but in what Foucault calls a 'general politics of truth'. A set of discursive rules emerge from an economy of epistemological production in virtue of which 'truth' may be differentiated from 'falsity'.[35] At issue in any such economy are competing interpretations of the language of truth, assertion, and representation—in short, of 'knowledge' and its relation to power.

Foucault suggests that 'nothing is more material, physical, corporeal than the exercise of power.' The authority of power cannot be something ideal. The drive to exercise authorial power—whether out of the pure pleasure of the expression or as a means to further ends—clothes itself in the theoretical fashions of rationality. Authority is established and exercised only by being vested with the force of discrimination, exclusion, and enforcement. If the canons of value and taste in which authority resides have the power to effect material ends, it must be that these canons themselves embody material force.[36]

Racialized discourse has for the most part dominated definition of otherness throughout modernity, and racist expression has largely furnished the material power for the forceful exclusion of the different. The institutional 'success' of racialized exclusion in its various forms presupposes a suitable authority to distinguish the beneficiaries of the entitlement (those who would enjoy the fruits of the endowment) from those to be restricted in their enjoyment or denied their rights, goods, and services. 'The sense of belonging together' is too vague alone to furnish a mode of discriminate differentiation and exclusion. If the sense of belonging is to have any force, it must either be manifest in or be predicated upon establishment of an authority (institutional or personal) in the body or person(s) of whom group members at least partially recognize themselves. By internalizing this authority and subjecting themselves to the law thus author(iz)ed and enforced, group members incorporate themselves and establish cohesion. In this way, the group so constituted coterminously acquires a privileged moral position.[37] When this authority assumes state power, racialized discourse and its modes of exclusion become embedded in state institutions and normalized in the common business of everyday institutional life.

To succeed so long in effecting the materiality of differential exclusions, racialized discourse has to be grounded in the relations of social subjects to each other and in ways of seeing, of relating to, (other) subjects. Voyages of discovery and imperialist drives may have prompted the presumption of general differences among conquering populations and the conquered. However, the rise of racist expression and its accompanying violence of material deprivation was rendered *theoretically* possible only by a change in paradigm from the seventeenth century onward for viewing human subjects. The new philosophical assumption that bodies are but machines naturally divorceable from minds, that minds are nothing more than physical machines, opened the way to some extreme novel developments in technologies of physical power and bodily discipline. These technologies of discipline and power were superimposed upon human subjects; they encouraged docility by reducing even *social* subjectivities, or at least some forms of social subjectivity, to physical dimensions and correlates.[38]

So racialized discourse may be seen to acquire unity in terms of bodily relations, that is, in certain forms of 'the investment of the body, its valorization, and the distributive management of its forces'.[39] This unity highlights the material force at racisms' heart. The distributive management of bodies enabled by some forms of color racism, for example, extended the space in which capital accumulation, the growth of productive forces, and the massive generation and redeployment of surplus value could take place. In other words, it is *in virtue of* racialized discourse and not merely rationalized by racist expression that such forced manipulations and exploitation of individual subjects and whole populations could have been affected. American Indians and inhabitants of Africa were imagined in European representations considerably before their exploitation as slaves took place. Indeed, these images and the discursive rationalizations attendant with them enabled the conceivability of Euro-enslavement of colonial inhabitants.

I am suggesting that racist exclusion finds whatever authority it has in a discourse of the body and that this 'body talk' (so to speak) forges an underlying, though abstract, unity for the discourse of race. It remains to be shown how the theory of the body materially grounds racialized expression, investing racist expression with its power of discrimination between and over the excluded and included, naturalizing and normalizing the violence of dismissal, dispersal, indeed, all too often, disappearance.

From the standpoint of human subjects, nothing is more 'natural' to think and speak about than the body. It is directly experienced, its deficiencies immediately felt; and it is usually taken as the receptacle or 'container' of pleasures and pains, desires and needs. The bodies of others are unproblematically observable, confronted, and engaged. In other words, the body is central to ordinary experience and offers a unique paradigm: It is a symbol of a 'bounded system', a system the boundaries of which are formed by skin at once porous but perceived as inviolable and impenetrable. Body parts and functions are accordingly related in a complex structure, their substance confined by boundaries and limits that are fragile, vulnerable, and threatened.

By extension, the body comes to stand for the body politic, to symbolize society, to incorporate a vision of power. Porous and permeable though the boundaried 'skin' of the body politic may in fact be, it is constituted always in terms of the bordered criteria of inclusion and exclusion, identities and separateness, (potential) members and inevitable nonmembers. Embedded as these criteria are in spoken or silent rules, they delineate and define social relations, reflect and refine the political body both internally and in its differentiation from other social structures.[40]

As a mode of exclusion, racist expression assumes authority and is vested with power, literally and symbolically, in bodily terms. They are human bodies that are classified, ordered, valorized, and devalued. They are human bodies that, because of their differences, are forced to work, alienated from their labor product, disenfranchised, or restricted in their right of social entry and mobility. Corporeal properties have also furnished the metaphorical media for distinguishing the pure from the impure, the diseased from the clean and acceptable, the included from the excluded. Classification of differences determines order. Hierarchy is established on the basis of a value of purity—whether interpreted biologically (in terms of blood or genes), hygienically (in terms, for instance, of body odor), culturally (for example, language as signifying the evolution of thought patterns and rational capacity), or even environmentally (virtuous character, like nose shape and size, determined by climate). Impurity, dirt, disease, and pollution are expressed as functions of the transgression of classificatory categories, expressed, that is, in terms of laws, as also are danger and the breakdown of order. Actively undertaking to transgress or pollute the given order necessitates reinventing order by way of confinement and artificially imposed separation.[41] For example, anti-Semitic representations have often been deployed to exclude Jewish bodies from European neighborhoods or active participation in European economies; the Palestinian presence on the West Bank, as well as the location of blacks under *apartheid* has been curtailed for the sake of law and order; and as I show in chapter 8, the 'native city' of colonial Africa was physically divided from European neighborhoods in the name of purity and the 'sanitation syndrome'.[42]

Instruments of exclusion—legal, cultural, political, or economic—are forged by subjects in relation to but never fully determined by specific local conditions as they mold criteria for establishing racial otherness. Racist expression is promoted—perhaps entailed—by this discourse of the body, with its classificatory systems, order, and values, its ways of 'seeing' particular bodies, and its modes of exclusion. Paradoxically, racialized discourse has often succeeded in drawing social subjects together. It has served to unify them as subjects of authority. Subjects have been able to recognize identity in terms of this discourse, as, too, they can be identified by it. The discourse of race furnishes a cohesive foundation for the body politic, a continuity in time and across authorities. It is a discourse that authors of the law might invoke as justification of entitlements or restrictions, endowments or lacks, incorporation or disenfranchisement.

Thus, racialized discourse has readily entered the domains of morality and legality, often silently, as foundational claims. Its asserted title to establish differences is taken as an objective basis of inclusion and exclusion, whether natural or historical. This is offered, in turn, as a primary ground of entitlements, of rights of accessibility (to enfranchisement, opportunity, or treatment), and of endowments (goods and the means thereto); and conversely, of denial (disenfranchisement or restriction), of prohibition (to entry, participation, or services), and of alienation (of goods and the means to them). In general, the discourse of race has served to 'justify', as it prompts the exclusion of others by making it thinkable to deny or ignore their respective claims. It encourages active interference in establishing what the excluded, the disenfranchised, and the restricted are entitled to and can properly expect.

These authoritative issues of racialized exclusion, entitlement, and expectation are exemplified most vividly by immigration policy. Eugenicists, for instance, addressed the political, legal, and moral issues of immigration from the standpoint of their 'scientific' findings. Earlier this century prominent eugenicists in the United States and Britain argued that members of alien racial stocks should be excluded or severely restricted from entering these respective countries to prevent weakening the biological quality of the local stock. In Britain, East European Jews were especially singled out;[43] in the United States, the national quota on population entry from any country in Europe was reduced to 2 percent of the residents of that origin in the United States in 1890. 'Orientals' were eventually excluded altogether, culminating in the complete ban on Japanese immigration in 1924. The European Bill had the intended effect of favoring immigrant stocks of the more 'desirable' English, Irish, Germans, and Scandinavians over the 'inferior stocks' of newer immigrants from Eastern and Southern Europe.[44] More recently, exclusion, disenfranchisement, restriction of entry and mobility, and denial of the means to fulfil needs and wants have been justified to varying degrees in South

Africa, Thatcher's Britain, and Israel. Though not for the most part racially explicit in formulation, the (re)new(ed) U.S. immigration restrictions (witness the Bush administration's forced repatriation of Haitian boat people), Germany's *gastarbeit* policy and vigorous antagonism toward asylum for foreigners in the wake of unification, and France's migrant labor system are racist in effect: They discriminatorily restrict entry or labor of members of those population groups considered undesirable—those who are identified, if only silently, in racial terms.[45]

I have argued that the formal apparatus of racialized discourse has multiple overlapping determinations. They include the economy of power and its relations pertaining to a prevailing spatiotemporal conjuncture that carries a new way of looking at bodies and new modes of speaking about others. This new mode of vision and expression is defined in terms of technologies of classification and the analysis of differences and identities, and it promotes new forms of institutionalized prohibition—for instance, on bodily contact implied by the concept of heredity or on land tenure implied by the appeal to historically granted land rights. As expressions of exclusion, racism appeals either to inherent superiority or to differences. These putative differences and gradations may be strictly physical, intellectual, linguistic, or cultural. Each serves in two ways: They purport to furnish the basis for justifying differential distributions or treatment, and they represent the very relations of power that prompted them.

The discursive unity of racialized discourse is promoted by the schema of preconceptual primitive terms laid out above and by the transformational structures effecting expressions on their basis. In specific sociohistorical contexts, this schema generates the concepts peculiar to the enunciation of racism at that time and place, and, thereby, the categories, stereotypes, expressions, metaphors, styles, and themes expressed in the field of racialized discourse and racist expression. To establish racism specifically as an expressive object of racialized discourse, however, the preconceptual schema must also give rise to racist hypotheses and presumptions, indeed, to racist implication, argumentation, reasoning, and rationalization.

If the widespread employment and influence of racist expression is to be fully comprehended, it is the *persuasiveness* of argumentation that must be accounted for. This suggests a factor of the racist discursive formation that remains to be analyzed. To show how agents have so readily taken up racialized discourse and resorted to racist expression, it must be illustrated how agents subject themselves to modes of expression, making these modes of expression their own; whom subjects direct these expressions and reasoning at and why; and what subjects might (aim to) gain from this way of expressing themselves.

The Racist Subject

Adoption of racialized discourse and racist expression has been widespread. They have been assumed across classes, nations, social and ethnic groups; in different places, at different times, and under widely varying conditions. This cannot be explained solely in socioeconomic, political, or sociological terms. Such explanations are singular in ignoring a central feature: the persuasiveness of racist expression, its compelling character for subjects. Similarly, the prevailing presumptions of racism's irrationality and of the 'false consciousness' of racists stress the psychosis of the racist personality rather than his or her persuasion, conscious belief and conviction, or rational willingness.[46] To comprehend this widespread domestication of racist expression, of the authority of racist articulation, the question of human agency and the formation of subjectivity must be addressed.

A primary factor in the formation of social groups is the self-recognition of (potential) group members in the image of an authority (whether institutional or personal). This recognition may be realized in terms of various media. *Interpellation* is the process by which individuals are hailed or called to subjectivity by others, and so it presupposes mutual recognition by individuals. The formation of subjectivity is thus inherently social. Emile Benveniste argues that individuals are interpellated as subjects in and by means of language.[47] This hypothesis raises the possibility of conceiving the constitution of the subject as the point of convergence or the bodily intersection of multiple discourses. Whatever properties and (Kantian) categories are thought to constitute humans *qua* human, individuals are defined and define themselves as *subjects* by way of social discourses. Discourses are the intermediary between self and society; they mediate the self as social subject.[48]

Discursive expressions like racism are the products of the economy of power, reflected in the interrelations of bodies, produced and refined in practice. However, social discourses do not just reflect the economy of power, with its characteristic relations of domination, subjugation, and exclusion. Once initiated, social discourses are placed in the arsenal of the 'practico-inert',[49] ready to be passed along, inherited, reproduced, and transformed to suit prevailing conditions. By converging with related discourses and interiorized by the individual, the discourse underlying racism comes to codefine not only subjectivity but otherness also. It molds subjects' relations with others. Subjects' actions are rendered meaningful to themselves and others in light of the values that this discourse, among others, makes available or articulates to the parties involved.[50] In this way, racialized discourse—reproduced, redefined perhaps, and acted upon—reconstitutes the relations of power that produced them.

Just as language furnishes a key for becoming conscious of oneself as distinct from the world, social discourse provides the means for social self-definition. Naming one's race, on the plane of racial identity, has come to function in something like the way that naming oneself at the level of self-consciousness and self-identity does. The possibility of the former necessitates self-recognition by the individual, bodily and culturally, in the image of the social fathers (e.g., white leaders, the nation's founding fathers, a Jewish Jehovah, the Aryan Superman), as self-consciousness presupposes self-recognition by youths in their own patriarchal (or matriarchal) figures. Each level of subjection—to authoritative discourses or to racial authority—is established by way of sociolinguistic symbols. These symbols incorporate general rules and taboos that represent The Law: the Law of Authority in general, or the Racial Law in particular. Once internalized, these discursive bodies of law, and others like them (nation, class, gender, religion, capitalism, democracy, and so on), give social definition to the subject.

The analogy I have drawn here between the forms of law constitutive of the social subject is obviously asymmetrical. The predominantly patriarchal Law of Authority is central to the constitution of human subjectivity, at least in its contemporary historical trajectory, in a way in which Racial Law and racist expression are not. The Law of Authority has perhaps come to serve as a model, an ideal, for the definition of individual subjectivity by social discourses. This is partially reflected in the fact that it is for the most part less wrenching to abandon the likes of Racial Law, to give up racialized discourse, than it is to transgress the Law of Authority, though of course there are times when these will be coincidental. This also suggests a reason why, once a discourse like this takes root in the definition of social subjectivity, it becomes so difficult to weed it out. The renunciation or shift to other discourses, like modifications internal to the discourse, might reflect more or less subtle changes in the economy of power. It is possible, nevertheless, that these shifts are sometimes determined by factors specific to the grammatical formation of the discourse itself. Monogenism, for example, began to give way in the second half of the eighteenth century to polygenism as the prevailing hypothesis of speciation. This transformation could not in any direct or simple way turn on changing social, political, or economic circumstances in Europe or the (former) colonies at the time. It was more directly related to developments in categorizing animal and human species, and thus to a dynamic internal to the discourse. The initial intraspecies ordering and valuation became, as the hypothesis emerged and unfolded, an ordering and implied valuation of separate species and their origins.

The social subject, I have maintained, consists in the intersection of social discourses in the body. The dimensions brought by the body to the equation are the (bounded) capacities to desire and to think. It is discourses, though, that furnish the media for thought and for articulation of desires. Kant's famous dictum may be emulated to express the state of subjectivity: Discourses without desires are empty, desires without discourses blind.[51] Because human subjects fail to act save on the impulsion of desires, discourses on their own would be unmotivated. Hence, they would be empty, in the sense of producing no effect. Conversely, a desire not yet defined by a discourse could only be blind (indiscriminate). The intentions, motives, dispositions, expressions, and acts of the racist are discourse specific. These determinations by discourse may be conscious and explicit, or inadvertent as with unconscious slips and misstatements that reveal repression and wish-fulfillment.[52]

On the conscious level, discourses articulate and thereby give definition to intentions, dispositions, reasons, and goals. The general intention, disposition, desire, or goal of the racist may be expressed as (relative) *racial exclusion.* The extension of this expression may include both specific racist goals and reasons (whether cited as justification or rationalization). Racists may intend, desire, or be disposed *inter alia* to exclude racial others with the goal in mind of domination or subjugation; of maximizing profit by maintaining a cheap labor force, a reserve army of labor; of reserving jobs for members of what they take to be their own race; or of maintaining indigenous culture. As reasons for or the general principles they take to inform their acts, racists may offer the goals themselves or various other categories of reason. These include, though they may not be limited to scapegoating (e.g., a conspiracy theory), rationalizations (like inferiority), or rational stereotyping (e.g., a normative judgment appealing to factual evidence). These racist motivations influencing a subject's acts are complemented by other factors. They include fear, whether brought on by the threat of physical force or psychologically induced; and conformism, that is, the behavioral disposition, imposed or merely encouraged, to conform to the needs of the community.[53] Such factors, in turn, may be prompted by racialized discourse or racist expression in the process of reinforcing or reinventing themselves.

The field of racist discourse, then, is a product of sociodiscursive *praxis* in determinate historical circumstances. The power of racist expression conjoins with the power of other discursive expressions—notably, though not only, those of class, gender, nation, and capitalism—to determine the subjectivity of individuals at established times and places. What begins to emerge from this racial subjectivizing is a subjection to violence. The violence of racisms afflicts both the objects of racist acts and the racist subject engaged in the expression. Violence is inherent in racist expression. Subjects are defined in general by the discourses of difference. So subjects recognize themselves for the most part only in contrast to others. Voltaire's or Kant's sense of their own racial identities are at once revealed in their respective views about 'fuzzy-haired Negroes' or Negroid intellectual incapacity.[54] The recognition of the self in the other remains at root an alienated identity, an 'identity-in-otherness'. Self-determination is a precondition for self-recognition or self-conscious identity. This assertion of self-determination may be thought to require that the other—literally the other's otherness—be negated or canceled. Where this 'identity-in-the-other' is racially predicated or defined by racial discourse, the drive to self-consciousness may become a negation or reduction of the racial other, the other's exclusion. Tabulating racial differences as an order of what Sartre calls 'alterity,' defining others reductively in such a way as to exclude them, is at once to constitute the other as enemy, to engage him or her in relations of violence.[55]

This establishment of the other *as* other is promoted by the initial drive to establish self-identity by identifying *with* the other. Negating others, *denigrating* them, becomes in part, thus, also self-negation and self-effacement.[56] The pleasure of violating another is not simply a product of self-assertion. It also involves, though often self-deceptively, the masochistic perversion of self-violation. By contrast, in responding to this violence the other may vacillate between the hardships of active resistance and the relative comforts of passive resignation. This hesitation signifies prior acquisition of the preconditions of the victim's own subjection and violation. The subjection at work here all too often presupposes acquiescence by the victims in the preconcepts of the discourse that motivated their exclusion: persecution approaching self-persecution (the 'persecution complex') and then projected as the vicious persecution of others. Anti-Semitism illustrates the point: The modes of Jewish subjugation are reproduced in Israeli exclusion and violence against Palestinians. Otto Weininger stands as the extreme example, viciously immolating a Jewish identity he finds inevitably impoverished while denying his own to the point of suicide.[57]

It is thus in the constitution of alterity itself that the hold of racialized discourse and racist exclusions over subject formation and expression is rendered possible. For it is in the very making of otherness by discursive technologies that the modernized modes of racial distinction and distancing can be invested in and through the bodies of social subjects and, accordingly, that this investment can be extended into the body politic. Racisms become normalized through modernity's discursive technologies of subject formation; they acquire their 'naturalism' in the creation of modern moral selves and social subjects.

Nevertheless, the self-assertive drive to determine one's conscious identity reveals an ambiguity in the determination of subjectivity by racial discourse. In negating another subject's *racially* defined otherness, the possibility of compatibility and solidarity beyond race may be entertained. The problem of dissolving racist expression is thus dialectically posed. It is this possibility that needs ultimately to be opened up. To reach the point where this can be fully addressed, however, the culture of race and its implications need further elaboration. The first requirement in this anatomy of racist culture is to specify what has been meant historically, both in popular discourse and in the social sciences, by the concepts of *race* and *racism,* and how they have become institutionalized in social reasoning. What is signified by the various social and theoretical articulations of race and racism? How has race been persistently able to structure and define transforming configurations of social relations? It is to these questions that we now turn.

4

The Masks of Race

'*While everything may seem to be negotiable, culture, education, and civilization are not negotiable.*'[1]

I suggested in the last chapter that of all the expressions making up racialized discourse some are more centrally constitutive of the discursive formation than others and, by extension, more primary to the forms of its reproduction and diachronic transformations. It may be predicted, roughly, that the more directly related a concept is to these central constituents of racialized discourse, the more likely it is to structure reproductive or transformative expressions in a racialized social order and so to effect their articulation of racist exclusions.[2]

This account may seem to suggest that there is no racism without or before at least some allusion to the concept of *race,* that the concept necessarily precedes the phenomenon of racism both conceptually and as a matter of historical fact. Nevertheless, it makes little sense to ask which came first, the concept or the disposition to distance and exclude that inheres at least historically in the constitution of racialized otherness. The transformations from one racism into another are closely entwined—as cause, as effect, sometimes only as affect—with the sets of changing social interests attaching to *race* in its conceptual variations from the sixteenth century on.

This way of looking at things suggests that it is a mistake to define race in terms of necessary and sufficient conditions. The prevailing concern here to show the normalization of racisms throughout modernity, in and through racisms' ties to transformations in the prevailing conceptions of *race,* implies that we should focus rather on a different set of concerns: How has the term 'race' been used at different times, what has it signified, and how has it served to articulate a conception for its users of self and group identity, of self and other?

To proceed in this way flies in the face of the prevailing methodology applied to the study of race in the social sciences. There are two basic ways to get at the meanings of socially significant terms. The first is purely conceptual: to stipulate definitions largely a priori on the basis of what the terms *ought* to signify, at least in relation to the conceptual scheme in which they are taken most convincingly to make sense, and then to look for empirical instances exemplifying the phenomena thus defined. The second way is historical: to lay out how the terms have predominantly been used, the sorts of implications and effects they have had, and how these have all and interrelatedly transformed over time.

Prevailing conceptions of race in the social sciences have largely proceeded in the former way. By contrast, definitions of racism since the 1940s have mostly mirrored perceptions of the term's popular usage, namely, as an irrational group prejudice assuming racial others to be inferior purely in terms of their biologically-conceived racial membership. I wish to invert this definitional process, and doubly so. I will proceed in the case of race by looking at the way the concept has been used historically and how these usages have changed over time. My concern is, thus, to see whether any transhistorical features common to these uses emerge, features which might be said to direct any further use of the concept, to set the limits to its transformative applicability and adaptability. In the case of racism, however, I will *stipulate* a definition. I argue in chapter 5 that this definition must be sensitive not only to the way in which the term has been variously used this past half century; more importantly, it must enable identification of racist expressions whenever they have been manifested this past half millennium. In the present chapter, I will be concerned with mapping the historically based significance of *race*.

Natural Kind, Social Creation

The concept of *race* seeped into European consciousness more or less coterminous with the exploratory voyages of discovery, expansion, and domination in the latter part of the fifteenth century. The French term *race* and the German *Rasse* derive from the Italian *razza* and the Spanish *raza*, general terms that came to reflect the discovery and experience of groups of beings very different from, indeed strange to the European eye and self.[3] From its inception, then, race has referred to those perceived, indeed, constituted as other. The earliest recorded English usage of the term 'race' occurs in 1508, in a poem by William Dunbar. It seems possible that the term's significance was a derivative of an earlier sense of race as 'root', applicable to vegetables or herbs (1450). Races were taken, loosely speaking, as population groups of different roots, suggestively rooted in the geographic soils of different regions. It is in this sense that the term assumed both medieval and modern cast: It reflected the revitalized Aristotelian concerns of the scholastics with plant and animal classification, and it increasingly defined the modern interest in differentiating newly discovered groups of people. Accordingly, from its earliest use 'race' has taken on both natural and social qualities.

It is this tension between its natural and social significance that predominantly marks the conceptual history of race. One finds this reflected in the two primary senses of the term: first, as a group of plants, animals, or persons linked by common origin or descent; and second, as a group having some feature(s) in common. While these features might be physical, they could equally be a characteristic style of speech or writing, manner or custom. So, in general, 'race' has been used to signify a 'breed or stock of animals' (1580), a 'genus, species or kind of animal' (1605), or a 'variety of plant' (1596). It refers at this time also to 'the great divisions of mankind' (1580) and especially to 'a limited group of persons descended from a common ancestor' (1581), while only slightly later to a 'tribe, nation or people considered of common stock' (1600).[4] Divisions, nations, and peoples may find themselves of common stock in virtue of shared social characteristics, ones perhaps deemed natural properties of the group. Thus, the primary senses of 'race' and the conflation of natural with the social kinds they promoted were already well rooted nearly two hundred years prior to the Enlightenment![5] Shakespeare's Caliban, for example, is characterized as belonging to a 'wild race/...which good natures/Could not abide to be with.' Like Sepulveda in his debate with Las Casas, Miranda conceives of the 'savage slave' as a 'brute', different in nature—in line of descent—from herself. Taught language, Caliban is nevertheless considered capable only of brute meaning, of taking orders.[6]

Pedigree and Population

Against the background of this early emphasis upon descent in terms of origin, breed, or stock, the general commitment to race as *lineage* was overriding.[7] This picture was at first prompted and promoted by an informal and nascent descriptive anthropology of travelers, adventurers, and imperial agents. Trading on the conception of a common European 'we' that coalesced in the 1450s, these travelogues—the means by which the wider public was teaching itself to read—played a key role in the commercial survival of the printing press a century later. At the same time, this literature popularized the interpretation of race in terms of ancestral relatedness. In the name of monogenism, this interpretation had already begun in the sixteenth century to dominate the 'philosophical' explanation of human origins. Monogenism considered all human beings traceable to common Godly origins. Racial distinctions were ascribed to group correlated geographic, climatic, and social differences.[8] Moreover, as I pointed out in chapter 2, the monogenist paradigm was consistent with, if not grounds for, a selective application of the prominent moral commitment to natural rights.

Michael Banton thinks that monogenism prevailed until 1800. However, a challenge was already materializing during the Enlightenment and can be traced back in inception to the heretical protopolygenic pre-Adamism of the seventeenth-century visionary, Isaac de la Peyrere. Pre-Adamism claimed that the

Bible represented only Jewish history and so established the origins of the Jewish species alone. It was hypothesized that following Jews' fall from God's favor and the incarnation of Christ, Christians were elevated over the Jewish *species* as the Chosen People. In addition, though, a stock of men were supposed to have lived an unspecifiable time in a Hobbesian state of nature prior to the creation of Adam. La Peyrere, a contemporary of Hobbes, was forced by the religious and political establishment to renounce these views publicly, though he never recanted them theoretically. Nevertheless, in the face of political and ideological reaction, the doctrine faded from public view.

By 1789 the attack against religion by reason had rendered possible a doctrinal revival. The data mounting against monogenism by then seemed overwhelming to Europeans. Francois Burtin, a Dutch scientist, had concluded from available fossil evidence that rational beings predated Adam, though he refused to deem them human. In 1800 Edward King (a member of the Royal Society) argued that biblical interpretation and scientific evidence revealed Adam to be the genealogical father only of that species of humans possessing the highest capacities of language and science. Pre-Adamism thus constituted the hypothetical bridge between religious presumption and scientific theory, the break between sixteenth century scriptural suggestion of monogenist origins and nineteenth-century polygenism. In the first half of the nineteenth century, the latter came to assume the status of *the* modern hypothesis of natural history and anthropological science.[9]

Though polygenism continued to read *race* in terms of origins, it differed from monogenism in emphasizing biological inheritance and hierarchy over pedigree. Classification of races proceeded on the basis of differentially ordered, heritable qualities and dispositions. In the eighteenth century even those who, like Kant, rejected the growing polygenist tendencies of the period were influenced by the central conception of hierarchical heritability. In matters anthropological, Buffon and especially Kant used 'race' centrally and liberally. Blumenbach, it is true, preferred to substitute the term 'varieties', while early in the nineteenth century Cuvier and Prichard used 'race' interchangeably with 'varieties', and Lamarck with 'families'. So Banton goes too far in claiming that 'race' was rarely used in the eighteenth century as a term of differential description, that the main increase in 'racial consciousness' occurred only in the latter half of the nineteenth century.

Banton is nevertheless correct in identifying the prevailing conception at this time as consisting in the view that among human groups varieties in character, behavior, and social condition reflected underlying invariant differences in natural kind, and these naturally given *types,* more or less superior, correlated with established geographical—indeed, continental—regions.[10] The shift from thinking of people predominantly in terms of their pedigree to conceiving them foremostly in terms of their group identity is reflected in the growing emphasis upon the concept of *population.* To be a member of a population was to be identifiable on the basis of invariant, heritable characteristics:

the principle physical characters of a people may be preserved throughout a long series of ages, in a great part of the population, despite of climate, mixture of races, invasion of foreigners, progress of civilization, or other known influences; and that a type can long outlive its language, history, religion, customs, and recollections.[11]

Europeans, or those of European type, had a view of themselves as 'civilized', while Africans were viewed as a 'barbarous ... ignorant and savage race'; to change the latter's customs 'requires a stretch of years that dazzles in the looking at'.[12] Civilized races were taken as having the capacity for self-determination; barbarous races, lacking self-control and autonomy, required direction.

In the monogenic view of race, the genesis of all human beings was considered to lie in the line of descent from Adam and Eve, and racial distinction was ascribable to environmental difference. Yet no account was forthcoming for the mechanisms by which races were environmentally determined. Polygenism resolved this difficulty by supposing racial difference to inhere originally in population groupings: Contemporary difference in type was a matter simply of inheritance. This view claimed initial corroboration from the natural history of the day: in the cranial comparisons and facial measurements of Dutch anatomist Pieter Camper, in the physiognomy or 'science of reading the human skull' of Johann Lavater, and in the phrenological plottings of skull shape, brain organs, and human character by the Germans Gall and Spurzheim. To this was added the influential authority of craniometry in France, Britain, and the United States, especially in the names of Paul Broca, James Hunt, and Samuel Morton respectively. It has recently been shown that each piece of claimed evidence imported into its structure aesthetic and pseudoscientific values and involved biased methods of measurement.[13] What raised grave doubts about polygenism in the second half of the nineteenth century, however, was a radically new way of thinking: The emerging evidence of evolution led to the introduction of a new notion of race.[14] Mere populations gave way to *breeding populations,* varieties or types to *subspecies.*

Breeding Populations and Gene Pools

Speciation in biology and natural history is part of the wider practice of taxonomy. This involves classifying groups or *taxa* according to established criteria. Groups consist of individual organisms collected together on the basis of similarities between them. These similarities are, in turn, thought to arise as a result of descent from common ancestry. A group or *taxon* incorporating substantially diverse plants or animals is called a *class.* The largest subunits of a class are *orders,* and the latter divide in decreasing levels of scope into *families, genera,* and *species.*

A species is a group of individual plants or animals of which the individual members bear the largest possible resemblance to each other. More specifically, it is a group of individuals whose members are *capable* of interbreeding with each other but not with members of other species.[15] A species, in other words, is a group whose members are reproductively isolated. A *subspecies* or race is, as the name suggests, a subdivision of the species. It consists in a group of individuals who bear resemblance to each other in some definable characteristics while diverging at least in these traits from other members of the species.[16] Breeding between members of different subspecies of the same species—plant or animal—may be feasible. However, interbreeding between different subspecies' members tends to occur less freely or frequently, at least in theory, than intrasubspecies breeding. Lines of demarcation between subspecies are accordingly often murky; at their periphery racial strains merge into each other.[17] Lack of miscegenation and reproduction may be due simply to geographical or, in the case of humans, cultural isolation. Long-term isolation may motivate classification of the isolated group as a race and in the very long term even as a species. Or so the story goes.

It was Darwin who reconceived species as breeding populations, and who imparted a fluidity to the taxonomic categories missing altogether from polygenism. Races for the polygenist were tantamount to species, fixed more or less since their separate inception and incapable of interbreeding.[18] In Darwin's view, species were breeding populations and races were simply subspecies. Both were capable of evolving; indeed, a subspecies might eventually evolve into a separate species. In terms of the earlier typological thinking, all members of the species were considered basically similar; character was set at the group level. For Darwin, by contrast, a breeding population was conceived as a system of interacting individuals. Evolution was analyzed in terms of the individual struggle and fitness for survival. The standard processes determining genetic inheritance—natural selection, gene variance, mutation, genetic drift—interacted with a wide range of specific environmental conditions to prompt a great variety of ways in which evolution might proceed.[19]

In due course, the conceptual relations at the heart of Darwinism came to be expressed genetically. Biologically related persons are those possessing genes, through inheritance, from a common gene pool. The genetic population consists in this common pool of genes from which individual members have each inherited a sample by way of their originating egg and sperm. Heredity is the pattern of gene transmission from ancestry which determines the individual's locus of possible responses to the environment. Races, in this view, are simply populations that diverge from each other in their relative gene frequencies or, in other words, in the relative degree of possessing certain inherited features. Racial similarities are merely agglomerations of individual hereditary characteristics (alleles or strings of genes), which even within a single population tend not to converge.

Races are thought to form biologically in the main (if they form at all) by imbalances in the equilibrium of the gene pool as a result of changes in relative gene frequencies caused by mutations, or by natural selection, by genetic drift, by population mixing following migration, or through geographical or social isolation. A race is supposedly capable, over a long period, of alteration in hereditary features. At best, then, race is not a fixed and static classificatory category. If they exist at all, races differ in relative ways, depending for their homogeneity and stability upon the relative constancy of the genes in question.

This raises an acute problem for classifying the human species in racial terms. Human beings possess a far larger proportion of genes in common than they do genes that are supposed to differentiate them racially. Not surprisingly, we are much more like each other than we are different. It has been estimated that, genetically speaking, the difference in difference—the percentage of our genes that determines our purportedly racial or primarily morphological difference—is 0.5 percent.[20] Stated more generally, intraracial differences are often much smaller than those between members of different races, interracial similarities often much greater than the similarities between those taken to be members of the same race.

Subject of Promotion, or Object of Analysis?

So the theory of evolution serves as a warning, though often ignored, to those who would proceed in rigidly classifying the human species into races on genetic grounds, and perhaps to those who would proceed in such classifications at all. The latter is a question to which we must return. The Darwinian conception of race as subspecies marks a watershed in race-thinking. On the one hand, those who would continue to think in terms of race began to assume the Darwinian language: 'Fitness for survival' in the case of Social Darwinians like Toynbee; 'hereditary hygiene' in the case of eugenicists like Francis Galton; and 'common gene pools' in the case of twentieth century thinkers ranging from proponents of the heritability of IQ like Jensen to sociobiological social theorists like Van den Berghe. Though one should take care not to collapse fundamental differences between these views, there is a utilitarianism underlying them: Natural selection and survival of the fittest are what will naturally maximize utility for the population at large. Thus, if nature constrains morality, there is a moral injunction, given these theories, to help nature along.

On the other hand, Darwinism issued the challenge to any theory investing explanatory power in the conception of race. And it did this at the very moment race had assumed discursive hegemony in colonizing social space. Race had set the parameters to what could be rational and reasonable, credible and utterable. It had drawn the bounds around common sense.[21] Nevertheless, prompted by Darwinism and at first tentatively, race began to occupy the position not of *explanans* but of *explanandum,* of the social object requiring rather than furnishing scientific explanation.

I do not mean by this distinction to deny the historical fact of other conceptions of race, for example, as blood. I want only to suggest that these are throwbacks, often confused and confusing, to earlier historical models. Great harm has been executed in their name this century. But in the face of social, political, and especially epistemological developments, such interpretations of race could no longer be paradigmatic. So in the case of reading race simply as blood, if the claim is taken literally it is construable—as it turns out, falsely—in genetic terms as blood type; if construed metaphorically the implication is of relatedness in terms of lineal descent. Gobineau's view is especially interesting, for he conflates race with basic linguistic group (and, by extension, with national identity). Here we are provided not so much with a different conception of race as with a marker, a kind of cultural phenotype, supposedly identifying descent relations:

> It is just because the connexion between race and language is so close, that it lasts much longer than the political unity of different peoples, and may be recognized even when the peoples are grouped under new names. The language changes with their blood, but does not die out until the last fragment of national life has disappeared.[22]

There are many examples this past century and currently, of work that begs to be taken seriously—as much so as in popular thinking—where race consists in this hybrid of significations: claims of descent or type mixed with assertions, often metaphorical, of spiritual or intellectual superiority. These examples furnish the more visible instances of the conflation of natural with social kinds that we have become used to identifying as racialized thinking. My wider point, however, is that they hardly exhaust the phenomena.

The social history of both strains in the last hundred years or so—the various applications of race genetically interpreted, alongside rejection of race as a concept fraught with genetic difficulties—has been well documented, and this is not my primary concern here. My focus, rather, is what race has been taken to mean. Given warnings (largely in the name of rights, but also conceptual and empirical) concerning race genetically conceived; given the virtual vacuity of race once defined in terms of interbreeding populations;[23] and given the growing recognition that racial phenomena require rather than provide explanations, some basic questions can be pressed: What shifts in significance did the notion of *race* begin to undergo, what prompted these shifts, and in what ways did these new senses infuse the explanations being offered?

Prompted by nineteenth century positivism, the primary methodological form assumed by explanations of social groups and their relations this century is reductionistic. The concern has been with ways to reduce relatively complex levels of group structure and relations to simpler explanatory levels taken to lie at their foundation; to explain entities deemed less real in terms of those thought to be more real. The less complex levels or more real entities may be held variously to determine, or to order, or simply to set the boundaries of the more complex structures and behavior, or of those entities considered less real.

Explanations of race and racialized phenomena in the past hundred years have tended to reflect two general forms. The first accepts the standard biological sense of race as subspecies genetically interpreted, of race as natural kind. It attempts to explain relations between real racial groups so interpreted, or their social appeal, or at least the social significance of such appeal by reducing the racialized phenomena to underlying social (or in some cases biological) terms or relations. These underlying terms are deemed more primary, more universal, more constitutive or basically motivating, and more fundamentally determining of social structure. Where these underlying levels are seen as biological, they are read as biological kinship or common gene pool.[24] By contrast, the other explanatory paradigm gives no independent content to the notion of race. It takes race as a social kind and interprets appeals to race as nothing other than recourse to social considerations and relations, again, like class or culture. If the first paradigm reifies race as an unquestioned biological given, the second conceives race and racial characterization of social relations as ghostlike. Lacking determining or motivational force of its own, any appeal to race is seen as mystificatory, a form of (self-deceived) false consciousness or misleading ideology.

Race as Class

Biological interpretations for the moment aside, the primary contemporary uses of race accordingly assume significance in terms of class or culture. *Qua* class, race can be understood to mean either socioeconomic status or relation to the mode of production. As status, race is simply an index of social standing or rank reflected in terms of criteria like wealth, education, style of life, linguistic capacity, residential location, consumptive capacity, or having or lacking respect. Status has to do with one's ranking in a social system relative to the position of others, where the ranking involves a criterial complex of self-conception and (de)valuations by others.[25] Those who are conceived as 'acting white' in these terms will be considered 'white'. There is a tendency here to equate race with class. Class position defines social distinction. It involves classification into groups occupying distinct social positions, and in the view at hand this is just what race does. It requires a further step to identify the class position at issue with racial configuration, but until recently this was—and in some countries remains—a relatively straightforward feature of *social* formation. This relative social identity of race and class may be thought true also of class defined in the second and narrower sense: as fundamental economic or structural relationships, in terms of relations to the mode of production and their corresponding interests. Race is conceived accordingly as masking the relationships and interests in question. So for those rejecting the biological connotation of *race,* races are identified with socially formed and materially determined class position. In either case—social status or material relations, race is considered empty in itself, and it supposedly assumes the sense of that class conception that is taken to determine it.

Now class analysis, whether in terms of status or modal relation, has made us more fully aware that social position is constructed and imposed rather than natural and necessarily inherited.[26] There are clearly ways in which social position is socially inherited, and the history of racial ascription has played a central part here. Illuminating race in terms of class, then, also reflects just this social feature of race. Nevertheless, it must be insisted that there are very definite limitations to any identification of race with class. While I will return in the following chapters to address the conceptual, methodological, and substantive relations between the two sorts of discursive formation, suffice it here to suggest that conceiving race in terms of class is tendentious. To insist on the identification tends to identify race misleadingly as class, as class under another name. This has one of two possible implications: It leaves unexplained those *cultural* relations race so often expresses, or it wrongly reduces these cultural relations to more or less veiled instantiations of class formation.

I suggested in chapter 1 that modernity can be characterized in part by an increasingly personalized, self-conscious, and atomized individualism. In contrast to the earlier emphasis upon localized forms of community,[27] the prevailing modes of social (self-)definition in modernity have been fashioned in terms of identities of anonymity. These identifications include class, but the more popular—nation, race, and gender—have tended in various ways to cut across class. They are, as I have said, ambiguous, if not always ambivalent. While forging general group definition and the outlines of social formation, these identities need not command individual commitment, at least not in any strictly defined, or direct, or obligatory sense (though obviously their proponents may try to make out the case). They are, it seems, identities of anomie and alienation. The group definition thus promoted sustains more or less loose cohesion, and it is emphasized as circumstances dictate. These social (self-)conceptions may become especially fraught in some social relations, especially (but not only) when material interests are at stake.

Cultural Race

Cast in these terms, another conception of race emerges: race as culture. As the biological conception has been increasingly attacked, the cultural is a sense (or a small set of senses) that has come to enjoy considerable commitment, though not without controversy. Generally, the cultural conception includes identifying race with language group, religion, group habits, norms, or customs: a typical style of behavior, dress, cuisine, music, literature, and art. Primarily at issue in such cultural differentiations are values and perceived behavior circumscribed by claimed group membership.

Such identifications in the name of race are not new. Strictly linguistic differentiations of racial groupings were popular in the nineteenth century and can be traced back a century before that period. Turning on the dictum that it is 'language that makes man',[28] European linguists at the time looked not to physical markers by which to classify races, but to affinities and differences in the system of linguistic representations of the various language groups. In 1808 Friedrich Schlegel argued that German, Greek, and Latin—and so French and English derivatively—were commonly rooted in Sanskrit. The ancient superiority of Aryan sagacity was to be inherited linguistically rather than biologically, via the classical grammar of the Greeks and Romans. The virtues represented by these classical grammars (like independence and self-reliance) were supposed by Müller and others to be relayed via linguistic acquisition to the bearers of modern civilization. 'Inferior' civilizations, derivative from Chinese or Semitic rather than from Aryan origins, were supposedly marked by linguistic incapacity and inability to assimilate. It was thought, for instance, that the 'wandering Jew' was culturally incapable of speaking German properly. This, in turn, was a development of an earlier view that identified as 'barbarous' the debased language, the 'vulgarity' of 'depraved people' (e.g., the common class or the nomadic racial other like gypsies or American Indian nations). Speakers of 'refined language', by contrast, were 'allegedly rational, moral, civilized, and capable of abstract thinking'.[29]

Since World War II, and especially in the past fifteen or twenty years, the cultural conception of race has tended to eclipse all others. It has become paradigmatic. But it has also largely suppressed hierarchical judgments of inferiority and superiority as the basis of exclusions, coding the exclusions it promotes in terms merely of racial difference. This raises a fundamental question about the cultural conception. Many insist that racial differentiation inevitably appeals, if only implicitly, to underlying *biological* claims.[30] Even where the surface expression is cultural, commitment to racial groupings is thought necessarily to be commitment to biological distinction. Thus, the only difference, if any, between nineteenth- and twentieth-century forms of racial differentiation seems on this reading to be at the level of surface expression.

Anthony Appiah is the most articulate representative of this biologically based view. Appiah insists that what differentiates ideas about race from earlier ideas about group difference and from claims about ethnicity is this: that necessary to the former, but missing from both of the latter, is commitment to the view that common racial membership entails shared 'biologically heritable, moral and intellectual characteristics' not shared with members of other races. In turn, this commitment has entailed the widespread claim, not necessarily but as a matter of historical fact, that 'some races were superior to others.' That racial differentiation necessarily presupposes a biological claim means that though Appiah's admission about the centrality of hierarchical judgments to the development of race thinking rests on historical grounds, the more basic idea is meant to be transhistorical. The latter is a transcendental claim about the nature of racial differentiation. Yet, it is a transcendental claim with distinct historical implications, for it necessarily implies that Appiah narrow the occurrence of race thinking primarily to its nineteenth-century apogee. In Appiah's view, neither *The Tempest* in the sixteenth century nor the current trend in U.S. and British law to accept as *racial* identification (for the purposes of census) whatever people take themselves to be turns out to be a form of race thinking.[31]

I do not wish to challenge Appiah's historical contention that ideas about race developed with a commitment to judgments of superiority and inferiority. He is right about the historical claim, though, as I suggested above, such judgments no longer prevail in racial ascription.[32] The underlying reason why Appiah admits that claims of superiority are contingent features of race thinking is that he wants to hold on to the undeniable point that cultural expression by the racially oppressed has sometimes also assumed racialized form, that the racially oppressed may assume racial self-identification not as a form of self-degradation but as a mode of self-advancement. Appiah wants to suggest that what separates such expression, which he benignly identifies as a form of 'racialism', from the extremities of racist expression is not the mistaken idea about biological inheritance but insidious judgments of superiority and inferiority.[33] What I obviously find questionable is the wider claim that ideas about race are inherently committed to claims about biological inheritance, whether of physical or intellectual or moral characteristics.

To see the narrowness of Appiah's conception of race and, by extension, of any view committed to limiting claims concerning race necessarily to presuppositions of biological heritability consider the transcendental argument he offers. The appeal in differentiating races to historical criteria, argues Appiah, must of necessity presuppose a belief in biologically distinct races as the only way of identifying the subjects whose distinct histories these are taken to be. To claim I am white in virtue of sharing a history with Thomas Jefferson, Calvin Coolidge, Enoch Powell, Margaret Thatcher, and P. W. Botha (to take any number of names not quite randomly) is only logically feasible, in Appiah's argument, if there is first some independent way to identify members of the racial group who are taken to share their history. If I share a history with them in virtue of group membership, I cannot consistently claim membership in virtue of sharing this history.[34] There must be an independent way of picking out group members who can then be said to share their history. And the only contestant for criterion of racial membership, thinks Appiah, is the false belief in biological heritability.[35]

In criticizing a transcendental argument, one needs to show either that it is *conceptually* possible to think otherwise about the phenomenon at hand or that there is at least a single *empirical* counterexample. Appiah's argument, I want to suggest, is wanting on both counts. Conceptually, consider the case of two pairs of people: Baldwin and Baker, and Buber and Benjamin. The parties of each pair consider themselves members of the same racial group, and the others as members of another racial group upon discovering (through reading the writings of each respectively) that they have suffered a pairwise similar form of oppression at the hands of some third, racially defined group of oppressors. Each pair agrees internally to use some relatively obvious but rough-and-ready visible marker, phenotypical or cultural, as an identifying *sign* of their pairwise common oppression (and of others who have a similar set of experiences), in contrast to different markers picking out both the other pair (along with those like them) and their oppressors. In accounting for the origins of their oppression and for the cultures of their resistance to it, Baldwin and Baker, in the one case, and Buber and Benjamin, in the other, are similarly willing to historicize the considerations they take to have motivated the commonality of their respective group statuses. Thus, in the contingent construction of racial identities no appeal need be made to or assumed about some biological factor. That the criteria of identification in each case may only be rough-and-ready may entail nothing more than what Appiah generally insists on concerning matters of race definition, namely, that it is at best a loose mode of group constitution.

Empirically, what is required is a single historical instance of race thinking that feasibly does not rely upon biological presupposition. Jews, for example, sometimes refer to themselves as a race fully cognizant of the fact that it can be no more than shared traditions and culture that binds them together, or at most a culturally defined law of maternal descent. Appiah might deny that this is a proper use of the term. He can do so, however, only at the empirical cost of denying the fact of such use. Nor can he insist that to characterize Jews as such is to turn them falsely into a racial group (implying that there is some other objective form of racial reference). As there are no real races in Appiah's view, all such references imply falsity, and so it cannot be this that differentiates the reference at hand from others.

Additional examples are not hard to find. In addressing the issue of immigration in the context of British politics in 1978, Margaret Thatcher identified the fear of native Britains of being 'swamped by people [from the New Commonwealth or Pakistan] with a different culture'. Here, race is coded as culture, what has been called 'the new racism',[36] making no reference to claims of biology or superiority. By contrast, in attempting more appealingly to uncover the possibility and existence of new forms of cultural identity, Stuart Hall emphasizes a style of cultural self-construction that is not just nostalgic but future oriented, not simply static but transformative, concerned not only with similarity and continuity but also with difference and rupture.[37] That this is *cultural* identity distances it from biological presupposition or implication. That such identities could be called races (though Hall is careful not to) is not testament to the biological grounds of such identification (they have, *ex hypothesi,* been denied) but to the fluidity of race as a concept. In its nonbiological interpretation, then, race stands for historically specific forms of cultural connectedness and solidarity, for what Appiah elsewhere acknowledges as 'feelings of community ... the feeling of people with whom we are connected'.[38] Appiah might want to insist that wherever race assumes cultural reference it simply disguises claims of biological difference. Nevertheless, the fact of the examples cited together with my conceptual counterargument suggest that the burden of proof now lies with Appiah.

Appiah is clearly correct that to talk of blacks or Jews (or anyone, for that matter) as a race is to take as homogenous large numbers of people with otherwise very different sets of experience and ideas, and that this could form the rationale for a dangerous exclusivist turn. This is a problem facing group thinking in general, and it is no doubt part of the reason Hall places such emphasis upon *self*-constructed identities. Nevertheless, it is not the point under contention here. What is at issue is the claim that ascriptions of race are inevitably reducible to a single, essential claim about biological heritability. I have argued, by contrast, that this is a misleading way of characterizing race thinking, conceptually and historically. It wrongly turns on a singular, unchanged, and transhistorical reading of the significance of race.

There is a wider point at issue concerning the liberal interpretation of race as a morally irrelevant category, an interpretation to which Appiah gives a sophisticated reading. Where race, or supposed racial characteristics, are invoked to distinguish people for distributive purposes, say, they serve not just simply but as signs, forms of shorthand for some further considerations. When a film director properly insists on casting a black actor to play the lead in a portrayal of Martin Luther King's life, 'race' stands for the commonality of experience, understanding, and empathy that would inform authenticity in the role. Any auditioning black actor who failed to exhibit these qualities would be as undeserving as a white one. So the consideration warranting desert is not the supposedly natural property itself but its place-marker for or development into the relevant skills. Even in picking out a person among a crowd in terms of skin color, we can only rarely be employing just skin color as the sole mark of identification. For 'black' and 'white' are never single shades of skin hue, indeed, are rarely properly black or white in color at all and are often confused with one another (as in the case of 'passing' and sun tans). What pigmentation often stands for in such cases of ostensive reference, as Wittgenstein may be read to suggest, is a range of encultured characteristics that include (but need not be limited to) modes of dress, bearing, gait, hairstyle, speech, and their relation.

Ethnorace

I am suggesting that *race* is a fluid, transforming, historically specific concept parasitic on theoretic and social discourses for the meaning it assumes at any historical moment. This way of looking at race seems to imply that it is simply a form of ethnicity. If it is, how can I continue to insist that racism and premodern forms of ethnocentrism differ?

In one sense, invoking the concept of race is inevitably ethnocentric. Ethnicity is the mode of cultural identification and distinction. Consider now the interpretation of race seemingly most antithetical to this construal, namely, the biological reading at issue in Appiah's contention. As Kevin Brown suggests, assigning significance to biological or physical attributes, in the way required by this conception of race, is a cultural choice. The biological in a sense becomes one among the possible cultural criteria for determining ethnicity. The influential distinction drawn by Pierre van den Berghe between an ethnic group as 'socially defined on the basis of cultural criteria' and a race as 'socially defined but on the basis of physical criteria' collapses in favor of the former.[39] It is not so much that natural and social kinds are conflated, though they may often be. Rather, the choice of natural kind as the criterion of group construction and difference is inevitably a social one.

There may be theoretical resistance to acknowledging as a form of race what for the sake of convenience I will call *ethnorace*. This resistance is due to the fact that the (self-)ascriptions of specific groups thus engendered as races turn out in their contours to be quite like those supposed to be biologically determined. This seeming convergence is largely the result of interpreting cultural connectedness in terms of what Sollors has named descent relations.[40] It is this claim of common descent that gives to ascriptions of race their affectation of natural and heritable qualities. However, it should be clear from the examples I cited above that ethnoraces can also be established by consent or domination by others. Here, membership turns more or less straightforwardly on choice and self-affirmation, on the one hand, or on the force of imposed classification, on the other.

Sollors remarks that many of the groups identified in the past as races are now commonly referred to in ethnic terms.[41] This reflects only part of the point I am getting at, for many (though not all) social groups now specified in the language of ethnicity may be and often are likewise identifiable as races. Why and when the terms are interchangeable in this way may have much to do with the referential history of the groups in question, though not necessarily. So Jews, Blacks, Hispanics, and Japanese in the United States may now be referred to as either race or ethnic group. Because of their connotative histories, the latter seems more benign. This may be changing, however, as the phenomenon of 'ethnic cleansing' in Bosnia suggests. (The extreme ethnonationalism at work there is noteworthy insofar as it has pointedly not been racialized.) Some in Japan continue to refer to themselves as the Yamato race, spiritually superior to others including Koreans and Taiwanese.[42] That races may emerge, submerge, or evaporate in the referential lexicon of social groups has in part and relatedly to do with the sorts of processes by which ethnicities form and emerge, with the (self-)explanation stressed for their formation, and with the politics of general group reference at the time in question.

The general processes of ethnic group formation, or what is generally called 'ethnogenesis', turn primarily on boundary construction and on the internalization and naturalization of identity by social subjects. Boundary construction involves the erection of more or less set divisions between groups identified as self and other. Boundaries are established by invoking the 'fact' of differences that may assume any combination of identifiable forms. These include mental, cultural, social, moral, aesthetic, kinship, linguistic, and territorial divides. Traditionally, the linguistic and territorial were taken to be of paramount importance, but if they ever really were, this no longer holds. Ethnicity, like race, cuts across geographical location; and Jews, like ethnic Italians (in contrast, for the most part, to Italian nationals), need not intraethnically speak the same language. The barriers thus constructed between groups, symbolic and actual, are historically specific in genesis. They may initiate from actual language differences or territorial claims; but these claimed differences may just as well be symbolic of some underlying power struggle. What is more important here than the ethnic content, as Frederick Barth insists, is the fact of the built boundary and the criteria of group membership.[43]

Ethnic content now tends to facilitate naturalization of the group formation and internalization by ethnic members of their group identity. This interactive naturalization and internalization is enabled primarily by a rhetoric of origins, ascribed or self-ascribed, that is reflected throughout the ethnic content. While often formulated in terms of relations of descent, it is entirely possible that the rhetoric of origins is expressed in the language of assent. In both cases, descent or assent, invocation of the law is fundamental to internalization of group identity: natural law in the case of descent, contract in the case of consensual agreement. Identities in the name of which social subjectivities express themselves are sedimented in the language of the law.[44]

These processes of ethnogenesis equally apply to the construction of racial differentiation. Like ethnicity, race may be viewed in terms of boundary formation and naturalization of social identity; and the criteria of racial differentiation may be identical to those for ethnicity. The language of race is likely to be invoked where group (self-)ascriptions tend to be fashioned on the basis of relations of descent, or where consensual relations seem 'naturally' to presuppose relations of descent. Ethnicity, then, tends to emphasize a rhetoric of cultural content, whereas race tends to resort to a rhetoric of descent. Nevertheless, these are rhetorical tendencies, not fixed conceptualizations. Like race, ethnicity may be cast and managed as much in terms of inherent as deeply historical identities, either of which may be claimed as the basis of sedimented and immutable differences.[45] And again, like race, ethnicity may serve to veil domination and exclusion via population disaggregation. The 1990 United States Census, for instance, identifies Hispanics, American Indians, and Blacks as ethnic groups, but not Anglos among Whites. Indeed, this tendency has a long social tradition: As the scribes of ethnic ascription, those claiming Anglo identity have projected ethnicity onto others and thereby naturalized their own as generically American.[46]

So whether any social group—Arabs or Aborigenes, say, American Indians or Irish, Blacks or Hispanics, Japanese or Jews, Polish or Gypsies—is identifiable as a race at any spatiotemporal conjuncture turns on the prevailing weight of interacting formative considerations. These considerations include (a) a history of being so named; (b) the processes and criteria of their boundary construction;

(c) the rhetoric of their genesis; (d) the sorts of contestational and exclusionary relations the group so circumscribed has with other groups at the time; and (e) the terms of self-identification and self-ascription, given (a) through (d). Latvians are usually identified as an ethnic, not a racial group, for (a) there is little if any history of racial identification; (b) there is little evidence, in contrast to related ethnic groups like Poles, say, of the racialization of their modes of boundary construction; (c) while the rhetoric of ethnogenesis invokes terms of descent, origins are not usually naturalized, and so historical self-identity (even where deep) may be insufficient alone to clinch racial categorization; (d) though relations with other groups (like Russians) may be experienced as exclusionary, they are in the context of historical circumstance recognized as irreducibly political and economic; and, finally, (e) self-identification and ascription tend explicitly to be in the name of ethnicity. Jews, by contrast, will sometimes be identified ethnically, at other times racially. Not only have Jews been identified by others as a race for exclusionary purposes, notoriously by the Nazis, we have seen that they may identify themselves as such. Moreover, the traditional rivalry between Ashkenazi and Sephardic Jews is now taking on racial form. New Soviet immigrants to Israel, for example, refer to Sephardic Jews derogatorily as 'Asiatics', and an immigrant cab driver arriving in Israel via New York is reported as characterizing Sephardic Israelis as 'Hebrew-speaking Puerto Ricans'.[47]

It follows that though I am claiming a much closer identification of race and ethnicity than is commonly assumed, I am not committed to their synonymy. I have argued, conceptually, that race is not just simply or straightforwardly a form of ethnicity, though neither is it reducible solely to claims of biology. I now want to insist that, historically, there are fundamental differences between premodern forms of ethnic differentiation like the ancient Greek or Hebrew and the forms of racial identification that emerged with modernity. First, identity is explicitly rendered in racial terms only in modernity, and this emerges with a specific set of socioeconomic, political, legal, and cultural relations that have no correlate in premodernity. Second, I have shown that racialization does not necessarily advance its claims cloaked in biology; minimally, it tends to naturalize as if seemingly given the relations so characterized. The environmentalism of monogenic presupposition might seem to mirror ancient Greek environmentalism by explaining similarities in terms of shared physical environment. But even here monogenic environmentalism (unlike the Greek) naturalizes similarities and differences, making them appear virtually unalterable. Third, racial identity need not differ from the religiously conceived Hebraic theocentrism only in terms of biological appeal. Theocentrism at least claims a special relation to God; race, by contrast, might merely commit its proponents to a (nontheistic) historical tradition of shared values. So the difference lies minimally in the basic kinds of values to which social subjects appeal.[48]

By insisting that race and ethnicity may at times be used synonymously, I am not suggesting that race be *explained* in ethnic terms. There are convincing reasons to avoid the lure of ethnic reduction, to resist the pervasiveness of what Omi and Winant identify as the 'ethnic paradigm'. Popularized by Robert Park, Gunnar Myrdal, Nathan Glazer, and Daniel Patrick Moynihan, this model has pervaded the social science explanation of race. It reduces racial formations to ethnicity and analogizes the future trajectory of the racial condition to the melting pot experience of immigrant assimilation. Nevertheless, the paradigm ignores the specific experiences of racially defined groups and differences within the groups so defined. Because it takes the formative experience of ethnic groups as generally similar, it overlooks the particular experience in a group's social constitution of oppressive conditions such as colonialism, slavery, exclusion, and in some cases virtual extirpation. Perceived failures of some racially defined groups to advance or integrate are then taken to turn not on dominant boundary construction, restriction, and exclusion but on the absence of certain kinds of values on the part of the group itself. This paradigmatic disposition to blame the victim implicitly reifies as given the very racial definition of otherness it is claiming to erode, much as it takes for granted the assumption of ethnic identification it valorizes. The racial other is necessarily different, but essentially alike within this categorical difference.[49] This, by the way, is central to the logic of *apartheid:* Circumscribe racial others as undifferentially Other in order to set them apart. But once in the majority, disaggregate the Other along ethnically defined lines so as to divide and rule.

In insisting that race sometimes (is made to) assume(s) ethnic connotation, I am not so much submitting an explanation of race in terms of the ethnic paradigm as I am suggesting one possible contemporary *meaning* for race. Thus, race sometimes takes on significance in terms of ethnicity, both (and relatedly) through ordinary folk usage and in virtue of the prevailing paradigm of social science reduction.

This paradigmatic sense of race now elaborated in terms of culture incorporates some of the prevailing features of racialized rationalization: the rhetoric of descent even as a cloak for consensual relations, claims of common origins, a sense of kinship connectedness and belonging, and the naturalization of social relations. These features, subject to the relevant qualifications, are also central to the force of national identity. This suggests another way in which *race* has been used and understood.

Race as Nation

Nation has both a conceptual and social history intersecting with that of *race*. Originally used to refer to those claimed to be of common birth or extended family (1584), the sense of *nation* simulated the early significance of *race* as lineage. The popular Enlightenment concern with national characteristics often explicitly identified these characteristics racially. Similarly, the great nationalist drives of the late nineteenth century, as well as their imperialist counterparts, commonly invoked the banner of race as a conceptual rallying cry; and legislation restricting immigration this century in Australia, Britain, Germany, France, and the United States—legislation imposed in the name of national self-consciousness—was in each case explicitly or implicitly racialized. That this should have seemed so 'natural' a conflation is attested to by the intersection of nation with native: Those properly of the nation are native to it, born and bred at its breast; Natives, by contrast, are those natural in racial kind to foreign, hostile, dominated lands. The latter are naive, simple, lacking art, culture, and the capacity for rational self-determination.[50] They are, in short, to be kept in their place, politically or geographically.

It follows that the relation between nation and race runs deeper than Benedict Anderson, in an otherwise stimulating analysis of nationalism, would have it. Anderson suggests that both are identities involving ties that are unchosen. This seems overstated, for one has at least some choice over national identity, choice which may be more or less constrained by impositions of race, class, and circumstance. There may also be some space in which to negotiate racial identity within and between *race*'s shifting connotations. Anderson is nevertheless correct in criticizing Tom Nairn's derivation of racism and anti-Semitism from nationalism.[51] Like Nairn, nevertheless, Anderson mischaracterizes the relation between race and nation—for reasons that have to do with Anderson's misleading insistence that 'ideologies of race have their origin in ideologies of class.' Underlying this insistent mischaracterization is a narrow construal of racial claims as univocally biological or 'physiognomic'. While Anderson takes the language of nation to be historical, that of race is deemed ahistorical because biological, eternal, and necessary. He thus insists that the language of race 'erases nationness' by substituting biology for it.[52] It should now be clear, however, that not only does this reading of race barely scratch the surface of racialized phenomena; it likewise fails to exhaust the changing historical connotations of *race* and so rides roughshod over its specific significance at various historical moments.

It is more illuminating to think of race and nation as signifying intersecting discourses of modernist anonymity. Sometimes these discourses express common connotation and cause, while at other times they are completely independent and occasionally are more or less at odds. As *concepts,* race and nation are largely empty receptacles through and in the names of which population groups may be invented, interpreted, and imagined as communities or societies. Under some interpretations, then, races (as population groupings) can—almost invariably do—cut across national boundaries. They are, in Zygmunt Bauman's compelling phrase, 'nonnational nations', truly *inter*national. Jews are a case in point. Where this lack of isomorphism is a necessary implication under one interpretation, national and racial boundaries may naturally be seen to map onto each other under another. Here, each nation must be taken to have a unique set of characteristics that constitute its nationhood, and these are considered just the characteristics that mark them off as distinct races. 'Englishness' is the example that quickly comes to mind (at least in conception, for if it exists at all it, too, can now only be transnational). So on the reading of races as 'nonnational nations' they are, to use Balibar's terms, *'supra*national'; while on the reading as 'boundaried nation', races ramify the spirit of the nation, by giving it specificity, into a *'super*nationalism'.[53]

Politicizing *Race,* Racializing Politics

I have argued that race is not a static concept with a single sedimented meaning. Its power has consisted in its adaptive capacity to define population groups and, by extension, social agents as self and other at various historical moments. It has thus facilitated the fixing of characterizations of inclusion and exclusion, imparting to social relations an apparent specificity otherwise lacking. To be capable of this, race itself must be almost, but not quite, empty in its own connotative capacity, able to signify not so much in itself but by adopting and extending naturalized form to prevailing conceptions of social group formation at different times. The historically specific connotations of the concept have been fixed by the insinuation of race into the paradigmatic views of group formation of the day. Initially, race meant root or pedigree. With the emergence of the formalized study of population groupings, race was used synonymously with variety, family, or type of population. In terms of the Darwinian revolution, it signified subspecies or breeding population or common gene pool. And with the shift in emphasis from explanatory principle to object of explanation, race first identified class or status and then more emphatically culture, ethnicity, or nation.

It follows that the prevailing meaning of race at any intersection of time and place is embedded in and influenced by the prevailing conditions within the social milieu in question. What is little noticed (though Banton for one is not guilty of this omission) is that foremost among these conceptually significant conditions is the history internal to racial thinking. This history sets the limits on the thinkable at that moment, on the evidence available, and on the acceptable range of argument and explanation. In fixing a historically specific meaning for race, what is as important as knowledge of social conditions at the time is the sociologic of racialized knowledge.

Michael Banton periodizes the study of race into three phases. The first phase establishes knowledge of races; the second elaborates expertise concerning management of intra- and interracial relations; and the third explains race sociologically rather than biologically. This rests upon the assumption that race is ontologically real, and so upon conceiving race as a singular and natural phenomenon. What alters historically in Banton's view is not the conception of race as such, but the way in which the phenomenon of race is explained, the theories of and about race. Race is a given; racial theories transform with time.[54] By contrast, if we see race as a fluid, fragile, and more or less vacuous concept capable of alternative senses, then we will not take the various notions identified above first and foremost as theories about race. We will take them alternatively as transformed and historically transforming *conceptions* of race, subjective identity, and social identification. Race, in this formulation, is ironically a *hybrid* concept. It assumes significance (in both senses) in terms of prevailing social and epistemological conditions at the time, yet simultaneously bearing with it sedimentary traces of past significations. Since 1500, then, race has been the subject of intense political and epistemological contestation in and through which it has variously assumed the symbolic power to colonize the prevailing terms of social interpretation, habit, and expression—to dominate, without quite silencing competing social discourses.[55]

It is crucially important to notice that, conceptually, race is almost but not quite completely vacuous, for its traces color all social and scientific theorizing into which the concept is insinuated. The minimal significance race bears itself does not concern biological but naturalized group relations. Race serves to naturalize the groupings it identifies in its own name. In articulating as natural ways of being in the world and the institutional structures in and through which such ways of being are expressed, race both establishes and rationalizes the order of difference as a law of nature. This law may be of human and not merely of biological nature.[56] In this way, race gives to social relations the veneer of fixedness, of long duration, and invokes—even silently—the tendency to characterize assent relations in the language of descent. As such, group formation seems destined as eternal, fated as unchanging and unchangeable.

Thus, race has been able, in and through its intersections with other forms of group identity, to cover over the increasing anonymity of mass social relations in modernity. Race brings together in self-conception individuals who otherwise have literally nothing to do with each other. In this, race pushes to its extreme the logic of national identification; hence, the gratuitous ease with which racism and patriotism seem to intersect.[57] This anonymity also facilitates, through the modes of distantiation inherent in it, the faceless forms of exclusion, exploitation, oppression, and annihilation that have so much accompanied the history of racial creation.

The question now arises whether, emerging from this analysis, any generally abstract characterization approaching definition can be given to the concept of *race*. It should be obvious from all I have said that race cannot be a static, fixed entity, indeed, is not an entity in any objective sense at all. I am tempted to say that race is whatever anyone *in* using that term or its cognates conceives of collective social relations. It is, in this sense, any group designation one ascribes of oneself as such (that is, as race, or under the sign) or which is so ascribed by others. Its meanings, as its forces, are always illocutionary.[58] In using 'race' and the terms bearing racial significance, social subjects racialize the people and population groups whom they characterize and to whom they refer. So to get at the specific connotations of the term in this process by which people and populations are transformed into races, one has to determine, in a sense both empirically and archaeologically, how the term is being used. The range of reference has largely turned on characteristics like skin color, physiognomy, blood or genes, descent or claimed kinship, historical origin or original geographical location, language, and culture.[59] This, nevertheless, is a fact of the historical condition; it could have extended and could extend beyond these. Thus, it could be, or could have been, that 'exclusion of women' was defined as racism, if women were, or would be, defined as a race.[60]

Accordingly, it is at once too constrained and too loose to define race, as Eipper attempts to, as socially conceiving a group 'on the basis of purported physical criteria, these criteria themselves being culturally derived'.[61] Too constrained, because physical criteria are not always what is taken to differentiate one race from another, the English say from Germans; and too loose, for in this definition football or basketball players may well come out being constituted as a race. Race, rather, is a form of imagined groupings of broad plant, animal, or human populations. It classifies together plants, or animals, or especially people in virtue of their sharing some purported and purportedly significant characteristic(s). The prevailing form of the grouping in question, especially in the case of human classification, assumes content influenced by established political, economic, legal, cultural, scientific and social scientific factors and relations but is not reducible to them. Here, the State may be deeply implicated in managing racial distinction. State implication may be of two kinds: The first concerns racial definition (most often through census taking or imposing racial criteria on immigration). The State may simply invoke and extend racial distinctions informally available from popular use or it may create and impose distinctions anew. The second sort of implication proceeds via state enforcement of the racial distinctions established independent of state initiation (primarily in managing opportunities concerning employment, housing, and schooling). In each instance, then, we should bear in mind the distinction Balibar insists upon between '(official) State racism' and *'racism within the State'.*[62]

So conceived, the concept that has assumed wide currency in characterizing the process by which human groups are constituted as races is *racial formation* (or more awkwardly *racialization).* Racial formation involves the structural composition and determination of groups into racialized form,[63] the imparting of racial significance and connotation at specific sociostructural sites to relationships previously lacking them. The particular conception of race that follows is taken by Omi and Winant to turn on struggles around competing political and ideological projects with differing preexisting and equally constructed racial dimensions.[64] While I am in some agreement with Omi and Winant's general formulation, I want to substitute for their notion of *racial formation* a designation that signifies a greater subjective dimension. In Omi and Winant's view, racial formation is *structural* in determination and so retains a form of the abstract social scientific reductionism it is trying to evade. Racial formation is to emerge seemingly magically out of political struggles, and somehow—we are never told exactly how—a different struggle involving a different set of contesting relations will produce a new set of racial categories. No place is cited/sited for (self-)constitution of the (racialized) subject. Hence I will speak of *race creation* (an act of anthropic gods) and of *racial constitution.*

Race creation emerges out of the creations—the fabrications—of real social actors in their constructed reproductions and transformations of established discursive formations and expressions. These creations are products of actual relations: It is real people, after all, who express themselves by means of a discourse or set of discourses, who make meaning and history. These social (self-)creations come as though given, fixed from on high, seemingly natural phenomena imposed almost unchangingly upon an innocent and so nonresponsible social order. Racial constitution is what gives one racial identity, what makes one (up as) a racial member, what inscribes one racially in society and in the law and identifiably gives substance to one's social being. It is, in short, what partly locates one as a social subject. This is borne out by the fact that debates about and struggles around race in a wide variety of societies are really about the meaning and nature of political constitution and community: Who counts as in and who out, who is central to the body politic and who peripheral, who is autonomous and who dependent?[65]

It follows from this way of conceiving things that though there is a sense in which race is arbitrary, there is another in which it is not. The arbitrariness appears most obviously in a wide range of individual dispositions to characterize racially, and it is straightforwardly logical. It is revealed by the fact that were one to line up all the individual members of the human species according to any usual racial criterion like pigmentation, there are no nonarbitrary points at which one might draw the lines of racial distinction. Indeed, to insist on drawing the line nonarbitrarily must presuppose having an independently defined conception of racial distinction to determine what color gradations fall on one side of the line or the other. Actually, not only will the persons on either side of the line differ in color imperceptibly from each other, those at opposite ends of the entire spectrum may well be identical in characteristics other than coloration. They may be the same height or weight, wear the same shoe size or have the same blood type, they may be sickly or lean, or score identically on some test of intelligence or adaptability or ability. If not separated on political grounds, they may attend the same school, work in the same capacity for some employer, be neighbors or (to the chagrin of some racists) lovers.

In another sense, however, it is unclear at the sociohistorical level of institutional structures that the application has been arbitrary at all. Of course, it is often *differentially* applied to render invidious judgments, usually to exclusionary ends. But one wonders whether this has been arbitrarily done, at least in many cases. I have argued that in the conceptual and historical dialectic between self, other, and social constitution race may be overdetermined both in conception and (often) in application. In some cases where race is invoked, it may simply be that the prevailing paradigm of race conception at the time, the common sense of the day insufficiently determines a conception for an individual in a specific context. Here, prompted by an alternative trajectory of social circumstance, another competing conception may assume prominence. For example, a person (self-)described as a white, Jewish liberal committed to ending *apartheid* in South Africa may nevertheless hold a view of Jews and Arabs as races with patently exclusionary implications.

I do not mean thus to justify exclusionary practices that are racially defined, only to suggest that the reasons they are to be condemned have little to do with their arbitrariness. The claim that race may be arbitrarily applied, that it is in other words a morally irrelevant category, fails to get at what is centrally abhorrent about racist lynching or epithets, discriminatory labor practices, segregated residential space, or voter misapportionment. To deem these sorts of practices wrong merely because race is appealed to as a mode of picking out their objects discourages further analysis of the nature(s) of the injustice(s) at issue. The implication is either that there is nothing more at issue than the arbitrariness of the category applied, or worse, that among wrongs they are not nearly the most evil.[66]

This raises once again the central question of the relation between racial thinking and racist expression. It is sometimes claimed that mere use of racial categories is inevitably racist, or at least racialist, and that all such uses are somehow irrational. Appiah, we have seen, makes these points. To be in a position over the following two chapters to address the complex issues involved here, a second point requires prior consideration, for the way in which we respond to the first set of issues turns in part upon resolution of the second. There are those, like Collette Guillaumin, who believe that to speak in racialized language 'implies the belief that races are "real"'.[67] So the question of the ontological status of races needs briefly to be addressed before turning directly to the concern with racism.

Racial Ontology

Ontological claims or denials of racial existence, if not explicit, are at least implicit in claims concerning the 'equality of races' or of human beings. In terms of the prevailing meanings of 'race', there seems to be a more or less direct relation between claiming all human races equal and denying that there are any races. Arguing for the inequality of races, by contrast, would seem to presuppose affirming their ontological reality, their existence in nature.[68] We should bear in mind, though, that arguments for the existence of races can be logically separated from hierarchical claims.

I do not deny that people differing phenotypically from each other evolved from phenotypically differing ancestors. Nevertheless, it needs to be stressed, in opposition to all those concluding from this the physical reality of races, that the evolution in question takes place at the level of the individual, not the group, and it involves unpredictable processes like random selection, genetic drift, adaptation, and mutation.[69] So where there are patterns, these can only be empirically established on the basis of a statistical run. They are not racially determined.

This is a very basic point denied by all those imputing biological determination to racial grouping. Recently, Pierre van den Berghe has argued that the human species has evolved sociobiologically, via natural selection, to the point where reproductive partiality to kin—to those genetically like oneself—maximizes the inclusive fitness to survive of the intrabreeding kin. Human organisms, in this view, are simply frameworks for the natural selection of reproductively successful genes; and genes favoring intrakin relations, biological history has proved, have selective advantage. Racial phenotypes and ethnic expressions are accordingly considered the most reliable markers, assuming current knowledge, of kinship or genetic relatedness. Nepotism, defined in terms of proportion of shared genes, is taken as the basis here of group constitution, and ethnic/racial interest is supposedly determined by the underlying 'interest' of genes to survive via reproduction.[70]

Van den Berghe simply extends the sociobiological argument from kin groups to ethnic and racial groups. The reason cited for this extension is that race and ethnicity are almost always based upon descent.[71] I have shown this to be generally questionable. However, van den Berghe has to establish something stronger, namely, that descent must be genetic. In attempting to do this, nevertheless, the sociobiologist tends to conflate claims about human organisms genetically conceived with claims about persons.[72] This is most clearly evident in two respects. First, there is ambiguity in claims about 'genetic interests' and individual human interests, for if it makes any sense to talk of genes having interests they are clearly distinct from those of persons: The 'interest' of my genes to reproduce hardly resembles my interest in getting an education or eliminating exploitation. Second, van den Berghe insists that culture evolves genetically and is thus causally linked to reproduction. So ethnicity and race, even where culturally based, are thought to be determined by the commonality of genetic interests.[73] This common claim confuses the level of individual biological reproduction with cultural reproduction, and conflates the general conditions for the possibility of culture—of any human activity—with the actual reproduction of specific cultural expressions. Stated slightly differently, van den Berghe fails crucially to distinguish between biological history and the history of social institutions and practices. Culture is not biologically transmitted or fully determined, at least not in any direct way. In setting the broad limits of individual capacity, biology at most provides the general parameters of cultural development for any period. Moreover, the fact that there is very little genetic difference between members of racial groupings, however defined, suggests that if the sociobiological argument carries any weight at all it is only to corroborate the truism that members of 'the human race'—the species—are disposed reproductively to seek each other out.[74]

Racial identity and conflict, of course, cannot be so easily denied or resolved, and racially ascribed status is not so simply avoidable. None the less, the fact that racially ascribed identity and status may be relatively undeniable or unavoidable has little if anything to do with the objectivity of their basis.[75] A belief that clearly distinguishable racial identities are grounded in biological nature has been shown above to lack all contemporary genetic credibility; and the ascription of racially based status involves only the social imputation of value to that claimed construction of difference. This is evidenced by the fact that those like M. G. Smith who are so committed to the claim invariably end up offering two contrasting sets of races at different times.[76] Observing *racial* differences between persons can only be successful if significant racial criteria have been presupposed, and so observation cannot be the grounds of the differentiation. And it is altogether incredible that the supposed significance of the differences lies simply in the observable 'givens' of nature.

For those who take races to be universal categories of nature, then, ethnicities are merely subdivisions of races. However, we have already seen that biologically imputed racial classification is simply one among other forms of ethnic differentiation, the form that assigns social significance to a biological criterion. This is not to suggest that ethnicity is in any way a given of nature, biological or otherwise. I mean only to insist that because ethnicity has its basis more firmly in the cultural, the consequent identities tend more readily (though not necessarily) to be considered immanent and historically formed.

It is because there is no biological basis to the formation of racial identities and because he thinks no other basis could be claimed that Anthony Appiah, like Ashley Montagu before him, thinks races biologically unreal and socially dangerous. Similarly, Robert Miles argues that any recourse to *race* necessarily rests upon a biological reference that lacks all objective and theoretical content, and so race ought to be analyzed as nothing more than an ideological construct. Any referential use of 'race' is eschewed for fear of reifying as real a nonexistent entity. Appiah urges we banish 'race' from all scientific discourse and prefers socially to speak of 'real civilizations'. Nevertheless, I have argued that Appiah construes *race* too narrowly, and consequently there is nothing inherent in the concept of *real civilizations* that prevents it being conceived as race, or of operating to exclude in the way race has mainly tended to.[77] Of course, the term is chosen because it reflects the collective value of identifiable cultural production and so is likely more (self-)affirmative. But then to call civilizations real seems little different than claiming the reality of ethnicity.

It may well be asked what difference it would make were races to be real, that is, were there to exist population groups relatively homogenous in some physical or cultural characteristic. We would be able to draw from this bald admission nothing about the relative values of the races in question, for to claim otherwise would violate the constraint of the naturalistic fallacy that from purely empirical presuppositions we can infer no normative conclusions. Further, although geographically located homogenous population groups may have seemed self-evident at the time of their 'discovery', the fact of 'discovery' and the ensuing intercourse of imperial domination quickly gave the lie to any naturally based conception of homogeneity. The dramatic shrinking of geographically obvious physical and cultural differences, of their interpenetration under late capitalism, should serve as adequate warning of the inevitable design in trying to sustain the thrust of racial homogeneity, whether biologically or culturally conceived.

The possibility of such design reflects conceptually the point I took pains to elaborate historically in chapter 3: Classification, valuation, and ordering are processes central to racial creation and construction. The ordering at stake need not be hierarchical but must at least identify difference; and the valuation need not claim superiority, for all it must minimally sustain is a criterion of inclusion and exclusion. It follows that race is irreducibly a *political* category. I do not mean by this what Omi and Winant do, namely, that races are formed and so their significance set in political contestation and struggle.[78] Rather, no matter how races form and whatever the meanings—and I've insisted that both the processes and the connotations are various and historically specific—racial creation and management acquire importance in framing and imparting specificity to the body politic. In this sense, race basically serves—sometimes explicitly and assertively, at other times silently and subtly—to define capacity for self-ownership and self-direction. It has established who can be imported and who exported, who are immigrants and who are indigenous, who may be property and who citizens; and among the latter who get to vote and who do not, who are protected by the law and who are its objects, who are employable and who are not, who have access and privilege and who are (to be) marginalized.[79]

Race continues to assume significance in this complex way. This is true even of the liberal legal mode of race definition now in place throughout the United States, codified by law and institutionalized by the State. Prior to the 1970s, definition of *black,* for example, had largely been set by the legacy of slavery in terms of the 'trace of black ancestry' (or less formally, the 'drop of Negro blood') rule. Since then, however, the general principle is no longer some form of ancestry but self-designation and self-ascription. You are what you take yourself to be (at least within the parameters of State-defined categories). That people generally continue to classify themselves as they traditionally have been, that they are even asked to classify themselves on this criterion, suggests that behind the principle lies the expectation that they will take themselves racially to be what they 'naturally' are. The depth of this presumption is, perhaps, revealed by the nervous laughter of students to my suggestion that on the criterion at hand I might (perhaps in some instances should) just as well declare myself black. Declaring myself, it seems, doesn't make it so.[80]

The fact that self-declaration of racial identity seems neither a necessary nor sufficient criterion for racial ascription reveals in two ways the indissolubly political dimension to race. First, the forced imposition of racial definition is reflected not only in acts of overt domination but also in more subtle formulations such as 'He acts like a Jew' or 'You're being Irish' or 'If you behave like a black you'll be taken or treated as one'. Second, it suggests what Appiah in part warns against, that race is also assumed as a category of political contestation, of resistance, a rallying point of the racially oppressed. Here, the criterion of membership is not self-declaration but a history of actual subjugation, a point that rubs up against the first one. Nonblacks and non-Jews can side *with* black persons or Jews, but this does not make them black or Jewish persons. This way of formulating the issue may tend to reify the very racial categories being contested; but the counterpoint is the crucial one that standing inside or assuming the categories of oppression has proved, at least in part, liberating both in itself and as a means to material emancipation.

In resisting racially defined oppression, Fanon, for example, uses those very metaphors of animality employed historically to rationalize subjugation of 'his kind'.[81] Fanon's point that racialized categories may be assumed, indeed invaded, as a fundamental challenge to racist exclusion and exploitation reveals, actually demands, that races have no ontological status. In the case of *race,* then, there is literally no object referred to, no 'given' phenomenon to be saved. That racialized objects are manufactured in the simulacrum of reference suggests that the issue is not the fact but the terms of asserted reference, its mode, styles, affects, and effects. The fabrication and manipulation of racial construction acquires significance purely instrumentally. It follows that elaboration of 'racial knowledge' need not serve, or be seen to serve generically political ends: Those concerned to create this knowledge might sincerely claim to be motivated solely by an epistemological drive. So Omi and Winant go too far in insisting that all racial categories and every racial distinction necessarily discriminate.[82]

Nevertheless, this knowledge and its uses fit into a historical order of racialized power. Any such use accordingly tends to reify and extend the conceptually necessary conditions of racially discriminatory power relations. Consequently, although an expression like 'There's a *black* woman standing over there' seems innocuous enough in a narrow sense, it reproduces on a structural level the set discursive conditions for racist expression to be perpetuated. At the same time, though, it must be acknowledged that assuming contemporary sociodiscursive conditions, this expression may be an emphatic affirmation in the most positive, nonvalorizing sense of the person's identity as both black and woman. However, a racialized category like 'black' bears with any use the history of its significations, the irrepressible traces of its repressive modes. This is all the more obviously so in the continuing employment of categories like 'Caucasian' on U.S. government affirmative action and census reports, or 'minority' in everyday discourse and political reportage. It is this return of the repressed, then, that metaphorically poses the dilemma for those wanting to invest resistant power in the assumption of these categories. There clearly seem to be ways to acknowledge the virtues of Jewish culture, say, without presupposing racial character. The question is whether we can affirm the vast value(s) in the culture taken as black, say, without invoking the presumption of race. More generally, can we speak in either way at this historical moment without reifying race?[83]

When we speak of or in the name of race at all, then, what we need first to clarify is which of its significations we are invoking. In this chapter I have undertaken to establish not only that the meanings associated with the term are various but that the dominant meaning at any time is related to its reinforcement of prevailing conceptions of self and otherness, of acceptability and excludability. It is the embeddedness of race in prevailing cultural and scientific conception, in the rationality of the day, that has enabled its renewable currency throughout modernity, that has underpinned its repeated and repeatable normalization. So if the significance of race (in both senses) is overdetermined in the ways suggested, if race is at basis a politically bound conception both in articulation and effect, then the prevailing vision of racism's singularity is similarly open to question.

To understand more coherently the relation between race(s) and racism(s), to be in a better position to see what range racist expressions cover, to specify their influences, determinations, natures, and consequences, and to bring more firmly into view the relation between racisms and rationalities in modernity's racializing normalization, a more precise picture of what is meant by racisms must be painted. To this task we now turn.

5

Racist Exclusions

If commentators have mostly assumed *race* to have a single transhistorical meaning, so too have they narrowed the concept of *racism* always to connote the same phenomenon. Racism, I have suggested, is not simply arbitrary, and it involves much more than merely invoking a morally irrelevant category. The fact that race is irreducibly a *political* category in the sense articulated in chapter 4 should warn us away from the standard conception to a fuller view of racism. It strikes me accordingly as altogether misleading to inquire into the determinants or causes of racism as such, for I want to insist that there is no generic racism, only historically specific racisms each with their own sociotemporally specific causes. There is no single (set of) transcendental determinant(s) that inevitably causes the occurrence of racism—be it nature, or drive, or mode of production, or class formation. There are only the minutiae that make up the fabric of daily life and specific interests and values, the cultures out of which racialized discourse and racist expressions arise. Racist expressions become normalized in and through the prevailing categories of modernity's epistemes and institutionalized in modernity's various modes of social articulation and power.

I do not mean to deny that we can give an impressionistic picture, as I have partly attempted to do in preceding chapters, of the broad and general discursive conditions that enable the emergence of racialized discourse and that promote the normalizing of racisms. Nor do I mean to deny that we can give a broad characterization of both the criteria for identifying racisms, however diverse, and of the ways in which racisms manifest, influence subjects, and victimize their objects. Indeed, such explication forms the focus of this chapter.

It is possible to identify in a tentative way general correlations between the historically specific connotations of race specified in chapter 4 and broad forms of racist expression. Very roughly, race as lineage may be identified with the discovery, physical and conceptual, of the racial other, of the initial empirical observation of significant difference in the drive to empire and domination. The specification of race as population is more or less coterminous with the maturing of the colonial condition, much as breeding population is with separation and extended subjugation of those racialized as other and gene pools with more formalized and often legally sanctioned segregation. By contrast, the explicit and emphatic transformations in meanings of race this century from natural to social kinds like class, ethnicity, and nation have been accompanied by increasingly sophisticated and subtle forms of economic and cultural racism.

This rough overview should suffice to discourage us from treating racism as a homogenous phenomenon. It entails not only that there is no single characteristic form of racism, but also that the various racisms have differing effects and implications. Racisms assume their particular characters, they are exacerbated, and they have different entailments and ramifications in relation to specific considerations of class constitution, gender, national identity, region, and political structure.[1] But the character and implicatures of each racism are also set in terms of its own historical legacy and the related conception of race. I will call the sum of these exacerbation effects and characterization influences by historicized identity discourses on the precise natures and characters of particular racisms the *multiplier condition*. This condition transforms the racist expression or formation from what it was, and it specifies the expression or formation spatiotemporally while differentiating it from what it might otherwise have been.

It follows that there may be different racisms in the same place at different times; or different racisms in various different places at the same time; or, again, different racist expressions—different, that is, in the conditions of their expression, their forms of expression, the objects of their expression, and their effects—among different people at the same space-time conjuncture. Examples of these varying types abound. The racisms that sustained as well as those that informed opposition to slavery in the United States differ from postslavery segregationism, and each differs substantially from contemporary racist expressions. The racisms that buttressed British colonial rule in South Africa differ in some fundamental ways from the establishment of *apartheid* in the 1940s, as well as from the sort of racisms indigenous to life in Britain now that 'the empire has struck back'; and as I argue in chapter 8, formalized *apartheid* will contrast increasingly sharply with the racisms now emergent in South Africa with the dismantling of *apartheid*'s more overt and formal institutions. I am not claiming that any one racism cited here emerged directly from the preceding one; nor am I contesting the fact that in each case the earlier racist formations enabled the later expressions in some direct or extended way. Causal relations in any microanalysis need to be distinguished from the natures of the conditions themselves. Thus, too, as Gramsci makes clear in his suggestive analysis, the racism in Mussolini's Italy differed significantly in its long-standing background conditions and in its manifestations from those in Hitler's Germany.[2] And as Bauman convincingly argues, the anti-Semitism of those designing and managing the Holocaust took quite another form from that of the general German population at the time.[3] This variety highlights the difficulty of definition.

Personal Prejudice and Social Structure

The methodological disposition one brings to the analysis of racism will influence, if not fully determine, its definition. The conception of the phenomena analysts take themselves to be addressing is circumscribed by the constraints of method. Studies of racism have tended to divide methodologically between those assuming an individually oriented and those accepting a structural approach. Taking individual beliefs and actions as analytically basic tends to commit one to viewing racism in terms of personal prejudice. Structural methodology, by contrast, sees racism embedded in, determined by, or emanating directly, even necessarily, from the prevailing constitution of social formation.

The individualist method tends to take racial prejudice as irrational and pathological, an 'infection' or 'cancer' of the body politic because it is predicated upon ignorance and self-deceit. The primary analytic issue here tends to be not the determination of whether, when, and how racism has emerged, but the description and analysis of *race relations* situations and problems, or the recording of individual prejudiced attitudes. On John Rex's influential formulation, race relations situations involve a structural relation in which two or more distinct, racially defined groups are forced by economic and social circumstances to engage each other in competition for scarce social resources. Social science analysis on this account primarily involves 'objective' description and microlevel explanation of prejudicial beliefs, attitudes, and discriminatory behavior and of the stratified relations of conflict, domination, and exploitation that result. Any condemnation of such relations as immoral is merely the personal judgment of the analyst and as such is beyond the purview of science. These studies may be used by politicians to manage the conflicts and improve the relations at issue,[4] but the analysis itself is to be as value free as the material permits. Michael Banton has argued, by implication, that because the term brings with it such emotive baggage, the concept of *racism* is largely useless as an objective tool of explanatory social science and should be avoided.[5]

This insistence to distinguish critical moral values from fact in the analysis of race relations presupposes veiled analytic values. First, however they may be defined or thought to arise in social relations, races are accepted as given. This is reflected in the commitment of race relations analysis to the management of race conflict. Relations between races presuppose objective racial groups between whom there exist better or worse relations. Second, assuming the claimed commitment to moral neutrality, nothing guarantees use of the analytic findings to eliminate, improve, or even to manage racism (whatever management may amount to). There is nothing save the unquestionably good intentions of those like Rex and Banton that prevents use of the research findings the better to dominate, exclude, or exploit those constituted as racial others. Third, historical analysis is invoked only narrowly to portray how groups in the race relations situation came to occupy their relative socioeconomic, political, or legal positions. As Banton puts it, historical knowledge is not 'as secure as [the] positive knowledge' of empirical research.[6] In subordinating the importance of the historical, we are given no critical understanding of the discursive practices by and for which populations are racialized or of the institutional structures that sustain racist exclusions.

Where race relations analysis tends to efface racism altogether as an acceptable category of analysis, structural methodology tends to reduce racism to an epiphenomenon of some basic component of social structure, whether economic or political. In each case, the range of racist expressions is restricted a priori. The phenomena are reduced to some purportedly more enduring individual or social condition. On this analytic stance, racism is mostly conceived as ideological, a set of rationalizations for sustaining exploitative economic practices and exclusionary political relations.

This is obviously the usual interpretation of standard Marxisms, and it has been variously criticized by those as much sympathetic to as those rejecting the tradition. Robert Miles has been the most recent defendant of this approach. In insisting that racism is an ideology, a 'representational phenomenon, distinguished from exclusionary practice', Miles emphatically denies that it involves any expressions other than a set of beliefs. There are accordingly no racist practices or relations, no practices or relations the effects of which are racially defined exclusion. After all, there are no such entities as races that can be objectively sustained. There are only socioeconomic and political exploitation and exclusion, rationalized by an ideology of racism.[7] Structural methodology, it is true, is open to historical analysis. Nevertheless, the meaning of racism is significantly narrowed to omit a range of expressions—namely, practices, effects, and implications—that I want to insist are properly constitutive of racialized discourse, in general, and (subject to the proper definitional constraints) to racism in particular.

Dominant Definitions

These restrictive approaches to the analysis of racism are influential in and exacerbated by the way most analysts set about defining their object of study. There are wide-ranging differences in the way the term is used. Bearing in mind the various qualified specifications, racism is most generally defined as the irrational (or prejudicial) belief in or practice of differentiating population groups on the basis of their typical phenomenal characteristics, and the hierarchical ordering of the racial groups so distinguished as superior or inferior. Typical phenomenal characteristics are largely interpreted in biological terms. The most usual and significant qualifications of this general characterization are twofold. On one hand, racism is considered exclusively as an ideology. As indicated, this is a view exemplified by Miles, among others. On the other hand, racism is considered necessarily to involve the domination and subordination of those groups deemed inferior. So we can distinguish five theses usual to the specification of the nature of racism (or what for the sake of convenience I am taking to be its terminological equivalents).[8] First, racism is irrational; second, the ordering of races it necessarily presupposes is predicated upon biological characteristics; third, this ordering is hierarchical; fourth, racism is an ideological phenomenon; and fifth, its design and effects are domination. This widely accepted way of construing the nature of racism is incomplete at best, misleading at worst. Consider briefly each of the claims in turn.

Irrationality

In criticizing the assumption that appeals to race are inherently arbitrary, I suggested earlier that some of these appeals are carefully designed to achieve well-defined ends. If this is so, then defining racism as irrational or as prejudice will fail to illuminate the full range of what I am going to insist is minimally central to the condition, namely, racialized relations of power. It is at least reasonable to inquire, as others have, whether some occurrence or interpretation of racism may be rational. (This inquiry, it should be emphasized, in no way commits us to acknowledging that some form of racism may be socially or morally acceptable.) The question of racism's rationality, at least intuitively, is not an ill-conceived one, and I address it in detail in the following chapter. It follows that as a matter of *definition* racism must be neutral in respect to its rational status. One cannot just will away by definitional fiat what may be an uncomfortable and uncomfortably enduring feature of social formation in modernity.

Biology and Hierarchy

We may press a similar point with respect to the claimed necessity of biological reference. Racisms of any kind must conceptually presuppose reference, however veiled or implicit, to race. I argued at length in chapter 4 that racial characterization and reference have long ceased to be thought of exclusively—and sometimes not at all—in terms of biological considerations. Those who insist, by way of the imperative of definition, that biological presupposition is conceptually central to racism will ignore those racisms predicated upon nonbiologically defined racial constructions. It should be clear, moreover, that racisms need not be premised upon hierarchical racial orderings of superiority and inferiority. Though this claim is historically prevalent, there are many instances (especially recently) of discriminations based simply upon racially defined *differences*. Examples abound. Robin Page, a British Member of Parliament, declared at the beginning of the 1980s that 'the whole question of race is not a matter of being superior or inferior, dirty or clean, but of being different'. And General Mark Clark, commander of Allied armies in Italy, 1943, insisted that 'the difference between us and [Asians] is our firmer belief in the sacredness of life—they're willing to die readily, as all Orientals are ... I wouldn't trade one dead American for fifty Chinamen.'[9]

Ideology

The claim that racism is nothing more than ideological is confusing or delimiting in a different way. It misleadingly leaves the deleterious effects of racist practices and institutions to be captured by some other term like racialism or racist discrimination. Alternatively, by insisting that the raison d'etre of the racist ideological structure is to hide some underlying form of economic, social, or political oppression, this widely shared claim refuses to acknowledge the materiality of racially defined effects in their own right. It fails to acknowledge, and so leaves unexplained, the fact that racist expressions may at times define and promote rather than merely rationalize social arrangements and institutions. Sepulveda's characterization of Mexican Indians as fit only for slavery enabled their enslavement to be conceived rather than simply serving to rationalize their exploitation *ex post facto*. I will undertake to incorporate the distinctions between belief structure, aims, practices, institutions, principles, and effects into a coherent characterization of the concept of *racisms*.

Domination

The claim concerning the centrality of domination, oppression, and subjugation does seem to capture a feature central to racism, namely, the relationships of power that racisms promote. Racisms may simply serve ideologically to rationalize relations of domination, or they may serve practically to effect such domination by defining who are its objects and what they may be subjected to. Racisms may be taken most centrally and generally as the condition of this domination and subjection, the mode and fact of racialized oppression. Even this misses a wider feature of racisms we need to hold firmly in view. At the very least, generically speaking, racisms need not be about domination so much as they are about racially predicated *exclusions*. And exclusions, even racially defined ones, do not necessarily involve domination and subjugation. Indeed, some exclusions may be for the sake of nothing else than holding the racially different at a distance. The reasons for such exclusion may be various. They have been made to include cultural preservation, or maintaining the size of relative economic distributions and benefits of the included, or fear of the unknown, and so forth. While domination may be at the heart of most exclusions, it is not necessary or necessarily a part of all.

Thus, the standard view of racism seems not to cover genuine cases. We might be tempted, as Frank Reeves suggests, to differentiate between more or less severe and extreme kinds of racist expression. Reeves distinguishes between a weak, medium, and strong form of racism. 'Weak racism' consists minimally in the set of claims that enduring races of human beings exist and that the differences are significant both because they explain existing social structures and because they have consequences for social policy. 'Medium racism' adds to this the evaluation, in terms of a scale of superiority and inferiority, of the different races identified by 'weak racism'. This qualification obviously involves implications for both explanation and policy recommendation. Where the rank ordering is taken to entail that the superior races should be entitled to more favorable treatment, Reeves thinks we have a case of 'strong racism'.[10]

These distinctions are clearly in keeping with the growing recognition that there are different kinds of racism. However, they fail to reflect (upon) an equally important consideration tying different racisms together. There is a basic sense in which the theories of racial difference, hierarchical evaluations, and related imperatives for differential treatment that distinguish Reeves's racisms from each other are all of a larger piece. Racial distinction, evaluation, and recommendation sustain each other both within sociosystemic constructions at specific historical moments and across the long historical duration of racialized discourse and racisms. So although the sorts of distinction suggested by Reeves may at times suffice to order priorities of response or resistance, they are potentially misleading. Perpetuation of a social formation in its racialized determination is enabled both by the microexpressions that constitute it—the epithets, glances, avoidances, characterizations, prejudgments, dispositions, and rationalizations—and by the accompanying racial(izing) theories, evaluations, and behavioral recommendations. They enable, in other words, common sense to be racialized and so the easiness, the natural familiarity of racist expression.

This is something to which Zygmunt Bauman is sensitive in his stimulating and provocative analysis of the Holocaust. However, trapped in a sense by the object of his study, Bauman narrows the range of racisms in another direction. Racism, he insists, is 'inevitably associated with' the estranging strategies of expulsion or extermination. These strategies, Bauman argues, are necessitated by racism's inherent commitment to the 'design of the perfect society and intention to implement the design'. Racism, in this picture, is conceived only as an end in itself, pursued for its own sake and never simply as a means for instituting other ends like profit or power.[11] This restriction of the range of racisms follows only if we accept the Holocaust as the paradigm case providing criteria against which to establish any other racist occurrence, not simply as one of the most extreme historical manifestations of racism. If we admit that there are such occurrences having nothing at all to do with (territorial) expulsion or extermination from the perfectly designed society, we are well along the way to admitting the proliferation of kinds of racism, of racisms.

Racisms

Thus, despite the difficulties facing his view, Miles is right to insist upon delineating what is common to different racist expressions, and his insistence is especially pertinent for those committed to a concept of multiple racisms. We cannot avoid asking what characteristics are common to racisms in virtue of which racist kinds of expression may be differentiated from other kinds across space and historical time. Unless we have some idea of the commonalities among different kinds of racist expression, we cannot identify any as such; nor can we characterize what makes one kind of historically specific *racist* expression differ from another.

I have suggested that explanatory presuppositions influence our conception of racism, just as this conception delimits the sorts of viable explanatory accounts of the phenomena deemed racist. For the sake of clarity, we should now distinguish between the contexts of definition, explanation, and rationalization. The context of definition involves spelling out the criteria in virtue of which some expression, person, or institution is racist; explanation involves advancing a clarifying account of why the phenomena so defined manifest; and rationalization tends to explain away, to excuse by legitimating, the occurrence of the phenomena.

Context of Definition

We require a characterization of the condition that does not commit us vacuously to finding racism everywhere but that nevertheless takes its systemic nature as basic. We need clear criteria for identifying individual responsibility for the various sorts of racist expression but do not tie the changing conditions of racisms too restrictively to individual intentionality. And we need an account that properly distinguishes between racialized reference or characterization and racist expression, for the burden of proof must rest with those wanting to hold that the former reduces inherently to the latter.

The definition of racism offered by Omi and Winant clearly takes in too much. Racism, we are told more than once, consists in those 'social practices which (implicitly or explicitly) attribute merits or allocate values to members of racially categorized groups, solely because of their race'.[12] So racist expressions include those like 'Blacks appreciate good music', or 'Blacks are as hardworking or intelligent as any other racial group', or 'I think highly of American Indian culture'. Perhaps in some idealized possible world it would be better not to use racialized expressions at all, and indeed racialized reference should be discouraged wherever possible while acknowledging *and* appreciating human difference. But in *this* world racialized reference is widely used in ordinary speech. It follows that any reasonable definition of racism must in principle be able to distinguish between racialized expressions that are more or less benign.

If race is a conception, then racism is a condition; or more precisely, where race is a set of conceptions, racisms are sets of conditions. Terminologically, the word 'racism' was first used in English by Ruth Benedict in the 1940s. Benedict, in turn, was influenced by the first use of *'racisme'* in France in the title of a book published in 1938. The use and meanings of both terms were strongly influenced by the wartime experience of anti-Semitism. 'Racialism', it is true, was used in the late nineteenth century. However, racist conditions clearly predate by a considerable time the emergence of a word in any language to refer to them: Conditions may exist whether named or not. By contrast, historically specific racisms necessarily presuppose and so cannot predate the conception of racial difference prevailing at the time. Thus, as I argued in chapter 4, the connotations of 'race' can only be established in terms of actual historical usage; here, on the other hand, any viable definition of racisms must be stipulated.

Racisms involve promoting exclusions, or the actual exclusions of people in virtue of their being deemed members of different racial groups, however racial groups are taken to be constituted. It follows that in some instances expressions may be racist on grounds of their effects. The mark of racism in these cases will be whether the discriminatory racial exclusion reflects a persistent pattern or could reasonably have been avoided.

Racists are those persons who explicitly or implicitly ascribe racial characteristics of others that purportedly differ from their own and others like them. These ascriptions, whether biological or social in character, must not merely propose racial differences; they must also assign racial preferences, or 'explain' racial differences as natural, inevitable and therefore unchangeable, or express desired, intended, or actual inclusions or exclusions, entitlements or restrictions.[13]

Persons may be judged (more or less) racist, then, not only on the narrow basis of intentions but also where the effects of their actions are (more or less) racially discriminatory or exclusionary. That is, persons may also be racist where their expressions fit a historical legacy or where the effects exhibit a pattern of racialized exclusion, and these are effects the persons should reasonably be clear about or it is a historical legacy to which they should reasonably be sensitive. The tendency to hold agents accountable in these cases becomes more acceptable the more reasonable it is to insist that they should have known better, especially once the nature of the effects or the tradition are brought to their notice and they refuse to acknowledge it is racist because they did not intend it so. Accountability will be especially difficult for someone to avoid where there are no other obvious grounds for the differential treatment than racial ascription, or where no other grounds could have been known to the one differentiating in the racist way. Where persons deny racist intent to bring about the racially differential effects in some case, their behavior can be checked in other cases to assess whether similar racially defined outcomes resulted, and whether they applied in other cases the nondiscriminatory principles they claim to be instituting in this case. Thus, there are ways of assessing the presence of racist acts, policies, or people, the (claimed) absence of individual racist intentionality notwithstanding.[14]

Racist institutions, by extension, are those institutions whose formative principles incorporate and whose social activities serve to prompt and perpetuate the racist beliefs and acts in question. Again, it is too restrictive to claim that institutions can be judged racist only if the institutional aim is racial discrimination.[15] If it is reasonably clear that some institutional practice gives rise to racially patterned exclusionary or discriminatory outcomes, no matter the institutional aims, and the institution does little or nothing to avoid, diminish, or alleviate these outcomes, the reasonable presumption must be that the institution is racist or effectively promotes racism of a sort. If the effect of an oil company's practices is a damaging spill despite stated aims, but the company does little to avoid, diminish, or alleviate these outcomes, we do not hesitate to accuse the culprit of engaging in hazardous behavior, indeed, of being environmentally culpable. The burden of proof rests with those who argue that the racist effects are unavoidable contingent and coincidental outcomes of otherwise permissible nonracist practices, aims, or institutional structures. For example, officers of a home owners' association who work to prevent low cost housing in their district for members of a racially defined group other than their own may not simply be, as Baier insists they are, concerned with their own (nonracist) economic interests. To escape the charge of racism, they must be equally prepared to exclude low cost housing for members of their own race, and it must be clear that they engage in such exclusion for reasons that are in no way related to some underlying racially segregationist end.[16]

Where there is a recognizable, institutionally governed pattern of racially predicated discrimination or exclusion, ongoing because unrectified, the presumption must be that the continuing exclusions are considered permissible by those institutionally able to do something about them. Similarly, the institutional officers who knowingly implement existing racist institutional rules, even if not for the sake of self-advantage, are implicated in the racism if they fail in some reasonable way to resist at least implementation of the racist rules.[17]

Consider the case of a student newspaper that publishes cartoons stereotyping black people as cannibals or monkeys. The material continues to appear even after vocal complaints by the university community of its offensiveness, or of the harm promoted by it. The newspaper cannot escape being characterized as racist by claiming that it has no racist rules governing its operation; or on grounds that the editorial board denies that its members individually or collectively have any racist intention; or by denying that the cartoons are meant to represent a generic image of blacks. No matter the claimed intention, the perceived and actual effect of their publication are perpetuation of exclusionary racial difference. The editorial board's insistence upon publishing the material even after they have explained to them the standing of such images in the history of racist expression may turn on the nonracist intention of its members to buck authority, or to exercise their First

Amendment rights to free expression. Nevertheless, this insistence does not simply suggest insensitivity to the interests and concerns of a group traditionally excluded on racial grounds. It indicates the continued promotion of such exclusion, no matter the intentions. Here, then, is an instance of a racist practice where the necessary and sufficient conditions for defining as such do not turn on the presence of racist intentions or racist rules.[18]

The dominant feature in this characterization of racist expression is exclusion on the basis of (purported) racial membership. The exclusion may be intended, actual, or (implicitly) rationalized. An expression will be more centrally and seriously racist the more directly, effectively, and usually it serves to exclude racially defined persons. Racist exclusion involves relative lack of access to, or absence from the distribution of, or lack of availability of goods or services, opportunities or privileges, rights and powers, even social responsibilities and burdens. These absences, lacks, and impediments by means of which exclusions are instituted must be explicitly or implicitly manifest in racially significant terms.

This captures in conceptually minimal form the sense of social power—again whether desired, actual, or rationalized—that centrally marks racist beliefs, practices, and institutions. Racist exclusions are not only done for the sake of gaining power in economic or political or personal terms. Power is exercised in the promotion and execution of the exclusions, whether intended or not. So racist exclusions need not be sought only instrumentally to control the socioeconomic resources; they may be sought also for the recognition of some imputed value in the exclusions themselves or for the sake of power in the execution of the exclusion.[19] This suggests that the proper yardstick against which to assess the degree of racist exclusion, the depth of the condition, is not simply the level of inclusion in and access to social resources. It is rather the fuller measures of incorporation into *and* influence upon the body politic, whether economically, politically, legally, or culturally.

Conceived in this way, racisms may service class exploitation. Exploitation of the poor by the rich involves two principles. The principle of economic oppression holds that the wealth of the rich depends upon the lacks or poverty of the poor. The principle of appropriation claims that the welfare of the rich depends upon the efforts of the poor, for the rich get rich(er) by appropriating as their own some of the productive effort of the poor. By circumscribing the opportunities and rights available to the racially defined poor, racisms have enabled the production and reproduction of the system of power and inequality required for class exploitation to take place. Not only do the racially oppressed have to work; limitation of their rights and possibilities have often thrust them into the kind of work that enables their product to be more readily appropriated.[20] However, there are racisms that need not be about exploitation in this strong sense of forcing or coercing racial others, or manipulating their situation to maximize surplus value for the ruling racialized class. While segregation was economically motivated in its historical emergence, racially defined separatism need not be. Economic exploitation requires at least partial inclusion of the exploited in a way resisted by the more or less complete exclusion of extreme racial 'apartness'.[21]

Nevertheless, the concept of exploitation may connote more than the sense implied by class relations economically conceived. Exploitation may involve the mere using of others, unfairly taking advantage of persons or of their situation. Those racist expressions that are exploitatively functional in this wider sense serve to ready for, or to rationalize, or to legitimate the exploitation. Racisms need entail no exploitation in this general sense either, for some racisms involve no using of those subjected to their expressions, either directly or indirectly. Again, many racisms have undertaken in theory (if not quite always so absolutely in practice) to place those subjected to the discourse, their racialized objects, outside the scope of use, separate and apart, lest they degrade the value of those socially incorporated. If exploitation is characterized more generally as *ab*use, as taking advantage of the lack of power others suffer, then most racisms may be exploitative in this sense. However, this tells us little about differences between various kinds of exploitation, between racist and nonracist kinds. And while exploitation implies that those exploiting gain by it, principled racists might gain nothing by acting on their views. In any case, a bald racist belief in one's racial superiority obviously need involve no exploitation provided one doesn't act on it.[22] So racism may sometimes be about domination in the sense of being in a position to exclude others from (primary) social goods (including rights), to prevent their access, or participation, or expression, or to demean or diminish their self-respect. Additionally, as I noted above, there are cases where racism will not be about domination primarily or at all.

In summary, racism excludes racially defined others, or promotes, or secures, or sustains such exclusion. Often racist exclusions will serve as a means to some form of exploitation, but there are times when the exclusions will be undertaken or expressed for their own sakes, for the recognition of the putatively inherent value the expressions are claimed to represent. In the case where persons insist that they are acting for the sake of racist principles, it is conceivable that exploitative acts will be a means to sustaining racist principles.

I am not committed by this characterization to maintaining that racists must appeal to a coherent conception of race. While some racists may, there are many for whom racial characteristics may be only loosely and perhaps unthinkingly ascribed of others. At the very least, it is of conceptual necessity that racists are (often only implicitly) committed to some notion of race. A child's expression, or a childlike one, will be characterized as racist in this view in part because of the (implicit) racial ascription involved, which it is the task of conceptual reconstruction to lay bare.

This raises a related question concerning the link between racialized conception and racist exclusion. Jews, for example, are sometimes characterized as a race and at other times as a religion, a nonracialized culture, or a nation. It would seem an odd implication to have discriminatory exclusion of some population group, in this case Jews, count as racist only where that group is directly racialized. In my view, exclusion of Jews will be racist where the underlying characterization of Jews is racialized either explicitly or by being linked to a history of racialized characterization. The characterization in question can then be said to stand in the tradition of such reference. The more central to the racist tradition are the categories invoked, the more fully can one say that their use is racist. So one's exclusionary act can be racist without quite realizing or intending it. As in the general formulation, one will be racist here to the extent one continues to characterize and act in this way, especially once informed that these expressions stand in a racist tradition, or where one refuses to acknowledge their racism and character once properly apprised of it, or where one should reasonably have been aware of it.

Two more general examples should serve to elucidate the scope of my account of racisms, and of their modes of applicability. The first concerns immigration restrictions. Maintenance and promotion of cultural tradition are widely considered morally acceptable ends. A general policy to foster these ends preserves prima facie regard for members of the various cultures in question. Some societies claim to find as a necessary means for realizing these ends the enforcement of immigration restrictions on members of 'alien' cultures. Quotas of this kind need not be overtly racist in formulation: Consider the ruling that 'only persons with families domiciled in Britain in 1850 will be granted British citizenship'. It is possible to universalize the policy without contradiction, for Tory parliamentarians have readily acknowledged that 'alien' cultures may want to protect their own heritage, that they ought to do so, and that this would necessitate similar immigration restrictions on their behalf.[23]

Consider also the case of a white district attorney in the United States who uses the majority of her peremptory challenges to exclude blacks from the jury in trials involving black defendants. The prosecutor correctly believes from long experience and statistical studies that she is less likely to obtain a jury decision in such cases the more black jury members there are.[24]

It might be argued that neither case is racist. There is no attribution to the excluded group of biologically determined characteristics that purports to render its members inferior or inept. This restricts racism to its older forms. Though neither case need be overtly racist in formulation, both turn out racist in my characterization. The first is racist in intending to exclude racial others, the second in effect. The prosecutor's professional aim is to secure prosecution. Should social statistics about black jury members alter, the prosecutor would be willing to change her strategy accordingly. So the prosecutor is clearly aware of the effects. Both cases pointedly involve exclusion of members of a racial group, and as policy both would adversely affect the excluded group. Because of racial membership, group members are (to be) excluded from entitlements available to others in a different racially defined group. In neither case is the policy self-defeating. Each is consistent and coheres with interests central to the society in question.

Both cases surely involve invidious undertakings. The former aims to and the latter does exclude on the basis of racial membership. The first case is tied to a pattern of historical exclusion, exploitation, and invidious treatment. As recognized by the U.S. Supreme Court in *Batson v. Kentucky,* the second case would go far, if generalized as a policy, in perpetuating blacks' exclusion in the United States from access to and active participation in the institutions of justice. The rights to equal protection of the law and trial by fair cross section of the community would be violated. Such a policy would increase the probability of procedural unfairness. Black defendants would be open to penalties in ways whites would not. Trial outcomes might be skewed by undermining the likelihood of jury divergence, for example, in interpreting the facts. In addressing the context of racial rationalization towards the close of this chapter, I will return to consider some of the more difficult questions concerning condemnation of racism.

These examples suggest what I have insisted upon throughout, namely, that a very wide set of conditions, often quite different one from another, make up the range of racisms. A key to formulating a typology of racisms involves construing this range in terms of the central concept of exclusions, qualified by the analytic contexts of definition, explanation, and rationalization. The kind of racialized exclusion forms one axis of the typology, context of analysis the other.

The formative typological distinctions will be at the definitional level and include the phenomenological differences between economic, political, legal, and cultural racisms. In the explanatory context, the distinctions will turn on what sorts of motivations and manifestations are taken to explain the rise or occurrence of racisms. These include sexual racism, symbolic racism, visceral racism,[25] the psychoanalytics of racism, class exploitative or economic racism, Balibar's distinction between a racism of extermination and one of oppression,[26] linguistic racism, and biological or genetic racism. Often, more general distinctions are drawn between overt and covert racism, intentional and instrumental racism, individual and institutional racism. They may be used to qualify the sorts of racist exclusions identified at the levels of definition and explanation. Finally, there are the ideological forms assumed by the rationalization of racist exclusions. These include theories like mono- or polygenism, social Darwinism, eugenics, or sociobiology, as well as practices like some IQ tests and ideologies like *apartheid* or 'Nordic racism'.[27] It remains for me here to say more about racist exclusions in terms of their contexts of explanation and rationalization respectively.

Context of Explanation

The fact that there is no single racist phenomenon or no phenomenon to which the variety of racist exclusions could be reduced entails that we should not expect a single explanation for racism. Different racist manifestations, racist exclusions at different times and in different places, will occur for different reasons. It follows that any explanatory account that seeks in every case to reduce the wide variety of the modes of racist expression to a more basic, underlying, singular social condition must likely be inadequate.

The undertaking to explain all manifestations of racism in terms of some basic underlying personal motivation or social condition I will call the 'principle of universal reduction'. It is in keeping with the general scientific concern to account for complex observed phenomena in terms of simpler, more fundamental conditions that may be said to give rise to them. The primary theoretical appeal of reductionism in the case of racism is the general insight that race has no ontological status: It is not a first cause.[28]

Some forms of explanatory reductionism concerning racism are so obviously inadequate as full accounts that they warrant little, if any comment. For example, the undertaking to explain every, or even the most pressing, sort of racist expression in terms of *men*'s rationalization of their fear of losing sexual partners raises counterexamples so obvious we need not dwell upon them. This is not to deny that some person's racism, or perhaps even a population's general expression, at some time may be at least partially explained in this way. Nevertheless, it clearly won't do as an explanation of nearly every such occurrence. Similar criticism applies to the attempt to explain racism in terms of the psychoanalytics of 'unconscious, symbolic, mysterious fantasies'.[29]

Despite their inadequacies, these sorts of individualistically based accounts reveal a deeper distinction between kinds of reductionistic explanations for racism. We can distinguish, as I did earlier, between explanations that take individual prejudices as analytically basic and those that identify constitutive features of social structure as fundamentally determining and so explanatory of racist expression.

In the former view, the basic component of racism is taken to be individuals' prejudices. A prejudice is an antipathic, hostile attitude, felt or expressed towards a person considered strictly as a member of a group. An individual object of the prejudice is presumed to bear those (usually reprehensible) characteristics supposed to define the group. The prejudicial judgment involves a faulty and inflexible generalization. It may be made in inexcusable ignorance of all the available facts, or it may involve logical error. The logical error consists in overgeneralization in one of two ways. Persons expressing prejudiced judgments may either improperly judge the object of their prejudice a member of the group in question, or they may wrongly infer that an individual is characterized by the designated properties because a member of the group. Thus, prejudice necessarily involves stereotyping; it is marked by intolerance towards the object; and it discourages modification in the face of further available information.[30]

The difficulties with this account will be discussed in the following chapter, in the context of the claim that racism is inherently irrational. Here, I wish to focus only on what in this account purports to explain all occurrences of racism. That I may hold a racist prejudice toward another says nothing about why I hold it. The usual answer to this question involves an appeal to emotions like fear, especially of the unknown, or of competition, whether economic or sexual. Pierre-Andre Taguieff, for example, reduces racism to a species of fear and resentment of the different—initially a natural, spontaneous, and perfectly general aggressive response to the presence of the strange and foreign. The fearful response is thought to be rationalized only ex post facto by a biological or mystificatory theory.[31]

This tells us nothing about why such fear and resentment assume forms so different as nationalism or homophobia, misogyny or religious intolerance, and in particular why they sometimes take the form of racism. The model necessarily fails to explain why racism only emerges with modernity. Even if it could be shown that racism afflicted antiquity, no principled account illustrates the differences between antique and modern racism.[32] Moreover, as I will detail in the following chapter, the model is unable to account for those racist exclusions that are calculated, brutally rational, and profitable.

This last criticism suggests that some form of economic reduction may offer a more viable, general explanation. I showed above that racisms cannot be defined as so many forms of economic exploitation. But as Bernard Boxill points out, the fact that they are differently defined proves only that they are different phenomena, not that the one cannot be reductively explained in terms of the other.[33] It may turn out that the underlying reason for any racist occurrence is to rationalize exploitative class relations.

'The element essential to understanding racism', notes John Rex, 'is that ethnic groups sometimes had identities imposed upon them to restrict their mobility and facilitate their exploitation and class oppression'.[34] Class in capitalist society may be lived out and expressed in terms of ideologically defined racial interests. Not only is the capitalist seen to be racially divided from the worker, the proletariat is split between the white-employed class and the black-unemployed 'underclass', or between white majority and black minority, or between white native and black immigrant. Intraclass divisions are introjected along lines defined on the basis of racial interests. By being adaptable to local geographic and seasonal considerations, racialized class relations enable the costs of both labor power and political disruption to be minimized. Moreover, racism facilitates reproduction of the established class relations by socializing future generations in the mode of past and present ones; and it rationalizes class inequalities as natural, inevitable, and so meritorious. Thus, just as prevailing specifications of politico-economic interest can be racially described, so any racialization of class interest can only be explained on the basis of its underlying relations of politico-economic power.[35]

This account offers powerful insights into some of the more deeply entrenched and troubling manifestations of racialized discourse and racist expression. It is also generally consistent with the explicit historical emergence and maturation of racism from the sixteenth century onward. Nevertheless, the sort of account it is in principle able to offer for racialized discourse and racist modes of expression is far from complete.

This incompleteness may assume various forms. First, there is a sense in which some racism could in principle promote, reify, and rationalize any social system incorporating differential relations of power and politico-economic exclusions. It should not be thought that racialized relations of power always are or need be those between capitalist and working class. It is at least conceivable that racism articulated the relations between antique slave and slave owner, serf and feudal lord, socialists in power and those who are not. Whether any of this has historically been the case, however, is an empirical question, and I have denied above that racism predates modernity. Second, some empirical evidence seems inconsistent with the theoretical claims that this form of reduction is committed to. In the past fifty years, for example, blacks in the United States have made major strides in the trade union movement and now occupy central union positions,[36] just as some blacks exercise considerable economic and political power among the bourgeoisie. The explanation at hand has great difficulty accounting for the specific triggers that require relations to the mode of production to be racialized and to be racially exclusive at specified space-times. Third, economic reductionism is equally unable to explain those forms of racialized discourse and racist expression that are not economic by nature, that do not manifest themselves in class terms and seem functionally unrelated to relations of exploitation. Examples abound of racially articulated power relations between individuals *within* a class and of ones that have little to do with class membership. Class accounts barely begin to explain the racialized restriction and denial by the political bureaucracies in the United States and Canada of Amerindian sovereignty and self-determination. Fourth, class reductionism is necessarily committed to the implication that racism cannot be eradicated 'until class societies are abolished'.[37] There seems ample evidence that racist expressions may sometimes have no identifiable class component. A bank's refusal to grant a home mortgage to a qualified black person is a case in point. So there remain the distinct possibilities that racist exclusions could be (largely) eliminated without eradicating class differentiations (the latter, recall, preceded the former historically); and that some forms of racist exclusion could persist despite eradicating classes.

In sum, the discourses of race and class, while intersecting in various important and codetermining ways, are at basis conceptually and effectively autonomous. There are fundamental differences in analytic emphases between class materiality and racial signification, between the material conditions determining exploitative class relations and the sorts of conceptual formation that racist exclusions must necessarily presuppose. Racist exclusions may cut across class divisions as much as they coincide with and carry forward class differentiation and exploitation. In some contexts, racist exclusions may enable class exploitation, just as class exploitation may (often) take the form of racist exclusion. Nevertheless, there are forms of racist exclusion—some interpretations of separatism again come to mind—that do not entail class exploitation, just as class exploitation need not require racist exclusivity.

It is undeniable that the history of race formation includes class collusion and that class constitution is carried forward in part by ideological ascriptions (witness the most recent reference to ghettoized urban blacks as 'the new underclass'). And it is true that, like race, the popular (nonacademic) language of class differentiation is unified as a discursive formation in terms of the abstract primitive terms 'classification', 'order', 'value', and 'hierarchy'. But this language plays only a supporting, not a defining, role in class constitution and exploitation. The difference between racist expression and class discourse is reflected in the difference between exclusion and exploitation. Both require social institutions for their respective effectiveness. Nevertheless, exploitation necessarily requires actual class differentiations, though not (necessarily) discursive rationalization; while racist exclusions invoke questionable differentiations and succeed only in so far as the terms they generate remain subjectively persuasive.

Racialized discourse and class discourse, intersected by gender in various ways, have altogether dominated the modern definition of otherness, the former furnishing the terms for the forceful exclusion of the different and the latter the relations of power for the exploitation of the powerless. It might be countered that this makes the very point of class-reductionistic accounts of racism. After all, the management of human subjects enabled by color racism extended the space in which capital accumulation, the growth of productive forces, and the massive generation and redeployment of surplus value could take place. This misses the deeper point I am insisting upon, namely, that it has often been *in virtue of* a previously articulated racialized discourse, and not merely rationalized by it, that such forced manipulations of individual subjects and whole populations could have been effected. The materiality of racist exclusions are not class confined; and the determinants of such exclusions have a material history that is not necessarily isomorphic with the material determinants of exploitative relations. The example of Las Casas reveals that one can invoke racialized expressions and promote some forms of racist exclusion even in resisting racist forms of class exploitation.[38]

I have emphasized throughout that racialized discourse, and the exclusionary acts and institutions they license vary widely. This should lead us to accept that no single causal explanation will be adequate for all expressions of racism; and sometimes even a single racist expression will be overdetermined. Conceptually, *race* is chameleonic and parasitic in character: It insinuates itself into and appropriates as its own mode more legitimate forms of social and scientific expression.[39] Racialized discourse is able to modify its mode of articulation. It can thus assume significance at a specific time in terms of prevailing scientific and social theories and on the basis of established cultural and political values.

The consequent resemblance of racisms' categorical functions to more acceptable forms of social and scientific thinking suggests one reason why these transforming racist expressions continue to enjoy social effect, if not always open endorsement. This mimesis renders some racisms seemingly more acceptable, consciously or unconsciously more normal, than their extreme forms sometimes suggest.[40] It implies not only that racisms insinuate themselves into, adapt to, and appropriate more acceptable cultural forms as their own modes of expression but also that there is a racist culture or set of cultures. Racist culture consists in the shared meanings, values, and norms that promote and sustain the variety of exclusionary acts, principles, rules, and institutions making up the range of racisms.

I have insisted that no single account will suffice to explain every expression of a racist kind. Nevertheless, the conceptual framework defined in terms of racialized discourse and racist culture enables some general remarks concerning the emergence, force and direction, the modes of operation, and the effects of racisms.

The expression of culture throughout modernity has been racialized in considerable part. This entails that racist culture has often defined the marks of civilization for modernity: scientific productivity and ingenuity, literature and literacy, subjects of a history and self-legislation. The self-transforming, chameleonic capacity of racialized expression means that it can adapt momentarily to the dominant mode of scientific and social articulation; and, once adapted, it can continue to assume the authority of the normal, the given, and the acceptable, if not the necessary and required. Thus, exclusions articulated, expressed, and rationalized in the name of racialized discourse become and remain central to social relations of power. Distribution of the images, metaphors, and meanings promoting and sustaining racist exclusions were made possible by the increasing importance of books and reading to the culture of modernity. Similarly, repetition, reproduction, and renewal of racist values in postmodernity is enabled by widespread teleliteracy. '[It] ain't what you do, or what you are but an image created by what you read.'[41] To take a simple, well-known example, witness the importance of the Willie Horton revolving-prison-door advertisement to the success of the 1988 Bush presidential campaign. And again, the disproportionate representation of racialized populations at the lower levels of the U.S. military reveals the inherent ambiguity in the successful telerecruitment campaign slogan: 'Be all that you *can* be. Join the Army.'[42]

So Bauman paints a misleading portrait in constructing a paradox of racism as both premodern in presumption and modern in practice. Racism, for Bauman, has a natural affinity with and is a convenient vehicle for antimodern emotions. Yet, racism cannot be realized in practice without the advancement of modern science, technology, and bureaucratic forms of state power. Modernity made racism possible by creating a demand for it. Racism, concludes Bauman, is 'a thoroughly modern weapon used in conduct of premodern ... struggles'.[43]

The drive to exclude is not antithetical to modernity but constitutive of it. Domination and exploitation assume new forms in modernity and postmodernity, not in contrast to an increasingly expressed commitment to 'liberty, equality, and fraternity' as well as to cultural preservation but as basic to the realization of such ideals for those espousing the commitment. Moreover, the self-conception of 'modern man' as free, productive, acquisitive, and literate is not delimiting of racims' expressions but a framework for them. It forms the measure by which racialized groups are modern and deserving of incorporation, or premodern and to be excluded from the body politic. Racialized expression seems to mirror modernist claims to universalist principles precisely in its own transterritorial and extemporal commitments. As Bauman distinguishes between the 'metaphysical' or 'conceptual Jew' and the 'actual Jew', so we can distinguish between the way the racial other is conceived and the actuality of those conceived as racial other.[44] The conceptual other is taken as the obvious and visible sign of the collapse of fixed order, certain and established values, eternal foundations and structures, and the breakdown of boundaries. It may have little to do in conception with the actual identity of the other beyond the racial fix, though everything to do with the felt effects of the model's imposition.

In this regard, the State has proved central to the reproduction and renewal of racist modes of expression and exclusion. Even where the State has explicitly opposed or moved to delimit forms of racist exclusion, racial conceptualization turns on continued State formulation, whether explicit or implicit. Thus, the spaces of social access and entry remain racially coded in terms of formally recorded data like birthplace, ethnic origin, residence, schooling, perhaps even consumption habits. As Kevin Brown notes, bureaucratic officers policing these spaces may be positioned into extending historical exclusions by doing nothing else than invoking seemingly innocent and innocuous task-defining criteria. 'By turning actual individuals into an amalgamation of bits of information, such formal processes invoke many more cues than the perception of physical difference alone.'[45] It follows, as Bauman notes, that postmodernity is likely inconsistent with modernity's more extreme racist expressions. For postmodernity is consumer oriented (market centered) and aims to diminish State bureaucracy.[46] This does not mean that racist exclusions will be relegated to relics in modernity's museums, only that they will increasingly assume more subtle, hidden, and implicit expression.

In resorting to racialized categories one is at once naturalizing social relations. One invokes an anonymous, abstract authority in legitimation of the relation, however skewed, and its rationalized expressions. In this, responsibility for the order of social relations is abrogated to a space which is reiterative, renewable, almost unspecifiable. Authorization is given, really invoked, by nature, inscribed in the laws of the universe, in the nature of things, in how the relations were naturally formed.

There is a conceptual analogy here between race and the law that enables the former to be insinuated or collapsed into, and so confused for the latter. Despite its idealized claims to fairness, objectivity, impartiality, and so integrity, the law is paradoxically alienating and dehumanizing. Qua universality, it opposes particularity and proceeds from a stance of anonymity. As Kant emphasized, a person is moral not in terms of any specificity but in virtue of exemplifying the abstract moral law. Law's efficiency is a function of its abstraction, of its capacity to be blind to particular circumstance and so indiscriminate, and of its charge to order social relations. Law's objectivity and impartiality are thus achieved by the distancing technology central to its mode of applicability. And in this, law is like race. It is no surprise, then, that those German citizens who objected to the mistreatment of the "'Jew next door'' … accepted with indifference and often with satisfaction *legal* restrictions imposed upon the "Jew as such"'.[47] Depersonalized and dehumanized in legal abstraction, people are reduced to mere objects, alien and anonymous.

This condition of alienation and anonymity, of what in relation to blacks Orlando Patterson and others problematically characterize as natal alienation, proceeds by rendering racialized peoples invisible, silent, and nameless.[48] To render invisible is to silence, and to silence is to erase the presence of those whose voices are drowned out. What is taken away is self-representation. Rubbed out is the articulation to oneself, to others like one, and to the world at large of who one is, of one's history, of a contesting set of values. One is denied the power to control one's names, what one is called or not, what one calls oneself. For example, traditionally named blacks under anglophone African colonialism and *apartheid* often suffer(ed) the indignity of being rechristened, usually by a white employer or official, with names of weekdays, with 'John', or simply with 'Boy'. These anglicized names are conferred because dominant whites have been too lazy, unimaginative, or uncaring to learn to pronounce or simply to ask for the person's given name. Blacks accept, perhaps tacitly assume, these nicknames because their employment may turn upon polite silence or response when addressed in this manner or upon offering a name easily understood if asked. So Nkathazo Mhlope will be changed to Wednesday because that's the day he's off, or to John, or to Boy because he's literally indistinguishable from all other gas pump or supermarket attendants.[49]

This raises once more the conception of power central to racialized discourse and racist expression. The relative conceptual autonomy of racialized discourse enables it not merely to serve and fuel relations of power but also to define them. Historically, race classification has been formulated, controlled, and assigned primarily by intellectuals and bureaucrats belonging to groups dominant in social relations. These agents usually, though not necessarily, take themselves to be 'racially' superior. Accordingly, the dominated often have imposed upon them and sometimes assume the racial schema; or while accepting the schema they may resist their assigned places of the domination and the oppression that accompany the categories. In the latter case, racial identity itself becomes the space from which resistance is launched, the stage of self-assertion.

It follows that although racisms are predominantly expressed by those who wield power, it is both conceptually possible and empirically evident that members of generally dominated racial groups can promote racial exclusions of nonmembers. But given the fact that the dominant by definition control the resources and social structures from which exclusions are advanced, racisms are largely if not altogether exclusively expressions from dominance. This also suggests two reasons why resistance to racisms is so often first and foremost cultural. First, the production, expression, and appeal of culture cannot be so easily controlled as material resources. And second, to wrest control over one's culture is at once to pry loose the hold over naming and (self-)representation. This is the first step to self-determination, and it is a necessary condition for taking command of the power to rationalize actions, conditions, and relations. I turn then to consider the question of rationalization.

Context of Rationalization

It should be evident that there are two interrelated senses of rationalization at issue here. The first concerns the processes by which the elements of social structure are rendered more coefficient, more productive, and more powerful. The second purports to provide a plausible covering reason to account for, legitimate, or explain away actions, relations, or social structure. Racial exclusion may be promoted as a means designed to bring about bureaucratic rationalization in the first sense, or it may occur as a patterned by-product of bureaucratization. In the second sense, racist exclusion may be rationalized as natural and so inevitable, as economically, politically, or culturally necessary, or as unfortunate but unavoidable.

Bauman shows that severity of the exclusion turns on implementing bureaucratic procedures like cost-benefit analysis, means-ends calculus, budget balancing, and universal rule application.[50] Exclusions mostly take place, as I have argued, not simply *because* of race but *in virtue* of racial belonging. This indicates that it is not, for the most part, the mere fact of racial membership that rationalizes racism in the second sense. Rather, it is what the racial belonging is made circumstantially to stand for that is usually taken as grounds for racially defined exclusions.

This latter distinction between exclusions supposedly determined by the raw fact of racial belonging and those rationalized by what race stands for only partially reflects Appiah's distinction between 'intrinsic' and 'extrinsic' racisms. Intrinsic racism claims that the raw fact of racial identity or difference, irrespective of any morally relevant virtue or lack this is supposed to entail, is sufficient reason for valuing one person over another. Extrinsic racism, by contrast, is the rationalization that racial members have or lack certain virtues and that such possession or lack is a relevant ground for differential moral treatment. Stated in this way, counterevidence that races and their members are not so characterized should suffice to disavow extrinsic but not intrinsic racists of their racist beliefs and behavior. The intrinsic racist is not concerned with morally relevant characteristics but with racial essences.[51]

However, exclusions extrinsically promoted in virtue of racial membership are not limited to false beliefs about moral character, racially defined. The exclusions may be about sustaining racially identifiable positions of power, privilege, or benefits, or about preserving a racially characterized worldview. Here, counterfactuals may have little effect in discharging racist belief and behavior, for at issue are not facts but values and relations of power.

Characterizing racisms in terms of exclusions entails that the injustices involved will mostly turn on more than merely picking out people for treatment on the basis of an arbitrary or irrelevant category. If no more than categorical irrelevance is at issue, the wrongs involved would be much weaker than racisms seem in many cases to warrant. Rather, the injustices at issue turn on the kinds of exclusions involved in each case. A specific racist expression may be unjust for different reasons than another one, depending upon the precise nature of the exclusion, its depth, the means of instituting it, and the nature of the violence involved.

Why, then, is there such resistance to acknowledging either the fact of racist occurrences or the severity of their injustices? There are related considerations in attempting to answer both aspects of the question. The reluctance has to do at least in part with racialized discourse and racist expression reinforcing themselves. This often assumes the minimal reactive form of a defensive mechanism, but it may at times be more proactive and vigorous. The resistance also has to do with the sorts of mechanism by means of which social relations are circumscribed and constrained, with how race negotiates (with) these mechanisms, and with how it helps to rationalize the exclusions that may follow.

The most extreme mode of rationalizing a racist exclusion is to deny its occurrence. Denial may be of the intention, occurrence, or pattern of exclusion. Holocaust denials offer the most visible example: Witness the claims of Robert Faurisson in France, the Historical Review Press and David Irving in Britain, Tom Metzger in the United States, and Ernst Christof, Friedrich Zundel, and the Concerned Parents for German Descent in Canada.[52] Only slightly less extreme, the exclusion may be acknowledged but its significance or effects trivialized, underplayed, or disclaimed. Mention was made in chapter 4 of Michael Levin's insistence that racial discrimination is far from the worst wrong people suffer. A corollary to this rationalization suggests that vigorous attempts to rectify the wrongs racism involves are likely to commit racialized injustices otherwise avoidable.[53]

By far the largest set of historical rationalizations ascribes the grounds for the exclusions to the excluded, in effect blaming those objectified by the discursive practices. This form of rationalization often turns on the suggestion that the exclusion is to be expected either because of the inferior physical or intellectual nature of the excluded or because of the victims' culture. A common rationalization in terms of nature involves claims about differences in measured intelligence. IQ testing of racial difference was an outgrowth of a long theoretical legacy that claimed to establish racial difference. Polygenism, social Darwinism, and eugenics were theories historically seeking to account for 'perceived' racial differentiation. As such, they 'established' the 'fact' of racial hierarchy. Racial character was then experienced through the filter of the prevailing theoretical veil. Once established, each theory was used to rationalize, to deem natural, or to explain away exclusions and exploitation. Similarly, intelligence testing set out to 'establish' racial correlations in IQ differences. But it was soon employed and continues only as rationalization for existing socioeconomic inequities.[54]

Contrasted with the rationalization from nature is the rationalization from culture. Racially defined or correlated exclusions are explained away as functions or outcomes of the cultural poverty of those excluded. In the past decade, for example, marginalized black people in the United States have been castigated by some for failing to exert effort, for relying on government, politics, social engineering, and the language of affirmative action entitlements rather than on developing individual initiative, self-sufficiency, and the competitive spirit of free and fair enterprise. The virtues of family are displaced by the vices of male irresponsibility, paternal commitments by the pleasure principle, the Protestant work ethic by drug dealing and dreams of the easy life. By waiting on redress for exclusions of past generations, blacks are thought to develop the 'help-me-and-hand-out' mentality, low self-esteem, and bitterness. Moral blackmail rather than merit is thought to be the proper mark of just advance. Thus, ongoing contemporary racialized exclusions are explained away or legitimated, precisely in the name of black, middle-class intellectuals, in terms of blacks' own misguided values and the abrogation of responsibility.[55] No matter that the standards of merit remain set in the terms of race and class; that the relative material conditions of racialized class are little different for many today than they were twenty or forty years ago; that socioeconomic exclusions are in many instances as racially entrenched as before; that the specificity and particularity of blacks is elided by an image no less essentialized in broad terms or in detail than that of the most extreme white racists; or that legal entitlements constitutive of justice as fairness remain far from secure or completely satisfied.[56]

The central foci of contemporary concern among those rationalizing racism in both natural and cultural terms are affirmative action policies. In undertaking to redress the wrongs of racism, policies of affirmative action are thought to commit the kind of wrong that they are supposed to be combatting, namely, privileging some over others on the basis of racial membership. Stated in this way, the criticism at the very least takes in too much. It fails to distinguish those features of affirmative action that are morally uncontroversial from those about which questions might be raised. Critics of affirmative action are invariably committed, at least in voice, to the principle of equal opportunity for all. Affirmative admissions, appointments, or promotions are considered to violate this principle. However, there is much that the principle of equality might justifiably require: that every effort be made to find candidates for admissions, appointments, and promotions from those racialized groups that remain relatively excluded; that availability of positions be openly advertized and characterized in non-discriminatory ways; and that admission, appointment, and promotion categories and criteria be nondiscriminatory in both principle and application. Thus, what is at issue here is not affirmative action policies generically but the form of preferential treatment that they are most often taken to assume. The objection is usually that the preferential treatment of groups whose members have been excluded from access to social resources amounts to unacceptable forms of reverse racial discrimination against those formerly favored (namely, white males).[57]

This raises a more general consideration concerning my characterization of racisms in terms of sets of exclusions. Are all racialized exclusions, and so seemingly preferential treatment programs, to be deemed objectionable because racist? Baier suggests one response to this problem. He insists that we distinguish between a 'morally neutral' and a 'morally committal' use of the term 'racism'. 'Compensatory racism', like a program of preferential treatment, is a morally neutral usage: It takes further argument beyond mere use of the term to establish whether it is necessarily objectionable. Accordingly, some racialized exclusions—some racisms—are morally acceptable. They cannot be rationalized away as merely legitimate but must be considered more strongly as justifiable.

There is another way of conceiving the issue, though. It may be denied that those cases where racism seems justifiable are properly cases of racist exclusion at all, even though there may be an appeal to the concept of race as a way of differentiating people. Baier rejects this option, without argument, as 'implausible'. It should be noted, however, that his definition of racism presupposes as a necessary condition appeal to the morally irrelevant category of race.[58] The question, then, is this: How are we to differentiate racist exclusions from those cases that may look like them but are actually only racially describable?

To deem preferential treatment programs racist, in the view I have articulated, people would have to be excluded from institutional opportunities in virtue of their racial membership. Certainly, it is not the aim of preferential treatment programs to exclude anyone on racial grounds; the undertaking is to *include* those who would otherwise remain racially excluded. So the determination must rest on whether such programs have the patterned effect of excluding whites. Critics would argue that this is obviously so. This charge necessarily presupposes that whites have a right to the positions in question, or at least to the opportunity to compete equally for the set asides. Competing on equal grounds is usually thought to involve being considered on individual merits. The criterion of merit, however, is similarly loaded. To serve as a principle of fairness, it must minimally presuppose that institutional access and opportunities, rights and liberties are equally open and available to all from the earliest moments of life, no matter racialized membership. Rhetoric aside, this is obviously not the world we have inherited and perpetuate. Thus, the actuality of equal opportunity under present conditions is perpetuation of privilege and discriminatory access. In light of this, it should be clear that preferential treatment programs do not exclude whites merely because of their whiteness. Rather, members of racialized groups who would likely continue to be excluded but for the program are given the possibility of access. The mark of inclusion is not the mere fact of racial belonging but what race stands for, namely, perpetuated discriminatory exclusion. Thus, Baier's 'compensatory racism' is not racism at all so long as there remain open to whites a range of opportunities that are not so readily available to members of those racialized groups whose opportunities continue to be curtailed.

I will return in the conclusion to address more fully the justifiability of preferential treatment policies. The more general point at issue here is that what distinguishes an experience describable in racialized terms from one of genuine racist exclusion is the way in which the case fits into a culture of racism. The primary questions to be faced in this respect include whether there is genuine exclusion taking place; whether that exclusion is part of a racialized pattern; its degree and depth; and what sorts of location in relation to the history of racialized discourse are occupied by the excluded and those prompting the exclusion.

The emergence and persistence of racist culture are enabled and exacerbated by mechanisms circumscribing and constraining the scope and applicability of law and morality. Those (to be) excluded are dehumanized. They are rendered abstract through the technologies of distantiation and depersonalization. The exclusions are often formally sanctioned by the law or bureaucratic procedure, and thus become institutionally routinized. Objects are faceless, silent, and invisible. Because the exclusionary effects may be experienced at some distance from their point of agent origination, anonymity is preserved: The agent of exclusion remains a stranger to the object, the victim simply objectified for the agent. Different sociotemporal contexts involve divergent 'logics of eviction' from the realm of justice.[59] Bauman identifies stages of moral repression underlying the intra-European drive to develop the bureaucratized 'machinery of mass destruction'. Population groups are defined as racially other; employees are dismissed, businesses seized; racial others are collected and concentrated, their labor exploited; finally, they are annihilated and their personal property confiscated.[60] A different logic of moral eviction operates in the colonial context where the dialectic of oppression is less univocal and unidirectional. Thus, 'discovery' gives way to (modified) definition and the technology of distantiation. Resource appropriation is accompanied by concentrated physical marginalization (townships, ghettoes, reserves), emasculation, and labor exploitation. Response, resistance, and revolution ultimately prompt redefinition and a modified dialectic of moral eviction. And a different evictive rationalizing is in process of erection in the postcolonial 'new world order' and the fitful emergence of European unity.

These logics suggest that the exclusions of racist culture become constitutive of worldviews, features of rational order and bureaucratic control. In this, racialized exclusions become normalized, routine features of modernity's everyday life and the sense of moral selfhood. This picture of racisms that are at least partially rational, of racializing processes that are normalized through the force of the rational, tugs rather heavily at the prevailing view that rests on the presumptive foundation that racism is inherently irrational. I turn now to address this central question of racism's rationality.

6

Racisms and Rationalities

I have been arguing that racial identifications and their attendant racist exclusions have been basic to modernity's sense of itself and that these exclusions are sometimes rationally authorized and endorsed. This is in sharp contrast to prevailing theoretical wisdom, for racism is widely considered to be inherently irrational. The common and related beliefs in a static conception of *race,* in the singularity of racism, and in racism's necessary irrationality have substantial support from the social sciences and careful philosophical analysis. Kurt Baier expresses a widely held view in considering racists irrational because their beliefs are 'hypothetical or deluded', as does Marcus Singer in insisting that 'the theory of racism … is self-contradictory as well as confused'.[1] From the moral point of view no more need be said: Racism is immoral because it is by nature irrational.

The general policy implication commonly drawn from this is that racism can be eradicated for the most part by education. Proponents point to the strides made since 1964 in the United States. Two sorts of critical consideration suggest some skepticism about this claim. First, though much ground has been covered in attacking racist expressions, the many effects of racist practices remain very much in evidence. To cite but one telling statistic, twenty years after the Kerner Commission black family wealth in the United States remains one tenth of that for white families. This clearly raises the central issue of racism's relation to power. Second, it is a fairly common assumption of studies supporting the thesis of racism's inherent irrationality that it is a social psychosis and that racists are socially sick. This assumption undermines moral condemnation of racism, for the mentally ill cannot be held responsible for acts caused by their disease; nor for such maladies do we usually think moral education the appropriate response. The fact that the prevailing metaphor for broadly characterizing racism is one of mental illness goes some way in explaining the social reticence to condemn and constrain private acts of racist discrimination. More generally, if racism is irrational in this sense, its emergence, persistence, and sometimes great viciousness must be inexplicable, as Zygmunt Bauman points out, because it is incomprehensible.[2] I will return to these questions of racism, power, morality, and education later in the chapter.

The question of racism's (ir)rationality goes to the heart of its acceptability throughout modernity. The paradigmatic picture of racism's inherent irrationality rests upon a presumption of Reason as embodying ahistorical and universal principles and standards of thought, and by implication as committing the 'Man of Reason' to objective, neutral, impartial, and universally valid sociopolitical and moral values. Recently, some feminist theorists have argued that the dominant criteria of rationality are socially constructed in historically male-defined terms. In the name of neutrality, dominant male standards, ideals, and values are inscribed as *the* (only, universal) rational standards, ideals, and values conformity to which is necessary if one is to be rational. The deeply historical character of reason, by contrast, need not commit its proponents to denying that some logical constraints like noncontradiction and consistency are minimally basic to any acceptable conception of rationality. Without reason we cannot make sense. Reason furnishes the broad conditions for making meaning at all and imparting sense to claims of any kind. At the extreme anything goes, including senselessness. Nevertheless, this does not constrain the conditions for sense-making to a single or perhaps even to a unified set, for sense can be made in a wide variety of ways. As Alasdair MacIntyre points out, satisfying logical conditions is at most necessary to but not sufficient for any viable notion of rationality.[3] Formalism commits us to no particular substantive normative conclusions. What is at issue for feminists, rather, is the set of values, emphases, 'metaphysical attitudes, epistemological principles, and cognitive styles' that are characteristically male.[4] Thus, to put it in the terms employed by Genevieve Lloyd, reason is used not simply to determine the truth value of beliefs, as universalists would have it, but to assess personal moral character. Nor is it used simply to furnish the criteria of truth but also to establish the requirements for being a person at all, indeed, for being a good person.[5] In this way, exclusion and domination of women have been sustained and authorized as rationally required.

Now it can be shown that just as ideals of rationality are gender constructed as predominantly male, so, too, are they racially constructed as exclusively white.[6] Historically, various sorts of racially defined non-Europeans, and more recently 'non-Westerners', have been excluded on racial grounds from membership (or at least full membership) in the human species. In large measure, the grounds for these exclusions have been Reason itself, or more precisely the claimed absence of Reason on the part of the excluded. Reason has dictated on principled as much as on instrumental grounds the moral rectitude of the exclusions. So just as Lloyd shows that the maleness of the Man of Reason 'lies deep in our philosophical tradition', so it could be demonstrated that the 'European-ness' (or the 'Eurocentered-ness', to use the current jargon), and more recently the 'Western-ness' of the Man of Reason, lies at the heart of this tradition also.[7] I do not mean thus to deny that any culture must presuppose the law of noncontradiction, say, to be able to make sense at all, either to itself or to others.[8] I want only to insist that the claimed universality of Reason, while perhaps undeniable at the level of abstract and thinly minimalist formalism, far from exhausts the nature and scope of rationality. To insist on Reason's universality to the exclusion of its historical or cultural particularity not only negates a large part of reason's ways. As MacIntyre makes clear concerning the Enlightenment, this insistence more problematically denies or refuses to acknowledge the particularistic cultural embodiment necessary to reason if it is to make sense or convince within a form of social life.[9] In this denial or refusal, 'universalist' Reason veils its capacity to dominate, to repress, and to exclude.

Thus, in spite—indeed, in the very name—of its universality, Reason expresses racialized exclusion. This should come as no surprise. The standards of Reason in modernity emerged against the backdrop of European domination and subjugation of nature, and especially of human nature. It should be equally unsurprising that the paradigmatic examples of rationality offered by the philosophical giants of an increasingly self-confident and assertive modernity should have been racialized. It is not my concern here to write this racial history of Reason; it is in part reflected in the historical references of chapters 2 and 3. Suffice it to conclude that the claim that racially characterized non-Westerners or those of purportedly non-Western origin are irrational, like the analogous claim concerning women, is not really that they are incapable of meeting standards of logical noncontradiction or consistency. Rather, it is the insistence that they fail to exhibit the values, metaphysical attitudes, epistemological principles, or cognitive styles of 'whitemales'.[10] The continued exclusions—sexist on the one account, racist on a related one—not only turn out rational, but are advanced (often silently and implicitly) in the name of Reason itself.

This coemergence in modernity of rationality and race as definitive constituents of human selfhood and subjectivity raises in acute fashion the question of the rationality of racialized expression, in general, and of racism(s) in particular. In this coemergence as usually construed there is contained in seed the seeming tension, sometimes violent, between modernity's expressed commitment to universal values and its more hidden particularism, that is, between the claims of rationality and irrationality. I do not wish to resolve this tension simply by resting content with a demonstration of the inadequacy in presuming rationality's singularity. I aim to show that even on a singular and narrow construal of Reason in the dominant mode of the 'Western' philosophical tradition, a significant body of racist expressions and rationalizations may be considered rational.

I argued in chapter 5 that racisms cannot be reducible to a single univocal model. Here, I will argue that the prevailing presumption about racism's (or, in my terms, racisms') irrationality is flawed. Jarvie and Agassi distinguish usefully between a weak and a strong sense of rationality, between rationality in action and rational belief. An action will be rational if there is a desired end or goal toward which it is properly directed. A belief is rational if it is consistent with some accepted and preferably the best available criterion of rationality, for example, if it meets sufficient evidence, avoids reasonable doubt, or is open to endless criticism and revision. Elsewhere, Agassi insists that only the radical Popperian commitment to open-ended criticism and revisability will render a belief fully rational. Nevertheless, not all criticism is rationally acceptable: The criticism dogmatists aim at the margins of their views so as to avoid challenging the center will, from a rational point of view, be unacceptable. As Jarvie and Agassi point out, a rational person accordingly may be one who acts or believes rationally, or both.[11] A theory will be rational if it consists in a set of rational beliefs. Here, one may distinguish, again as Popper did, between the rationality of the theory itself and the rationality of accepting the theory. A theory that is rational may under some circumstances be rationally rejected by everyone. It may turn out that members of a society the institutions of which are thoroughly racist are not irrational in accepting these institutions, and this may be so whether such members are privileged or disempowered by the social structure. Theories are rational if they are able to offer imaginative possible solutions to problems produced by the cultural background.[12] A racist theory offered to capitalists in an economy of inflationary labor costs will be rational if, by dividing the work force along racial lines and producing a surplus labor force, it is able to drive wages down. This suggests that we distinguish between rationality as a problem-solving method and rationality as a framework. One may be highly rational within a framework and still be irrational, for the framework itself may be irrational and one may hold onto it dogmatically.[13] One of the primary reasons racism has been considered by nature irrational is that it has been taken to consist always in the same perennial set of prejudiced beliefs that the racist has been unwilling to renounce. I have shown that this is a deeply misleading view of racisms. It rests on an underlying picture of rationality that is equally blinding. Here, rationality is taken to be the means of apprehending a set of fixed, unchanging truths about the universe that Reason commits one singularly to holding.

I will argue negatively that the set of irrational racist beliefs and practices is considerably smaller than commonly believed, that racism is not inherently irrational; and I will show positively that some forms of racism, some racisms, will turn out rational in both the weak and strong senses. In light of this, those who continue to insist that racism is by nature irrational reproduce a dogmatic myth about modernity that liberalism has done much to produce and perpetuate. It is a myth, I want to insist, that now largely stands in the way of understanding the nature of racist thinking and practice and, by extension, of suggesting imaginative means to resist and eradicate them.

Lest my motives be misunderstood, I should emphasize that it is in no way my aim to provide a rationalization for any form of racism. Rather, the fact that *some* racist expressions are capable of meeting otherwise acceptable standards of rationality means that a different sort of social condemnation than their irrationality will have to be offered. Indeed, the implication of the line of analysis I am pursuing here is that particular and directed attacks on racist manifestations in highly specific sets of conditions must replace the largely unsatisfactory reliance upon a general condemnation of racism as irrational. Only by way of microresponses will the rationalized normality of racisms be (re)moved. The same point can be made about other forms of aversive social discrimination and exclusion, such as sexism.

Whether racisms can be rational in any circumstance turns on the rationality of the racist beliefs, ascriptions, and acts at issue. Generally, two classes of arguments are offered to support the contention that racism is by nature irrational. For the sake of convenience, I refer to these as logical arguments and moral arguments, respectively. Each class consists of two subclasses. The logical arguments divide between accusations concerning stereotyping and those concerning inconsistencies. The former divide in turn between those stressing the centrality to racist thinking of category mistakes, on one hand, and empirical errors from overgeneralizations, on the other. Accusations of inconsistency divide into claims of inconsistencies between attitude and behavior, in the first instance, and contradictions in racist beliefs, in the second. The arguments from morality claim that racisms are always imprudent, failing as means to well-defined ends, on one hand and that racist acts achieve ends other than moral ones, on the other. In a general and perhaps unsatisfactory way, then, what I have designated 'logical' arguments for the most part represent concerns with individual psychology, while the 'moral' arguments largely represent concerns pertaining to intersubjective and social relations.[14]

The Logic(s) of Racism(s)

It is generally agreed that racisms are commonly expressed in terms of stereotypes. So in addressing this question of the logic(s) of racism(s), we need an account of stereotypes and their relation to categories.

Social psychologists and philosophers commonly hold that placing sensory data under categories is central to human experience. Application of categories enables human cognition by the ordering of data that we would otherwise find chaotic. The data organized are so large that they would be impossible to assimilate if considered monadically. Categorizing simplifies the complexity of the surrounding world: It condenses potentially overwhelming data to manageable proportions, it enables identification, it serves ultimately as a guide to action, and in modernity it extends to human beings a sense of social control, of being in control. In this view, scientific classifications are simply natural extensions of our ordinary cognitive facility.

Basically, the same cognitive functions pertain for social cognition, for the same general purposes (categorizing and identification) and reasons (simplicity), and to the same general ends (a guide to action). In perceiving and thinking about others with whom we have social contact, the economy of thought demanded to navigate the complexity of social experience is promoted and reinforced by characterizing individuals in terms of groups—classes, ethnies, races, genders, and religions. The less familiar we are with the individuating characteristics of the persons in question, the more likely we are to treat them in terms of their ascribed group membership.

It may be objected that this account captures only ethnocentric ascriptions, not racist ones. While ethnocentric characterization may weaken with familiarity, the very point of racist ideology, in terms of which racial ascriptions get their force, is to maintain exclusions—either by stiffening or altering their form—at the very points at which the exclusions threaten to evaporate. This is no doubt true in some instances of racial categorizing. However, it is inadequate as a general account of the differences between the ethnocentric and the racial on two counts. First, some forms of ethnocentric ascription may function in just the same ways—for example, fundamentalist characterization of more liberal religious practices. Second, not all racisms are rigid in this way. For example, in becoming more familiar with blacks, some white South Africans now concede that 'we would not mind black neighbors as long as they can afford it'.[15] Here, race as the dominant grounds of exclusion gives way to class which nevertheless remains racially defined.

It is necessary to find some criterion for differentiating acceptable forms of categorizing from the unacceptable, the rational from the irrational. A general proposal is to conceive stereotypes as transgressions of the rational limits of category utilization, that is, as irrational categories. In the past, prominent social psychologists assumed stereotypes to be false generalizations involving oversimplification, rigidity, and bias. This is just another version of the usual presumption that stereotyping is inherently irrational, and it still requires that criteria of rational categorizing be offered. Social scientists now generally consider stereotyping to be a species of social categorizing, for it involves fundamentally the same kinds of purposes, reasons, and ends identified above for categories in general.[16]

Stereotyping, nevertheless, is thought to involve an 'economy and efficiency of thought only at the expense of accuracy'.[17] Yet stereotypical categories differ from the categories of ordinary functional thought in respect only of their *tendency* to rigidify, to harden our attitudes towards others, not in any necessity that they do. 'Rigidity' consists in the social subject's refusal to admit to alteration in the light of countervailing evidence or in the denial that any such evidence in fact exists. While many cling resolutely to their stereotypes, thereby establishing their apparent stability over time, it cannot be assumed that this rigidity is an essential feature of stereotypes. Completed studies largely fail to exclude the distinct possibility that the rigidity may be caused in the particular case at hand not by the stereotype but by some individual feature of the agent's personal character.[18]

Accordingly, stereotypes may be defined in neutral terms as those beliefs concerning the characteristics or attributes of persons in virtue of their group membership. Prejudice, by contrast, is a negative attitude or disposition towards others in virtue of their differential group membership. Prejudice will tend largely to employ negative stereotypes of other groups. But stereotypes need involve no prejudice. It should also be noted that prejudices may at times be justifiable or at least understandable, as in the case of negative stereotypical attitudes on the part of the racially excluded toward extreme racist groups.[19]

So rational and irrational stereotypes can only be differentiated on the basis of whether they commit errors—conceptual, logical, or factual—when ascribed in respect to the data base at hand. It is commonly considered that racist stereotyping and thinking invariably commit such errors and, hence, that they must be irrational. A representative text claims simply that 'anti-Semitism ... consists of faulty habits of thought characterized by simplism, overgeneralization and errors of logic'.[20] Difficulties arise in ascribing each of these errors generically to racist thinking. Or so I will argue.

Basic Errors

Conceptual Errors and Category Mistakes

Racisms appeal *ex hypothesi* to the concept of *race* as the basis for discriminations. Many find here the grounds for their objection to racisms. A racist tends to explain the behavior of others by attributing it causally to racially transmitted dispositional traits of the agents in question rather than to the effects of environmental conditions in which agents find themselves at the time. But race, so the argument goes, is a spurious taxonomic unit of the human species. This 'fundamental attribution error' functions by replacing the proper set of conceptual factors in the causal explanation of the behavior with a set that is only apparently more appropriate.[21] To attribute human social differences causally to racial membership, as racists must, is to commit a category mistake: It is to confuse social kinds with natural kinds. Actual differences are thought to be explained in terms of some ghostly group biology, and so racisms must be irrational.

This criticism ignores what I have alluded to above, namely, that nobody seriously objects to discrimination *between* members of different races, only *against* them. We speak of 'black business' and 'black self-respect' or 'Jewish political interests' without thereby demeaning members of the group to whom we refer. And there seems little to object to in legitimate social science or media polls of racially identified attitudes. A casting director for a film on Martin Luther King who differentiates between black and nonblack applicants for the main role does so properly provided that casting a black person here is central to cinematic authenticity. So a nonblack applicant would not be discriminated against if he (or she, for that matter) failed to receive consideration. Requirements of the role determine not that the white actor be excluded, simply that black persons alone be considered for the role. Thus, any nonblack candidate would fail to qualify for consideration on the same grounds as the white. However, if the casting director refused to consider a white (or black) model because of racial membership though the person's ascribed racial grouping is irrelevant to the film role or product advertized, this would amount to a case of racial discrimination against the person(s) in question.[22]

Committed Kantian-style liberals go so far as to insist that even in the case of the King role, race should be an irrelevant consideration. Adrian Piper, for example, has suggested to me that racial consideration may improperly exclude the best available actor, a white member of the Royal Shakespeare Company, say.[23] The wonders of makeup artistry may render some semblance of plausibility to this view, though only in terms of a broadly defined sense of fine acting. Nevertheless, it strikes me as highly dubious that a white Shakespearean, excellent actor though he or she may be, would impart authenticity—in look, manner, speech, and so on—to a black public figure like King. In social structures whose social relations show a semblance of being racialized, even subtly or implicitly, it may turn out that the criteria for fine acting are likewise racialized. It was, after all, just seventy years ago that Vasco da Gama, the famous Brazilian soccer team then consisting of all black players, was expelled from the Brazilian league for refusing 'to whiten' themselves for games by being doused with talcum powder. The first black person to play 'America's game' at the highest professional level broke into national baseball less than fifty years ago. It is not beyond comprehension that, against such a background, a fine actor like Richard Harris, say, may be chosen, preposterously, over Paul Winfield to play the part of King. It is possible, of course, that a white actor may be able 'to pass' for a black character. The likelihood of 'successful passing' will generally be greater the more the actor is able to assume—or has assumed—as his or her own, not just emulating in acting the cultural habits identified with 'blackness'.[24]

Interpreted as statistical generalizations across phenotypes, race may perhaps be viably employed as a taxonomic unit, though only with extremely limited scope. Actual racial classification of, say, black and white may differ according to the phenotypical markers employed or stressed. Racist implications follow only if the putative racial memberships are supposed to include or exclude persons from some favorable or unfavorable social arrangement or are signs of some inherent qualities or abilities. The notion of 'passing for white' reflects such a racist social arrangement: Historically, it has been deemed preferable to be considered white. It is interesting to note, *en passant,* that as blacks increasingly define and dominate contemporary cultural fashion, one finds more attempts by whites to assume—some may say to appropriate—the cultural expression of blacks. Might we not take this as a form of 'passing for black'? We should not forget, however, that racial membership determined by near ancestry is a central part of a racist historical arrangement. The Texas Statute Book of 1911, for example, defined as 'black' any person with but 'a drop of black blood'. Nevertheless, determination of racial membership by ancestry is not necessarily racist in conception. An evenhanded application of the criterion carrying no socially biased implications need not discriminate against anyone *qua* racial member. Such an application would be strictly neutral between placing a person with one white and one black parent in the racial group 'black', 'white', or some third category. A person need not be racist, then, merely by use of some version of the concept 'race'. So it cannot be the mere use of race which is objectionable.

The accusation of category mistake must rest upon the assumption that racists inevitably impute biological determination to individual behavior. Racists need not make the causal claims central to this 'fundamental attribution error'. The error is characterized by social scientists as a 'tendency' of racist reasoning. Though cited as a 'logical fallacy', social psychologists offer only *examples* of the error in place of objective criteria for acceptable causal reasoning. This is not to deny that racists sometimes commit the 'cognitive bias' of 'illusory correlation', namely, that they wrongly judge there to be a relationship between two variables, one of which is racialized. Such error may lead to the development of a racial stereotype by insinuating itself into the initial cognition of racial differences.[25] But racist stereotypes may develop without illusory correlations or other cognitive bias, and illusory correlations need not give rise to any stereotype at all. On the other hand, racists may resort to racial categories as simply signifying descriptive differences. These differences are taken in turn not as biological attributions but as the social basis or signs of certain modes of exclusion. Though it may be accused of introducing many demons, then, racism cannot be so readily condemned as irrational for encouraging conceptual ghosts.

Overgeneralizations and the Facts of the Matter

In the standard view, racist thinking always functions by way of stereotyping. It is assumed that individuals are squeezed into hard and fast categories by the rigid application to them of racial stereotypes. Racial stereotyping is taken to overgeneralize from a narrow data base of empirically perceived racial characteristics to their assumed status as core traits of the alien racial stock. The characteristics in question are then supposed to harden into a stereotype of the other race, its ideal features, which any individual identified as a member is thereby thought *a priori* to possess. Thus, racial stereotypes are defined as overgeneralizations from persons' experiences of members of another race. Stereotypical or 'category-based' identification is considered to be fundamentally inconsistent with the 'individuating processes' of identification. Individual members of a race are stereotypically ascribed racial characteristics they may in fact fail to reflect. Treatment of all racial members is enjoined on the basis of possessing these characteristics, and so those members who lack the relevant traits will be treated—perhaps adversely—on grounds inapplicable to them.[26]

Two related claims are embedded in this argument. The first is that unavoidable factual errors arise in ascribing the putative racial traits to individuals, especially where the ascribed traits are aversive. The second is that every form of racial stereotyping suffers the fallacy of universalizing from particular characteristics or from individual members. Problems of scope afflict both claims.

The argument underlying the first claim is that racists fail to notice the extent of individual differences in respect to a given property (e.g., ability, or intelligence, or culture) within the group under observation or that they deny the degree of overlap in respect to such traits between members of the observed group and those of the racist's own. This supposedly leads racists to be too readily convinced of the accuracy of their racial attributions. Where available evidence conflicts with their stereotypes, racists may be led to distort the evidence—via selection, accentuation, and interpretation—and thereby to corroborate the applicability of the stereotype at issue. It has been found, for example, that factual information about a group with which one affiliates is more readily remembered than information about a group one rejects. And once one has applied categories to such information, the categories used become more influential in subsequent social judgments concerning the groups in question than the factual information. In short, this demonstrates the power of social—and in particular racial—discourses to define and color those social facts considered relevant.[27]

Racists often fail to recognize individual intragroup differences and intergroup similarities. However, nothing in the standard view of racist thinking establishes the much stronger assertion that it *necessarily* fails to recognize these differences and similarities. Nor is it established that stereotypes inevitably involve factual errors. In some cases (for example, 'Oriental or Western eyes' or 'blacks tend to be better at popular dancing than members of other groups'),[28] a bare stereotype without any associated or imputed value may reflect the facts rather accurately. Stereotypes usually arise on the basis of some empirical observations, however thin and value laden these may be. It was just this sort of consideration that led me earlier to offer a morally neutral definition of 'stereotype' as those beliefs concerning the characteristics or attributes of persons in virtue of their group membership. Moreover, it is not necessary to racist thinking that racial stereotypes be substituted for observation. I noted above that the racist may use the stereotype simply to assist in observations of others' characteristics, to order data otherwise potentially overwhelming. Where relevant information is unavailable and decisions immediately pressing, there are cases in which the agent may rationally appeal to the stereotype at hand. Bertrand Russell's statistically based claim that more people of genius tend to be Jewish may prompt a granting body to award a Jewish scientist rather than a non-Jewish applicant, other things being equal and no further information being available. It is not clear either that racial stereotypes necessitate in those holding them a dogmatic conviction of accuracy and validity in their racial attributions or that they inexorably distort counterevidence. Again, the dogmatic convictions and tendencies to distort may prove in many cases to be agent specific rather than due to 'racist stereotyping'.

Racial stereotypes may lead to factual errors, and in those cases they may be dismissed for the most part as irrational. It is not essential to their nature that they involve such errors, and there may be instances where the person expressing the stereotype cannot reasonably be expected to know better. These may be instances of Aristotle's acting *by reason of* rather than *from* ignorance. Because a person cannot be expected to know better, at least given the data and the relative reliability of the best available methods for data accumulation, responsibility for the act is mitigated. Stroebe and Insko point out, for example, that there may be considerable delay in the transformation of stereotypes to reflect changes in the empirical conditions and behavior of the target group. Someone justifiably unaware of the changes may use the old stereotype without being morally culpable. Things are more complex even at this level of explanation than Stroebe and Insko's example entails. They suggest that black people may still be considered lazy now because this was their condition under American slavery. Nevertheless, the authors fail to explain why this characterization arose under slavery, for the judgment of laziness involves not only the passivity due to lack of incentive to work but also and perhaps more fundamentally slowness as a form of resistance.[29] Moreover, the explanation Stroebe and Insko offer for the perpetuation of this stereotype of laziness ignores the distinct possibility that such a stereotype continues to be used today because of the *contemporary* interests it represents. In any case, as R. A. Jones points out, the factual errors often committed in stereotyping are not indicative of deficient categorizing or processing functions. The errors follow largely from shortcuts that for the most part operate ably in ordinary information processing and which render our categorizing easier. It follows that the basic operations of stereotyping need be no different from those of categorizing.[30]

The fundamental issue in establishing agent irrationality on the basis of factual errors in racial stereotyping, then, concerns the determination—in cases of lack or falsity of information about races—of the agent's culpability: Ought the agent properly to have known more about the racial group or individual in question? Like other questions of culpability, the verdict here can only be established contextually. In this respect, racist thinking appears to be no different than other forms of social thought.

There are similar problems with the scope of the overgeneralization claim. Claims of particular races may be characterized in terms of probabilistic or statistical generalization of trait possession by their supposed members. So it is open to the racist to discriminate on the same basis against a race and its members. Stereotypes may be read as probability estimates of differential group trait characteristics. They are constructed accordingly as abbreviated measures of the believed degree of trait incidence among members of specified groups compared with the person's comparable beliefs about the population at large. People may believe, for example, that 'Jews are stingy' or that 'Blacks are lazy', that 'Arabs are sly' or 'American Indians are alcoholics' to varying degrees: that all or 60 or merely 30 percent of the racial group are characterized as such. This degree of belief or estimate is furnished by plugging the person's many relevant judgments into a Bayesian statistical formula. Given the availability of objective statistical data (e.g., contributions by Jews to secular charities, productivity levels of blacks and whites at the same level of employment, and so on), the degree of accuracy of people's stereotypes may be computed. There is potentially available, then, an objective measure against which to assess the validity of social judgments.[31]

This formulation solves problems confronting any analysis of racial stereotyping. Social subjects are not committed to extending the stereotyped beliefs about a group to all its members; they can allow exceptions to the generalization. In this way, someone may hold a stereotypical belief about a group, treat the relevant proportion of the group accordingly, and yet consistently insist that though some of his or her best friends are group members they lack the characteristics in question. A person may believe, for example, that his or her Jewish friends are generous while adhering to the stereotype 'stingy Jews' (to the degree, say, of 0.6). This suggests that stereotypes have only partial extension, altering and corroding the more familiar agents become with group members. Clearly, this model represents much more closely the way people tend to respond to others—as individuals and as groups members—within the complexity of social relations.

A measure for the degree of rationality of a person's social stereotypes can be constructed in light of the relevant group information objectively available and taken into consideration by the individual. Familiar with members of a race that they are capable of identifying 'macrodiacritically'[32]—for example, blacks— racists may construct an aversive stereotype on the basis of their fairly extensive experience of group members in relation to their experience of the population at large: for example, '40 percent of blacks encountered in some city are unemployed compared with 20 percent of whites'. Racists may construct from this a predictive estimation of their future experiences and probable behavior responses. They may even be open to careful modification of their behavior as a result of failed predictions and new experiences. Thus, they would seem to meet Jarvie and Agassi's strictest demands on rational agency.[33] The stereotype may tend to skew the underlying explanation for the condition it represents, that blacks are lazy, say, rather than to identify the prevailing reasons for the condition, that blacks have few employment opportunities available to them or that they are mounting resistance to their conditions of existence. But, again, this is a tendency of stereotypes, a direction encouraged, rather than necessary to them.

It follows that racist thinking is not simply a matter of overgeneralization grounded in conceptual mistakes and generating factual errors. It is not simply the impaired psychological functioning of an authoritarian personality as opposed to a tolerant one. Racist thinking is capable, at least in some cases, of avoiding both primary features of stereotyping, that is, the tendency *to rigidify* our conceptions of individuals *by ignoring* their differences in the face of some idealized group conception. Researchers seem to agree that changing stereotypes of people will be more effective the more closely related changes are to the stereotype holder's self-interest. Thus, it must follow also that holding a stereotype will be individually rational the more it is consistent with, especially the more it is a means to instituting, the person's self-interest.[34] This conclusion that racist beliefs do not necessarily transgress criteria of rationality will be corroborated by a careful examination of the second subclass of logical arguments cited to support the contention that racisms are inherently irrational.

Logical Errors

The prevailing presumption that the logic of racisms is commonly characterized by inconsistency and contradiction assumes two forms: first, that there are undeniable inconsistencies between the relevant attitudes of agents and their behavior; and second, that racist stereotyping and thought consist in contradictory beliefs about members of the race in question. There are shortcomings with both formulations of this 'racist logic'.

Attitude-Behavior Inconsistency
Social psychologists generally hold that there is an inconsistency between the relevant attitudes of agents and their behavior. Though racists may express overtly benign attitudes towards members of another race, it is claimed that their behavior will sometimes be inconsistent with these expressed attitudes. By contrast, logical theory reveals that only propositions (or their bearers, such as statements or sentences) may be inconsistent, not disparate entities like attitude and behavior. More directly, social psychologists have treasured this claim of 'attitude-behavior inconsistency' as a scientific thesis generating research programs. Yet subsequent research in social psychology has failed to furnish any clearly defined results in support of the hypothesis.[35]

The common assumption underlying these inconsistency claims, at least in the social psychological literature, is that the beliefs constituting the attitudes in question are alone capable of causing behavior directly and uniquely. However, attitudes *(qua* beliefs) are incapable alone of determining behavior directly. More than the bald beliefs, attitudes may express intentions, dispositions, or desires—generally motives—to act. There is nothing about the nature of racists that necessitates inconsistencies between their racist motives to act, truly admitted, and their acts. Indeed, it is doubtful that the claim of such inconsistency is coherent. Without the relevant disposition, intention, or desire to impel action in accord with, or to aim at, the consequences projected by the belief, the attitude alone can have no direct determinative (causal) effect upon the agent's behavior. Attitudes in the narrow sense of beliefs can only affect actions indirectly—by fashioning desire or expressing a motive in the relevant way.[36]

It follows from the conjunction of these logical and conceptual truths that persons can harbor only inconsistent beliefs. The beliefs in question are either reflected in particular premises (for example, descriptive claims about the member of a race, or the race as such, against which the agent bears a grudge); or in moral or prudential universals (believing, for instance, that members of a race ought both to be treated with respect and to be used merely to the individual's own ends). The universal claims can only be inapplicable, strictly speaking, to particular premises; a person's desires or motives can only conflict with each other (where one has two mutually exclusive motives to act). Consider someone who reveals truthfully that he or she has a nondiscriminatory attitude toward a race or member at a specified time. If, then, at a later time he or she is seen to act towards that race or member in a manner that conflicts with this attitude, the general reasons must be these: Either the person's attitude has altered, or a competing attitude has come at least momentarily to exert greater influence, or the introduction of some desire or changed motive has now taken hold.[37] In other words, racist action will generally (though not exhaustively) turn out rational in the weak sense of aiming at a desired end.

These conceptual confusions underlie the failure of the psychological research to establish the claimed 'attitude-behavior inconsistency'. The failure may have to do, at least in part, with the fact that cognition and behavior follow different rules of operation.[38] Liska concludes that recent research reveals 'a significant relationship between attitudes and behavior'. He admits, however, that it is completely unclear from the research whether the relationship is such that behavior affects attitude or attitude affects behavior. The supposed inconsistency is not 'an anomaly' nor is it 'an insignificant datum'.[39] It is simply no inconsistency at all.

Contradictions in Beliefs

The dominant view of racist logic is that it consists in straightforwardly contradictory and hence irrational beliefs. This 'contradictory belief thesis' is not merely a hypothesis about the psychological state of individual racists. It represents the logic of racist beliefs and must be assessed as such. Gordon Allport is the clearest and most influential representative of this widespread view, and so I will concentrate on his presentation.

Relying upon results reported in *The Authoritarian Personality*, Allport cites the following set as a paradigmatic instance of contradictory beliefs:

J_1 'Jews tend to keep apart, excluding gentiles from Jewish social life, remaining a foreign element in American society.'

and

J_2 'Jews pry too much into Christian activities, seeking too much recognition and prestige from Christians, going too far in hiding their Jewishness.'

Allport admits that 'there is somewhat less self-contradiction' in respect to 'Negro' stereotypes, yet insists that 'contradiction is by no means absent' as witnessed by:

B_1 'Negroes are lazy and inert.'

and

B_2 'The Negro is aggressive and pushing.'

Alternatively, the following set is deemed inconsistent:

B_3 'The Negro knows his place.'

and

B_4 'Force is needed to keep the Negro in his place.'

Items of the kind J_1, B_1, and B_3 constitute a 'subscale of seclusiveness'; those of kind J_2, B_2, and B_4 a 'subscale of intrusiveness'. Since in *The Authoritarian Personality* Adorno and his collaborators had found that the two subscales converged to the degree of 0.74, Allport concludes that the same racists who believed that Jews or blacks are seclusive *tended* also to believe that Jews or blacks are intrusive.[40]

Nevertheless, contradictions are subject to far more stringent logical prerequisites than Allport acknowledges. First, in strict terms, contradictions assume the form 'a & –a'. Second, the person must hold both constituent beliefs of the contradictory set in respect to the same people or well-defined group, not some vaguely constituted and shifting population. Third, the beliefs must be held within the same delimited time span. Allport's conception of contradiction clearly violates each of these strict criteria. At best, the 'subscale of seclusiveness' could only indirectly contradict the 'subscale of intrusiveness', that is, where the properties constituting one subscale, given the appropriate context, controverted those making up the other. Now the measure of 0.74 suggests that the same people tended to believe that the racial group in question was marked by apparently contradictory characteristics. But the study eliciting this correlation failed to establish whether the racists tested held these beliefs about all members of the race in question, and if they held these views only about some, whether the contradictory beliefs were predicated of the same group members. Further, *The Authoritarian Personality* fails to confirm whether the apparently contradictory beliefs were held simultaneously, or at least within a narrowly defined time span. Each person surveyed marked off the properties considered characteristic of Jews or 'Negroes' in the abstract—in terms of what, following Bauman, we may call 'metaphysical Jews' or 'metaphysical Negroes'—without reference to specific individuals. That a racist may believe 'a' and that, given some other background setting, may believe '–a' does not entail that the racist believes 'a & –a'. As I pointed out earlier, there need be nothing irrational in believing Jews in general to be stingy while admitting that one's close Jewish friends are generous.[41]

In particular, the properties Allport offers as examples do not exhibit the proper logical form: Jews, it is believed, only *tend* to keep apart, remaining foreign to *American* society (J_1) while seeking too much from *Christians* (J_2). Tendential judgments in terms of differing predicates cannot contradict each other. It may be that under some interpretations 'laziness' and 'inertia' (B_1) contradict 'aggression' and 'pushiness' (B_2); or that 'knowing one's place' (B_3) contradicts 'needing force to keep one in one's place' (B_4). But it is not obviously so. The study failed to establish that racists predicate these claims of the *same* 'Negroes' or in respect to the same kind of behavior of the racial group. A racist may consistently believe that 'a Negro' is lazy and inert when it comes to work, but aggressive and pushy about rights.

The logic of racist thought is characterized less by contradictions and internal inconsistencies than commonly assumed. This is corroborated by the fact that group (racial) stereotypes and what some social psychologists now call 'discriminatory speech acts' do not arise randomly. As we have seen, they are determined by the relative probabilities of trait possession by members of a (racial) group, by the nature of historical contacts between those expressing discriminatory speech acts and members of the stereotyped group, and by the dynamics of group identification and membership identity, as well as by sociopolitical, economic, and cultural conditions. These factors include the cognitive social processes promoting social discrimination, like distancing, dichotomizing and stressing differences, debasement and degradation. The use of 'demonstratives of distance' like 'they' and 'them' both reflect and exacerbate the discriminatory conditions.[42] Deeply influenced by this intricate web of specific factors which serve to define any social actor, the (potential) racist may construct what amounts to an implicit yet coherent theory of character for members of the group in question. It is in light of this picture that group members' behavioral expectations and the racist's responses are projected. The point to be underlined here is that 'the implicit theory generally is *internally consistent* and is unlikely to contain any sharply contradictory traits'.[43]

So racisms are not inherently irrational on logical grounds. They need involve no inconsistency between attitudes and acts, for such inconsistency is ill conceived. Nor must an individual racist hold contradictory beliefs, for clearly a racist need not. This highlights prior conclusions. On one hand, a racist act may conflict with an affirmative or neutral attitude expressed at an earlier time by the racist. Here, however, it must be that the act is effected by a changed attitude in relation to the specific desire or motive at issue or that the act conflicts with a currently held belief. In the latter case, an aversive desire or motive on the racist's part is most likely at odds with the belief in question. The racist can be considered irrational in this but not in the former instance where the attitude has changed in the relevant way. On the other hand, where a racist holds contradictory beliefs about a race or (some of) its members, he or she is in this respect clearly irrational. But where both beliefs are conscious, it is unlikely they would be held together. Finally, racisms need not function by way of stereotyping in the narrow sense of employing the techniques of dismissal, rigidity, and plain ignorance. It is not simply that the 'logic' commonly ascribed to such stereotyping is inapplicable to the general operations of racisms but rather that the 'logic' is inadequately formulated itself.

We have failed to establish that racisms are necessarily irrational on the grounds of individual logic and psychology. I now turn to inquire whether the claim to racisms' irrationality can be established on the wider intersubjective and contextual bases of prudential or moral reasoning.

Racisms, Prudence, and Morality

An agent is irrational, in the standard account, if the ends, aims, and purposes proposed and pursued are mutually coherent and the means utilized to attain them are conducive to fulfilling these pursuits. These two conditions of agent rationality—the prudential considerations of means-ends consistency and the coherence of ends—are interdependent in a number of ways. Nevertheless, in determining whether the various racisms are capable of meeting these conditions, clarity requires that they be addressed seriatim.

The Imprudence of Racism

The prudential condition obviously rests upon the way in which ends are circumscribed. The clearest attack on the rationality of racisms on grounds of imprudence has been economic in nature, and so it will prove useful to cast the discussion here in terms of the economic end of profit. Determination of the means appropriate to maximizing profit will include defining investment possibilities, predicting probable outcomes for each, and specifying the optimum conditions (for example, labor hiring and wage policies and working conditions) under which each of these policies may be instituted. What has to be decided are the institutional forms and behavior conducive to the highest possible returns on investment, presupposing prevailing market conditions. The objection that racisms are economically irrational translates accordingly into the claims that racist expression—the 'taste to discriminate'—ultimately proves unprofitable; that assuming certain social factors, the neutral calculus of economic profit never discriminates on racial grounds; and that where discrimination occurs, it is always extraeconomic or 'exogenously determined'.[44] Thomas Sowell states the argument thus: 'Short, empirical evidence confirms what economic analysis would predict: that regulated industries have more discrimination than unregulated industries when this depends only on economic considerations.'[45]

Rentals in government-controlled, nonprofit housing schemes in a racist society, on this account, would more likely discriminate against tenants from generally excluded races than would private landlords. The inefficiency supposed to arise from the discrimination is of less concern to the nonprofit sector than to the profit-seeking one, for private landlords are out to maximize the rent they receive, and if rational they will be unconcerned with the race of the highest bidder.

Nevertheless, it is now a well-established historical fact that racially discriminatory laws and practices in some societies have periodically enabled the profit ratio to be maintained or increased both on the micro- and macrolevels. Indeed, discriminatory laws and practices have often been intentionally introduced with this end in mind. While we must view his hypothetical calculations with considerable caution, Lester Thurow estimated that white economic gains or 'Negro' losses from discrimination in the United States amounted to approximately \$15 billion annually. The massive gains to South African whites from *apartheid* are inestimable.[46] It might be suggested that *apartheid* is now disappearing precisely because the costs to whites in material terms are clearly outweighing the benefits. This is no doubt part of the explanation, but it does not deny—indeed, it reaffirms—that most whites in South Africa were willing to hang on to *apartheid* so long as it proved economically rational. And while traditional *apartheid* may be crumbling, white South Africans still 'express tastes' for other kinds of racist expression. Neoclassical microeconomic theory of the sort underlying claims to racism's economic irrationality rests upon the simplifying assumptions that people's tastes and racism are both unchanging. The model is thus incapable of explaining the facts that continued white power and privilege in South Africa are a legacy of *apartheid,* despite the mounting contemporary costs of holding on to it, and that the kinds of racist expression and its attendant benefits have altered. Discussions of the instrumental rationalities of racisms, then, often overlook the crucial fact that any viable analysis of economic rationality must be time-relative, but also diachronic.

A closer look at the prevailing claims from 'economic reason' will reveal the terms under which some racisms may prove to be prudentially rational, that is, rational in the weak sense identified above. I am concerned here only to specify the broad and prevailing conditions of racisms' economic rationality, and this should not be thought to imply that racisms have no extraeconomic influences.

In a review of two provocative books by Thomas Sowell, Christopher Jencks distinguishes between four kinds of economic discrimination: myopic, malicious, statistical, and consumer directed.[47] *Myopia* is the refusal to employ any properly qualified member of a specified racial group because of a misjudgment about the job performance of some group members. As many neoclassical economists are quick to point out, this is economically irrational, for it causes the discriminating employer to hire less-qualified workers without decreasing the wage bill. *Malicious discrimination,* against the group as a whole but not directly against any individual member, is considered economically irrational on the same grounds. In support of this claim Jencks offers the example of an individual employer who refuses to hire a more-qualified black for fear that extending some economic power to blacks will undermine white social supremacy in general. Similarly, middle-income whites who support economic discrimination against blacks as a whole are deemed irrational for it can be shown that the former also experience loss of income as a consequence of the discrimination.[48] However, it is not clear that malicious discriminators need be irrational, for white social and political supremacy may be both a cherished and a tested means of maintaining the profit ratio or social benefits above the level otherwise attainable. Third, it has been demonstrated already that what Jencks calls *statistical discrimination* may meet ordinary standards of rationality. Jencks admits that the employer who refuses to hire members of a racial group on the basis of statistical evidence that its members are generally less productive or more likely to fall foul of the law is acting rationally in the economic sense. The wage bill in relation to productivity and the costs of turnover will likely be higher by employing such group members.

Fourth, *consumer directed discrimination* is that form of discrimination motivated not by antipathies of the discriminating employer or supplier but by consumers of the product or by those wishing to maintain the good's value. For example, a real estate agent serving a prestigious neighborhood acts in his or her own long-term economic interest, and perhaps in the best economic interests of his or her clientele, by refusing to sell property of one client to members of a particular race where it is clear that this would result immediately and inevitably in lower property values for the neighborhood in general. Implicit here is the realistic assumption that only a small percentage of the restricted racial group could afford housing in such a neighborhood. Of course, the agent may thereby delimit the highest price for that client and so act contrary to the latter's economic interest (unless the client owned other property in the area). Yet this objection cannot be generalized from *any* particular client to a denial of maximized profit for *all* clients. The temporal consideration necessary for the generalization to be effective transgresses the condition that property values fall more or less immediately. More clearly, consider the case of Jewish employers who are not themselves antagonistic to Arabs but who refuse to hire Arab personnel because all businesses in the community have been threatened by boycott should they employ Arabs. These employers are hardly proceeding contrary to good economic reason by acting accordingly.[49] Stephen Carter, in discussing Shelby Steele's controversial book, *The Content of Our Characters,* argues that while they may be rational, neither the real estate agent nor the shopkeeper in cases like these are racist, for they do not express nor can we impute to them racist preferences. All they are doing, in Carter's account, is rationally 'acknowledging the force of society's racism'. Carter contends that this acknowledgment is to be distinguished from identifying and learning to live with the racism one finds in society.[50] Perhaps so, but both the real estate broker and shopkeeper (as well as the professorial landlord Carter and Steele discuss) are extending, by being agents of, the continuing exclusions of those each identifies racially. And in my account this amounts to a kind of racism, to perpetuating racist exclusions.

The analysis of general conditions in which instrumental economic rationality may turn out racist has been given more formal social scientific expression in terms of the widely employed rational choice theory. Generally, the rational choice paradigm seeks to explain and predict social behavior on the basis of the following set of assumptions: Self-interested social actors with stable and unchanging tastes or preferences seek to realize the greatest sum of their preferences by employing the smallest proportion of their available resources. In assessing the rationality of any potential undertaking, then, the central calculation of the rational choice model involves assessing whether the expected rewards will outweigh the expected costs, and more so than any alternative employment of resources by the person. If the discriminatory act involves a net profit to the racist, the act will be ruled rational. Thus, the lower the benefits of discriminating, or the higher the cost, the less likely a rational racist will engage in it. By contrast, the more a person's discriminatory preference is deeply cherished, if it is what Sen terms a 'commitment', the higher will have to be the costs of holding the preference before the person will be prepared to give it up.[51]

If we accept for the moment the terms of the model, there are many examples of racist expression that will appear rational. A white employer, landlord, or lending agent has a taste for discriminating against 'nonwhites'. Assume that the market wage rate, rent, or interest rate is M, and that D represents the degree to which a person in a specific circumstance is willing to discriminate (what the person may be willing for that reason to forego). So if whites receive a wage or are charged rent or interest M, then a person who is not white would be employed only if willing to accept $M - D$ and would get the apartment or the loan only by being prepared to pay $M + D$. In each case, the racist would be instrumentally rational either if the person deemed nonwhite were willing to receive less or pay more; or if not willing, were another person willing to accept or pay market rates. A similar analysis must apply to a white shopkeeper, school teacher, or white parents with discriminatory tastes. Each would relocate professionally to a neighborhood considered nonwhite, or allow their children to be bused to a school conceived as nonwhite, only if the rate of compensation received by way of profit, or salary, or property tax reduction, or school cost reduction, say, were sufficient to offset the degree of discriminatory preference. It should be pointed out, too, that those not white in these examples would act rationally in the model were they to resist the discrimination and the 'public bads' that may result to a degree commensurate with but no greater than the felt weight of discrimination they are subject to.[52]

I do not mean to deny that the rational choice model is exceptionally limited, that there are features of social action having to do with racial groupings that are irrationally motivated in various ways, or that various racisms may be instrumentally irrational in one way or another. As I noted in passing, the theory of rational choice assumes fixed preferences, and it is completely unable to account for changes in taste. Moreover, in its commitment to narrow instrumentality, the theory is completely ahistorical. It assumes as given the effects of past actions and the values thus presupposed, and it is unconcerned with how those values arose, how groups came to assume their identity, and how the values in question came to be attached to these groups. The theory thus ignores the institutional positions of actors, structural constraints upon their abilities to act, and the forms of legitimacy that grant subjects the eligibility to act in specified ways. While rational choice theory may be able to account for individuals rationally serving their own group interests, it seems hard pressed to account for the undeniable rationality of a state, or state agents, serving racialized interests all the while gaining legitimation from public condemnation of racism.[53]

It should be noted, nevertheless, that the assumptions central to rational choice theory—isolated, self-interested individuals seeking to maximize their preferences—are those that likewise dominate modernity's picture of the subject. In particular, these assumptions are basic to the liberal conception of morality from Hobbes to Kant, and from Bentham and Mill to Rawls and Gauthier. A basic implication of these assumptions, it turns out, is that many manifestations of racist discrimination may facilitate the general end of profit or utility maximization. These forms will be considered economically rational. This conclusion could be exemplified by analyzing the rationality of white workers who defend the maintenance of job color bars to guarantee their own jobs and preserve higher wage levels by eliminating competition.[54] It is a conclusion that may be generalized: Where ends, aims, and purposes are predetermined and rationality is weakly defined in purely instrumental terms, racist expressions that engender the ends in question must be rational (provided the ends themselves meet prudential requirements).

The instrumental rationality of bureaucracy is central to the structures of modernity. It is the mode of rationality that in its committed formalism makes possible the Holocaust and genocide, organized slaughter and the weapons of mass destruction, the social orders of *apartheids* and racialized ghettoization. For, as Bauman argues so poignantly, instrumental rationality reduces all that it addresses to questions of cold calculation, to numbers and charts and schedules and formulae, to problem solving and hypothetical imperatives. Those occupying offices and playing roles in the culture of modern bureaucracy are thus shielded from assuming personal responsibility by their distance—physical and psychological and existential—from the point of destruction. And the formalized abstraction of instrumental rationality offers both the means to and the rationalized legitimation of this alienated distantiation. It stands at once as the peak and the death valley of the modern condition.

The microlevel analyses of racisms' rationalities thus far addressed are perhaps subsumable under a macrolevel account. It may be claimed that the psychological, social, and cultural rationales for racist expression are to be explained in the last analysis only in terms of their functionality for the capitalist mode of production, as 'rational ideological response(s) to the realities' of capitalism. In this view, racisms have both systemic and ideological implications, for they structure, strengthen, stabilize, and legitimize relations of class privilege and racial exclusion.[55] In short, racisms are rational only in so far as they serve the interests of capital and white privilege.

Viewed in this way, all forms of racism are treated as 'false consciousness', as a 'system of beliefs and attitudes that distort reality'.[56] So though racisms may prove rational at the level of individual psychology, or personality formation, or accumulation of wealth, they involve intellectual defects by distorting and undermining real social and human interests.[57] Despite the recognition that racist ideas are distasteful, blacks, for example, continue to remain structurally subordinate both intra- and internationally. At the wider level, then, racisms turn out to generate contradictions, in general, between their functionality and disfunctionality. Racisms may serve to maintain profit, power, and privilege; yet they do so only at the cost of long-term resentment, reaction, and instability. Thus, at the macrolevel racisms seem generically irrational.[58]

There is much I agree with in this picture of racism. Many have demonstrated that the rise of racism is coterminous with the development of capitalism and colonialism and that changes in the forms racism has assumed can largely be related to transformations in the capitalist mode of production and its class relations.[59] But while these determinants, for the most part, account for the genesis of racisms, I have shown that they fail to exhaust the range of racisms' possibilities and transformations. At some point, offspring assume autonomy from progenitors. There are cases where exclusion takes place *in virtue of* and not merely rationalized by racist discourse.[60] This is reflected in the fact that racist discrimination may occur intraclass, as it may interclass, and that racisms could conceivably afflict nonclass societies. It is possible, then, that some form of racism could persist despite eradicating classes or capitalism, just as racisms could be eliminated without eradicating (capitalist) class differentiation.[61] Moreover, the maintenance of profit, power, and privilege may not be inconsistent with resentment, reaction, and instability. The greater the risk, the higher the rate of return: The latter may turn out to be the conditions under which maintenance of the former are truly put to the test. And as I noted, a racist mode of production may prove exceptionally profitable in the short or medium term, and may be readily abandoned once it ceases to sustain profitability in the long term. Thus, while racisms are highly likely to exacerbate social inequities and tensions, it is not clear that they need promote (dialectical) contradiction.

This leaves the claim of racisms' inherent irrationality to consist in the general incoherence of racist ends. I turn now to assess the set of claims this assumption entails.

The Immorality of Racist Ends

I argued in chapter 2 that modernity exhibits a variety of competing conceptions of morality. Though there are important differences between these views, central to each is the presupposition that moral subjects are rational and that morality consists in the proper application of the rational faculty. In a nonobjectivist view of values, individual ends considered in isolation are arbitrary and subjective. The only way to determine whether a person's end is rational is on the basis of its cohering with some established system of ends. The question here is whether discriminatory exclusions considered as ends-in-themselves—as racist beliefs held and practices undertaken for their own sakes—are capable of cohering with our other ends. To hold racist beliefs or undertake racist practices as ends-in-themselves and not merely, say, for their profitability is literally to adhere to and act for the sake of the racist principles. It is to believe or act thus not because of any advantages these expressions may afford, but in the face of conceivable or actual disadvantages. Where social ends are racist, social institutions are fashioned in their light, and this, of course, enables realization of these ends. Social structure in South Africa attests to this. Now there is no inherent inability of exclusionary racist principles to cohere with other ends like social affluence, retention of state power, domination, and the like. It follows that the view of racisms' inherent irrationality is left to depend upon the argument that racist ends or principles are inconsistent with moral ones.

This argument must hold generally that moral ends conjoin in a body of universal principles—honesty, truth, justice, liberty, and so forth—determined by perfectly rational, legislating subjects constrained only by common, objective—that is, rational—laws. No principles other than these or those consistent with these principles are moral, for no other principles are socially rational. Exclusionary racist principles would not be chosen, in this view, for they are inconsistent with principles of liberty and justice. Hence racisms, whatever form they assume, must be irrational.

In this argument, an end is a proper member of the empire of ends by virtue of being rationally chosen by an ideal legislator. To determine whether a racist principle would be morally acceptable, it must first be established whether it is rational. We cannot, on pain of circularity, simply claim its immorality *a priori* and infer its irrationality from this. Nor may we presume so readily that any racist principle will be inconsistent with principles of liberty and justice. It is at least conceivable that a policy of separate development might meet rational standards of freedom and equality. Though the policy separates social, political, and cultural institutions on racial grounds, it could guarantee distributively equal levels of resources to the separate institutions. This may include separate institutions for the group forming as a result of mixed marriages. The son of H. F. Verwoerd, architect of *apartheid,* continues to insist that this egalitarian separateness represents the proper spirit of his father's vision. Such a conception of an exclusionary race-based social structure cannot be attacked by appealing to principles of liberty and equality, but only on grounds of the overriding value of genuine mutual incorporation, whether the value is established on consequential or intrinsic grounds. Of course, this 'egalitarian *apartheid*' is merely a conceptual possibility. Nevertheless, it cannot be objected that experience has proved otherwise, and this for two reasons. First, though historically separatism has been proposed for the most part by and in the interests of dominant groups, it has received some support among those dominated (e.g., blacks, Palestinians). Second, the general form of the argument at hand is an *a priori* one. It follows that rational possibility is a sufficiently strong counter.

The benevolent utilitarian has a more appealing formulation of the argument. Concerned with maximizing benevolent treatment for all, the utilitarian can extend equal liberty and justice to each as a means of maximizing utility, average or aggregate. Maintenance of liberty and justice would be guaranteed for all and, by implication, so would moral indictment of institutional racism.

The assumption of equal liberty and justice for all as a means to utilitarian ends must realistically presuppose an economy of scarce resources. From positions of equal liberty participants compete for the same goods. It is then open for some to argue in justification either of their claims to the goods or of their successful domination of the competition that they deserve the disproportionate distribution on *empirical* grounds. These grounds might include race-based claims. The utilitarian could appeal, for instance, to needs based upon putatively racial characteristics. More fundamentally, the claim could be rationalized paternalistically, as we saw earlier John Stuart Mill rationalize it, in the following way: Despite equal rights to liberty and justice abstractly considered, the 'less civilized' level of development of some races renders their members incapable of the best administration of their resources from the perspective of maximizing their own utility.[62] So there is no necessity in terms of this utilitarian principle to condemn racially exclusionary practices. One possible response open to the benevolent utilitarian here is to insist that liberty and justice have intrinsic utility. But this is no longer a factual claim, and the utilitarian retreats thereby to deontological high ground.

As Stanley Cavell makes clear, the standard view of deontological deliberation determines a unique moral obligation for each act context by reasoning from a premise to which all rational agents would assent, via intermediate steps (description of context, and so on) that anyone would be capable of comprehending to a conclusion with which all would agree and hence are compelled to accept. To fail to accept the conclusion signifies either incompetence or irrationality. However, formulated in this way, moral reason is even more stringent than the concept of rationality basic to the strictest sciences. Rationality in science consists in suggesting hypotheses and undertaking to revise them by checking them against established facts. In any case, the scope of morality itself seems to belie such rigor: In keeping with scientific reason, one of the marks of the moral is taken to be that disputes remain open to rational disagreement, that moral claims are revisable.[63]

It might be argued that racist contentions are not something that there can be *rational* disagreement about. They transgress the revisability condition and so must be irrational. In this view, racist beliefs are intrinsically indisputable, and those who espouse and act upon them are not open to being persuaded otherwise. There is nothing in the nature of racist beliefs that render them inherently indisputable: Some continue to claim that even *apartheid* can be reformed.[64] Not only may extreme racists be rational within their racist framework, they may also be rational about the framework. So the argument seems to reduce to a question about the dogmatic nature of racists. Racists may respond, not insincerely, that they are open to being persuaded otherwise; they simply have not been offered reasons compelling enough to overthrow their racist beliefs. For example, after long and vehement commitment to *apartheid,* the Nederduits Gereformeerde Kerk (Dutch Reformed Church) recently declared it inimical to the spirit of God. Similarly, Peter Urbach once argued that the hereditarian research program concerning intelligence is progressive in the sense of anticipating novel facts, while the environmentalist program could only account for these facts on an ad hoc basis. The anticipated facts Urbach had in mind included the degree of family resemblances in IQ, IQ related social mobility, and most notably a ten-to-fifteen-point IQ differential in sibling regression for American 'Negroes' and whites. Urbach's arguments presupposed the prevailing data at the time furnished by Burt, Shuey, and Jensen. The data have since been discounted as fraudulent and biased.[65] Presumably, Urbach would be concerned to revise his thesis, if not to renounce it, as a result of these later considerations. These examples also suggest that there are cases where racist beliefs turn out rational in the strong sense of consistency with the supposedly best available explanatory theory and formally established evidence.

The revisability objection to the possibility of racisms' rationality can be interpreted in strictly moral terms. Here, the objection is not equivalent to the logical one that racisms refuse revision. Nor is it tantamount to the criticism that racisms conflate natural and social kinds, that appeals to race as biological grounds for exclusionary social treatment always involve unjustified values as the motive for such differential exclusions. Nor, again, is it just the point of empirical sociologists that racists are found never to alter their views. Rather, the objection consists in the moral claim that race never commands categorically: It is incapable of grounding a moral imperative. *Race* is, by definition, a 'morally irrelevant category', and discriminations on the basis of race are thus irrational.[66]

The Rawlsian formulation of the objection is the strongest, and I will restrict my remarks to it. Rawls may be right in insisting that any appeal to racial considerations be excluded from the *ideal* principles of justice rationally chosen in the original position, though it may be debatable whether nonexclusionary uses of race should be so excluded. Nevertheless, appeals to racial considerations turn out irrational, and hence immoral, in Rawls's view because the impossibility of their coming out rational is assumed to be a structural feature of the hypothetical choice situation itself. Rawls assumes away contingent differences between people that in actual contexts could conceivably make a moral difference. *Race* turns out to be a 'morally irrelevant category' because it is presumed to be. Alan Gewirth formulates a similar criticism of Rawls in terms of rational choice: Rationality of one's choice behind the veil of ignorance is in question when one is ignorant of one's particular identity, and self-interested rational persons will hardly be motivated to pursue ends they have chosen blind to their own particular goals.[67]

The difficulties facing the strict moral rationalist here are highlighted in those cases where agents find self-interested prudential considerations competing with rational choices made behind the veil of ignorance. Like Kant, Rawls's moral argument assumes the overriding compulsion of moral claims in conflict with prudential ones. Nevertheless, as Philippa Foot has argued, the claim that moral considerations are overriding from the moral point of view is tautologous and uninteresting. Common cases can be cited where an agent may be deemed rational for acting on prudential considerations in the face of competing moral ones and, one may add, where the prudential considerations can be racially characterized.[68] The moral rationalist who holds ideally to the irrelevance of *race* is hard put to distinguish between the moral unacceptability of 'discriminating against' and the oftentimes permissible 'differentiating between' members of some supposed race. As liberals in the United States are just beginning to discover, this makes it more difficult, at least prima facie, to justify race-based preferential treatment programs. Nevertheless, as I suggested in chapter 5 and will argue in conclusion, such programs are not on the face of it irrational nor need they be irrelevant.

I do not mean to imply by this set of arguments that rationality can play no part in establishing the unjustifiability of racisms. There are clearly cases where racist beliefs and the exclusionary practices with which they are inextricably tied may be dismissed as unacceptable because they turn out irrational. Nevertheless, irrationality can serve only as a sufficient condition for racisms' social unjustifiability. The unacceptability of racisms turns for the most part on something more substantive than the rational status of the beliefs and practices in question. We usually condemn racisms not because they fail to satisfy formal requirements of rationality, like consistency, nor because race is an irrelevant moral criterion. Rather, we condemn racisms because they pick out persons so as to exclude them from rights or entitlements we think should be available to all or to subject them to treatment we think nobody should suffer. Even in those cases where racist beliefs and acts are dismissed as irrational, this seems to signal a deeper disapprobation. Mostly, we find racisms wrong because they are somehow unfair or unjust, because people are improperly excluded from application of the relevant social principles, or from the moral realm altogether. In short, we dismiss racisms on grounds of commitment to deeply cherished values.

One way of trying to sharpen the distinction at issue is to deem racisms wrong for the *unreasonable* claims and behavior they encourage or cause. The distinction between rationality and reasonableness is embedded in the contemporary moral tradition: It is explicit, for example, very early in Rawls's work, and many moral theorists intend the latter when using the former. 'Rationality' is largely formal in extension, setting the standards for 'explaining, arguing, proving and deliberating'.[69] Reasonableness includes formal criteria like rational consistency, coherence, conceptual clarity, and generalizability. But it signifies more than this, including substantive conceptions of fairness, moderation, genuine autonomy, support by grounded reasons, emphasis upon nonfatalistic ideas, and respect for persons and counterclaims. A reasonable person is one open to being persuaded otherwise by the best available arguments. In short, a rational person might not be reasonable, though a reasonable person cannot help but be rational. Thus, while some racisms need not be irrational, all forms are inherently unreasonable and as such unacceptable.

Now it may seem immediately apparent that this hypothesis is faced by difficulties similar to those I have shown afflicting the view that racisms are inherently irrational. This line of objection becomes especially pertinent given Gewirth's undertaking to establish not only that it is reasonable to be rational but that it is rational also to be reasonable. For Gewirth, rationality consists centrally in the principle of noncontradiction. Any rationally self-interested persons take as their basic self-conception that they have rights to freedom and to pursue their own well-being. This self-conception furnishes the minimal necessary conditions for persons to act to satisfy their purposes. But in claiming these rights as necessary conditions for the satisfaction of their own purposes, rational agents must admit them, on pain of inconsistency, likewise as the conditions of all other persons' purposive actions. So, concludes Gewirth, if rational, persons must be reasonable by respecting the basic or 'generic rights' of other persons.[70]

Even if by accepting his construal of 'generic rights' we admit the tight conceptual link Gewirth seeks to draw between rationality and reasonableness, there is a fundamental point this argument fails to address, and it is central to the question of racism's rationality. There are various ways we may think it reasonable to restrict the freedom of others for their own well-being. In general, we proceed in this way for persons we deem not fully rational (sometimes we proceed thus even for all persons where we think it is likely many may be irrational, as in laws requiring seatbelts). Historically, races deemed 'nonwhite' have been considered less than fully human, or judged to be species lower or different than Homo sapiens, their members not rational purposive agents. So just as the application of rationality has been circumscribed in relation to race, gender, and class, so too could reasonableness be curtailed. The only relevant difference between the two, for Gewirth, is that reasonableness is thought to rest in having certain dispositions, namely, the moral ones, while rationality consists minimally in the formal principle of noncontradiction. This concedes the point Gewirth is contesting, for it suggests that rationality is at most a necessary but not a sufficient condition for being reasonable. More directly, though, as Gewirth admits, it cannot guarantee the success of reasonableness where rationality fails, for we are concerned here with the scope of its application, and I have suggested that this may be restricted in respect to the racial other in just the way it has been for rationality. The criteria for being reasonable may be historically and culturally racialized in much the fashion I have suggested concerning rationality.

Nevertheless, the inherent unreasonableness of racisms in contrast with their sometime rationality does seem borne out by the following consideration, which I owe to Laurence Thomas. What one comes to consider reasonable or unreasonable is tied up with a range of experiences one has across a life. Some of what one deems reasonable or unreasonable, then, will not be open to persuasion, for to be persuaded here would mean denying deeply cherished life experiences. It may be difficult to persuade racists of the unreasonableness of their racist commitments, to dissuade them of those commitments, in something like the way one cannot convince a person who has had no experience of love or art or music that a life with them far outweighs one without. On the assumption that racism is inherently irrational, the widespread occurrence of racisms can only remain mysterious: The fact that they are so pervasive and impervious to dissuasion is literally beyond explanation. One's refusal to be persuaded out of one's racist commitments, by contrast, is a mark for the most part of one's unreasonableness, not necessarily one's irrationality, which can be put down to one's experiences. And for one's experiences, or at least for the influence they are taken to have on one's life, outlook, and character, one is for the most part responsible.

This raises a deeper point about the nature of racisms. I argued in chapter 5 that racism has come to designate a very wide range of phenomena. So though we may be able to say roughly what in general we find wrong with racism, there may be no single social condemnation strictly appropriate to all types. This would commit us to developing multiple strategies for revealing that all racisms are socially unacceptable. A particular racist token would turn out unjustifiable by reflecting a type that has been shown for some reason to be wrong; it may differ from the reason another racist token of a different type turns out unacceptable. The existential hurt suffered by the victim of racist exclusion and its characteristic wrongfulness may differ for different kinds of cases. Certainly, they will not just have to do with the ascription of morally irrelevant characteristics. In some cases the hurt and wrong will be turn on being made the object of categories from which there is no escape. If one is called stupid, there may at least be ways of showing why the characterization is wrong—in this or other cases. By contrast, if one is deemed incompetent for racist reasons, the most one can often hope to show the racist is that the designation is unfitting in spite of one's race. But here one can think of at least two different sources for the hurt and wrong. On one hand, they may turn on having the culture, history, and products of the group to which one is committed being demeaned, dismissed, or disregarded; on the other, they may be a function of being placed in a group to which one chooses to show no allegiance. The first is a straightforward case of disrespect; the second a case of denying autonomy.[71] The first excludes the group to which one chooses to belong from full consideration or worthiness; the second excludes one, in virtue of one's purported racial belonging, from the self-determination supposedly characteristic of human agency or personhood. Again, these may or may not differ from cases where the cause of hurt is tied to the historical weight of being called 'a nigger' or 'kike', deemed 'a sly Arab', considered incapable of more than athleticism or entertainment, or slighted as a usurious money lender. Circumstances must establish whether the accompanying wrongs here are instances of disrespect or lack of autonomy, or simply rationalized instances of the denial of a right to equal treatment. The blanket notion of irrationality at best serves to hide these distinctions, and at worst draws attention away from the wrongfulness of rational racism, leaving uncontested and so seemingly legitimate any racist expressions not clearly irrational.

Thus, the conceptual, logical, prudential, and moral arguments supporting the thesis that racisms are inherently irrational fail under scrutiny to exhaust the entire range of racist propositions, beliefs, and acts. There are clearly many examples where racist actions turn out rational in the weak, instrumental sense of effecting ends or goals. A fuller account of social rationality involving a more complete specification of human psychology and the structures of social life will bear this out. Here, beliefs will turn out rational in terms of their ability to comfort and protect against anxiety, to organize vague feelings, to provide a sense of identity, and to facilitate participation in a cause.[72] The view that many racist acts turn out weakly rational assumes greater plausibility in this light.

Moreover, some racist beliefs or theories could turn out strongly rational, if they satisfy widely accepted formal criteria of rationality. I have already suggested that Urbach's hereditarianism, structured in terms of Lakatosian methodological considerations, is an example of this sort. Pierre van den Berghe's commitment to a sociobiological explanation of racism provides a more recent example. As I showed in chapter 4, the sociobiological paradigm holds that, like other animals, members of the various human races have reached the point, via selection, of kin preference. One is purportedly drawn for reproductive purposes to kin, for this maximizes the inclusive fitness of the intrabreeding group members. Human organisms are simply frameworks for the natural selection of reproductively successful genes, and genes favoring intrakin relations have purportedly exhibited selective advantage. Racism, under one interpretation, emphasizes genetically heritable phenotypes in selection of sexual partners, and all other fraternal relationships are for the sake of this reproductive end. Racial phenotypes are accordingly considered the most reliable markers of kinship or genetic relatedness. Racism, on this reading, turns out to be genetically functional.[73] The sociobiological implication is that racial exclusion is understandably universal in both the temporal and spatial senses. As with Urbach's hereditarianism, sociobiology makes a natural phenomenon of racism. Explanation of its occurrence becomes rationalization of its inevitability. Theoretical commitment to sociobiology under this interpretation implies rational commitment to racist beliefs.

That forms of racist expression may sometimes turn out rational in both the strong and weak senses has implications for how racisms are conceived and resisted. Thus, we should not be too optimistic about the effectivity of moral education. Moral education may turn out to be an appropriate way to respond to some forms of racism, but its scope and effects are likely to be very limited. First, as Prager points out, there is no necessary relation between the growth of knowledge and its effect on the dominant representation of others, probably even less on more subtle discriminatory articulations.[74] The limits of moral education in combatting racism will likely be magnified in those cases where racism is more deeply embedded in the social structure and its accompanying discourse of articulation. Here, nothing short of structural transformation and discursive displacement will help. Second, moral education aims to encourage subjects to give up racist behavior by altering racist feelings and thoughts. This line of attack seems inverted: One can never be sure that or when the moral education has been effective, and there are all sorts of ways to restrict exclusionary expressions directly without having first to alter thinking.[75] Third, moral education is always undertaken in, and so is likely to reflect, a specific social context. In a racist social setting, there is an increased tendency for racial constructs to insinuate themselves into the presuppositions, language, and thinking of public morals.[76]

This insinuation of racialized language, presuppositions, and implications into social relations is prompted, facilitated, and perpetuated by prevailing discourses that order our conception of the social, of self and other identity, of inclusion and exclusion. Conceiving the realms of sociality and morality in this way delimits the power of appeals to how the social relations *really* are. Realist appeals to social or moral truths may at most rule out some empirical appeals to racist and racialized claims. But, against a background of the practical indeterminacy of moral claims, one has to be far more circumspect about realism's capacity to rule in some specific claim. While some claims may be so outrageous as to be self-evidently false, more subtle representations—even those serving established relations of racialized power—often have considerable perspectival plausibility. Calls to stand outside these profitable perspectives, ultimately calls to assume 'the view from nowhere', may turn out as partial or as ungrounded as the claims being rejected: 'partial' insofar as they represent specific interests in the imperial name of universality, and 'ungrounded' insofar as they represent no interests at all.

Rationality, thus, forms the centerpiece of enlightened modernity's self-conception and self-representation. Racialized discourse and its attendant racist expressions, I have argued, are centrally and uniquely constitutive of the modern condition. It stands to reason, then, that racisms should intersect with and advance their claims in terms of modernity's rationalities rather than merely by the expression of raw power. Racisms are accordingly not some throwback to premodern social formations, not necessarily marginal to the constitution of modern liberal democracies, not antithetical to the processes of social modernization. Racisms, I have suggested, define at least in part what modern social actors take themselves to be, just as they are often taken to exhaust definition of those persons modern actors would include with themselves in the body politic. It turns out that the emergence of social knowledges in the development of modernity and the elevation of their importance in the processes of modernization, both as theoretical discourses and as empirically based sciences, have been crucial to the reproduction and transformation of racialized body politics. It is to a more direct demonstration of these relations between social knowledge, racial formations, and racist exclusions that we are now drawn.

7

Racial Knowledge

I have argued that race has been a constitutive feature of modernity, ordering conceptions of self and other, of sociopolitical membership and exclusion. It has identified exploitable individuals and populations for subjection, and it has been used to rationalize and legitimate domination, subjugation, even extermination. The forms of racist exclusion, more or less extreme, have been enabled by the embedding of transforming racialized distinctions into the ordinary processes, categories, and outcomes of reasoning, into Reason itself. And these exclusions have been executed in terms of the imputation of race into various conceptions of morality, into conceptions of what sorts of behavior morality requires, and into accounts of the Moral Subject—who is capable of moral action and who is subjected to it, who is capable of moral autonomy and who should be directed. Thus, I have largely been concerned so far with conceptualizing the logics of racializing discourse and racist expression. In chapters 7 and 8 I will be concerned with what can be called a sociology of these logics, with showing how these processes of racial formation and racialized exclusion continue to be extended subtly through formalized production of knowledges in the social and humanistic disciplines and in the production of spacialized configurations.

I demonstrated in chapters 3 and 4 how eighteenth- and nineteenth-century social science and humanities ordered racial creations, in chapter 5 how these creations have enabled and extended racist exclusions, and in chapter 6 how race colonizes and is extended through rationalities. I will be concerned in this chapter and the following one with an engaged and concrete exemplification of the central conceptual thematic of the book, namely, of the normalizing of racisms in and through the transforming sociologics and rational(izing) modes of modernity. My immediate focus will be directed to contemporary (re)production and transformation of racialized knowledge in the social and humanistic disciplines, while in chapter 8 I will be concerned to show how social space is configured in and through racially conceived terms. In chapter 9, by extension, I will conclude with a pragmatic account of oppositional resistances to racist culture in all domains.

'Methodological Eurocentrism' consists primarily in the claim that prevailing Eurocentric values in the social sciences like economics, psychology, and social anthropology apply universally. There is much in the contemporary critical analysis of this presupposition that is convincing.[1] My primary critical concern in the present chapter, however, will not be with this methodological presupposition. Rather, I will illustrate how, through various primary ordering concepts and root metaphors, contemporary knowledge production reinvigorates racialized categories or launches new ones and so subtly orders anew the exclusiveness and exclusions of racist expression.

Racial Knowledge and Power

Knowledge and the Production of Otherness

In the seeming informalities of its modes, literary and cultural production is particularly well-placed to mold, circumscribe, and stamp racialized identity, since racial significations are deeply implicit in the signs employed and employable. Racialized connotations are embedded in the locus of ordinary social meanings that cultural expression reflects in the various space-time contexts of modernity.[2] Knowledge, in particular knowledge of and about the social, is not produced in a vacuum. Knowledge producers are set in social milieus. The political economy and culture of their productive practices act upon the categories employed, and so they inform the knowledge being produced. By furnishing assumptions, values, and goals, this economy and culture frame the terms of the epistemological project. Once produced, the terms of articulation set their users' outlooks. The categories that now fashion content of the known constrain how people in the social order at hand think about things. Epistemological 'foundations', then, are at the heart of the constitution of social power.[3]

What I am calling 'racial knowledge' is defined by a dual movement. It is dependent upon—it appropriates as its own mode of expression, its premises, and the limits of its determinations—those of established scientific fields of the day, especially anthropology, natural history, and biology. This scientific cloak of racial knowledge, its formal character and seeming universality, imparts authority and legitimation to it. Its authority is identical with, it parasitically maps onto the formal authority of the scientific discipline it mirrors. At the same time, racial knowledge—racial science, to risk excess—is able to do this because it has been historically integral to the emergence of these authoritative scientific fields. Race has been a basic categorical object, in some cases a founding focus of scientific analysis in these various domains. This phenomenon has no doubt been facilitated by the definitive importance of difference in modernity's development of knowledge. As Foucault remarks:

> [A]ll knowledge, of whatever kind, proceeded to the ordering of its material by the establishment of differences and defined those differences by the establishment of an order; this was true for mathematics, true also for *taxonomies* ... and for the sciences of nature; and it was equally true for all those approximative, imperfect, and largely spontaneous kinds of knowledge which are brought into play in the construction of the least fragment of discourse or in the daily process of exchange; and it was true finally for philosophical thought.[4]

Racial knowledge consists *ex hypothesi* in the making of difference; it is in a sense and paradoxically the assumption and paradigmatic establishment of difference. An epistemology so basically driven by difference will 'naturally' find racialized thinking comfortable; it will uncritically (come to) assume racial knowledge as given.

Power is exercised epistemologically in the dual practices of naming and evaluating. In naming or refusing to name things in the order of thought, existence is recognized or refused, significance assigned or ignored, beings elevated or rendered invisible. Once defined, order has to be maintained, serviced, extended, operationalized. Naming the racial Other, for all intents and purposes, *is* the Other. There is, as Said makes clear in the case of the Oriental, no Other behind or beyond the invention of knowledge in the Other's name. These practices of naming and knowledge construction deny all autonomy to those so named and imagined, extending power, control, authority, and domination over them. To extend Said's analysis of the 'Oriental' to the case of race in general, social science of the Other establishes the limits of knowledge about the Other, for the Other is just what racialized social science knows. It knows what is best for the Other—existentially, politically, economically, culturally: In governing the Other, racialized social science will save them from themselves, from their own Nature. It will furnish the grounds of the Other's modification and modernization, establishing what will launch the Other from the long dark night of its prehistory into civilized time. The wiser, the more knowledgeable the governors are about subject races—at home or abroad, colonially or postcolonially—the less will their administrative rule or government require raw force. 'Good racial government' thus requires information about racial nature: about character and culture, history and traditions, that is, about the limits of the Other's possibilities. Information, thus, has two senses: detailed facts about racial nature; and the forming of racial character. Information is accordingly furnished both by academic research and through practical expertise, through reading and observation, in schools and universities, in courts and prisons.

Production of social knowledge about the racialized Other, then, establishes a library or archive of information, a set of guiding ideas and principles about Otherness: a mind, characteristic behavior or habits, and predictions of likely responses. The Other, as object of study, may be employed but only as informant, as representative translator of culture. The set of representations thus constructed and cataloged in turn confines those so defined within the constraints of the representational limits, restricting the possibilities available to those rendered racially other as it delimits their natures. The spaces of the Other—the colonies, plantations, reservations, puppet governments and client states, the villages and townships, or the prisons, ganglands, ghettoes, and crowded inner cities—become the laboratory in which these epistemological constructs may be tested. Even the literature, art, languages, and general cultural expression are appropriated as proper objects of 'scientific' evaluation. They are judged not as works among works of art in general, but the works or languages or expressions of the Other, representative of the cultural condition and mentality, of the state of Otherness—artifacts not art, primitive formulations not rationally ordered linguistic systems, savage or barbaric or uncivilized expressions not high culture. Learned societies linked to the colonial condition, even disciplines emerged for the sole purpose of studying various racial Others, or the racial Other as such, *its* metaphysical being. These societies have served to inform the colonial or urban administration on whose account they have flourished, but they have also been defined and confined by the relation: what they could experience or represent, who and under what conditions objects could be approached, engaged, studied. Knowledge, accordingly, is socially managed, regulated by the general concerns of social authority, and self-imposed by the specific interests and concerns of the disciplinary specialist.[5]

So the central role of scientific authority in constituting Otherness cements such constitution into an objective given, a natural law. The characterizations accompanying, promoting, or instrumental to such constitutional creation of Others become reified, objectified as unalterable, basic parts of people's natures. In this way, the various divisions of racialized personhood become set as naturally given, as universal and unavoidable. This epistemological manufacture of Otherness mirrors the abstraction typical if not inherent in philosophy's constitution of its discursive object, namely, pure concepts indicative of universal, objective truths. Here, in the philosophical setting and interrelations of personhood (of mind and body), of civil society, and of the State, it is not that the Other is necessarily denied or abnegated (though this has often been so). Rather, in the abstraction of ideas about persons, society, and politics, the philosophical abstraction becomes objectified, once objectified reified as natural, and so extended universally. Part, indeed, an idealized part, is substituted for the whole, and the specificity of the Other, of Otherness itself is silently denied. Those thus rendered Other are sacrificed to the idealization, excluded from the being of personhood, from social benefits, and from political (self-)representation.[6] Erased in the name of a universality that has no place for them, the subjects of real political economy are denied and silenced, ontologically and epistemologically and morally evicted. The universal claims of Western knowledge, then, colonial or postcolonial, turn necessarily upon the deafening suppression of its various racialized Others into silence.

This process of silencing furnishes the solution to what Bauman identifies as the 'technological challenge' faced by social knowledge in the face of the erratic, and so unpredictable behavior of an Other unruled, or insufficiently ruled, by Reason. Admitting the Other's subjectivity is at once to give up epistemological and political control; it is to admit scientific and administrative inefficiency. To retain control, the scientist as much as the administrator, the theoretical expert as much as the advisor and consultant has to control the variables, to manage the environment. The outcomes must be predictable, the more strictly so the better. Calculation is methodologically central, the more formalized the more acceptable. As Foucault remarks, 'Recourse to mathematics, in one form or another, has always been the simplest way of providing positive knowledge about man with a scientific style, form, and justification.' Racialized knowledge in the nineteenth and twentieth centuries has been no exception: witness phrenology, the measurement and weighing of skulls, IQ testing, and crime statistics.[7]

Implicit in these remarks is a hint of the relation between formally produced racialized knowledge, especially at the hands of social science, and the State. Etienne Balibar insists that the relationship to the Other at the heart of modern racism is necessarily mediated by State intervention.[8] One of the basic modes this intervention assumes is concern over production of racialized knowledge. State conceptual mediation is as old as the category of *race* itself: recall the debate between Las Casas and Sepulveda discussed in chapter 2. But state mediation basically reinvents itself with each of the major conceptual developments in racialized thinking: with polygenism and the colonial encounter, with social Darwinism and eugenics, with IQ testing, and, as we saw, with race relations analysis. We should pursue the conceptual relations between racialized social science and the State a little further.

Race, Social Science, and the State

Social science is important to the modern State both *functionally* and *ideologically*. In the former sense, social science furnishes the State and its functionaries with information, and it is often employed in formulating and assessing State policies to satisfy social needs. Ideologically, the State often invokes expedient analyses and the results of social science, whether by collaboration or appropriation, to legitimize State pursuits and to rationalize established relations of power and domination. I do not mean to suggest that the functional and ideological exhaust State support of social science, still less that these forms exhaust social science itself. The State may support a research program because of its scientific value; and much social science may have little formally to do with the State as such, though work that studiously avoids *the social* barely deserves the name. More important, the State—or some particular state—may be the object of a *critical* social science concerned with uncovering and attacking modes of repression. So State Functional and State Ideological Social Science could both be objects of critical analysis.

What I am calling State Functional Social Science can be conducted *in virtue of* or *in service of* State ideology. Consider, for example, two related claims: 'People [in South Africa] ... do define themselves, in the first instance, as members of a population group'; and 'The research ... showed that population group/race/nationality are first-order interpretations, categorizations or characteristics in terms of which others are perceived'.[9] These assumptions are so deeply entrenched in South African state ideology as to be unquestioned, and they are unquestioningly endorsed by the research that reproduces them. The claims hold, if at all, only *in virtue of* accepting the premises that ground the ideology; and in turn they give foundation to the conclusion that possible 'solutions' to the South African dilemma must be limited to producing 'constructive intergroup relations'.[10]

Consider, by contrast, the claim that white settlers arrived at the Cape of Good Hope at the close of the seventeenth century coincidentally with African tribes migrating from the north. Asserted by amateur colonial historians Theal and Cory early in the twentieth century, common in most school history texts, and until quite recently propounded by serious Afrikaner scholars, this claim was made *in service of* state ideology.[11] (Perhaps it should be said that the claim *functions* as ideology.) It was designed to substantiate the idea that whites originally laid equal claim to the land with blacks and historically acquired control over (at least) 87 percent of South African territory by way of a 'just', and so justified war. The deeper insinuation here, of course, is one of white superiority.

It seems obvious that State Ideological Social Science—the development and use of (a) social theory to rationalize, legitimize, or conceal repressive or unjust modes of social relation and expression—has functional value. That is, ideologically State Social Science need not merely define but may serve given state interests. It remains an open question, however, whether State Functional Social Science—social science prompted by State defined purposes and structures—signifies ideologically. One is tempted to say that the ideology expressed by a State committed technocratically to functional social science is a form of *instrumental* pragmatism. Here, knowledge is treated as strictly instrumental to predefined State purposes, never as sustaining critique. Untheorized pragmatisms either generate or (more usually) cover up underlying ideological rationalizations of events, relations, and structures.

The relevance of these distinctions to an understanding of racialized social science should become apparent as I proceed. Yet their application is seldom quite so straightforward. For example, during the 1980s, many South Africans were fond of citing data showing that the majority of that country's black population did not support the call to disinvest. It is difficult to establish, without knowing considerably more and in the context of political hegemony, whether the data and, more significantly, the studies that produced them were functional or ideological;

whether the studies were performed in virtue or in service of (function as) state ideology, or simply from the desire to know; and whether the *use* of the data thus collected was purely pragmatic, or in virtue, or in service of state ideology.

The distinction between data and their use is one the positivist might appeal to in objecting that State Ideological Social Science is not social science at all; and I suspect that one who pursued this line of criticism would conclude likewise for functional social science in the way I have defined it. But this form of positivistic critique misses the deeper point that needs highlighting, namely, that social science—the study and analysis of human beings past, present, and future in their social relations—is affected in all kinds of ways by the *Weltanschauung* in terms of which it is conducted, that it is often conducted by and for the State, that it may be formative in constructing the 'imagined community' of racialized State- or nationhood, and that once collected the data has to be interpreted before conclusions about social policy or action can be drawn. In short, there is nothing remotely resembling pure social data whose meaning and truth are incontestably self-evident.

Racialized knowledge production, and social science in particular, has been integral to State designs in both functional and ideological terms. It has often been noted that anthropology was handmaiden to colonialism. In furnishing information about those societies under the colonizing gun, anthropology both serviced the perceived needs of colonizing states and rationalized colonization as morally necessary for the sake of the colonized. Nevertheless, as Foucault reminds us, it should not be concluded that anthropology is nothing but a colonial discipline.[12] This was, understandably, the general sense of many suffering at the hands of anthropologizing colonialisms. This conclusion might be implied from the fact that with independence, especially in Africa, anthropology departments were replaced largely by sociology faculties at local universities. It should be remembered, though, that while Western governments may have withdrawn from former colonial territories, Western social scientists clearly did not. With the growing move to independence in those states marked as racially Other, political scientists were substituted for anthropologists in representing the functional and ideological interests of the West. Capitalism required new markets, and capital investment presupposed political stability. Western models of state formation were offered as necessary preconditions for the takeoff stage[13] of modernizing economic development: Rational political organization—for example, the Westminster model for former British colonies—would rationalize efficient use of economic resources. Indigenous political organization reflected prehistory, objects for anthropological study not modernization. Once the battle for ongoing political allegiance had been more or less won by the lure of capital, economists almost automatically replaced political scientists as the prevailing postcolonial experts of choice. If imperialist direct rule was replaced under colonialism by indirect rule (a prototype of the sort of independence to follow), the outmoding of indirect rule by independence was accompanied by the institution of rule by other means—by economic control. The influence of economists, of direct representatives of Western capital, and of local technicians trained in the West furnished the skills necessary to rationalize control, in both senses of the term.[14] More or less radical social science, while undertaking to alter the thrust of epistemological colonization, has nevertheless done little to transform the terms of racialized knowledge production.

The terms used by social scientists to represent the racialized Other in the nineteenth and twentieth centuries reflected popular representations in dominant Western culture at the times in question. This truncated and all too partial reading of the history of social science in colonial and postcolonial control shows that the terms of popular representations of racialized Others were in many cases set by prevailing modes dominant in social science at the time. What follows is a critical reading of three conceptual schemata hegemonic in the production of contemporary racialized knowledge that now define and order popular conceptions of people racially conceived: the Primitive, the Third World, and the Underclass. These terms and the conceptual schemes they mark are the most prominent and general in silently ordering formal and popular knowledge of the Other in and through the study of cultural, political, and economic relations.

Conceptual Orders

Each of the terms, together with the conceptual presuppositions they signal, invoke (by cutting across and so abstractly uniting) a range of social scientific disciplines. *The Primitive,* Wolf's 'peoples without history', is threaded through anthropology, ethnography, art history, legal and cultural studies and criticism. *The Third World* brackets political economy and political science with sociology and development and area studies. *The Underclass* brings together sociology, politics, policy studies, justice studies, and urban planning. All three connote in social scientific and popular discourse more widely than in their racial delimitations. There is a dual sense, however, in which this fact serves to normalize, seemingly to legitimize their racial connotations. Their noncontroversial meanings offer to their racialized ones the aura of respectability, just as their racial connotations spill over silently, unself-consciously, and so unproblematically into their nonracialized ones.

The Primitive

The word 'primitive' was first used in the late fifteenth century to refer to origins. In that sense, it assumed the connotations that were thought to accompany the image of an early, ancient, or first stage, age, or period: old-fashioned, or rough, or rude. (It later acquired more neutral technical meanings in relation to the original words in a language, or members of the early Church.) The Enlightenment interest in human origins was, as we've seen, largely defined in physical terms. Original peoples or races were thought to have little or no social organization or cultural achievements worthy of mention, and the meaning of 'primitive' at the time seems to reflect this. It was in Darwin's wake that scholarly interest in the 'original' social and cultural condition of society really flourished, though even at this time the concept of *the Primitive* was not necessarily racialized. Many of the major theorists of 'primitive society' in the late nineteenth century initially approached the object of study as a set of legal issues, the standard for which was an analysis of Roman law. Included in the conception, accordingly, were Greek and Roman societies, those societies taken to be the primitive or early forerunners of modern Europe. The influence of this scholarly bent is reflected in the fact that art history initially included in the extension of the term 'primitive art' only pre-Renaissance Italian and Flemish painters. By the end of the century, the term had been broadened to include all ancient art; and by 1920, art's historical connotation had assumed the racialized reference it had long had beyond the boundaries of that discipline, referring strictly to art of non-Western cultures: Africa, Oceania, and South America.[15]

The idea of a *primitive society* invented, as Adam Kuper points out, by nineteenth-century legal anthropologists referred to some primeval origin to which society could be archaeologically traced. The idea reified the 'existence' of its referent through the crafting of a set of specialized instruments, ultimately those of applied mathematics, to get objectively at the 'real' nature of primitive society. Like *race,* then, the concept of *the Primitive* proved theoretically adaptable, appropriating novel theoretical developments as its own by being appropriable as a concept central and so seemingly necessary to theoretical advance. Almost as vacuous in connotation as *race, the Primitive* transformed in meaning as *race* did.[16] The Primitive assumed synonymy with the racial Other, a technical nomenclature for a popular category. Popular and scientific discourse merged, mutually influencing the terms of discursive formalization and expression. Indeed, the set of meanings that attaches to contemporary usage of 'the Primitive' and 'primitive societies', and by extension to 'Primitivism' is a legacy of this past century of scholarly and popular coproduction. Its transformative capacity makes it particularly suited as a basic trope, a primary element of racist expression.

Formally, primitive societies were theorized in binary differentiation from a civilized order: nomadic rather than settled; sexually promiscuous, polygamous, and communal in family and property relations rather than monogamous, nuclear, and committed to private property; illogical in mentality and practicing magic rather than rational and scientific. In popular terms, nonwhite primitives have come to be conceived as childlike, intuitive, and spontaneous; they require the iron fist of 'European' governance and paternalistic guidance to control inherent physical violence and sexual drives.[17] If, Platonistically, there is conceived to be a primitive lurking deep in the soul of the civilized, it is ruled by Reason, contained and controlled by civility and the institutions of civil society. For the Civilized have a history, but the Primitive have none: their histories are frozen.[18]

It is a remarkable conceit, this, to think of 'a people' having no history, no past, no movement from one time to another, frozen stiff like a wax figure in Madam Tussaud's or the Museum of Man. Remarkable in its arrogance, in its abnegation of those seemingly so unlike themselves that *they* can assume away humanity, banish it to the shadows of their assumptions about what human beings are or are not; remarkable in its lack of self-conscious skepticism about their own limits and excesses, their own warts and odors and blemishes, of what they can or cannot do or know, of their own productive capacities and incapacities, developments and destructions. Remarkable, too, in its denial of the invented relationships between Self and Other in modernity and now postmodernity that have been necessary in making possible the standard of living achieved by the 'civilized', 'developed', 'progressive', 'historical' beings. If the Primitive has no history at all, it is only because the theoretical standard-bearers of Civilization have managed first to construct a Primitive Subject and then to obliterate *his* history.

I do not mean to deny the importance of the anthropological critique of the primitivist discourse throughout much of this century. Two related points need stressing about the counterdiscourses. First, if Kuper is correct, although primitivist ideas no longer dominate anthropological theory, they continue to stamp initiation into the discipline and to be circulated at the fringes. Indeed, they continue to structure popular ideas about the racial and distant Other, as in the Blair brothers' popular 'Adventure' public television series, or National Geographic features, or coffee table books.[19] Second, this popular discourse of the Primitive has partially been sustained by the fact that the anthropological critique of the discourse is *internal,* so much so that it reproduces (even if it transforms) key concepts: primitive society, the primitive or savage mind, totemism, and animism. Contemporary sophisticates often know all too fashionably the critical references but are largely ignorant of their content. This partial, superficial knowing promotes reproduction of the categories under critique rather than internalizing the point of the critique itself.

There is an important sense in which this latter criticism also applies to scholarly production about the Primitive that borrows from, but is strictly beyond, anthropological confines. Two examples, quite different in various ways, will illustrate the point. The first is Marianna Torgovnick's widely cited book, *Gone Primitive,* to which I have already referred in passing. The second is the controversial Museum of Modern Art exhibition on 'Primitivism', and its accompanying two-volume catalog. While Torgovnick discusses the MOMA exhibition in considerable detail, I will analyze each in turn.

Torgovnick is concerned with the way modernists and postmodernists construct notions of the Primitive and import them into contemporary culture. She studies the various ways in which the discourse of primitivism signifies, both in racialized terms and in ways that have little if anything to do with racialized conceptions. In spite of her self-conscious resolve to distance herself from the discourse, it silently takes hold of her. On one hand, Torgovnick insists that in constructing a notion of the Primitive 'we become primitive'. One would think she would accordingly take more seriously Kuper's warning that there never was anything like a 'primitive society', that there is no coherent way of specifying what it is, that the history of the discourse is 'a history of an illusion'.[20] On the other hand, Torgovnick repeatedly, if tentatively, reaffirms the existence of primitive cultures that differ from 'our' modern or postmodern ones.[21] A critique of primitivist discourse that so readily reiterates the discursive terms at issue tends to reproduce the terms it is committed to resisting.

In an interesting and revealing discussion of the Tarzan phenomenon as primitivizing texts, Torgovnick offers a good example of the penetration of social scientific categories of racial Otherness into, and their distribution by, popular culture. Edgar Rice Burroughs, Tarzan's American author, conducted nonprofessional research on plant and animal life in Africa, and he was no doubt familiar with popular anthropological knowledge in the first half of the twentieth century. So, as Torgovnick points out, the reticence and ultimate denial of miscegenation that Burroughs constructs of Tarzan's sexual relations with female apes is reflective of and reinforces prevailing dispositions in the United States toward interracial intercourse. But it is one deeply reflective, at the same time, both of the polygenic presuppositions lingering from nineteenth-century anthropology in popular literature and of eugenic dispositions socially influential in the United States well into the 1920s.[22]

Torgovnick's understated commitment to the categories of primitivist discourse is reflected in her appreciation of Burroughs having Tarzan join the Waziri of West Africa in *'their* dance and fashioning within *their* societal norms'. There is an unstated assumption throughout that the reader is one with the postmodernist 'we', that the Primitive is in no position to read such a text. The 'we' here, of which Tarzan represents a recent predecessor, is identical with the anthropological 'we'. Indeed, Tarzan may be read as the figure of an anthropologist. He enters the 'primitive' world of Africa 'to learn what hierarchies exist in the human world and by suppressing his doubts about their inevitability and basis'.[23] This is the anthropological drive, and the implication of this 'realist' ethnography— seemingly neutral in its objectivity but masking the imperialist imperative—is the affirmation of 'Western hierarchies', of superiority and subjection.[24]

Thus, *Gone Primitive* becomes an example of the production of social knowledge reproducing certain sorts of established presuppositions about relations between racialized natures. Torgovnick approves of what she takes to be the central thematic of the Tarzan series: leaving nature as it is, being true to nature, living in 'harmony with nature, without troubling relations of hierarchy and otherness'.[25] It is as though this utopian naturalism escapes racist expression, which may yet be advanced through the assumption of natural difference. It also leaves resistance to racisms unproblematically coming to terms with nature, with what Torgovnick leaves (and one is left to assume she takes) as natural difference, with the differences of racialized natures—analogized in keeping with a long history of racist expression in terms of apes! 'Going primitive' in Torgovnick's reading, then, is ultimately to 'go home' to a space of comfort and balance, to a space that is supposed to save us from 'our estrangement from ourselves and our culture'.[26] While this domesticated construal at least centralizes the inventedness of the Primitive, it uncritically recreates the notion of the West's power over its creation, its appropriation as its own, as 'home' precisely, a place of comfort, a 'return to origins'. If this is a place to which it belongs, to which it has privileged access—or which belongs to it—the Western self must surely be justified in its appropriation. What is missing from the text is an account of the expense of the appropriation, the real life and death expense, for those so constructed as primitive.

This absence turns in part, I think, on a deeper methodological shift that has taken place under the growing hegemony of postmodern knowledge production. A crude reading of the postmodern presupposition that the world is a text, the text a world invokes a new form of reductionism. It is a reductionism of methodologies in the production of human knowledges to the methods of textual analysis, of political economy to the economy of the written word, of politics and production to the politics of literary production. The sum total of political economy Torgovnick produces, in a subject begging for politico-economic integration, consists in a facile paragraph projecting third-hand facts about colonial expropriation, exploitation, and extermination, a kind of neopositivistic empiricism taken as authoritative validation.[27]

If *Gone Primitive* is a postmodern text, the exhibition and catalog of 'Primitivism' in art at the Museum of Modern Art (MOMA), New York, in 1984 are representative in their drive to impose a single interpretive narrative, a grand theory on 'primitivist' artistic production, of 'high' modernism. In representing ethnographic objects, a museum stakes a claim as the bridge between social science and public consciousness, knowledge and ideology. As consumptive demands of the public are met in galleries, the museum's mediation of social science shapes ideology, just as ideological dimensions in the practices of social science open it to the possibilities of such mediation. Ethnographic museums and exhibitions both reflect and form the ideological consciousness of popular and professional expression of Otherness. They refine the Primitive, freeze it for a public demand of an Other spatially and temporally different.

Art museums in the West since the nineteenth century have traditionally expressed only Western art or culture, or Western interests in art of the racialized Other. This latter art found its way, for the most part, into anthropological or natural history museums, or occasionally into anthropological rooms in art museums. There is a sense in which it has largely been considered not art at all. In the nineteenth century, for example, 'artifacts' produced by the Other were deemed barbarous or grotesque.[28] This points to a deeper divide between Western self-representation, the Western I/Eye, and the non-Western one, articulated in terms of the Hegelian trinity of art, religion, and philosophy as the highest forms of civilized expression. In each case, the Primitive is lacking. Lacking art, the Primitive has only craft; lacking monotheistic religion, the Primitive is pagan; and lacking self-reflective texts, the Primitive is prephilosophical, *he* can neither write nor read. Unable to read the Good Book, the Primitive must be preached to, saved by conversion, or condemned to deathly defeat or extinction.

State (self-)representation in South Africa provides the extreme case in point. The South African Museum in Cape Town, projecting the national heritage, presents the early history and social organization of black 'tribal' groups—what is taken literally to be South Africa's prehistory, undated because undatable—together with displays of indigenous animal life. The latter include stuffed animals and skeletal bones of mammals like whales and dolphins. What is furnished here is the natural: natural fauna and flora, indigenous 'peoples' in their natural habitat. Life-size models representing members of each of the claimed tribal groups are displayed in their 'natural', their racial settings. The models that populate the displays, manufactured in 1912 by taking plaster casts off actual group members and then painted the representative racial hue, presuppose that 'primitive' physical differences divide the various ethnic groups so represented. Whites, however, are notable by their explicit absence. They are the representers, the anthropologists whose displays fill the cabinets and whose explanations adorn the walls. The history of those taking themselves to be European in racial origin, by contrast, is reserved for the South African *Cultural History Museum*, a quarter mile away down Government Avenue, adjacent to the Houses of Parliament. Here we find housed the cultural property of post-seventeenth-century colonization.

The MOMA event circumvents rather than confronts these historical ironies. Torgovnick characterizes the exhibition as assuming that 'it existed in a postmodernist, and *hence* postcolonialist frame of mind'.[29] That postmodernism is thought necessarily to entail postcolonialism, as much in the minds of the event's directors as in Torgovnick's, is true only in the sense that they are historically coterminous. They are concerned with more or less the same periodization. But the necessity of the presumed relation implies much more: that as a postmodernist one is, in practice as much as in theory, anticolonial and not just a-colonial; that the postmodernist has more than neutral feelings about colonialism. In proclaiming the necessity of being against colonialism, the postmodernist can safely proceed to ignore any of its manifestations, for the manifestations of colonialism are historically speaking modernist, and postmodernists by definition have 'transcended' modernism.[30]

William Rubin, curator of the exhibition and editor of the seductive two-volume catalog, insists that Primitivism (which is supposed to be capitalized throughout the two volumes) refers only to *art* of *tribal* cultures. Primitivism is contrasted with Western (capitalized) art, and 'primitive' (noncapitalized) is taken to refer to 'peoples' and societies. Primitivism, it turns out, signifies Western interest this past century in 'tribal' arts. The fact that from its inception Primitivism carried with it an affirmative connotation is supposed to legitimate its usage. For example, we are told that Picasso referred to it as 'superb art'.

Rubin acknowledges the pejorative connotation linked to the word 'primitive'. He nevertheless assigns such negative judgments to the eighteenth- and nineteenth-century traditions expressed ultimately in terms of cultural evolution, and he insists that it has nothing to do with the art historical connotation of 'Primitivism'. Like his principal collaborator and chief theorist, Kirk Varnedoe, Rubin contrasts the notion of *the primitive* with *Primitivism*. They link the latter to a countertradition emerging out of the Enlightenment. This countertradition, which they find to be attitudinally affirmative, the collaborators trace to its philosophical expression in Rousseau's *noble savage* (which Rubin capitalizes and explicitly refuses to flag). In Rousseau's hands, 'the Primitive' (suddenly capitalized) becomes a concept of philosophical critique. It is supposed to contrast critically with the degenerate nature of existing European societies during the Enlightenment. Accordingly, Rubin takes the concept as a critical tool in the hands of a small, educated, bourgeois intellectual elite, much as one is led to believe that Rubin sees himself in relation to the vulgar of the contemporary art world.[31]

To interpret Rousseau's *noble savage* in this way is totally to flatten its complexity. The notion of *the noble savage* signifies a primitive, necessarily unattainable, pristine state of contemporary society, an idealization abstracted from a simpler social formation under construction at the time by emergent ethnographic science. *The noble savage,* then, invokes the very terms at issue: progress, development, civilization, rationality. These terms are associated in Rousseau's view, it is true, with some negative connotations. Though negative, the terms nevertheless express for Rousseau a necessary stage in human development. To affirm some of the virtues of an earlier, simpler, purer condition, as Rubin and Varnedoe do, is to reaffirm this earlier condition as a state of nature, unfree and determined, not a state of culture or politics. The state of nature, the primitive state, is one in which people lack autonomy and self-determination. The point of Rousseau's social contract, then, is to reinfuse some of these lost virtues into a free and self-determined democratic order. Rubin and Varnedoe resurrect the terminology of the Primitive, popularize it for the cultural capital of the civilized world—via the mammoth exhibition and equivalent two-volume intellectualization accompanying it, via a semipublic conference, public lectures, newspaper articles, reviews, seminars, and classroom discussions. In the context of contemporary race politics and international political economy, the effects of all this energy is to reinvigorate the terminology and assumptions of the Primitive, to reinvent in subtle ways the distinction between high and low or mass culture, expertise and popular (mis)conception, to control by expropriating the cultural expression of the racialized Other. Once again, Otherness is defined and refined, reified and dominated; once again, the absent Other is spoken to and most of all for.[32]

In ways analogous to Torgovnick's qualified appreciation of Burroughs's Tarzan, Rubin toasts 'the voyagers, colonials, and ethnologists' to whom 'we owe the arrival of [tribal] objects in the West'. No account, however, is offered by him, indeed, no acknowledgment even of the conditions under which these objects were appropriated, how they found themselves into galleries and museums, of the stripping of cultures in many cases, of the fact that they were often the spoils of wars, colonial domination, trickery, and the exercise of pure power.

For many, Rubin's two volumes have become seminal documents on primitivism, and on the Primitive. There is, as James Clifford notes, plenty of art historical value in them. Nevertheless, they are framed by the primitivizing premises of Rubin and Varnedoe. Their language reproduces even as it flags the use of racialized reference. These texts, then, are a primary filter through which the art production of the Other has been represented, as witnessed for example by the 'Primitivism and Affinities' exhibition that followed not long after in Phoenix at the Heard Museum of Native American Art. Rubin and Varnedoe fail to understand that, read in terms of its historical context, any use of the term 'primitive' in a straightforward referential sense carries value: the value of aggregation, of undifferentiatedly taking groups, cultures, and their art production as a single whole, a whole confined to a distant past that lacked progress or development, sophisticated technology, and the sort of rationality associated with it. No use of 'primitive', especially when contrasted with 'Western' or 'European' or 'modern', no matter how affirmative, can escape these sedimented significations.

Similar arguments can be fashioned around the notion of *tribe*. (The subtitle of Rubin's two volumes is *Affinity of the Tribal and the Modern*.) As Jenkins notes, tribe can operate as another distancing notion in both temporal and geographical terms. It has a double movement: It enables differentiation between a modern and a primitive condition, between 'the West and the rest'; and in this differentiation between a primitive Them and civilized Us, it establishes a unity, a likeness among all those who are otherwise (inter)tribally distinguishable.[33] There is, nevertheless, a moderating qualification in the respect of 'tribal' that is absent in the case of 'primitive'. Some, like certain American Indians, identify the importance of their own group belonging in tribal terms, fully aware of the connotative weight borne by that form of identification. That some in Africa—Nigerians, for example—strongly reject the language of tribal categorization while elsewhere—as in Botswana—it may be accepted, attests to the almost inevitable politicization of relations that racialized terms produce.

If all group naming seems so politicized, how then may we refer nonracially to those traditionally racialized in this way? An immediate suggestion is to use the self-nominated terms by which particular social groups prefer to refer to themselves. Terms like 'primitive' or 'traditional' or 'tribal' society mostly efface differences within the category as they resurrect bald differences between all members of the category and nonmembers. These notions should be referentially invoked only in critical analysis of the social and theoretical conditions that gave rise to them. However, one may query whether there is any noncontroversial way to invoke useful generalizations across conditions of similarity between any society and its members. One more or less recent mode of such reference is 'the Third World'.

The Third World

The theory of three worlds was first proposed in 1952 by a French demographer, Alfred Sauvy, writing in the newspaper *L'Observateur*. Sauvy provocatively suggested that the notion of the 'Third World' was a product of developing superpower antagonisms expressing themselves in terms of the cold war. The notion came to reflect superpower anxiety about escalating postcolonial conflict, the fear of expanding rival spheres of interest over vast territories, numbers of people, and resources. It also expressed alarm among the newly decolonized or decolonizing at revitalized control by the iron fist of superpower domination. In this sense, as Pletsch argues, the concept of a *Third World* is nothing more than the by-product of aggression between the First and Second worlds.

This threefold division has been accompanied by, indeed, it has been defined in terms of sets of accompanying characterizations.[34] For social scientists and political theorists who have been seminal in constructing the model, the First World is strictly modern, scientifically and technologically ordered, ruled by utilitarian decision procedures. Governed by the laws of economic nature, of rational self-interest, it is unconstrained and self-regulating, the embodiment of the liberal, autonomous Kantian state. Of all societies, it is (as Pletsch says) the most natural, that which all others should seek to emulate, for it is guided by the invisible hand of universal Reason. The First World is thus efficient, democratic, and free.

The Second World, the space of (once) communist domination, is conceived as modernized and technologically developed, and so partially rational. But it is stricken unnaturally by ideology and by a socialist elite who must rely upon repression to maintain its privileges. This ideological veil and repressive reliance prevents the Second World from being completely efficient, and unless it emulates the First World, it is destined sooner or later to stagnate. (The recent economic and political devolution of the Second World is being taken in many ways as triumphant vindication of the naturalism of the First, and so as confirmation of the model.)

The Third World is also defined in economic and political terms. The accompanying geographical, environmental, and psychological characterizations are more or less expressly linked to racialized premises. Pletsch suggests that, but possibly for 'left' and 'right', the three-world division is 'the most primitive' scheme of political classification in social science. The rootedness of racialized discourse in modernity and the centrality of 'black' and 'white' within this discourse suggests that these racial designations are classificatory 'primitives' as basic perhaps as 'left' and 'right'.[35] It is in virtue of this racializing of the Third World that the First and Second worlds also silently assume racial character. The Third World is located baking beneath the tropical sun in contrast to the moderate climate of the Northern Hemisphere so conducive to intellectual productivity. It is the world of tradition and irrationality, underdeveloped and overpopulated, disordered and chaotic. It is also non-European and nonwhite.

There has been considerable debate about how the world should be divided in three. Different configurations will result when one employs only economic or only political criteria, or some mix. The divisions will differ again from one interpretation of economic criteria to another, from level of production or development or technology, say, to capacity of the rich countries to exploit the poor. The climatic-geographic consideration, historically associated with race, has led a country like Greenland, for example, to be considered part of the First World, while others like Korea or Singapore or Taiwan, Kuwait or Saudi Arabia, at least until recently, to 'belong' to the Third World, and still others like some Southern European countries to hover politically, and economically, and ideologically between the two. States with populations considered racially polarized, like Israel or South Africa, are ambiguous: Under one interpretation of the criteria they turn out to 'belong' to the First World; under the other, to *be* Third. I am not interested here, at least not primarily, in pursuing the theoretical politics of representing the three worlds. Rather, my concern is to indicate how in its conception and articulation this tripartite division is racialized; how it perpetuates, conceptually and actually, racialized relations—relations of domination, subjugation, and exclusion.

From the outset, the concept of *the Third World* captured the popular, political, and scientific imaginations. Journalists took to the term like vultures to a slain carcass. It came to dominate the way social science conceived of the world, of the basic differences between states, of what Pletsch calls the division of labor within the social sciences. The three-world scheme ordered the focal object of each discipline: Mainstream economics, sociology, and political science respectively concentrated on wealth, status, and power, especially in capitalist societies. Communist studies and international relations focused on the Second World. Area studies, development economics, and anthropology analyzed the 'underdeveloped' and 'traditional societies' of the Third World.[36] The study of Western civilization, the classics, or the Great Books is regarded as foundational, as the base and structure for knowledge, value, morality, and good citizenship. By contrast, area studies, and in particular specialization in geographical and cultural fields concerning Otherness are standardly taken to have little if any intrinsic value. They are, if anything, deemed only instrumentally valuable. They are not pursued as knowledge *of* the field for its own sake, for the value inherent in it. At best, they are thought to furnish knowledge *about* the Other, the better to deal with *him*. This amounts to 'knowing *how*', not 'knowing *that*', to use a well-known epistemological distinction. The instrumental knowledge promoted concerns how to civilize, how to approach and relate to the Other.

More significantly, perhaps, the terms 'First World' and 'Second World' are rarely used. States so conceived are usually called capitalist or (formerly) communist, the West or the East, and their populations are termed European, (North) American and, generically, Westerners or East Europeans. 'The West' is similarly a sliding sign. Initially designating countries west of the iron curtain, its scope came to include those countries and their inhabitants that are capitalist in their mode of production, politically free with democratic institutions, culturally modernized, and largely white. Thus, the designation usually includes Australasia, which is almost as far east as one can go without being west, but excludes Japan (surely a First World state if there are any) and does so implicitly on racialized grounds, as in the title of a recent book by a British official with the European Community, *Japan Versus the West*. Indeed, 'the West' has included South Africa insofar as that country has been considered white or non-African. (Under *apartheid*, Japanese have been considered, for obvious reasons, 'honorary whites'.) The grandson of H. F. Verwoerd, for example, expressed a common sentiment among whites in South Africa when he once explained to me that he had 'gone over to Africa' (he meant Zambia). This is reiterated in a plaque at the Afrikaans Language Monument near Cape Town (which ironically is located on a hill across from the prison, in the valley below, from which Nelson Mandela was finally released): 'Afrikaans', the plaque reads, 'is the language that links western Europe and Africa; ... it forms a bridge between the enlightened West and magical Africa.' Implicit in these claims is a deep-seated presupposition that South Africa is a European country (in racial, cultural, political, and economic commitments), not an African one. Within a historical context of political economy, power, and dominant culture, this characterization strikes me as highly suggestive.[37]

By contrast, 'Third World' is the generic term of choice in referring not only to those states that are taken to be underdeveloped but to populations considered traditional in their productive and cultural ways. Sometimes, 'the Third World' carries no racialized connotation: Argentina, for example, is often regarded as a Third World country (though not one that immediately comes to mind when using the term generically), and its population is not usually considered to be racially Other. Yet here, too, racial characterization can take over: Argentinean players in the 1990 World Cup were repeatedly described by British football commentators, in a reinvocation of the themes of the Falkland campaign, as 'naturally violent', displaying the sort of behavior to be expected of 'the Latin temperament'. Equally, the 'exotic' players of the 'Cinderella team' from the Cameroon—some players sported dreadlocks and wore 'traditional' jewelry—were characterized as 'exciting', but 'wild' and 'undisciplined'.[38]

The racial connotations carried by the ascription, 'the Third World', are captured most clearly in their usage by those in the United States and Europe who warn that blacks, the *Gastarbeiter* immigrants, and asylum seekers are turning their respective societies economically and culturally into Third World countries. In the political and cultural theater of the United States, Kirk Varnedoe is not that far from David Duke or Patrick Buchanan, or indeed from George Bush, in claiming that 'Third World nations have intensified their concern for the integrity of their own tribal arts'. As a range of conservative political figures portray an undifferentiated blackness or Otherness for political effect and reduce it to an unspecified Third World, so Varnedoe reifies an undifferentiated Third World and reduces it to the level of the Primitive. In a recent *New York Sunday Times* article on the declining fortunes of Detroit, Ze'ev Chafets draws a similar analogy between what he describes as the tragic decline of that city under black rule and the inevitable decline of independent African nations.[39] In a similar vein, the racialized situation of guest workers in Europe, not that different from Mexican migrants in California, is increasingly obviated against the reconstructed measuring stick of a European identity. Their strictly economic status as guest workers transforms into a supranational, superracial one against the backdrop of a European identity. Europe, after all, was central to the initial manufacture of racialized identities and racist exclusions. It is an irony too great to be bypassed that the unification of a European 'we', racially exclusionary in reinvented fashion, occurs exactly half a millennium after the voyages of discovery that prompted the initial manufacture of racial Otherness. Whereas European racism might initially be described as exclusion at a distance, it is now what Balibar terms 'internal exclusion', and it takes place at the world level.[40] Migrant labor, then, is nothing else than racialized exploitation, an off-the-books form of what Worsley calls 'cost-free aid from the Third World to the First'.[41] The analogy with South Africa is accordingly worth pursuing (indeed, I will argue in the following chapter that central features of *apartheid* furnish a basic trope for racialized location in the West). Insofar as South Africa is considered a black country, it is 'naturally' designated Third World. In a recent visit to South Africa, I found whites widely bemoaning their observation that 'the new South Africa' is fast becoming 'a Third World country'. It follows that the notorious migrant labor system *apartheid* merely formalized must be a form of relatively free service to those identified as (ex-)European.

There is a point to be made here about progress and its lack as indexes of world status. Progress has been tied to obvious technological prowess and modernization. However, since its inception in the fifteenth century, the term 'progress' has assumed moral and cultural judgments of civilized superiority. This assumption has had to do, in part, with the self-identity of the West, of its self-confident superiority, its imperial successes, its dominant colonialism, and its postcolonial dominance. It has also had to do, at least in part, with the projection of European Enlightenment values as universal, as the standard against which all judgments should be measured. The beacon of progress came to conflate undeniable developments in science, technology, and the sorts of spectacles wealth could sponsor with moral, political, and aesthetic values. The former were taken to entail, to justify the latter. A critique of this self-assertive and dominant progress need not rest with demonstrating this naturalistic conflation. Progress has mixed results, to say the least, at the technological level, too. Technology may have enabled some people to live considerably better lives than their predecessors. At the same time it has created environmental and political crises, as well as the possibility and actuality of mass destruction beyond the premodern imagination. Appeals to the virtues of progress must ring very hollow to Filipino women brought to the United States with the promise of better lives, who then find themselves in Philadelphia sweatshops working weeks and months without a break; or to migrant miners in South Africa, forced off the land by cash taxes or soil erosion or the lure of gold, who find themselves huddled in grim township ghettoes or in hostels, fearing for their lives as orchestrated faction fighting terrorizes all touched by it; or to the victims of the Holocaust and Hiroshima, of precision bombing in the Gulf War, or of any number of repressive governments with the means to purchase instruments of terror and torture. The variety of racialized devaluations accompanying modernizing progress has facilitated—in some cases made conceivable—the extremity of so many of the victimizations carried out in the name of civilization and morality.

Social comparisons are obviously useful. Where some society faces a pressing social problem already faced by another under similar conditions, it will help the former to know about the difficulties faced by the latter and about the resolutions. Social comparisons are also prompted by theoretical imperatives. Generalizations serve social science as a bridge to, if not as, the construction of social laws. Laws are the mark, the embodiment of the claim to scientific status, to objectivity, predictability, and epistemological progress. In intersocial relations, generalizations are furnished via social comparisons; they are the outcome of the drive to discover similarities. The pressure to establish sameness across a domain lurks behind the disposition to *see*—to find—identities. Where the object of study has traditionally been racialized, as is the case with 'the Third World', similarities are often predisposed, virtually assumed, and conditions of identity discovered where expected.

We may accordingly inquire what terms might be substituted for 'the Third World' that would better reflect the comparisons, the identities and differences it is considered justifiably to evoke. 'Underdeveloped' at least has the theoretical virtue of calling into question the processes of expropriation, exploitation, and exclusion that inform the histories by which societies so designated have assumed that state. Nevertheless, as with its more euphemistic analog, 'developing societies', it is governed by economic and technological standards that metaphorically assume dominant political, cultural, and moral value. Like 'peripheral', 'postcolonial' usefully conjures up the history of contested relations between colonizing and colonized societies, while it recalls the historical grounds of postindependence racialized conditions in both. Relatedly, the term 'former colonies' indicates similarities in historical experience and a commonality of contemporary interests. Notably, this could include comparison with the U.S. experience, a former colony (or more accurately, set of colonies). Similarly, 'debtor nations' now includes the United States, a fact that might be useful in trying to generate a deeper appreciation of difficulties facing deeply debt-ridden and poor economies.[42] The latter may also serve to remind us that relations of production and accumulation within societies, First or Third World, as well as between them are invariably more complex than their serialized characterization suggests. To say that there are classes in Third World countries that may be characterized as First World, and Third World class fractions in First World countries is a signal of class relations and tensions within and between states that the baldness of the numerical designation elides. This is not to deny that use of the term 'the Third World' may properly signify, as Pat Lauderdale forcefully reminded me, that people channeled into relations of dependence are forced at the same time into 'third rate quality of lives'. I want only to suggest that the set of connotations more usually tied to the term's use tends to efface the critical thrust that may be intended here.

A further point should be highlighted. That we should so much as ask what substitutes are available for terms like 'the Third World' or 'the Primitive' presupposes that they identify something real, some natural condition that is virtually given and unchangeable. A primary aim of my critique is to shift the burden of proof. I have been following the standard procedure of those who would replace notions like 'the Third World' with some other designation or scheme of classification by undertaking to show why the substitute escapes the difficulties of those it seeks to replace. I am suggesting that the onus here should not so much be upon the insurrectionary terms as more firmly upon the incumbent ones. The burden should rest with those who would continue to use the model of the three world divisions, and others like or associated with it, to show why it is necessary, how it advances knowledge of the political economy of worldly divisions, relations, and conditions, how it promotes human (rather than partisan) interests, and what it does for those states relatively excluded in racialized terms.

I turn now to demonstrating that similar constraints face the concept of the *Underclass*.

The Underclass

The notion of *the Underclass* has been present in social science literature for some considerable time. Myrdal used the term in passing in *The American Dilemma* and returns to it more firmly nearly twenty years later. Myrdal's use was strictly economic, designating the persistently unemployed and underemployed, those marginalized or completely excluded from the postindustrial economy.[43] With structural transformations in the capitalist economy that began to be obviated towards the close of the 1970s, the connotation of the term in social science shifted from degrees of unemployment to deep-seated, chronic poverty. This shift signaled a series of conceptual chains forged as much by the popular media as by social scientists. The Underclass population came to be characterized in behavioral terms, as a set of pathological social attitudes, actions, and activities. The outward, visible sign of these pathologies was race. Thus, the notion was relinked to the nineteenth-century conceptions of the 'undeserving poor', the 'rabble', and the 'lumpenproletariat'.[44] Accordingly, 'the Underclass' has come to signify not just the unemployed but the permanently unemployed and unemployable. It has come to include, particularly in the popular but also in the academic and political imaginations, those poor considered unmotivated to work—especially, women on welfare, vicious street criminals, drug pushers and addicts, hustlers and urban gangs, winos and the mentally deranged homeless. If these conditions are permanent, then they are necessary, and necessarily unchangeable, and so it would seem there is no responsibility for doing anything about them save improving the criminal justice response.

The conditions of the Underclass are accordingly reduced to individual pathologies and the poverty of culture that generates the social disease of deviance. '"Underclass" describes a state of mind and a way of life. It is at least as much a cultural as an economic condition.'[45] The claim that the Underclass consists of pathological individuals is 'established' by way of comparison with the 'deserving poor', those adult, law-abiding, two-parent families that, despite steady male employment, are unable to make ends meet.[46] The supposed fact that the underclass condition is produced by the poverty of culture is 'explained' in terms of the absence of moral virtues disabling individuals from 'deferring gratification, planning ahead, and making sacrifices for future benefit'.[47] So the social conditions of the undeserving poor can be blamed upon their own character.

The interpenetrating lists of individual pathologies and cultural poverty that have been taken by social scientists and journalists alike to make up the Underclass condition carry patently racialized connotations. Though technically and historically the Underclass is purported to be 'interracially' constituted (poverty is supposed to know no color), it is obvious that blacks are for the most part being thus chronically identified. If there is a single identifying criterion of Underclass membership, it is *idleness*. And as J. M. Coetzee makes clear in relation to the history of white South African writing, idleness has long expressed a central idea of racialized representation.[48] In group terms, blacks in the United States, Britain, and now South Africa are often aggregated into Underclass characterization by the term's conceptual extension: by police, on the street, in the media, at school. And they are so referenced whether they technically meet the sliding criteria or not.

Inner city culture conjures up the very real political economy of racialized space that the concept of *the Underclass* is assumed to be theorizing. The individual pathologies and wanting culture of the Underclass are seen to be expressed against the blighted backdrop of the urban ghetto. Causal responsibility for the set of

Underclass conditions nevertheless is largely traced not to urban location—this is thought to be a mere manifestation, a symptom—but to the pathological population, to its culture. It is this causal inversion that William Julius Wilson undertakes to rectify in his important work on the Underclass.

Wilson has been careful to evade the poverty of culture thesis. He conceptualizes the Underclass as the set of individuals lacking training and skills, those experiencing long-term unemployment, and those not part of the labor force. Wilson seeks to explain the social position of the Underclass primarily in terms of the 'mismatch' hypothesis.[49] Inner city residents in the past two decades have been caught by structural changes in the U.S. economy that have left them without the technological skills necessary for the financial service jobs their spatial position would otherwise give them access to. This dislocation has two main effects: The 'concentration effect' results in a large number of single parent families, the unemployed, and criminals ghettoized into a relatively small and intense urban area with diminishing social services. The 'isolation effect' leaves these people cut off from the ameliorating influence of a middle class, black and white, who have fled for the suburbs.

Though Wilson dismisses the poverty of culture position, he has not found the case for individual pathologies quite so objectionable. Included in his underclass membership are street criminals, welfare mothers, and other social deviants. His notion of *the Underclass* is thus identified against a paradigm of a healthy body politic from which the Underclass population by definition diverges.[50] Although Wilson stresses that the Underclass includes many nonblacks, he is equally clear that his work focuses on the much larger black segment of the Underclass. These considerations prompt two implications for Wilson's analysis. The first is that he racializes the concept almost in spite of himself. The weight of Wilson's scientific stature behind the use of the concept authorizes even its more dubious, racially obvious policy and popular usages, no matter Wilson's own guarded qualifications. The second implication is at the explanatory level. Wilson predicates his structural economic analysis of the state of the Underclass on the idea of isolated, albeit spatially concentrated individuals. It is this methodological assumption that leaves Wilson holding on to the descriptive schemata of individual pathology. And it is in part this assumption that leads him to downplay the place of racism in his explanatory account of the black Underclass, as well as to de-emphasize race-specific programs as viable solutions.

Wilson finds it important, particularly in his more recent work, to recognize the effects on the black Underclass of racism, past and present. Nevertheless, his overriding emphasis throughout has been to stress the relatively greater weight of class considerations in the explanation of Underclass conditions. Class *structure* is specified in terms of individuals' 'attachment to the labor force'; in terms, that is, of *individual* job opportunities or access to job network and information systems.[51] Contrast this, for example, with Marx's notion of 'the proletariat', which is conceived as the *group* whose members own nothing but their labor power. This individualist methodological presupposition—perhaps it is even ontological—forces Wilson to underplay the influence of group effects. Similarly, Wilson thinks nonracialized programs aimed universally at alleviating poverty have far better political prospects in the racially tense political arena of the United States than race-based programs, which he takes to be racially polarizing. However, it is well-known that universally cast legislation and class- rather than race-specific antipoverty programs end up benefiting the white poor far more than the black.[52] One explanation for this is the ongoing perception among enforcers and administrators, linked to the prevailing image of the Underclass, that the former are deserving poor, the latter undeserving. Wilson has undertaken to integrate structural factors in the plight of the Underclass with individual and cultural ones. This is a commendable undertaking, but it is Wilson's peculiar mix that proves troubling. Thus, while he acknowledges racialized experiences and racism, they are almost completely untheorized in the explanatory schema and openly criticized in relation to policy considerations.

Wilson's analysis has been widely influential, even upon critics of his work. One of his deeper influences is related to this individualizing that is at the heart of his conceptual and explanatory account. In a set of interesting critical remarks on Wilson's work, Jennifer Hochschild praises Wilson's courage for insisting on the disturbing shift in the social values of the inner city, black poor. As evidence of this shift, Hochschild quotes from unpublished work of the urban sociologist Elijah Anderson. Anderson notes the 'general sense of alienation, lack of opportunity, and demoralization of certain aspects of the black community'. Nevertheless, Anderson seems to be noting something more subtly complex than Hochschild is implying, namely, that the shift in values among the urban black poor is structurally related, a frustrated response to the perception of perpetuated, racially defined limits the black poor find themselves facing. The frustration has become especially acute in light of the failed promises the civil rights era seemed to hold out.[53] Anderson's structurally defined observation is at odds with Hochschild's ambivalent individualism, an individualism that becomes highlighted in Hochschild's analysis of possible courses of action. Here, she locates responsibility for responding to the plights and problems of the racialized poor primarily with those closest to the problems: the individuals directly in touch with those whose values are seen to need transforming. These include parents, schoolteachers, social workers, police, potential employers, and local politicians. True, Hochschild proceeds from here to structural considerations and state obligations, but the latter are secondary, an afterthought, though a recognizably necessary one. Hochschild individualizes the issues by locating the nexus of both the problem of poverty and of the starting point for transforming its complex of individual and structural considerations with the poverty of culture. She works out from this localized individual space of responsibility, expanding the universe of obligation outward from the 'problematic individual' ultimately to the political.[54] This presupposes that the problems lie foremost with deviant individual expression and only vaguely with policies, prejudice, economic structure and political self-interest, the failure of moral imagination and application, and the poverty of political discourse.

Experience might have taught us that where technologies of conceptualization create distance between what is needed and those with the responsibility and means to respond to the needs, little is likely to be done. The virtue of Wilson's work is its recognition of the complex interaction all the way up and down, so to speak, between individual responsibilities (local *and* distant) and transformed structures. *The Underclass,* I want to insist, is one conceptual technology that stands in the way of fully satisfying that recognition. Naming the Underclass makes the Underclass, nominates it into existence, and constitutes its members at once as Other.

Wilson's understating of the force of race and the effects of racisms in the account of contemporary poverty in a deeply racialized social order like the United States rests upon his underestimating the perpetual disadvantages blacks continue to suffer, irrespective of their class position. Employment opportunities for whites are considerably greater than for blacks across the class spectrum. Geographically defined unemployment rates for blacks are often double that for whites. The rates of unemployment for both male and female blacks with one or more years of college are greater than those for whites who failed to complete high school. Unlike the experience of inadequately educated immigrants, many educated blacks have to settle for relatively poor jobs, while uneducated blacks have to live with no legitimate work at all. As Fainstein concludes in his subtle and convincing analysis of Wilson's 'mismatch' analysis, racism pervades the U.S. economy. It is

> built into the routine decisions of employers: the way they organize the division of labor, how they allocate men, women, blacks, and whites among jobs; what they decide to pay different kinds of workers, and the implicit criteria they utilize in hiring and promotion. Combined with virulent racism in housing markets, which keeps blacks concentrated in residential ghettoes in central cities and increasingly in suburban jurisdictions, outright discrimination along with more subtle forms of channeling in labor markets goes a long way toward explaining black economic disadvantage.[55]

Managing inflation through unemployment, for example, is a tax on the poor and, in the context of deeply racialized employment differentiation, upon blacks in particular.[56] This further disadvantages the truly disadvantaged, and it benefits those relatively well-off in ways analogous to the largely free aid Third World migrant labor finds itself 'forced' into furnishing the First World.

So, in general, the notion of *the Underclass* explicitly erases the exclusionary experiences of racisms from social science analysis while silently enthroning the demeaning impact of race-based insinuations and considerations. It distinguishes the especially impoverished from the ordinary poor while aggregating together those whose conditions of experience in various ways—in terms of race, gender, and class—may be quite different. It thus promotes a single policy solution for perhaps very different difficulties and social problems people find themselves facing.[57]

In a society whose advantages and opportunities are racially ordered, a concept like *the Underclass* will almost inevitably assume racial connotation. No matter the protestations of social scientists of Wilson's standing, race will likely be tied to pathological considerations of an *under*class. As others have noted, in analyses where there is an underclass, there too implicitly must be supposed to be an overclass. However, we find both in social science and popular accounts no mention of this.

The justification Wilson offers for using the concept turns on its identification of the structurally marginal position of some people in the labor force and the linking of this economic marginality to spatial location. He rightly criticizes Hochschild's substitute, 'the estranged poor', for failing to reflect the relationship between people's experience in the labor market and their neighborhood environment.[58] If Wilson's notion of *the Underclass* passes for the most part silently over the racial characterization of this relationship, Hochschild's term seems to erase it altogether. I would like to suggest *the racially marginalized* as an alternative. It explicitly captures the class dimension of economic marginality; it references the ghetto as the spatial location of the racially marginalized (Wilson admits that the white poor seldom live in ghetto areas); it differentiates those who are racialized but nonmarginal from those who deeply experience the material effects of exclusion, namely, the racial poor; and in foregrounding the processes of marginalization, it refuses moralistic judgments as first causes of the marginal condition. Accordingly, it directs analysis properly away from individualized character traits, or their lack, to what Hughes identifies as the 'isolated deprivation of the (impacted) ghetto'. The concept of *the racially marginalized* thus clearly captures the intersection of race and class that multiplies the depth of structural dislocation.[59] It also bridges the imaginary conceptual divide between those ghettoized in the racialized locations of urban sites, the 'urban jungles' throughout 'the West' and those marginalized in 'the Third World', between those situated as the 'Underclass' and those whose (supposed lack of) history is reduced to 'the Primitive'.[60]

There is a further dimension to the power of social science in effecting the 'objects' of its studies, one that is especially pertinent in the case of the racially marginalized. Debates in social science concerning important policy-related questions take place over a specified time span—a decade, say. During this time, the exchange becomes more precise—in the conceptual apparatus used, in hypothesis specification, testing, data accumulation, and analysis. Wilson's 'mismatch' hypothesis is a case in point. In the meantime, *en passant,* policy decisions are implemented on the basis of one or another of the contesting positions in the unresolved debate, a debate that may never see satisfactory resolution. The policies are necessarily partial (in both senses), just as the debate is incomplete. Researchers proceed to new issues, driven by perceived social needs, or their own interests, or available funding. Monies for research on the black super poor, or for that matter on black racial attitudes[61] have been notoriously difficult to come by, especially after the Moynihan and Kerner reports were issued in the late 1960s. Of course, there are real lives that are affected by the policies. So all too often the resolution of the issues under debate, insofar as there is resolution at all, is embodied in the lives of those trapped between the threads of tattered policies.

Blauner and Wellman emphasize the political and economic power major research universities represent to poor black populations whose neighborhoods are often adjacent to and controlled by the university trustees. University researchers are seen by communities to stand in positions of control, power, and exploitation, with little or no benefits accruing to the 'objects' of the research.[62] I have argued that racialized power is primarily conceived through conceptual orders like the Primitive, the Third World, and the Underclass. These are constitutive metaphors of racialized experience, the power of which consists in their ability to order and order anew racialized exclusions. In terms of social science, power is here expressed, managed, and extended in and through representing racial Others—to themselves and to the world.

As with 'black', it may be possible for those objectified by these categories to appropriate them, assuming the categories in assertive self-ascription. This appropriation is what I earlier called 'standing inside the terms', making them one's own, giving new meaning to and thereby redirecting them as forms of political engagement and critique. Of the three notions, 'the Third World' has come closest to this, perhaps because it is less deeply positioned in the history and rhetoric of racialized discourse than the other two. Nevertheless, it has to take extraordinary effort on the part of all, or nearly all, so characterized to redirect the original connotations the three terms carry. For a term like 'primitive' this would prove exceptionally difficult. Where it is still used, its referential scope proves to be partial and vague, temporally vacant and spatially diffuse. Those so referenced are rarely in a position of power, politically and technologically, to take on the category as a form of self-reference, even should they choose to. In the case of 'the Underclass', the lack of representational power seems equally obvious. Indeed, it might be added that to the extent that people so referenced assume some semblance of representational authority, they cease under the imposed criteria to be 'underclass' or 'primitive'.

As we have seen, it is not necessary that members of any group get racialized, though some groups—blacks and American Indians especially—are more likely than others to be. Nor once racialized does it necessarily follow that all members will be treated in racial terms or that any one member be so treated all or even much of the time. Once a group is racialized, and especially where the racial creation of the group runs deep into the history of its formation, however, the more likely will it be that the group and its members are made to carry its racialized nature with them.

Thus, not only is it the case, as Bauman observes, that the great effort exerted by the social sciences in studying race and racism has done little to alter the self-conception of the social sciences;[63] it is perhaps more emphatically the case that the social sciences have done much to create, authorize, legitimate, and extend both the figures of racial Otherness and the exclusions of the various racisms. The ways in which the production of social knowledge in the name of science continues more or less silently, more or less explicitly, to do so will be obviated by analyzing two contemporary texts produced in and representative of differing though not unrelated racialized contexts. The first reads race strictly as Africa; the second undertakes to normalize racial comprehension in/of South Africa by reinventing it in terms of 'Western' social science.

A Dying Racism?

Terence Ranger has long been concerned with representing Africa to and in the West. Where earlier social scientists engaged in what Mudimbe properly calls inventing Africa,[64] Ranger is committed to reinventing it. In the text I want to focus on here, his definitive statement on 'race relations', Ranger re-presents the civilizing mission of liberal good works in terms of charity beginning not at but from the home. Like earlier social science about the Other, then, it could be said that Ranger pursues Torgovnick's primitivizing search for (a) home in modernity's space-time of 'transcendental homelessness'. And as before, the invention of this idealized home can only be sustained by the destructive denial of the Other's actual home.

The auspicious occasion of Ranger's remarks is his inaugural lecture in 1987 as (Cecil John) Rhodes Professor of Race Relations at Oxford University. Ranger might thus be permitted some largesse, but the form the lecture assumes is the metaphor of a reimagined imperialism. In the address, 'Rhodes, Oxford, and the Study of Race Relations', Ranger engages in a range of metaphorical transmutations: metaphorical in the literary construction of his lecture; metaphorical in standing for the epistemological reproduction of the rule over Africa (which by implication cannot epistemologically rule itself, for it requires Oxford once again to know it, to be represented to itself); and metaphorical again for the place of racialized representation in Britain, in the terms of Ranger's, of Rhodes's Oxford.

Ranger's lecture transposes the Rhodes Chair of Race Relations into a Central African Kingdom; the Oxford pro-vice-chancellor, the highest-ranking university representative present, into a tribal elder; Ranger himself into an ascending king, a ruler over the domain of African Studies, not just at Oxford but universally; thus, Race Relations (itself a severe circumscription of a domain and a reification of its terms of representation as givens) into a certain sort of African Studies; race into what *others* are; and finally, Cecil John Rhodes, of all people, into a 'tutelary deity', a 'patron divinity' of Africa, of Race Relations as African Studies.[65]

The rhetorical medium of Ranger's transmutations is the description of the figure of Rhodes as deity of African Studies. Ranger admits the Janus-faced nature of the figure: At once appealing and fraternal, paternalistic and condescending to local Africans, Rhodes approached African leaders as equals and as servants. Expressing a desire to live as peaceful neighbor or landlord, Rhodes was consumed with the drive for and expression of personal, political, and economic power. This figure of contradictory power Ranger contrasts with an antidotive figure, a 'companion deity' with whom Ranger more easily identifies, a figure representing 'abnegation and powerlessness'. This is the figure of Arthur Shearly Cripps—British, white, a missionary (though 'radical'), and above all 'a quintessential Oxford man'. Yet, concludes Ranger with just a hint of melancholy, Cripps's humanism—his 'pastoralism and medievalism', traveling on foot in his missionary Africa 'like *his* African *flock'*—is inadequate to salvage Africa for Oxford; it is unable 'to conceptualize Africa'.[66]

The moral of Ranger's narrative for Oxford—the University, that is—is neither to save nor ruthlessly to modernize (Rhodes's) Africa. 'Oxford must settle for a relationship of equality (if it is not in itself absurd to speak of equality between a university and a continent).'[67] It is self-evidently absurd to speak in this way. But Ranger, recall, is speaking not anymore of a university but of the Oxfordian Kingdom, not of Africa but of African Studies, not of Africans but of Race Relations, over all of which he is assuming titular control. In moving to the concluding moments of his inauguration, to the assumption of his throne, Ranger reveals the state-to-be of the study of race relations at Oxford: an African Studies Centre not in the mold of any white divinity of the past—a Rhodes or Cripps or Smuts—but with the view to the need for understanding Africa 'as much as Africa needs to understand us'.[68]

It is unclear in whose name the 'us' is being spoken here—Oxford, Britain, Europe, or the West. Postmodern irony and self-consciousness are not beyond the assertion of postcolonial power. What is clear is that Ranger refers by 'race' only to Africans, to the traditional Other; and clearer yet what his intentions are in representing Africa: to bring Africans to Oxford so as to be able 'to render [them] accurately—to speak of, sometimes even *for* Africans in Oxford'.[69] The power of representation remains fit for the king. In his construction of race and ethnicity in the name of Rhodes, not a word about race in contemporary Britain, about the 'empire striking back' or the 'lack of black in the Union Jack'; no mention of the vast study of race relations and the critical debate about racial construction and exclusion. Not a word, that is, about the state of British race analysis impossible to ignore beyond the shadows of Oxford's ivied bastions. No reference to race in the city of Oxford, of the testy relation between racialized town dwellers and the wearers of the university gown. Nothing about the fact that there are more African students attending Oxford than there are black British students, nor about the almost total lack of black faculty representation.

Ranger is at one with Oxford's past, the appropriate wearer of Rhodes's crown: Race is Africa! The World Bank would do no better than to respond to Ranger's explicit appeal, to buy its knowledge of Africa—of an undifferentiated Africa if the language of this document is anything to go by, and despite all its qualifications—to fund his Centre. Ranger's Kingdom is a market, a place to trade, to bring Africans once more to sell—this time their intellectual energy and their knowledge[70] (though sometimes, too, the Other must understand, knowledge will have to be given them, they will have to be re-presented). Once more, African labor, this time intellectual, becomes foreign aid for the glorification of the great white man's rule.

Thus, where the likes of Leonard Doob's social scientific exercise was to prepare liberating Africa for self-chosen Western economic and cultural penetration, Ranger's racialized recreation serves to ready the African as an epistemological object for postcolonial consumption while rendering race locally invisible within the West. The text of a South African report on 'intergroup relations', by extension, serves in its own way to normalize these (de)racialized relations of *apartheid*.

In the first half of the 1980s, a large study on 'intergroup relations' was undertaken in South Africa under the auspices of the Human Sciences Research Council (HSRC), the body governing the production of social knowledge in that country. The HSRC report, published in the United States in 1985 with the assistance of and a foreword by Leonard Doob, was concerned with reinventing *apartheid*. It undertook, in other words, not to transform *apartheid* out of existence, beyond all manner of racialized exclusion, but rather to normalize its forms of racialized expression in the sense of bringing them in line with those more or less acceptably practiced in the West. It was thus involved in rendering South Africa respectable, recreating it for Western consumption. This may seem less surprising in light not only of pragmatic imperatives like ending economic sanctions, but also in terms of the discursive relations between *apartheid* and dominant racialized formations in the West. In general terms, we may here emulate Said's provocative suggestion that Zionism is an ideological extension of nineteenth-century European colonialism.[71] Assuming all the appropriate qualifications, *apartheid* may be interpreted as the extremely local, but logical, extension of European colonialism in the South African context. It is subject to these parameters that the HSRC report on intergroup relations is to be read.

As the governing body of the production of formalized social knowledge in South Africa, the HSRC receives virtually all its funding from the state. It was, at the time of the report, ruled by a council of ten whites appointed by the minister of national (that is, white) education. Since its establishment in 1969, however, it has claimed autonomy from state control concerning its research interests and scope:

> In the Republic ... social science research is not a dogma superimposed from above as an instrument of national policy; and the aim of the HSRC is to encourage and stimulate research in the social sciences by free and independent scholars whose labours ... will lead to a fuller satisfaction of the needs and aspirations of the various peoples in our country.[72]

Indeed, in the study of the status and prospects of 'intergroup relations' in South Africa, the HSRC professed, and appeared, to challenge established state policy. Nevertheless, this report, *Investigation into Intergroup Relations,* reveals the deeper functional-ideological order the practice of HSRC social science serves to perpetuate.

In 1980, 'intergroup relations' was identified by the HSRC as the most important issue of national concern requiring objective scientific investigation. As means to generating 'constructive intergroup relations' the report recommends *inter alia* the abolition of all racial restrictions on *economic* access, racial deregulation of *economic* land use, respect for and protection of 'human dignity, life, liberty and property of all'.[73] If these suggestions were intended as policy recommendations, the break with tradition seems dramatic, if not stunning. In the past, HSRC investigations had prompted shifts by the state both in policy and in the terms of rationalization. Here, by contrast, noted liberal opponents of *apartheid* participated in the research program. These considerations rekindled a glimmer of hope that political moderation in South Africa would prevail. However, far from breaking radically with its past or politico-economic base, the HSRC has become more sophisticated in its mode of representation.

The lines of organizational structure and authority underpinning the *Investigation* are hierarchical. A Main Committee controlled all final decisions concerning investigative policy and management. This committee consisted of twenty representatives of conservative Afrikaans universities and institutions, six from more liberal English-language universities, two black representatives both with conservative community affiliations, and one representative of business. Demarcation of the areas of investigation was determined on the basis of the recommendations of a subcommittee consisting of eight senior Afrikaner academics, only one of whom was affiliated with an English-language university. Work committees were appointed for each of the ten research areas demarcated, and they developed reports on the basis of commissioned individual research projects. In all, 116 commissioned Project Reports were produced by 208 scholars. Of these reports, 69 were written in Afrikaans, the rest in English. Though there were a number of reports about the conditions of existence for blacks, only one was written exclusively by a black researcher (another was cowritten in Afrikaans by a black person with Afrikaners). One report, by a South African Indian, was about Indians in South Africa, and one report by a Chinese person about Chinese. The definitive final report, surveying the various findings of the work committees and of the individual works they commissioned, was compiled by a subgroup of the Main Committee with no black contributors. In short, as in South African society at large at the time, all meaningful forms of black self-representation are stripped away: The black majority is never properly represented, never allowed to speak for itself, but is always authoritatively spoken for and to. Far from being considered autonomous agents, black South Africans are treated as little more than problematic objects of research.[74] By contrast, the Report proved so controversial among whites simply because a blue ribbon, state-sanctioned inquiry acknowledged openly and emphatically that *'apartheid* is dead' and that resolution of 'the black problem' is necessary for sustained prosperity and security.

This underlying political economy of the final report is reflected in and reproduced by its content as well as by the way the content is structured. Individual work projects were published by the HSRC in South Africa, where their style and content restricted their circulation to an academic audience. The final report summarized the conclusions of the individual projects and the findings of the work committees without revealing their sources or processes of data accumulation. This final report is aimed at a wider public readership, both nationally and internationally. Thus, while the report explicitly seeks to project an image, politically and intellectually, of democratic pluralism, the individual reports are mediated by the authority of the Main Committee. Conclusions, especially those of the more critical studies, are torn from their argumentative contexts, re-presented, altered. For example, the work committee report, 'Juridical Aspects: *Law and justice and intergroup relations'*, critically analyzes the form and effect of law in South Africa, concluding that racial and ethnic population categories cannot be defined and sustained by and in the law.[75] The basic premise of the final report, however, is to provide ways of accommodating conflict and managing inter*group*—that is, racial—relations. So, even in its discussion of the subreport on law, the final report assumes the very categories that the Working Committee on Law rejected.[76] The effect is nothing short of sophisticated censorship.

Accommodation and management of 'good intergroup relations' in South Africa presuppose those group categories definitive of formal *apartheid* that remain informally constitutive of social relations in South Africa today. Group identity and group perceptions in terms of ethnicity and race are presumed by the report to be essential principles of social organization.[77] That they structure social existence and relations in South Africa is considered an undeniable fact of historical and social observation. Once presumed, this 'fact' serves to reify existing social relations; it acts as a boundary condition of criticism and reform. The effect is to *naturalize* domination, power, and control—and their causes—in South Africa, to render them direct implications of natural events, relations, and forces. 'South African society', it is claimed, 'is characterized by people who have become isolated from one another.... [This isolation] is determined to a large extent by the particularly segmented or divided composition of the country's population.'[78] No analysis is offered of the prevailing relations of power, of domination and exploitation, and by extension no critical account of the set of discourses and ideology in the name of which 'the separation of peoples' was historically effected. Oppression is reduced to 'long-term conflict', which in turn is *explained* (away) as the result of the raw fact of 'ethnic differences' accompanied by 'conflicting economic interests'. Of course, 'where ethnic and class differences coincide', in South Africa as elsewhere, conflict may *naturally* be expected: 'Conflict is inherent in any industrialized society. South Africa cannot escape centuries of racial polarization ... without periods of disruptive conflict.'[79]

These attempts to naturalize established social relations and events in South Africa are underscored by selective comparison with other societies, most notably other African countries and the United States. Thus, economically South Africa's blacks are compared favorably to the rest of Africa; while socially, riots in the black townships are explained (away) as expected responses to modernizing reforms and liberalizing white attitudes in just the way that riots are supposed to have been instigated in U.S. cities in the 1960s.[80] This cross-comparison normalizes current events by stressing the mainstream nature of the contemporary South African experience. However, in so far as there are proper analogues of comparison at all, they seem reversed here: Perhaps a more fruitful economic comparison could be made with the United States, while social comparisons with revolutionary colonial forms seem to offer wider explanatory scope. We may often learn as much from the disanalogies of comparison as from similarities. In this light, the presumption that objective economic comparison for South African blacks is with other blacks in Africa rather than with all South Africans, white or black, smacks of racism: The observation that blacks throughout Africa are generally poor is meant to imply that the poverty of South African blacks is their natural condition. This racism is mirrored in local comparisons of coloureds and whites in the legal system. It has been *found* by '[h]ighly innovative research' that 'coloureds' are 'less able to structure their [court] evidence according to coherent narratives than whites' and thus are 'potentially unreliable' witnesses.[81]

Now the question of comparative study raises the more general issue of the insistent self-legitimation of the report as science. The investigation is conceived as a *scientific* undertaking to produce *objective*—that is, politically independent—accounts of the South African experience. However, the epistemological authorization in terms of 'general agreement ... among scientists' lends official stamp not to objective knowledge but to the Report's general mandate to generate '[c]o-operation between groups to form constructive relations'.[82] This instrumental and ideologically bound conception of social science is reflected most dramatically in the report's use of statistics, and in its treatment of ethnicity.

On the face of it, numbers appear neutral, and so they may be easily manipulated. Stephen Jay Gould reminds us that 'numbers suggest, constrain and refute; they do not ... specify the content of scientific theories'.[83] The report omits or transforms embarrassing or inconvenient statistics. For example, in discussing demography the illegal populations of shantytowns are dismissed (and continue by the State to be discounted, as occupying 'informal housing' and engaging in an 'informal economy'), while the residents of 'homelands' are counted among the population of South Africa only for favorable purposes.

This raises the issue of official group designation under *apartheid.* Color symbolism aside, 'whites' and 'blacks' are generally used beyond South Africa as definite descriptions. Formal use in South Africa would have it otherwise. There, 'whites' has tended to be used as a mass noun, resembling 'human hair' more than, say, 'water'.[84] When contrasted externally with blacks as a group, 'whites' include all group members, ignoring ethnic, linguistic, or ancestral distinctions. In this, it resembles distinctions between human hair and dog or coconut hair. Distinctions between Afrikaner, English, Portuguese, and so forth as subgroups are drawn largely informally among whites, and only when they have little bearing on more fundamental political relations (the analogy here is with brunettes, blonds, and so forth). Legally ordained identification in terms of the Population Registration Act never differentiated among white ethnic groupings. In its external formal relations, accordingly, 'whites' has designated similitude.

'Blacks', by contrast, has largely been taken as a sign of difference. The differences ascribed are triply overdetermined. First, unlike 'whites', 'blacks' in the past formally designated, and continues informally to designate, in its external relations a group essentially different from whites. This much is understood as self-evident. Second, it is a 'fractured concept', and third, a 'numerative plural'.[85] It is fractured in that 'blacks' is divided by whites pragmatically into 'coloureds', 'Asians', and 'Africans'. The attempt has been to establish 'browns' and 'yellows', by preferential political, economic, and social treatment, as a buffer for whites 'against African aggression'. 'Blacks' is a numerative plural in that Africans, by far the largest constituent of the black majority, is deemed to divide naturally into nine ethnic—'tribal'—groups. So 'whites' is a mass category that is considered more or less united, while 'black' insinuates division. Use of the fundamental terms of racialized categorization seem to serve different ends. On one hand, they are used to divide the majority African group into manageable components; on the other, they combine members of the minority white group into an effective political unit. Clearly, the ends that actually continue to be served by the categories, whether formal or informal, are in a deeper sense identical: to divide and rule. One finds this reflected in the concern, introduced in the report and still effective, that rapid black population growth would place an undue burden on state provision for African education: The state is thus excused from providing equal if not improved educational resources for blacks.[86] Once more, discursive objects are blamed.

Concerning ethnicity, general scientific agreement is claimed for the garbled assumption that it includes '[a] common race-semantic norm image'. 'Race', in turn, is interpreted as marking 'external physical characteristics and therefore

Racial Knowledge

differences in biological history'. Accordingly, all talk of 'ethnicity' in the report reflects a 'genetic and physical sense'. Moreover, African ethnicity is largely reduced to 'tribal solidarity', which is seen to generate 'open clashes'.[87] So the report accepts the spurious race conceptions of folkways, state ideology, and *Volkekunde* (national folk anthropology) as established in the presumed objectivity of scientific literature.

State social science in South Africa bears both instrumental-functional and formative-ideological dimensions. Clearly, the HSRC report accepts the terms and premises—it is an instance—of *apartheid* social science. The instrumental functions of the *Investigation* are self-evident (e.g., the overriding concern to suggest ways of controlling conflict), as perhaps also is its role in ideological reproduction. Ideologically, a further role emerges. While the report rejected the terms of *apartheid* in the *narrow* sense of post-1948 legislation that explicitly invokes discriminatory categories, it presaged a novel language in virtue of which the state began increasingly to rationalize its power and domination over existing relations among the body politic. In this sense, the report prefaced seemingly deep transformations in the language of rationalization, legitimation, and representation in South Africa. It pointed political and popular thinking in a new direction, an apparently nonracialized and superficially antiracist one that seems, at first tentatively and now more firmly, to have taken hold of the terms of social relations and representation. Nevertheless, while formalized racisms may have in many respects been set aside, the terms and implications of the 'new South Africa', of the 'post*apartheid*' social order, remain deeply coded in racial terms.

Since the publication of the report in 1985, the terms of state representation have stressed the 'complex, deeply segmented ... and plural' nature of South African society; that the consequent 'structural conflict' needs to be 'regulated' if it is 'not to increase in extent and intensity'; and that 'constructive relations, regardless of the differences' need to be promoted. In the broad, this remains the rhetoric of rationalization. The 'homelands' are deemed 'national states', which 'are given real opportunities to develop political and administrative structures'. (This seems paradoxical, for if they are independent nation-states why do they have to be *'given* real opportunities'?) Like other developing countries, they receive 'developmental assistance' from the benevolent South African state. (The South African state, it should be pointed out, now refers to the homelands as 'the self-governing areas'.) The government is 'open to dialogue ... [with] everyone who reject[s] violence as a means for change'. South Africa seeks to forge 'a participating democracy' in which the 'legal system' is to 'provide assurances on protection and safety' of all citizens and groups. Ironically, '[s]uch a participating democracy ... cannot yet be realized in South Africa, since the majority have not yet had the opportunity to realize their political aspirations'. The assumption here is that a participatory democracy can only be satisfied in South Africa in terms of inter*group*—that is, interracial—relations.[88] While the stress on racial groups is now being underplayed, the informal expectation of a group-defined resolution remains strong. The weight of this expectation is carried by the presumption that people will naturally identify themselves and be identified for the most part with what they 'really'—that is, racially—are.

The report's influence is evidenced by the State's reaction to it. In the copublished response, the government acknowledges 'a special calling and responsibility to promote sound intergroup relations and ... peaceful coexistence'. The 'complexity of conditions in South Africa' consists in its 'ethnic group basis'. Conflict resolution is taken to require that 'rights and interests can best be protected and promoted on an equal basis within a group context. Recognition of such groups also contributes to the full development of groups *in accordance with their own needs, aspirations and potential.*' Constitutionally, the 'government is committed to democracy', which requires 'dialogue and negotiation with those concerned'.[89] We seem to be witnessing at present the application, the living out of the report's central resolutions, though perhaps a living out that has assumed a logic of its own.

The report dismissed—it openly renounced—the discourse of explicit discrimination, that is, the language of formal *apartheid* in the narrow sense. For the terms of this discourse it substituted—indeed, colonized—the more benign if not problematic language that appears consistent with the Western tradition of plural democracy. This newly annexed discourse—of constructive ethnic relations and conflict resolution—remains embedded, nevertheless, in a background conception of the general relations of *apartheid* that leaves, and will foreseeably continue to leave the structure of power in South Africa, if not the dynamics, effectively in place. So the politically contestational character of racialized categories persist under informal *apartheid.*

It is not only that social policy in South Africa restricts the practice of social science; in both its functional and ideological capacities, state social science informs and defines the limits of social policy. Functionally, the HSRC report services state ideology; but the *Investigation* was conducted also in virtue of state ideology, just as the report redefines it. The instrumental concern to restrict conflict and efficiently manage intergroup relations in part reflects and in part renews the ideological concern to legitimate existing relations of exploitation. The 'disciplinary powers' of social science in South Africa (re)articulate the terms of social cohesion and dominance among the body politic, as they (re)produce the forms of coercive and coerced social relations.

It would be too easy to dismiss as pseudoscientific the notion of State Social Science outlined here. Obviously objections can be raised, as they have been, to biases in underlying assumptions and against the skewed and sometimes inconsistent content to which they give rise. Ultimately, these objections rest upon criticism of the exclusionary interests which the science serves, and the objections take moral and political form. It should be recognized, however, that State Social Science in South Africa employs the methods of traditional neopositivist science, on one hand, and *Geisteswissenschaften,* on the other. It produces knowledges the *use* of which constitutes individuals as social subjects—at once of and to the law. Moreover, much of social science practice in South Africa is reducible by mandate to or consistent with *apartheid* social science. The accompanying *appeal* to scientific authorization underwrites state policy and rationalizes claims to reform in labor and influx control, in economic deregulation, in the constitution, in education, and in daily life. Exercise of the raw power of repressive state apparatuses is difficult enough on its own to face down; the 'normalization' of disciplinary coercion and control sanctioned by this State Social Science prompts a social collaboration of faceless and silent subjection that only a radical epistemological and axiological transmutation may be able to dislodge.[90]

So racial knowledge is not just information about the racial Other, but its very creation, its fabrication. Racial knowledge has been a foundational structure of the social sciences and humanities, even as it has been denied. It has fenced off in scientific and popular imaginations researchers from research objects; writers from those written about; liberal representatives of civilized modernity's most advanced forms of scientific spirit from less-civilized primitives; epistemological kings of Western civilization from racialized subjects; mature Westerners from infantilized *non*-Westerners; citizens marked by civility and decorum from the criminal and the vulgar; and urban sophisticates from dwellers of the jungle and the urban jungle. It is in the contemporary sense that *apartheid* represents a dying past, a past the West has passed beyond, that I now want finally to invert by analyzing the more or less universal constructions of racialized urban spaces. The ultimate and effective material manifestations of racial knowledge, then, are expressed in the related forms of representational and spatial ghettoization. It is to a demonstration of this that I now turn.

8

'Polluting the Body Politic':
Race and Urban Location

'If I were to wake up one morning and find myself a black man, the only major difference would be geographical.'[1]

The category of space is discursively produced and ordered. Just as spatial distinctions like 'West' and 'East' are racialized in their conception and application, so racial categories have been variously spatialized more or less since their inception into continental divides, national localities, and geographic regions. Racisms become institutionally normalized in and through spatial configuration, just as social space is made to seem natural, a given, by being conceived and defined in racial terms. Thus, at the limit, *apartheid* space—so ab-normal and seemingly unnatural—will be shown to be the logical implication of racialized space throughout the legacy, colonial and postcolonial, of the West's hidden hand (of Reason). The material power of the categorical exclusions implied and produced by racializing discourse and social knowledge will accordingly be exemplified.

Power in the polis, and this is especially true of racialized power, reflects and refines the spatial relations of its inhabitants. Urban power, in turn, is a microcosm of the strengths and weaknesses of state. After all, social relations are not expressed in a spatial vacuum. Differences within urban structure—whether economic, political, cultural, or geographic—are in many ways magnified by and multiply the social hierarchies of power in and between cities, between town and country. These sociospatial dialectics underline the fact that social space is neither affect nor simply given: The rationalities of social space—its modes of definition, maintenance, distribution, experience, reproduction, and transformation—are at once fundamental influences upon the social relations of power.

Conquering space is implicated in and implies ruling people. The conquest of racialized space was often promoted and rationalized in terms of (where it did not itself prompt) spatial vacancy: the land's emptiness or emptying of human inhabitance. The drive to racialize populations rendered transparent the people so racialized; it left them unseen, merely part of the natural environment, to be cleared from the landscape—urban or rural—like debris. The natural and built environments, then, as well as their modes of representation are made in and reify the image and architecture of what Foucault aptly calls 'pyramidal power'.[2]

Citizens and strangers are controlled through the spatial confines of divided place. These geometries—the spatial categories through and in which the lived world is largely mapped, experienced, and disciplined—impose a set of interiorities and exteriorities. For modernity, inside has tended to connote subjectivity, the realm of deep feelings, of Truth; outside suggests physicality, human difference, strangeness. The dichotomy between inside and outside also marks, as it is established by marking territory; and in settling territorial divides, connotations may transform, splinter, reverse. Boundaries around inner space may establish hegemony over that space, while they loosen in some ways but impose in others a disciplinary hegemony over the map outside the inner bounds. As the boundaries between inside and outside shift, so do their implicit values. Inside may have concrete certainty, outside the vast indecisiveness of the void, of nothingness, of nonbeing. Outside, by contrast, may avoid the phobic confinement of inner space.[3]

This dichotomy between inner and outer intersects with and is both magnified and transmuted by another one central to the condition of modernity: the dichotomy between public and private. The truncated spaces of a privatized moral sphere may prove to be a refuge from the imposed obligations of the public ethic; the obligatory policies citizenship may impose often cover (up) the exclusionary practices extended in the name of a private sphere. Public diversity may give way to private univocality; inner multiplicity may reduce to a segregated singularity and divide off from differentiated outer homogeneity. Inner and outer may thus face multiplied connotative inversions. Private inner subjective space may serve as sanctuary from exposure to public inner city space; the public inner city may accordingly 'necessitate' avoidance by flight to outer suburban space, where the public realm is largely reduced to instrumentalities. Here, public outer space circumstantially assumes the privatized virtue of relative autonomy from bureaucratic imposition. The private order and harmony of subjective inner or suburban space commands (legally authorized and enforced) protection at its limits from the incursive dangers of inner urban violence spilling over from center to periphery. The means invoked to effect this include rendering the center peripheral. Thus, peripheral space may at once prove liberating and alienating, free and enclosed, open but empty.

One's place in the world is not merely a matter of locational coordinates, nor just a demographic statistic, nor simply a piece of property. It may be also taken, in Krieger's suggestion, as a trope for fashioning identity.[4] Where the colonial was 'confronted' by vast hinterlands to be opened up—in the Americas, Southern Africa, Australasia—the rivers of red, brown, and black blood required by settlement were representationally wiped away by two bleaching agents. In the first instance, they were cleansed by myths of 'virgin land' and 'just wars'. In the second, those identifying themselves as Europeans turned in whitewashing their histories to the civilizing mission of 'saving the impure' and extending God's order over heathen lands. Whether the bodies of the racialized Other were to be killed or colonized, slaughtered or saved, expunged or exploited, they had to be prevented at all costs from polluting the body politic or sullying civil(ized) society.

Impurity, dirt, disease, and pollution, it may be recalled from chapter 3, are expressed by way of transgressing classificatory categories, as also are danger and the breakdown of order. Threatening to transgress or pollute established social orders necessitates their reinvention, first by conceptualizing order anew and then by reproducing spatial confinement and separation in the renewed terms. The main modes of social exclusion and segregation throughout maturing capitalism and modernity have been effected in terms of racialized discourse, with its classificatory systems, its order and values, and its ways of 'seeing' particular bodies in their natural and social relations.

I will assess the institutional implications of racialized discourse and racist expression for the spatial location and consequent marginalization of groups of people constituted as races. The materiality of racialized relations—of relations between knowledge and power, rationality and exclusions, identity, opportunity, and availability—are most clearly in evidence here. In the spatial delimitations of these relations it is human bodies, racialized human beings, that are defined and confined, delineated yet (dis)located. This will provoke some remarks also about the spatial affects of racial (dis)location on the preservation of and transformations in racialized discourse.

The Terms of Spatial Marginalization

Colonizing City Space: Producing Urban Peripheries

It seems uncontroversial to claim that the roots of the racialized postmodern city can be traced to the end of the colonial era. Not until this juncture did the metropolises of the West have to confront directly the 'problem of the racially marginalized', of (re)producing racial marginalization in its own spaces.[5] Throughout the colonial era, racial Others were defined in terms both of a different biology and a different history, indeed, where those 'othered' were considered to have a history at all. Colonial administration required the bureaucratic rationalization of city space. This entailed that as urbanization of the colonized accelerated, so the more urgently were those thus racialized forced to occupy a space apart from their European(ized) masters. The doctrine of segregation was elaborated largely with the twentieth-century urbanization of racial Others.[6] By contrast, European cities remained until fairly well into this century, from the viewpoint of residence and control, almost as 'white' as they had been in the Renaissance. By the close of World War II and the sunset of direct colonialism, this had largely changed: (Im)migration of colonial and country people of color to the metropoles of Europe and the Americas was well under way or had already run its course.[7]

In the 1950s and 1960s slum administration replaced colonial administration. Exclusion and exclusivity were internalized within the structures of city planning throughout the expanding (cos)metropolises of the emergent 'West'. Fearing contamination from inner city racially defined slums, the white middle class scuttled to the suburbs. The 'tower of Babel' was quickly superseded by the 'tower of the housing project high rise' as the appropriate *image* of racialized urban space. Local differences notwithstanding, the racial poor were simultaneously rendered peripheral in terms of urban location and marginalized in terms of power.

This notion of *periphractic* space is relational: It does not require the absolute displacement of persons to or outside city limits, to the literal margins of urban space. It merely entails their circumscription in terms of location and their limitation in terms of access—to power, to (the realization of) rights, and to goods and services. The processes of spatial circumscription may be intentional or structural: They may be imposed by planners upon urban design at a specific time and place, or they may be insinuated into the forms of spatial production and inherent in the terms of social rationalization. Further, the circumscribing fences may be physical or imagined. In short, periphractic space implies dislocation, displacement, and division. It has become the primary mode by which the space of racial marginality has been articulated and reproduced.

In the 1960s and 1970s a convoluted but ultimately consistent inversion of urban space developed along racially defined class lines. The white middle-class suburban flight left the racially divided inner-city residential neighborhoods to poorer whites and to the racially marginalized. The segregated suburbs were graded in terms of their distance from industry and urban slums and their proximity to the conditions for leisure and consumption: seaside, lake, mountain, countryside, and shopping mall.[8] The openness of the extended urban outside pressed in upon confined racial ghettoes. Outer was projected as the locus of desire, the terminus of (upward) mobility; inner was painted as bleak, degenerate space, as the anarchic margin to be avoided.

The inevitable gaps in urban order nevertheless provide the soil for cultural proliferation, while suburban uniformity stifles it. Lured by the image of music, drugs, and sex, suburban teenagers became avid consumers of city culture. By the late 1970s young professionals entering the job market no longer wanted to live an hour from the workplace in the central business district, or from the sites of fashionable recreation in the inner city. Personal preference schemes are hardly maximized by time-consuming, crowded commutes. What followed was a reversal of the pattern of white flight: The postmodern inner city may be defined in terms of urban renewal and *gentrification*—and so also in terms of their absence and denial. The anarchic margin of the inner city was revitalized, a part here and a piece there, into an urban center. The racially marginalized have spent much time and effort trying to improve the built environment they found themselves forced to accept. They are now increasingly displaced, their housing 'rehabilitated'—often with public collusion, if only in the form of tax breaks—and rented or sold at considerable profit.[9] Outside colonizes inside; unable to afford spiraling rents, the inner are turned out, homeless, onto the street. Any urban location represents a potential site for the realization of commercial profit and rent. And profit maximization tends to be blind both to history and to social responsibility. As the social margins are (re)colonized or cut loose, the peripheral is symbolically wiped away. With no place to gather and dislocated from any sense of community, it becomes that much more difficult for dispossessed individuals to offer resistance both to their material displacement and to the rationalizing characterizations that accompany the dislocation.

Racial marginality may assume various forms. Economic instantiations are invariably definitive. The racially marginalized are cast most usually in economic terms: lack of employment opportunities and income, wealth and consumerability, housing and mortgage access.[10] These are factors also defining class position. This highlights an important aspect of racial marginality. It is only necessary to the process of marginalization that some (large) fraction of the racially constituted group be so marginalized, not that all members be dislocated (though for reasons concerning personal and cultural identity, the alienation affect for the group at large tends to be almost universal). So, for example, professional blacks may be accepted as neighbors or colleagues by whites, or as more or less full members of the body politic, while the larger fraction of blacks remains displaced to the periphery. This clearly raises questions about class location. While my focus here is to identify those determinations of periphractic marginalization that are specific to *racialized* discourse and racist expression, this will necessitate some identification of the intersection of race with class, and the attendant multiplication(s) in social cause, effect, and affect.

Roughly coincidental with changing forms of racial marginalization this century are shifts in the raison d'etre of urban planning. Until World War II, urban planning objectives were swept under the banner of the 'city beautiful'. In the early postwar years (until 1960), this concern with environmental aesthetics gave way to demands of social efficiency. This was refined in the 1960s into a 'rational systems model' that set out to define rules of rational decision making for effective urban development and resource allocation. By the 1980s efficiency considerations in the state planning apparatus had largely succumbed to economic interests. This runs so deep now that it largely determines what is or is not *technically* feasible: Decisions are defined without public debate by the expertise of professional bureaucrats in terms for the most part of returns on capital investment. Even state penetration of urban development has been reduced to privatized corporate commodification: Public space has come effectively to be controlled by private sector land and property development interests. As Dear comments, 'planning serves to legitimize the actions of capital'.[11]

Planning ideology did not develop in this way either solely in response to or as a directive for the concerns of racial marginalization. Obviously other determinants and an internal logic of its own are formative. Nevertheless, it seems clear that concerns of race have played some considerable part in the unfolding of planning rationale. Kushner, for example, describes how local planning authorities required suburban housing plots to range between half an acre and three acres, thus encouraging development of larger and more expensive housing beyond the means of the racialized poor. At the same time, where apartment buildings were permitted in these suburban towns at all, they were restricted to small one- or two-bedroom units so as to discourage families, and expensive design features required by the building code effectively excluded the racialized poor.[12]

The Significance of the Slum

Consider in this light the contemporary history of the concept of *slum clearance*. The racial dimensions of the idea were set at the turn of the century by colonial officials fearful of infectious disease and epidemic plague. Unsanitary living conditions among the black urban poor in many of Africa's port cities were exacerbated by profiteering slumlords. Concern heightened among the European colonists that the arrival of the plague, which devastated the indigenous population, would contaminate them. As fast as the plague spread among the urban poor, this 'sanitation syndrome' caught hold of the colonial imagination as a general social metaphor for the pollution by blacks of urban space. Uncivilized Africans, it was claimed, suffered urbanization as a pathology of disorder and degeneration of their traditional tribal life. To prevent their pollution contaminating European city dwellers and services, the idea of sanitation and public health was invoked first as the legal path to remove blacks to separate locations at the city limits and then as the principle for sustaining permanent segregation.

When plague first arrived at Dakar in 1914, for example, the French administration established a separate African quarter. This was formalized by colonial urban planning as a permanent feature of the idea of the segregated city in the 1930s. The urban planner Toussaint formulates the principle at issue: '[B]etween European Dakar and native Dakar we will establish an immense curtain composed of a great park.'[13] Leopoldville (now Kinshasa) was strictly divided into European and Congolese sectors by a *'cordon sanitaire'* of empty land. The aim was to restrict contamination of the former areas by African disease. Epidemic plague in the early part of the century caused the division of urban blacks from poor whites in Salisbury (now Harare) and their removal to a separate location. This developed into the government policy of residential segregation in

Rhodesia (now Zimbabwe). Soon after discovering outbreaks of the plague in both Johannesburg and Cape Town, African slums were razed and their inhabitants expelled to peripheral locations on sewage farms. These locations, materially and symbolically nauseating, later grew into permanent segregated townships at the city limits.

Fanon identifies the general mechanism centrally at work in each of these cases: 'The European city is not the prolongation of the native city. The colonizers have not settled in the midst of the natives. They have surrounded the native city; they have laid siege to it.' In the postwar years, active state intervention in urban development of Euro-American and colonial cities was encouraged, by means of apparatuses like nuisance law and zoning policy, to guarantee the most efficient ordering and use of resources. Thus, the principle of racialized urban segregation insinuated itself into the definition of postcolonial city space throughout 'the West', just as it continued to inform postindependence urban planning in Africa.[14]

Accordingly, administration of racialized urban space throughout those societies identifying themselves as 'the West' began to reflect the divided cityscapes produced by colonial urban planning. The massive urban renewal and public housing programs in the United States in the late 1950s and 1960s started out explicitly as the exclusive concern for slum clearance. This concern is reflected in the titles of the bureaucracies directing the programs: In terms of the heralded Housing Act of 1949, urban renewal was to be administered by the Division of Slums and Urban Redevelopment; the country's largest urban program in New York City was originally headed by the Slum Clearance Commission and in Chicago by the Land Clearance Commission. The experience of the Philadelphia Housing Authority is typical. The federal Public Housing Authority rejected slum locations in the 1950s as the sites for (re)new(ed) public housing projects. However, they did little to generate available alternatives. Strong resistance to encroachment by white neighborhoods, a strict government unit-cost formula, shrinking federal slum clearance subsidies, and high land costs (caused in part by competition from private developers)[15] left the Housing Authority with one realistic option: to develop multistory elevator towers on slum sites. The effects were twofold: on one hand, reproduction of inner city racial slums on a smaller but concentrated scale, but now visible to all; on the other, massive removal of the cities' racial poor with no plan to rehouse them. Inner city ghettoes were centralized and highly rationalized; the larger proportion of the racialized poor had to settle for slum conditions marginalized at the city limits. The first effect turned out to be nothing short of 'warehousing' the racially marginalized; the second, no less than 'Negro removal'.[16]

This notion of 'slumliness' stamped the terms in and through which the urban space of the racially marginalized was (and in many ways still is) conceived and literally experienced by the Other's racial and class other, by those more or less white and to some degree middle class. The slum is by definition filthy, foul smelling, wretched, rancorous, uncultivated, and lacking care. The *racial* slum is doubly determined, for the metaphorical stigma of a black blotch on the cityscape bears the added connotations of moral degeneracy, natural inferiority, and repulsiveness. It serves as an example of the spatial contradictions identified by Foucault's notion of *heterotopia*. The slum locates the lower class, the racial slum the *under*class.[17]

Apartheid's Urban Areas

In terms of structural formation, then, the planning prototype of project housing and slum reproduction for the racially marginalized throughout those societies ideologically identified as 'the West', I want to suggest, is idealized in the Group Areas Act of the *apartheid* polis. This hypothesis will be considered by many to be purposely provocative and obviously overgeneralized; by others it may be thought trivially true. The standard assumption is that the racial experience of South Africa is unusual. My point here is to invert this presumption, to show just how deep a certain kind of experience of racial marginality runs in 'the West'. Nevertheless, to avoid misconception, I should specify what I do *not* mean by this suggestion.

First, I am emphatically not claiming that urban planners and government administrators outside of South Africa have necessarily had *apartheid*like intentions. Indeed, though there may have been exceptions at the extreme, motives seem to have been mixed, and expressed primary intentions in the public domain appear mostly to have been to integrate neighborhoods along class lines. Second, the planning *effects* under consideration in 'the West' have not been formalized or instituted with anything closely resembling the precision of the South African state; urban movement, racial displacement, and segregated space outside of South Africa have more often been situated as the outcomes of privatized preferences and positioned as responses to the 'informalities' of market forces.[18] Third, I do not mean to suggest that project housing (or ghettoization, for that matter) ever was or now is considered a single residential solution to 'the Negro problem' or to 'the problem of the underclass'. Fourth, and most emphatically, my aim is not to exonerate *apartheid* morally by *normalizing* it, that is, by rendering it in terms analogous to common (and so seemingly acceptable) practice in Europe and North America. Rather, I am concerned in invoking the comparison to condemn segregation wherever it manifests by calling attention to the practice of reinventing ghettoes (whether formally or informally) and its peripheral dislocation—and thus reproduction—of the racially marginalized. The implication I intend here is that repeal of the Group Areas Act in 1990 and other cornerstones of formal *apartheid* will leave urban space in South Africa emulating the sort of racialized location 'West-wide' for which, I am claiming, *apartheid* has offered a model. Finally, I am not claiming that all elements of the *apartheid* idea of Group Areas are manifest in the practices outlined above, only that they embed key elements of the *apartheid* structure.

Pragmatics of Segregated Space

The key structural features of the Group Areas Act of 1950 that I wish to emphasize here include:

a. A residential race zone or area for each racial group;

b. Strong physical boundaries or imagined barriers to serve as buffers between racial residential zones. These barriers may be natural, like a river or valley, or human constructions, like a park, railway line, or highway;

c. Each racial group should have direct access to work areas (industrial sites or central business district), where racial interaction is necessary, or to common amenities (like government bureaucracies, airports, sport stadiums) without having to enter the residential zone of another racial group. Where economies in furnishing such common access necessitate traversing the racial space of others, it should be by 'neutral' and buffered means like railways or highways;

d. Industry should be dispersed in ribbon formation around the city's periphery, rather than amassed in great blocks, to give maximal direct access at minimal transportation costs;

e. The central business district is to remain under white control.

'Racial groups' in (a) are most widely interpreted as being constituted by 'whites' and 'blacks'. But, as we have seen, the informal extension of 'black' differs widely. For example, in Britain it has included Asians, while in the United States it excludes Hispanics. This simply underlines what I have been insisting upon, namely, that race is fabricated. In keeping with my usage above, I will qualify 'racial group' in this context in terms of class position. A racial group will acquire specificity as a class or class fraction that has come to be conceived in racialized terms; a class or class fraction, by extension, is partially set by way of its racialized delimitation. So those subjected to project housing and ghettoization are defined here as the 'racially marginalized'.

Examples of physical boundaries or imagined buffers, (b), abound. Harlem is divided from southwest Manhattan by Central Park and Morningside Park, as well as by double-lane, two-way-traffic cross-streets (110th and 125th streets; most east-west streets in Manhattan are one-way). The South Bronx is divided from

Manhattan by a river and from the rest of 'respectably' residential Bronx by a steep hill. Black public housing in the racially split and discriminatory city of Yonkers is all to the west of the Saw Mill River Parkway, the railway line, and a large reservoir park; white middle-class housing is all to the east. Examples of this sort in other cities or countries can easily be multiplied. South Africa, again, provides the limit cases. In the black townships dormitory hostels that house migrant workers, usually consisting of one ethnic identification, are divided by wide streets from 'more respectable' township housing often occupied by those whose ethnic identification is different. And the white residents of one wealthy Johannesburg suburb have literally walled themselves in; all access to the suburb is strictly controlled and patrolled.

The strong buffer zones of *apartheid* urban order ideally make spatial allowance for each racial residential zone to expand. In the urban metropolises where the residential race 'problem' emerged and where space is at a (costly) premium, this ideal has not been an option. It is replaced, in the scheme of things,[19] by a testy area of racially overlapping, common class residential integration (as, say, in South Philadelphia). Examples of neutralized transversal routes across the residential space of the racial Other, item (c), include the West Side Highway and the East River Drive along the sides of Manhattan, the I-95 and Schuykill expressways in Philadelphia, Chicago's Lake Shore Drive, and the system of transversal routes cutting across Los Angeles County (the San Diego Freeway, I-10, the Long Beach, Santa Ana, and Pasadena freeways).[20] Johannesburg provides an interesting inversion of this latter principle: Three highway ring roads circumscribe the city as a form of laager defense against 'alien' invasion. The motto here, formerly 'lest native restlessness spill over', has been silently recast in post*apartheid* terms as 'lest the underclass externalize its frustrations'. This racialized containment maximizes as it imparts new significance to the (socioracial) control over what Foucault identifies as the 'three great variables of urban design and spatial organization': communication, speed, and territory.[21]

With the informalizing of racialized exclusions, organization and control of racial space in post*apartheid* South Africa is becoming increasingly complex. Central Johannesburg, to take just one example, has quickly transformed into a city inhabited by black South Africans, into what many descriptively or disparagingly refer to as 'a black city'. The instigation of this process predates repeal of the Group Areas Act. It was prompted by slumlords in the inner city seeking the highest rent the market would bear, in conjunction with the demand of blacks who wished to escape the bleak and blighted townships located a costly and dangerous commuter ride from work. As formalized *apartheid* ended, whites likewise inverted the *apartheid* process, much as they had done two decades earlier in Detroit, by fleeing first for the suburbs and then for Cape Town, where for historical reasons the presence of black people seems dramatically diminished. One might refer to this as 'normalizing racism' in the face of 'ending *apartheid*'. Racialized exclusion is being deepened by the informalities of private preference schemes. It is, as elsewhere, being rendered the (in)advertent outcome of private choice and informal market mechanisms. The state simply facilitates this privatizing process. For example, the pending Residential Environmental Bill seeks to maintain 'norms and standards in residential environments' and to curb community disputes, disturbances, and physical or offensive nuisances. Power is ceded to residents, local authorities, and to a board with wide-ranging powers to be appointed by a cabinet minister. Effective control thus remains in the hands of whites. The aim of the law is to furnish the state, its agents, and those it represents with the power, first, to contain the dramatic spread of informal, shantytown residential space by black urbanizing poor and second, to maintain and manage the boundaries of rigidly racialized neighborhood space within urban settings. Thus, the law enables owners of an apartment building to establish a bylaw restricting residence in the entire building to families with no more than two children or no less than an established income level, as long as two-thirds of residents agree. Blacks in South Africa tend to have significantly larger families and lower incomes than whites.[22]

In seeking to privatize the choice of and control over defining racialized urban space, South Africa seems to be invoking a long-standing principle of racially exclusionary relations. When formally sanctioned exclusions are no longer politically possible, private preferences to exclude may be sustained under more generally acceptable principles like freedom of expression, or association, or uncoerced property contracts dictated by free market forces. For example, when racial zoning was rendered unconstitutional in the United States, some property owners and real estate developers entered privately into what became known as 'racial covenants'. The agreements restricted sale or leasing to blacks of property in specified areas for stated periods of time. They were used not only to prevent blacks from moving into a neighborhood but spatially to ring black ghetto areas so as to prevent their street-by-street expansion. While judicial enforcement of the covenants was declared unconstitutional by the Supreme Court in 1948, it was not until 1972 that the recording of racially restrictive covenants was rendered illicit. Thus, prior to 1972 such agreements had to undergo the effort and expense of a legal challenge in order to render them unenforceable. Their widespread influence on racialized urban spatial arrangements was as effective at the time as the juridical limitation of racism to intentional discrimination is proving for exclusionary employment practices now.[23]

The illustrations of (b) and (c) are not meant to imply that city parks, highways, or reservoirs in the United States developed for the purpose of dividing urban space along racial lines or to deny that (racialized) communities have their own internal logics of formation. The historical determinations of urban structure are multiple and complex. But once in place, these urban facilities were explicitly used or, at the very least, facilitated physically reifying the symbolic divides of racialized city space.

In terms of (d), the placement of industry and employment, the suburbanization of capital in the 1970s further 'whitened' the work force as travel costs and time proved prohibitive for inner city blacks. The reversal generated by gentrification, as I noted earlier, has doubly displaced blacks, whether formally or informally. The drive to settle the central business district residentially, (e), is class-determined. Displaced from inner city living space, the racially marginalized are removed once more from easy urban access to a workplace. It is, as Duncan and Mindlin bear witness, costly to be poor and more costly in almost every way for black poor than for white poor.[24]

The living space of poverty is best described in terms of confinement: cramped bedrooms sleeping several people, sleeping space serving as daytime living rooms, kitchens doubling as bathrooms, oftentimes as bedrooms. The segregated space of formalized racism is overdetermined. Not only is private space restricted (if not completely unveiled) by the constraints of poverty, so too is public institutional space, and purposely so: cramped corners of upper galleries in movie theaters and court houses, the back seats of buses or minibus taxis, overcrowded classrooms, emergency rooms, and prison facilities. The restriction of formalized racism has done little to alter most of these conditions for the racially marginalized. Indeed, the privatization of racism, the continuance of informal racist expression, may have done much to extend confined conditions in the inner cities. Moreover, shopping malls and large discount supermarkets are invariably placed at locations convenient to white middle-class residential space or in the relatively 'safe' central business district. Thus, the racially marginalized may be drawn at some inconvenience and increased expense to seek out such shopping sites. Whites, of course, are almost never drawn to shop in racial ghettoes, in what are invariably perceived as 'slums'. In this, inner city racial space bears uncomfortable affinities with urban space in *apartheid* and post*apartheid* South Africa.[25] It is difficult to imagine how this racialization of space would differ in the 'new South Africa'. Consider only the fact that all concern to date has focused on how upwardly mobile blacks might penetrate what effectively remains white residential space. Nobody has raised the question, perhaps for obvious reasons, of a reverse or counterflow.

In every case the construct of separate (racial) group areas, in design or effect, has served to constrain, restrict, monitor, and regulate urban space and its experience. The spatial economy thus constituted along racial lines determines a discipline, 'a type of power [or] technology, that traverses every kind of apparatus or institution, linking them, prolonging them, and making them converge and function in a new way'.[26] *Apartheid* circumscribes township 'locations' with barbed wire fences and entry checkpoints. Racialized urban sites throughout Europe and the United States are distanced, physically or symbolically, in the master plan of city space.

Projects and Periphractic Space

Social Pathologies and City Projects

The sort of similitude I have identified here between the southern tip of Africa and the northwestern hemisphere reveals issues that otherwise remain obscure. Spatial control is not simply a reaction to natural divisions and social pathologies in the urban population but is constitutive of them. So certain types of activity are criminalized—hence conceived as pathological or deviant—due to their geographic concentration in the city. Because of statistical variations in location, 'other kinds of crime are either not important, not widespread, or not harmful, and thus not really crimes at all'.[27] This localization of crime serves a double end: It magnifies the image of racialized criminality, and it confines the overwhelming proportion of crimes involving the racially marginalized to racially marginal space.[28] Spatial constraints, after all, are limitations on the people inhabiting that space. These delimitations extend discipline over inhabitants and visitors by monitoring them without having to bother about the intraspatial disciplinary relations *between* them. Nevertheless, as the example of Johannesburg ring roads suggests, this mode of controlling racialized urban locations presupposes a repressive source of disciplinary self-control and self-surveillance set in order by those in power. In watching over others not only are these Others forced to watch themselves, but the Masters (and Madams) limit and locate their own set of liberties. In the emerging spatial economy of post*apartheid* South Africa, for example, the depth of paranoia among upper-middle-class whites is reflected in the high prisonlike walls swallowing up the houses they seek to hide, in the perspicuous burglar bars, very public displays of sophisticated alarm systems, and vicious guard dogs trained to react only to the passing presence of blacks. The prevalence of theft as a coping mechanism for extreme racialized poverty and as a sign of the breakdown of (whites' obsession with) 'law and order' is coded in white public consciousness—in the endless cocktail hour reports of such 'incidents'—as something 'they' (blacks) do. South Central Los Angeles, it seems, is but a metaphorical stone's throw away from suburban South Africa.

The racialized image of urban squalor is taken to pollute the picture we are supposed to have of the body politic by reflecting itself in terms of other social pathologies like crime, drug abuse, prostitution, and now AIDS. The poverty of the inner city infrastructure provides a racial sign of complex social disorders, of their manifestation when in fact it is their cause. The idea of *project housing* has accordingly come to stand throughout 'the West' as the central mark of racially constituted urban pathology. Tower projects assumed high visibility as the housing solution to a set of bureaucratic problems: lack of vacant sites at the urban periphery, unaffordable center city plot costs, and overwhelming low income demand for decent housing.[29] These economic considerations were complemented by strong social reaction on the part of neighborhoods even to low density public housing infiltration. The high rise project resolved bureaucratic concerns that assumed both economic and social form by building low cost, high density buildings in slum areas where resources and morale have traditionally tended to limit resident reaction.

It is with the *idea* of high rise project housing, however, that I am primarily concerned. The racially marginalized are isolated within center city space, enclosed within single entrance/exit elevator buildings, and carefully divided from respectably residential urban areas by highway, park, playing field, vacant lot, or railway line: Hulme in Manchester, the Bijlmermeer project outside Amsterdam, Federal Street in Chicago, Jacob Riis in New York, the Baltimore project at the margins of the very popular Harbor Place development,[30] Southwark Plaza in Philadelphia, and the various projects for 'Coloureds' scattered around Cape Town—Manenberg, Hanover Park, and Ocean View, which barely lives up to its name. In the extremity of their conditions, the inwardness of their spatial design, their relative spatial dislocation, and their alienating effects, the Cape Town projects provide something of a prototype. They also serve as a perpetual reminder of the racialized grounds of projects' formations. The projects present a generic image without identity: the place of crime; of social disorder, dirt and disease; of teenage pregnancy, prostitution, pimps, and drug dependency; the workless and shiftless, disciplined internally if at all only by social welfare workers. The marginal are centralized in this faceless space, peripheral at the social center.

The *project* is conceptually precise: a plan to place (a representative population) so that it protrudes or sticks out. The economies of condensed Bauhaus brick or concrete are visible from all sides. Project housing, then, is in more than its economic sense public: 'We' always know where the project is, if only to avoid it; and while familiar with the facade, 'we' can extend our ignorance of the personal identities of its inhabitants. Its external visibility serves at once as a form of panoptical discipline, vigilant boundary constraints upon its effects that might spill over to threaten the social fabric.

The thrust of this argument applies equally to the construction of Chinatown as an idea and a location in 'occidental' urban space. Kay Anderson has shown that the formation of Chinatown as an identifiable and contained place in Vancouver—and the same must go for San Francisco, Los Angeles, New York, Philadelphia, London, or the Latin Quarter in Paris—is likewise a function of that set of historical categories constituting the idea of the project: idealized racial typifications tied to notions of slumliness, physical and ideological pollution of the body politic, sanitation and health syndromes, lawlessness, addiction, and prostitution.[31] Chinatown is at once of the city but distanced from it, geographically central but spatially marginal.

The idea of project housing is in principle periphractic for it contrasts sharply with the prevailing norm and surrounding practice of housing throughout the extension of 'the West'. This norm and the practices it generates are best characterized as possessive individualist home ownership. This sensibility is well-expressed by Frank Capra's characters in *It's a Wonderful Life:*

> George Bailey (to his father): Oh well, you know what I've always talked about—build things ... design new buildings—plan modern cities...

> Pop: You know, George, I feel that in a small way we are doing something important. Satisfying a fundamental urge. *It's deep in the race for a man to want his roof and walls and fireplace.*[32]

Home is a place of peace, of shelter from terror, doubt, and division, a geography of relative self-determination and sanctity. Lacking control over housing and common conditions, lacking the recognizable conditions of homeliness, tenant commitment to the neglected and confined rental space of the project is understandably negligible. By contrast, enjoying relative autonomy over private property and the benefits of tax incentives, homeowner resentment to the permanence of project housing is fierce. A preferred bureaucratic solution repeats another structural feature of *apartheid:* Recourse to perpetual removal and turnover of the project population prevents incubation of solidarity and a culture of resistance.

At the extreme, whole groups or neighborhoods may be moved or removed, as in the destruction in South Africa of Sophiatown (a Johannesburg shantytown and vibrant cultural enclave in the 1940s and early 1950s), Cato Manor (the Indian equivalent in Durban), and District Six (a thriving Cape Town inner city 'Coloured' and Muslim neighborhood), or ultimately in the gentrification of a project. Sophiatown, Cato Manor, and District Six were destroyed by the state because they stood as living expressions of cultural resistance. On a more practical level, all three were densely populated and organically formed. Thus, management of everyday life was far more difficult to order than it is when subjected to the grid geometry of the townships to which their inhabitants were relocated.[33] Similarly, and in keeping with the logic of privatized exclusion, there has been real estate talk in Philadelphia of turning Southwark Plaza housing project into a home for the aged to sustain spiraling property values due to gentrification in the adjacent Queen's Village or to temper falling values in an economic downturn.

It should come as little surprise that urban housing administration in 'the West', and the idea of the housing project in particular, reproduces central structural features of the expression of Group Areas. I have been arguing that despite local variations and specificities, a common (transspatial) history of racist expression proscribes the range of acceptable city planning for the racially marginalized and circumscribes the effects of such plans. Against the background of the discursive link of *apartheid* to the history of Euroracism, the Group Areas Act is not only not foreign to the Eurocentric *Weltanschauung* but, with the optimal set of social conditions for a racialized social formation, to be expected as the norm. And South Africa has furnished nothing if not the ideal(ized) conditions for the reproduction of racism.

Degeneration and Gentrification

I noted earlier that this extended analogy between the informal affects of implicitly racialized urban housing policy throughout 'the West' and the Group Areas Act is implied in a set of terms common to historical and present-day racist expression: pollution, sanitation, purity and cleanliness, degeneration and gentrification. It is not that these terms bear the same connotation whenever and wherever they have occurred. It is precisely because of their conceptual generality, malleability, and parasitism that they have managed both to reflect prevailing social discourse at a specific time and place and to stamp that discourse with their significance.

Degeneration appears to be the binding principle here, at work even if only implicitly. In the nineteenth century, the concept was central to fundamental discourses of collective identity and identification. It found expression in biology, including evolutionary theory, in sociology, criminology, economic and psychiatric theory, in discourses defining sex, nation, and race. Herbert Spencer most clearly expressed the key idea: In sex and society, biology and race, in economic and national terms, physical, mental, and social defects 'arrest the increase of the best, ... deteriorate their constitutions, and ... pull them down towards the level of the worst'. The racial assumptions presupposed decay, the extent of which was defined by racial type. Races accordingly have their proper or natural places, geographically and biologically. Displaced from their proper or normal class, national, or ethnic positions in the social and ultimately urban setting, a 'Native' or 'Negro' would generate pathologies—slums, criminality, poverty, alcoholism, prostitution, disease, insanity—that if allowed to transgress the social norms would pollute the (white) body politic and at the extreme bring about racial extinction. Degeneracy, then, is the mark of a pathological Other, an Other both marked by and standing as the central sign of disorder. Stratified by race and class, the modern city becomes the testing ground of survival, of racialized power and control: The paranoia of losing power assumes the image of becoming Other, to be avoided like the plague.[34]

These assumptions are apparent in the popular rhetoric surrounding public housing in the middle and late twentieth century. Thus, Mayor Lamberton of Philadelphia in 1940 noted: 'Slum areas exist because some people are so utterly shiftless, that any place they live becomes a slum.' The beneficiaries of public housing, he concluded, should only be those capable of 'regeneration'. A *New York Times* article in 1958 about the 'public housing *jungle*' characterizes tenants of a New York City project in the language of the Primitive, 'deprived of the normal quota of human talent needed for self-discipline and self-improvement ...

a living catastrophe ... [breeding] social ills and requiring endless outside assistance'. The comparison between the 'respectability, diligence and moral superiority of [white] homeowners' and the 'disreputableness, slothfulness, and property-endangering' tenants of [black] projects is often repeated: from Philadelphia public hearings on project housing in 1956 to the American *apartheid* of Yonkers, circa 1988, and the contemporary media characterization of 'the Underclass'.[35]

If degeneration is the *dark,* regressive side of progress, then 'regeneration' is the reformation—the spiritual and physical renewal—but only of those by nature fit for it. And *gentrification* is the form of regeneration which most readily defines the postmodern city. Gentrification is a structural phenomenon tied to changing forms of capital accumulation and the means of maximizing ground rent. It involves tax-assisted displacement of longtime inner city resident poor (usually the racially marginalized), renovation of the vacated residential space, upscaling the neighborhood, and resettling the area with inhabitants of higher socioeconomic status. The structural changes occur not only on the ground, so to speak, but in terms of capital formation (capital is shifted from less profitable yet possibly productive sectors into real estate) as well as in terms of labor formation and relations in the city (shifts from productive to service workers and from blue collar to white collar positions).[36]

Obviously, the implications of gentrification may vary from one inner city sector to another. If project residents are naturally slothful and dangerous, if these are their natural states, then the imperatives of gentrification demand not merely project containment but its total transformation, together with the ultimate displacement of the residents. This is the extreme form of the Group Areas Act. Sophiatown was redeveloped into a suburb occupied largely by white members of the South African police force and triumphantly renamed 'Triomf'. Cato Manor was until recently largely laid bare. Parts of District Six, like other areas reclassified as white residential space, have been gentrified by white real estate developers who have remodeled the dilapidated, multiresident houses into single-family Chelsea-style cottages. Similarly, single room occupancies in Philadelphia's Center City were redeveloped under a tax abatement scheme into 'elegant' townhouses, just as they were converted in Manhattan into 'desirable' studio apartments. With the repeal of the Group Areas Act in South Africa, gentrification will likely be available to a proportion of the black population no larger than it has been in the urban centers of the United States. By contrast, the exoticism of Chinatown's marginality may be packaged as a tourist attraction and potential urban tax base. Thus, urban revenue requirements—fiscal costs and benefits—combine with lingering racist language to determine the fates of urban dwellers: Expenditures and the discourse of pollution and decay demand displacement and exclusion in the first instance; revenue enhancement, the discourse of exoticism, and exclusivity prompt urban renewal and 'beautification' in the second.

The Power of Place

We now live the postmodern condition mostly in polarized cities, atomized ethnic neighborhoods and racial locations divided 'naturally' from each other. The sprawling pockets of racialized poverty are contained, but for the growing holes of homelessness that spill forth a future we would rather not face. It is in virtue of the kind of notions I have outlined here and the superficially neutral surface expressions to which they give rise—most recently, 'the underclass'—that members of 'pure' groups are distinguished from the 'impure', the 'diseased' and 'different' are differentiated from the 'clean' or 'clean cut' and 'acceptable', the 'normal' set apart from the 'abnormal', the included divided from the excluded. Covert rearticulations of these concepts continue to provide criteria and rationalizations for differential inclusion in the body politic—for the right to (express) power, for urban location and displacement in the process of gentrification—and in the differentiation of urban services. In this resurrection of segregated city space, in these 'imagined geographies',[37] the expressive content of racialized discourse and racist terms are invented anew.

This extended spatial affinity between 'the West' and the *apartheid* polis is also reflected in the similitude of racialized iconographies of resistance and reaction in the United States and South Africa, in the particularities of South Central Los Angeles and Soweto. Far from 'senseless', the horrifying phenomenon of 'necklacing' in the political lexicon of South African township symbolism assumed significance, if not justification, by emulating the act of placing the mayoral chain around the neck of governmental collaborators. Setting alight the rubber tire was akin, then, to melting the chain of collaboration, to wiping away the symbol of white authority, as it at once reduced to human ashes the body in whom collaborationist authority was vested. In Los Angeles, the torching of buildings and businesses, not quite randomly, also seemed to reflect a rage against a class-defined collaboration in perpetuating the subjugation of the racially marginalized. In the delirium of the momentary, the innocence of homeliness was reduced in a flash of fire to the common denominator of homelessness as the contrast between home ownership and project dwelling was instantaneously laid bare. Liquor stores were trashed not simply in a drug-crazed drive to feed a habit but as in South African township uprisings nearly a decade earlier, because they so clearly represent the spirit of surplus value soaked in degradation, the pursuit of profit with no regard for the consumptive effects upon people. And finally, that vicious beating of a defenseless white truck driver by young black men overlooked from afar by inactive officers of the peace, was frozen in the media representation as a photographic negative of Rodney King's brutal beating at the hands of white policemen. Both images boasted the power to transgress, to be outside the law. The latter image was boosted beyond belief by the policemen's acquittal; the former was mediated, in contrast, by the distance of helicopter reporters, whose journalistic objectivity prevented any intervention in the deadly event, just as this and a second attack on a truck driver at the same intersection were mitigated only by the largely unreported fact that both truck drivers had escaped death by being escorted through the mob by young black men and women at considerable risk to their own safety. Unbridled anarchy is the ultimate price of acquittal in the court of injustice. The formal lawlessness, the ungovernability of and loss of control over *apartheid*'s racially marginalized townships reveal the inherently political dimensions to racial configuration. In this sense, race is more than simply the site of stratification, for the latter merely presupposes the establishment of levels of socioeconomic being. The politics of racial identity and identification constitute rather the sphere(s) of subjection and subjugation, the spaces in and through which are created differences, gradations, and degradations. By extension, they become the spaces from which resistance and transformation are to be launched.

Coincidentally, this account highlights one reason, often overlooked, why public policy in nation-states taking themselves to be of 'the West' has been so readily complicit with the reproduction and renewal of *apartheid*. Distance is not, at least not primarily, to be interpreted spatially or geographically but in terms of difference—and so in terms of the reinvented articulation of racist concepts. 'Generative metaphors' of sameness and otherness rule spatial relations. Consider the spatial image of civic duty inherited from modernist morals:

> I am [a] pebble, the world is the pond I have been dropped into. I am at the center of a system of concentric circles that become fainter as they spread. The first circle immediately around me is strong, and each successive circle is weaker. My duties are exactly like the concentric circles around the pebble: strongest at the center and rapidly diminishing toward the periphery. My primary duties are to those immediately around me, my secondary duties are to those next nearest, my tertiary duties to those next, and so on. Plainly, any duties to those on the far periphery are going to diminish to nothing, and given the limited resources available to any ordinary person, her positive duties will barely reach beyond a second or third circle. This geographically based ranking of the priority of duties seems so obviously correct to many people that it is difficult for them to take criticisms of it seriously.[38]

Center and periphery need not be literally located: White South Africa may be part of the (implicit) interpretation of center, the racially marginalized United States part of the periphery; Japanese once at the outer limit now seem to be more centrally—if ambivalently and ambiguously—placed. Distance and diminishing duties are inversely proportional to a common history and culture, as well as to the interests they define. Universal norms are circumstantially qualified and so delimited in terms of the racialized metaphors that are insinuated into the historical formation and reproduction of spatial differences. In racializing part of the population, the autonomy of the group thus 'othered' is mediated, if not completely denied. Recasting the terms of the moral in the postmodern fashion of community, tradition, and localized particular may serve here solely to magnify the racially exclusionary effects.

The racialized postmodern city differs from its modernist counterpart in that we have embraced its atomized spaces,[39] that we have become habituated to the recurrent removals, displacements, boundaried racial and ethnic territories, and that we have become chained to and by home ownership and its vacating implication of homelessness. It is not just that the limits of our language limit our thoughts; the world we find ourselves in is one we have helped to create, and this places constraints upon how we think the world anew. That we continue to imagine and reproduce the racially marginalized in terms of shiftlessness, laziness, irrationality, incapacity, and dependence preclude important policy options from consideration, literally from being thought. Homesteading has been successfully practiced on a small scale in various urban communities (for example, in Northwood, Baltimore), though its successes have largely been limited to the middle class and there has been no attempt to generalize the undertaking. Modest plans in Palm Beach County, Florida, to desegregate school districts by attracting black families to acquire local housing are being criticized by some realtors for encouraging racial steering, the illegal practice of directing racially identified home seekers to particular neighborhoods. Though such modestly imaginative attempts to overcome the effects of historically discriminatory housing and schooling practices are already constrained by the presumption of 'integrating minorities into a dominant status quo', they are nevertheless being cynically forestalled in the name of principles or laws designed to delimit discrimination.

Here, as elsewhere, the law's necessary commitment to general principles, to abstract universal rules, to develop objective laws through universalization, is at once exclusive of subjectivities, identities, and particularities. It is exclusive, in other words, of people's very being, erasing history—both one's own and others'. So when the law in its application and interpretation invokes history the reading is likely to be very partial, the more so the more politicized the process becomes. And race, I am insisting, necessarily politicizes the processes it brackets and colors. In its claim to universality and objectivity, the law effaces the being of legal agents, of principals and their principles. It effaces agency itself and so veils different agents' pleasures and sufferings, which are often causally, if silently linked. In commanding anonymously, the law hides those in and issuing command, just as it denies the violence it may perpetrate upon those commanded. The only satisfactory response that seems available to this dilemma of the legal and moral domains, to the dilemma of sameness and difference, universality and particularity, is to insist that moral expression intersect pragmatically with political, metaphysical, and cultural contestation. This is a point I will return to elaborate as the central claim of my conclusion.

That the State in the name of its citizenry insists on overseeing—*policing*—the precise and detailed forms that housing must take for the poor and racialized suggests that we really are committed to the kinds of disciplinary culture that inform current practice. The principle of agent autonomy so deeply cherished at the core should not, it seems, extend to the periphery; the racially marginalized should not be encouraged to exercise independence (least of all with public monies). The 'Detroit Expedition' of the late 1950s set out *with* the urban poor to determine which problems of urban housing were most pressing and which solutions acceptable.[40] The political resistance of public policy creators to emulating this undertaking with the racially marginalized reflects the deep-rootedness of a racialized discourse reproducing itself in its more extreme mode. It stands as a visible mark of the depth to which political imagination and a will economically driven have been colonized by the discourse, the degree to which is explicable only in terms of a culpable silence, blindness, and complicity.

I have undertaken here to identify the formative relations between the conditions for the subjective experience of 'knowing one's (racial) place' in the contemporary city,[41] on one hand, and the social structures and discursive formations of (racial) space, on the other. Now place, as Raymond Williams remarks, is a crucial factor in the bonding process of individuals, groups, and the oppressed.[42] Resistance to racialized city space, to the very grounds of periphery and center, is restricted by state containment, *intra*spatial conflict and conditions, and the forces of removal. State initiatives concerning the racially marginalized have proved mostly unreliable: If the above is anything to go by, they drip with the divisive discourses of race and class. One emerging alternative is the assumption of 'given' peripheral places as sites of affirmative resistance—in much the way that 'black', say, has been assumed affirmatively as a designation of resistance. It is in the final analysis only on and *from* these sites, the social margins, that the battles of resistance will be waged, the fights for full recognition of freedoms, interests, claims and powers, for the autonomy of registered voices, and the insistence upon fully incorporated social institutions, resources, *spaces*. After all, and against the apologists of *apartheid*, to change one's geography—not only to move from but equally to transform one's spaces and its representations—may well be to change one's world.

9

Taking Race Pragmatically

Racisms and Representation

I have argued that the conditions of racialized discourse and the variety of racist exclusions prompted in specific contexts are deeply embedded in the shifting space-time conjunctures of modernity and postmodernity. Race has fashioned and continues to mold personal and social identity, the bounds of who one is and can be, of where one chooses to be or is placed, what social and private spaces one can and dare not enter or penetrate. Race inscribes and circumscribes the experiences of space and time, of geography and history, just as race itself acquires its specificity in terms of space-time correlates. Changing one's place in the world will in this sense likely change one's world. Nevertheless, the history of racialized expression has served to fix social subjects in place and time, no matter their spatial location, to delimit privilege and possibilities, to open opportunities to some while excluding the range of racialized Others. And in so fixing, these imposed and imagined histories freeze not only the racial Other but also those so privileged into *given* identities, perspectives, and dispositions.

What seems fixed in this freezing is also, as I argued in chapter 8, the boundaries of and the bounds of experiencing racially defined space. Significantly, the early taxonomies of racialized (in)humanity by the likes of Linnaeus were territorially defined: *Homo afer, americanus, asiaticus,* and *europeus.* A rhetoric of space thus came to frame persons' basic identities, and with it the limits of their opportunities. Once established, this rhetoric set the limits—territorial and social, spatial and moral—that some continued to define and control, to police and reproduce, as others dared to negotiate only if beckoned or at their own peril. The presumptive conceptual architecture ordering epistemological construction in modernity and establishing the grounds of identity and (self-)identification has prompted dispositions to create and insinuate, to magnify and emphasize racially significant categories. It has enabled the racializing of personhood and social space, personal relations and the body politic.

The passages from classical liberal modernity to 'postmodernist bourgeois liberalism'[1] have signaled shifts from the fundamental public commitment to ignore difference and particularity in the name of universality to a public celebration of diversity and an openly acknowledged and constantly recreated politics of difference. In these shifts, racialized spaces and their differential cultures continue—often silently—to reproduce even as they transform the culture of race, to situate as they anchor those they continue to mark or mark anew. Racialized space positions people in public political space, just as racialized identity circumscribes social space, as they identify the included from the excluded, the (relatively) empowered from those (largely) powerless and peripheral, the enfranchised from the disenfranchised and disinherited.

These shifts from modernity to postmodernity pull in different directions. The emphasis on cultural diversity that has now taken root intersects with legal developments and capital's new demands for 'flexible accumulation'.[2] The sociocultural and spatial boundaries that serve as the skin of the body politic have accordingly become more porous. The conditions of possibility for moving through, for transgressing, the established racialized limits of spatial confines and political imagination have seemed to broaden. At the same time, though, commitments to diversity in the public domain have been displaced and delimited by privatizing univocality, exclusion, and exclusivity. Racial identities and racist commitments have to a much greater extent become privately circulated, more or less silently distributed rather than properly silenced. Racist expressions are rendered visible or audible more generally where the claim to unhindered private exchange gets expanded into the public space—in restaurants or airplanes, cinemas or on the street, and then into more formal settings like universities, implicitly or inadvertently licensed by explicit media reportage of racist 'incidents' or political campaigns.

Those political perspectives, views, or theories that unambiguously and self-confidently proclaim the end of racism restrict the range of pertinent expressions to a shrunken totalization of an uncontested Truth. That Judge David Souter can proclaim *unchallenged* during the Senate Judiciary Committee hearings to confirm him as a justice of the U.S. Supreme Court that there is 'no racism in New Hampshire'; that the director of the British Information Service in the United States can respond in 1978 to the controversy surrounding the film *Blacks Britannica* that 'racism is not a significant factor in British life and politics';[3] that Thomas Sowell can imply in 1984 that institutional discrimination is no more[4] can only be grounded in the totalized closure of the Truth claims themselves. They are grounded, that is, in the exclusions marked by totalized criteria (lack of intentionality or institutional rules), or in the exclusive totalization of formal methods by which claims to racial Truth can be established (social science surveys and attitude studies of personal prejudice, or legally sanctioned reports of discriminatory institutional rules).[5] The denials and delimitations accordingly entailed erase the exclusionary experiences of racialized subjectivities, the effects of racist patterns of discipline and deprivation, and the marginalizations and periphraxes insinuated into the racial ambiguities of social practices. Totalized racial Truth excises differentiated experience, extends the silences of those racially othered, wipes away as it claims to clean up the historical subjectivities and subjections of racialized Others, of othering, of otherness itself.

I suggested in chapter 7 that central ordering concepts and root metaphors in contemporary knowledge production have served to reinvigorate stock racialized categories or to prompt new ones. These concepts and metaphors inform as they cover up racializing technologies, constituting a lexicon of racialized power. These generative ideas within racialized discourse have served, as they continue silently or explicitly, covertly or vociferously, to order anew and extend the exclusiveness and exclusions of racist expression. Knowledge production, in general, and the social sciences, especially, have thus done much at various watershed moments to create, authorize, legitimate, and license the figures of racial otherness, the fabrication of racial selves and social subjects. They have serviced the rhetoric of racial order(s) that at once rationalize(s) and recreate(s) racialized exclusions, that are expressed in (terms of) and through the claims and chains of rationality.

What I have called racial knowledge may be extended socioscientifically through the use of racialized categories. I argued in chapter 6 that racialized knowledge may also be 'advanced' by using stereotypes—even reasonable ones—where what is significant is not simply their use (after all, a person may use the same stereotype with no racist implication at all) but what (unreasonably) the stereotype is taken to show, to warrant. So, for example, the stereotype that blacks tend to be good entertainers or sportsmen and sportswomen will warrant for the racist that blacks have little intellectual capacity—that they need affirmative action programs to get ahead yet often still fail. The racist and non- or antiracist may proceed here from the same stereotype. What makes one a racist, what distinguishes the racist from one who is not, thus, cannot be the formal irrationality of the beliefs at issue. Rather, as I concluded earlier, it is the unreasonableness, the lack of warrant, in this case of the inference drawn from the reasonable generalization.[6] Similarly, social science often prompts or perpetuates characterizations of social groups that either initiate or extend their racialized condition and accordingly license misleading generalizations about the group's members. As Don Nakanishi makes clear, social science has done much to popularize the image of Asian Americans, in general, and Japanese-Americans, in particular, as a 'model minority'. Presupposing the contested standard of melting-pot assimilationism and assuming the European immigrant experience as the appropriate model, this image prompts two unreasonable (because unwarranted) implications: first, that Asian Americans as a totality no longer experience structural forms of racist exclusion; and second, that those who continue to face such discriminatory exclusions have only their own pathological deviance to blame.[7]

Racial knowledge, then, gets extended socioscientifically through invoking certain assumptions or employing established methodologies that tend to entail racist or racially determined conclusions or outcomes. This may be exemplified by what I will call the 'informal fallacy of blaming the marginalized'. The fallacy manifests itself in the work of social scientists setting out with the assumption or to prove (often these are hard to distinguish) that the marginalized position of some racial group is tied to a set of damaging (or damaged) cultural values; to a culture of racially specified poverty; to a poverty of the racial culture in question; to cultural deprivation; or to an unrealistic, outmoded, and self-defeating ideology. Analogously, social scientists who focus methodologically on individuals in order to account for discriminatory group exclusions will likely resort to explanations in terms of prejudice and individual pathologies. They are thus likely to miss the group and structural dimensions in determining the extent of exclusionary occurrence in their explanations for the exclusions, and in respect to the question of reasonable redress.[8] In these and other ways, then, I have illustrated how the exclusions of racist culture become constitutive of worldviews, features of rational order and bureaucratic control. In a word, they become normalized. They enter into and mold, ground and order, the shared values, meanings, and norms of a social formation. In turn, racist exclusions are promoted, sustained, and extended. They are expressed often under the veil and in the name of more acceptable social and scientific discourses.

So there is no single explanation for racism, for there is no single racism to be explained. This raises the question, in turn, as to how we may distinguish an experience that can be described in racialized terms from one that amounts to racist exclusion. I have suggested that this distinction turns generally on the way in which the case at hand fits into a culture of racism. It turns, that is, on whether we have a case of genuine racially characterizable exclusion according to the set of conditions stipulated in chapter 5, whether the exclusion at hand fits a pattern of such exclusions, and on the degree and depth of the discriminatory exclusions. Yet, it also requires specifying, and this perhaps most centrally, the relation of the case in question and of the parties in the case to the history of racially exclusivist expressions and to racialized discourse more generally.

This history of exclusions is tied in inextricable ways to the emergence of and transformations in racialized discourse, to the changes in use and meanings of 'race', to the various ways in which race has intersected with authoritative discourses, and to the means by which it has naturalized social relations (see chapter 4). It is tied, that is, to the politics of meaning and the meanings imputed in and to politics, and through all of this it is more than anything else tied to (the expression of) power, to how power gets to be articulated. Race has been able to colonize the social and political imaginations more or less throughout modernity by managing in (re)new(ed) ways to express prevailing interests, by specifying the content of otherwise abstractly universal conceptions of rational personhood and moral claim, and by insinuating into these conceptions (through its multiplying intersection with other exclusivist discourses of modernity) the identities necessary to sustain and legitimate (if not quite to justify) the exclusions and exploitations, the interests and institutions at stake (see chapters 2 and 3).

Taking Race Seriously

Racial identities, like other forms of social identity, have become increasingly ambivalent and ambiguous, even (or especially) as they are asserted with such visible self-assurance, tremulous confidence, and power. Since its inception at the turn of the fifteenth century, race has emerged as an identity of anonymity, identifying social subjects conceived by modernity (and so self-conceived) as radically individualized. Race extends a tremulous identity in a social context marked by uncertainty—the uncertainty of a future beyond this life, the uncertainty of situatedness, or at least of its lack, and the uncertainties of self-assertion and assertiveness in a world of constant flux, power shifts, neighbors and nations next door one day and gone the next. Identities like race, especially of race, offer a semblance of order, an empowerment, or at minimum an affectation of power.

A racist modality, that fragile structure of racist exclusions at a space-time conjuncture, is sustained not only by the power of socioeconomic interests but also by 'the microexpressions and strategies that cement the social identities, and by the indispensable intersection of discursive fields and strategies of demonstration, evidence, and reason with those of contrasts, threats, and accusations'.[9] The contemporary modality, signaled since the beginning of the Reagan-Thatcher era as the 'new racism', reflects as it cements the structural alterations and current contingencies of the order of postmodernity. Here, race is increasingly fluid, the racist exclusions it suggests diversified (like the portfolios from which it has supposedly been erased) and implicitly intensified. As disciplinary regulations in the age of apparent deregulation and privatization get rearticulated, as they become more fluid and more hidden from obvious view, as freedoms and powers become more constrained while made to seem more readily available, so do social identities become refixed: They are reset as they are made to seem more fluid, imposed as they are made to seem self-chosen, frozen as they are made to appear evaporative. Embedded in the histories of modernity, central to modernity's possibilities and impossibilities, racialized identities become reconstituted, reascribed as they are made to seem self-ascribed and splintered, reaffirmed as they are supposed to be rendered irrelevant. Race accordingly traces out the routes for, as it maps onto, 'the mobile idea of freedom'.[10]

Race has been conceptually well-placed to characterize freedom's routes, to channel freedom's mobility, and so to thrive in this age of ambiguity, for as I have made clear it is by nature (insofar as it has one) a concept virtually vacuous in its own right. Its virtual conceptual emptiness allows it parasitically to map its signification of naturalized differences onto prevailing social views and scientific theories that are readily acceptable and accepted, to articulate and extend racialized exclusions in the name of and legitimized by discourses seemingly neutral and impartial. Race has thus been able more or less continuously since its emergence to naturalize difference and to normalize exclusions.

This prevailing historical legacy of thinking racially does not necessitate that any conceptual use of or appeal to race to characterize social circumstance is inherently unjustifiable. What renders an appeal to racial categorization racist is not that it need be arbitrary. Rather, its racism turns on whether the categorization is constitutive and promotive in the case at hand of racialized exclusions. In other words, what distinguishes a racist from a nonracist appeal to the category of race is the *use* into which the categorization enters, the exclusions it sustains, prompts, promotes, and extends. Foucault argues instructively that no technology, technique, or architecture necessarily restricts freedom or is naturally liberative. In the final analysis, the only and necessarily contingent guarantee of freedom is the practice of freedom itself, is freely living out the conditions of expressive space.[11] Analogously, I want to suggest that though race has tended historically to define conditions of oppression, it could, under a culturalist interpretation—and under some conditions perhaps must—be the site of a counterassault, a ground or field for launching liberatory projects or from which to expand freedom(s) and open up emancipatory spaces.

Nevertheless, though one may be able now to get all, or nearly all, to agree that racism, or at least some extreme form like *apartheid,* is necessarily unacceptable, it will not follow, and for a variety of reasons, that the days of racist expression and practice are thus numbered. First, it does not follow that all will agree to racism's conceptual extension, that each understands by the term exactly what others do, either in general or in the particular case. For example, the South African government openly declared in the late 1980s that *apartheid* was already dead because the central laws constituting the *apartheid* state had been repealed. By contrast, those in opposition like Archbishop Tutu or the African National Congress insisted then, as they do now, that *apartheid* was very much in place in the institutional structures and common sense that socially continue to locate and determine the possibilities of people racially identified and identifiable, even absent the laws. The South African case reveals, second, that agreement may not be forthcoming on the seriousness of the wrongs involved, or perhaps even on their nature. Third, and relatedly, there may be no consensus concerning permissible means of resistance, or alleviation, or compensation in combatting the racisms at issue. The alternatives have ranged from 'any means necessary' to nonracial considerations alone, from 'compensatory racism' to colorblind options only.

These contestational considerations in defining both the field of issues and the range of conceivable responses reflect what I earlier characterized as the inherently political nature of race and the sets of exclusions it underpins. Racial identities, recall, are fashioned and fabricated in the contestations of individuals and groups in their struggles for or to sustain power, in the drive to effect, advance, or perpetuate exclusions from the benefits of the body politic. Contesting these exclusions, their modes, and—where necessitated by the demands of praxis—the racial identities in whose name the exclusions are ordered, must be political in the broadest sense as well.

This suggests that neither the formalist universalism of modernist morality nor the particularism of the postmodernist independently sustain the value and practical commitments necessary to condemn and resist, to restrict or eliminate all racist exclusions and expressions. Universalisms offer the virtues of principles generally acknowledging the injustices of broadly construed racist expressions. However, they hide in the claims to universal values the inherent limitations of their lack of specificity, and they deny the value in culturally construed particularities inconsistent with the putatively universal principle. For example, if the universally construed criteria for land tenure in a prevailing legal system (even inadvertently) exclude 'nomadic' conditions, nonsedentary indigenous people will be deprived both of their land (in what have been construed as 'just wars', or treaties to end wars or their threat) and, in the ensuing representational battles, of mounting any legal claim to the land.[12] Particularisms, by contrast, recognize the virtues of communities, traditions, and specific cultural values, but they may find themselves incapable of offering any principled restriction of exclusivist expressions mounted in their name.

It may be thought that in the absence of any resolution to this dilemma of the universal and particular, of sameness and difference, the resulting indeterminacy or underdetermination of the moral will leave social space open to racially exclusivist expressions. Attempting to resolve this tension theoretically through principled (over)specification will render moral theory practically useless for ordinary social subjects (for all nonphilosophers, that is, and perhaps for most philosophers also if only we would own up to it), or it will so restrict the realm of practicable application that a range of exclusionary practices will inevitably escape condemnation. It is better, I think, to admit moral indeterminacy as a necessary feature of social praxis. The lead in condemning, resisting, restricting, and ultimately clearing social space of racist expressions will accordingly lie in social praxis, a practice in which values are embedded and through which commitments are articulated, revised, and refined in relation to the changing tasks at hand.

Consider the case of a burning hotel. One hundred people are caught inside, but there is the possibility of saving only fifty. If this is all the information we have, race must be irrelevant to the choice. Commitment to the universal value of nondiscrimination would suggest that rescuers proceed on the basis of random selection. Now imagine that a conference at the hotel has left stranded there the last fifty surviving members of some racial group (interpreted as culture, though phenotype may help to pick them out): the San, say. It seems that a strong case could be made for first saving the San as a means to perpetuating or attempting to revive the culture. This is not a case where the numbers count so much as it is one where race (interpreted at least as culture) does. Commitment to a universal principle rejecting any appeal to race as arbitrary must obviously entail rejecting such an argument: This, after all, is a matter of life and death. Rational self-interested agents behind the veil of ignorance would likely dismiss making an exception in cases of this kind, for were they to do so they could possibly be signing their own death warrants, and this seems self-interestedly irrational in the extreme. But we are not bound to accept the Rawlsian determination here, for this outcome simply reflects the narrow individualism of the Rawlsian assumptions, and as I argued in chapter 6, we are not bound on pain of putative irrationality to accept these. Dismissing as morally irrelevant the particular historical conditions that have reduced the likes of the San to virtual extinction is to ignore the legacy of colonization that so reduced them and for which they are not responsible. It would amount, in short, to perpetuating and extending the legacy of those conditions.

Nevertheless, whether we are moved in a case like this by the universal principles or by the force of facticity will not be resolved in the end within an established theory. Nor should we encourage relief workers to be haggling over appropriate action at the scene of the disaster. Assumption of a theory already commits us one way or the other. Thus, resolution lies ultimately in what sorts of ends we would achieve by our social practices, in what sorts of values we find ourselves committed to in undertaking the practices themselves, most importantly in what sort of (transforming) vision we have of the body politic, and by extension in what sorts of means we deem warranted in facilitating the ends, values, and vision.

Underlying this is an issue of scope. Liberalism tends to assume that there are pockets of injustice, in particular of racial injustice, that a liberal or enlightened meliorism will progressively overcome. I am suggesting, by contrast, that racist exclusions, though not exactly everywhere in contemporary racialized social systems, are discursively far more pervasive and diffuse than liberalism is willing or able to acknowledge. Racialized modes of social definition and exclusion in such social systems tend to be so systemic and fluid that piecemeal meliorism is unlikely to go very far in uprooting the culture that promotes and sustains them.

As I have said and as I argued at length in chapter 5, there is no single unified phenomenon of racism, only a range of racisms. This lack of any more than a general identity to instances of racialized discourse and racist exclusions expressed in their name has implications for a politics of resistance and an ethics of transformation. Just as a plurality of strategies may be required for moral condemnation, so no single mode of resistance to racism will succeed exhaustively. Racism's adaptive resilience entails that we have to respond with sets of oppositions that are found in and through praxis to be appropriate to each form racism assumes. Institutionally, overcoming *apartheid* must take on forms different from opposition to racist jury practices or discriminatory employment and housing practices in the United States; ideologically, the appropriate kinds of response to claims of racial superiority or inferiority will differ from those to racially interpreted cultural differences; and scientifically, critical attack on racist metaphors and concepts insinuated into standard theoretical articulation will differ from the responses appropriate to scientific theories supporting racist hypotheses.[13] Countering the specific marginalizations of racialized women must sometimes require different strategies than those necessary to resist racist exclusions in general and those of men in particular.[14] In general, the ways in which we are to resist rational articulations of racism will diverge from critical opposition to irrational racisms, as indeed will also the appropriate responses to rational racisms in the weak and strong senses (see chapter 6). Ethical resistance to racism must necessarily assume political, legal, economic, and cultural forms. Equally, any such form of resistance to racism must be underwritten by personal ethical commitment. Given the basic practical indeterminacy of moral reason, the terrain of resistance to racisms cannot merely be moral or sustained merely by moral appeal narrowly construed. In general, the struggle against racisms must be played out on the political terrain broadly construed as general sets of relations between social subjects. Resistance to racisms, if it is ultimately to make a difference, must assume any and every form taken on by racist expressions and exclusions in these social relations.

Racisms and the Pragmatics of Praxis

This generalized commitment to the specificities of particular antiracist practices can be reflected theoretically only in the flexibility of philosophical pragmatism. Recently, pragmatism has emerged as the theory of choice among those known in sociolegal theorizing as 'Critical Race Theorists'.[15] The suggestion is that in contrast to liberalism's universalism and postmodernism's communitarian particularism, a commitment against racisms must seek to resist specific forms and expressions of exclusion, exploitation, and oppression, to transform particular racist social formations in the name of general principles of sociopolitical transformation. These principles will acquire specificity within the political culture in terms of the struggles and envisioned standards, social relations, and at least remotely achievable ideals of established milieus. Those actively committed to resisting racisms cannot define their resistant or transformative projects in terms of abstract, transcendental ideals, atemporal universals, or fixed social foundations. Nor can the transformative projects seek grounding in terms of the universalist appeal to the Sameness of a transhistorical Subject. Rather, the emancipatory ideals and the means to their institution must be considered provisional and revisable, situated in the transformative and transgressive possibilities of the sociohistorical contexts in which social subjects generally find themselves struggling individually and collectively. Kimberle

Crenshaw notes in her perceptive critique of the limits of the Critical Legal Studies project, for example, that blacks launched the Civil Rights struggle in the United States fully cognizant of the ways in which legal rights had been circumscribed to exclude them. Nevertheless, many blacks at the time properly found legal reform the most 'viable pragmatic strategy ... confronted with the threat of unbridled racism on the one hand and cooptation on the other'.[16] Similarly, the decision by the African National Congress in 1960 that its only available option, given the conditions facing the people it represented in South Africa at the time, to resort to armed struggle aimed at strategic state targets, while being careful to avoid noncombatants, was one reflecting this pragmatics of praxis; as also was its decision thirty years later to suspend the armed struggle and to engage the South African government in negotiations toward a new, nonracist constitution that would ground the democratic institutions in which all South Africans could participate.

I hesitate to invoke here the optimistic spirit of pragmatism. The notion is taken by many to carry connotations of an unprincipled instrumentalism, a technological tampering that services power and control. My ambivalence is fueled by the tendency of some of its more sophisticated and eloquent proponents to praise pragmatism as licensing the unquestioned comforts of bourgeois liberalism or for representing a properly 'American' self-representation, both of which are historically tied to various forms of racist expression.[17] Nevertheless, I am moved by the principled pragmatist's commitment that we not be primarily concerned with the abstract, formalistically rational grounds for a just social order, or with theoretical establishment of indubitable and epistemological social foundations. Pragmatism directs us philosophically, some say banally, away from the search for transcendental foundations of knowledge, morality, and politics, away from the foundational orientation that distinguishes appearance from reality, and towards establishing in theory and practice the contingent social circumstances and relations of cooperative power that would at specific space-times best facilitate human flourishing and self-development. As Richard Rorty notes, principled pragmatists replace the appearance-reality distinction with descriptions by the oppressed and excluded of prevailing social conditions and relations of power. Though these descriptions are not epistemologically privileged by the pragmatist, they nevertheless contest the oppressor's characterizations.[18] Against unprincipled and expedient instrumentalism, the philosophically principled pragmatist may be characterized as deeply concerned with historically specific social arrangements without being historicist. Pragmatism, in other words, refuses any grand teleological narratives specifying in deterministic fashion either the social state in which history must supposedly terminate or any utopian condition in which all social tensions and difficulties will purportedly be resolved. Pragmatists are thus committed, both philosophically and practically, to oppose all forms of oppression and domination and to avoid, resist, and reject all hierarchical orders in modes of thinking and social formations. They are concerned, that is, with and about the contingent and transforming relations between knowledge and power, with resisting the discursive conditions and determinations of domination and exclusion, and with setting the contingent grounds for instituting and promoting liberatory self-determination for all people.

In this sense, we might characterize pragmatists philosophically as skeptical realists. They are skeptical because experience has prompted a healthy disdain for extreme and untenable positions and for valorizing marginality without doing much to transform it. They recognize, as Gerald Torres has put it, that marginality is to be resisted but does not in itself constitute resistance. Marginality is an effective space from which much resistance may be mounted, but the social, political, and economic margins do not in and of themselves guarantee resistance or its success.[19] Indeed, often the fact, degree, and success of marginal resistance will be related to the degree of political and cultural hegemony. The point, then, is not to be narrowly ideological; it is, rather, to be critical in a transformative way of any theory or practice that unjustifiably restricts freedom or promotes exclusion. And pragmatists are realists not in the sense of being tied to a metaphysical theory of truth but in undertaking to effect strategies for social liberation, and in the realization that liberative transformation does not come all of a piece but is to be made and remade, that it is never ended but open ended.[20]

It is these features of a principled pragmatism that I want to invoke as general guiding principles for resisting racisms. What we need is a theoretical and sociopolitical praxis sufficiently fluid to recognize and respond to racisms' renewals and to articulate broad principles of renewable and revisable social relations committed to resisting the emergence and refinement of racist thinking and practice. This contestational 'pragmatics of praxis' is defined and renegotiated through the reiterable intersection of informing principle and sociopolitical practice.

Now the general differences between the liberal and the neopragmatic view of the kind I am pressing on the question of race may be summarily highlighted in terms of the distinction between the former's universal ideal of *nonracialism* and the latter's practical principle of *antiracism*. The liberal (and this seems equally true for the postmodern bourgeois liberal) takes any appeal to race to be arbitrary. The idealized liberal polity will thus be defined, among other things, by the absence of any such appeals, by the failure to recognize racial distinction. The African National Congress's longstanding (and, it seems, increasingly idealized and unrealistic) commitment to a nonracial South Africa is a thoroughly liberal one.[21] The concern, of course, has been to avoid the sorts of exclusionary outcomes projected by the deeply racialized commitments of *apartheid*. However, the ANC's nonracialism, typical of liberalism generally, is idealized in the sense that it refuses to acknowledge, let alone confront, the exclusionary practices and concerns that in a variety of fashions will continue to be racialized by social subjects, though now less formally than before. Further, it idealistically presupposes that racism assumes a single form that may be constitutionally legislated out of existence, here one day, gone the next. And, it fails, finally, to entertain the transformative, the liberatory possibilities that may nevertheless emerge from and in terms of thoroughly, or a thoroughly reformulated though still racialized, social formation.

What is necessary, by contrast, is a firm commitment to the practical reasoning, the intersections of theory with practices, required by antiracism. The concern is to end racist exclusions and the conditions that give rise to and sustain such exclusions, however and whenever they manifest. This may sometimes call for recognizing nonexclusionary racial distinctions as a (potential) site of resistance or (self-)affirmation, while in other contexts it may also necessitate resisting the imposition of racial categories, of racializing. For the liberal, the standard of nondiscrimination necessarily entails a commitment to nonracialism, to ignoring race. Antiracisms, on the other hand, recognize the possibilities of multiple manifestations of racist exclusions, of exclusionary resurgences and redefinitions, of newly emergent racisms or expressive recurrences, of different discursive impositions or terminological transformations. It is in this sense that antiracists must repeatedly recommit themselves to root out the weeds of racist cultures, though not necessarily the culture of race, wherever they may sprout.

This should not be taken to deny that the antiracist, like the pragmatist generally, can resort to ideals as guiding principles. Just as the pragmatist need not be committed to a crass instrumentalism, so ideals for the antiracist are nothing else than the best available, the most warranted, guiding principles for social action and transformation. They are to be taken, as I have said, not as foundational but always as revisable, not as necessary truths or universal essences but as warranted assertions and contingent generalizations. The legal principle of 'equal treatment before the law', for instance, has been interpreted by liberal jurisprudence in terms of Aristotelian identity: like should be treated alike. Differences are set aside, ignored or collapsed, in order to squeeze cases deemed suitably similar under the same principle. While this represents an advance over allowing wildly irrelevant considerations to serve exclusionary ends, Gerald Torres rightly points out that it nevertheless reduces similarity to sameness. It effaces difference to ensure an identity that hides or represents the power of partiality. Interpreting the standard of equality in terms of equivalence does not necessitate identical treatment by the law but proportional treatment in relation to the specificities of the persons' differing circumstances.[22] A jurisprudence of equality may be particularly effective in recognizing exclusionary wrongs and establishing the formal grounds for ending them. It seems less capable, precisely because of its formalism, of recognizing and eliminating the historical and continuing effects of those exclusions. In its recognition of historical and contemporary particularity, a jurisprudence of equivalence would be explicitly committed, at least at this historical moment in the United States, to recognition and redemption of the practices and effects of unwarranted, unreasonable, and so unjust exclusions.[23]

In broader social terms, critical antiracists should be similarly committed to generating and thinking through new possibilities, to disrupting familiar and settled ones, or to reinventing by giving new meaning or renewed vigor to old but still viable ventures. Antiracism encourages inventing new ways of expressing or speaking about social identities, of breaking out of the dualisms in conceiving relations between social subjects: between black and white, Arab and Jew, African and European or American, men and women, and so on.[24] We must accordingly be prompted to think the once unthinkable: that whites, to take Timothy Maliqalim Simone's suggestions seriously, be intellectually *and* culturally influenced by the thought of black people; that whites and blacks think through the conditions of possibility for being black, indeed, for whites to be black. I formulate this as such rather than in the language of formal equality, for blacks have long had to ask themselves, as a matter of survival, what whites want, what it means to be white, how to assume the position of whiteness. This thinking of, through, and beyond the condition of otherness presupposes that, relatively speaking, we de-emphasize the liberal insistence upon autonomy in favor of mutuality, relation, and reciprocity, that we loosen the hold of necessity over social identities in favor of transgressing imposed identities by assuming ourselves into the situations of others and so beyond Otherness.[25]

At the same time, though, we have to bear firmly in mind, indeed, to stress that conceivable possibilities are those opened broadly *at the moment* or through the possible transformations available to the specific conjuncture at hand. The range of possibilities is not to be artificially constrained and confined, narrowed to fit the terms of what the status quo takes to be 'naturally' available. Possibilities are established rather in terms of the whole spectrum of political economy, spatial configurations, and culture; in relation, that is, to the entire rainbow of prevailing and potential norms and theoretical articulations. The antiracist will test the limits of the given by pressing at its boundaries, expanding outward from within, pushing critically against the walls of the assumed and taken-for-granted from without. This brand of expansionary and insurgent antiracisms runs together in the name of the possible what is considered practicable at any moment with—and against—the conceivable of and beyond prevailing paradigms. Critical antiracism thus centrally involves 'boundary crossing, from safe circle into wilderness: the testing of a boundary.... It is the willingness to spoil a good party and break an encompassing circle, to travel from the safe to the unsafe.'[26]

There is a tension here for any pragmatically inclined view: On one hand, we find the finitude and particularities of changing racist expressions and practices, their fit into different sociohistorical contexts, their differentiated effects across place and time. On the other hand, there are similarities and identities between racist practices and expressions from one place to another or across times, in spite of the specific differences. The broad identities enable comparison and solidarity in resisting racisms. The emergent identities and similarities, the broad family resemblances suggest general principles for an effective antiracist social commitment and political ethos and for possible sorts of antiracist social practices. At the same time, the pragmatist recognizes that whatever general principles of social relation are articulated, they will be open to interpretation and revision in keeping with local prevailing conditions and transformative possibilities.

Consider the transformations this century in prevailing standards for relations between racialized social subjects in the United States. Once it became legally and politically viable to address institutional exclusions of black people in the 1940s and 1950s,[27] the standard of equal treatment for blacks (still conceived as 'Negroes') came to mirror the melting-pot model for ethnic immigrants, namely, *assimilation.* Prior to this, the model was thought not to apply to 'Negroes' at all, precisely because they were deemed inherently unassimilable. The United States was taken to have a core set of cultural and political values, and assimilation meant giving up all those 'un-American' values in order to be able to assume those that would make one as American as the construction warranted by the average statistic. The core values were those of the class and racial culture that historically had become hegemonic. Blending into the mainstream melting pot meant renouncing—often in clearly public ways—one's subjectivity, who one literally was: in name, in culture, and as far as possible in color. The language of race relations and racial harmony, as Bhikhu Parekh notes in a slightly different context, served the racial interests of those with power; those, that is, who continued to define what the acceptable core values were and required the powerless to content themselves with the generosity of charitable handouts.[28]

With the civil rights and countercultural movements of the 1960s, the prevailing assimilative standard gave way to the new one of *integration.* Here, the model left cultural groups (including races) effective control of their autonomous cultural determinations and expressions at the social margins, while maintaining a supposedly separate, and thus neutral, set of common values to mediate their relations at the center. The common values were to furnish the grounds for cohesion, the conditions of Americanness. The dualism of this model is reflected in its pluralist allowances at the margins with its univocal core insistences at the center. The central values continued to be defined hegemonically by those who were politically and economically dominant. Where racially insurgent cultural expressions emerged, as in the self-representation 'Black', they were either quickly suppressed or diluted through the tokenism of economic and cultural appropriation. This was effected, as Torres makes clear, by translating particular needs into the neutral language of interests and by then applying something like a utility calculus to balance interests with the view to maximizing utility—or control. Those in command of the calculus, of the mechanisms of power and its distribution, continue to define what gets included in the social good, and it continues to exclude those whose numbers and interests fail to count. As in the case of the assimilative ideal, 'race awareness training' in the integrative mode has focused primarily on alleviating racial conflict and tension, improving race relations via intergroup management, and on more or less genuine attempts to define and service improvements in conditions for those who continue to be identified as 'minorities'.[29]

Cultural diversity and multiculturalism under their liberal interpretations constitute advanced stages of this (dis)integrative stage. They are administrative instruments that serve to contain and restrain resistance and transformation as they displace any appeal to economic difference by paying lip service to the celebration of cultural distinction. The corporate culture of integration is defined through determinations by legal authority of what it takes to meet the letter of the law and thus avoid complaints of discrimination. Similarly, cultural diversity in the academy is invoked as a necessary recruiting mechanism at a time of decreasing enrollments and shrinking federal dollars.[30]

A different standard, an antiracist one, is just beginning to emerge in the struggles of cultural transformation. To contrast this with the standards of assimilation and integration, I will refer to it as *incorporation*. The principle at issue here involves the dual transformations that take place both in the dominant values and in those of the insurgent group, as the latter insists on more complete incorporations into the body politic and the former grudgingly gives way. Incorporation, then, does not involve extension of established values and protections over the formerly excluded group, either a liberal bringing into or a Habermasian collectivist extension of the status quo. The continual renegotiation of sociocultural space is not fixed in and by a contract, a momentary communicative agreement that reifies relations. The body politic becomes a medium for transformative incorporation, a political arena of contestation, rather than a base from which exclusions can be more or less silently extended, managed, and manipulated.

The body of political relations is irreversibly altered as new parts attach themselves to and then work their own ways into its mechanisms of power and cultural expression. Incorporation undermines the grounds of integration and marginalization, for it empowers those once marginalized in relation to the dominant and forceful of the body politic. It extends transformative power, not just to alter or end marginalization but to undermine and alter from within the dominant, controlling, confining, and periphractic values of the cultural dominant. The central issue here, as Patricia Williams notes, 'is precisely the canonized status of any one group's control'.[31] Evidence that this incorporative ideal is now emergent may be found in the cultural struggles over the literary canon and the curriculum, in the stresses over defining and control of legal pedagogy, in (re)writing histories, and in the power of African-Americans to (re)name, to represent themselves. And perhaps the central value of this standard is what Bhabha calls 'hybridity', a displacement of the histories that constitute its moment, thrusting forth new 'structures of authority, new political initiatives', promoting the emergence of 'a new area of negotiation of meaning and representation' that is incomprehensible and unrecognizable in terms of prevailing knowledge.[32] In this sense, incorporative undertakings are transgressive, engaged by definition in infringing and exceeding the norms of the racialized status quo and transforming the values and representations that have held racist culture together.

The insurgency of the antiracist insistence upon incorporative politics over some exclusionary social standard does not turn on its standing as inevitable conclusion to rational deduction. Liberal arguments may be offered to the effect that incorporative politics map out the social conditions most likely to maximize well-being or that they specify the social processes most likely to be agreed upon by all rational agents choosing in their self-interest. Yet ultimately there is little one can say from the foundations liberalism claims as its own to a moral or political skeptic who may consistently deny the grounds of utility or contract. Pragmatic responses differ from foundational theories in acknowledging indeterminacy of moral and political theorizing, in requiring a specific action or institutional arrangement for some established context. In place of a formula or algorithm, pragmatic antiracisms are committed to specifying the conditions of possibility for resistance and transgressive transformation to succeed, to articulate the full range of possible alternatives available, and to indicate against the general standard of self-determination which of the alternatives is most warranted in the circumstances.

So, faced by a nihilistically inclined skeptic, pragmatic antiracists would tend to respond in two ways. First, they would argue that incorporative political projects fashion the general social conditions, the acid test, for delimiting restrictions on human flourishing, for social and individual well-being. Social institutions and the responses to racisms they promote that block incorporative strategies would be dismissed prima facie as inadequate. Similarly, institutional responses to racisms that fail to encourage or execute conditions of possibility for incorporative undertakings to emerge should be avoided. Adopting a conception of personhood, on this account, need be concerned only with whether it is prima facie incorporative rather than exclusionary in its characterization of human agency and in the human inclinations it prompts. Pragmatic antiracists must also insist in the face of nihilism that antiracist incorporative practices require political *commitment* to their effectivity beyond illustrating their theoretical or personal desirability. There must be an affirmation of the values central to incorporation and an active undertaking to institute them.

Incorporative undertakings turn on the practical understanding that social subjects will confront and critically 'engage the relational and contingent character of the identities that constitute them'.[33] They require that social subjects strive reasonably to represent the values of their self-ascribed identities in a vigorous but open contestation and will be prepared to revise their commitments, even deeply held ones, to alter their values, ultimately to transform their identities in relation to the critical pushes and pulls of the incorporative dynamic. The assumption of voice by diverse expressions of value in the politico-cultural clash will open up cracks in the hegemonic walls of standardized cultural identity.

Racially defined cultural distinctions may force their way into and between these cracks, thereby exacerbating the processes of incorporative transformation of the dominant by the different. Yet incorporation signals transformations not only in the hegemonic culture and center of power but also in the insurgent one through the dialectic interaction that transpires in the cultural clash. Not only is the dominant interpretive community moved to transform; so are the values and interpretive modes of those seeking to displace the culture of dominance. As the cultural impositions of dominance are (re)moved, a (re)new(ed) culture of interpretation and action will be called for(th).

It should not be thought that the principles of incorporative politics are the natural outcomes of the processes of modernity or postmodernity. The principles involve the interaction of idealization and realpolitik. They are idealized in so far as they turn on a set of values or ideals to be specified in practice, to be affirmed by commitment, to be strived for through social institutionalization effected by way of praxis. These values leave open self-conscious racial creation as a viable option, as a mode of resistance and self-affirmation. Incorporative principles engage in realpolitik, then, in articulating the set of processes and practices necessary at some conjuncture for political contestation by the racialized of their racially defined exclusions, for recognition in and on their own terms, and for politico-economic and cultural transformation of the racist culture into which they are thrust.

Racist culture is fluid and often manifests itself in covert and subtle forms. Its transforming natures are deeply connected as cause and manifestation to reconstructed and restructured identities, to changing conditions in social structure and organization, as well as to anxieties about impending changes. I have argued that racial identification and racist exclusion could emerge in or define almost any social formation, though they are less likely to do so for some forms and under certain characteristic conditions than others. So a political economy that is more egalitarian, not just formally but substantively, is less likely, other things being equal, to involve deeply racist exclusions, for competition and its representative forms of class power and imposition will likely be less prevalent, and these are primary (yet not nearly the sole) determinants of racist discriminations and exclusions. Similarly, societies for whom identities and identifications have readily been established in racialized terms, that have a long history of racial creation and discrimination, societies—to use Stuart Hall's well-known phrase—that are 'structured in dominance' will more readily be open to exclusionary extensions than those societies not so historically defined. A society deeply class divided and historically racialized will be more likely in times of economic strain to abandon commitment to assisting the deeply distressed. Where people in the society are racialized, or where the conditions are available for their racializing, the economically distressed will likely be or become the racially marginalized. Indeed, they will likely be turned, in the figure of the welfare class, into what William Connolly convincingly characterizes as 'a dispensable subject of political representation and an indispensable object of political disposability'. The racially marginalized will accordingly be constituted in 'the theatricality of power' as the pole around which the terms of political accountability to the effective electorate can be organized by promising to cut a program here or reduce a program there.[34]

A society more readily committing itself to the transformative institutions and practices of incorporation will likely resist recourse by its members to engage in practices of racialized definition for exclusionary purposes. Open incorporative standards will discourage individuals or groups from extending their values over others as though they constituted a human or social essence, a natural condition. The society would be committed to working out institutional forms and practices that inhibit imposing representations upon others while encouraging self-representation, to promoting difference not for disciplinary purposes but to restrict and delimit definitional normalization. Incorporative politics corresponds to Connolly's 'politics of the paradoxical'; it furnishes 'the medium through which the independent antinomies of identity and difference can be expressed and contested'. The point is not simply to neutralize identity claims because they are ambiguous and ambivalent, as the liberal would, but to affirm their transformative and incorporative values and their implicative possibilities while denying the normalized simplifications, disciplines, and exclusionary orders they so often tend to license. We are not to convert the contingeny of prevailing identities into those deemed ethically essential by universalizing them. Rather, we are actively to resist and displace the various instruments of definition and power employed to convert 'difference into otherness'.[35]

I have run together two forms of incorporation that bear distinguishing. The first is inclusion in the status quo and an undertaking, though enticed by the riches of appropriation, to transform it while actively engaging the institutional arrangements it makes possible. The second is more radically transformative than it is reformative. It consists in negotiating the bases for a new social order, one altogether different in form and substance. The Civil Rights Movement in the United States represents a case of the former, the contemporary constitutional convention in South Africa a case of the latter. By the same token, we can distinguish between two modes of resistance to racisms. One consists in resisting attacks on antiracist gains already achieved, like the Reaganite assault aimed at restricting through redefining civil rights. The other involves counteracting continuing degradation, subjection, and repression. While the liberal nonracialist is committed for the most part to little more than ignoring race, the pragmatic antiracist is concerned with opposing racisms and protecting social subjects against delimitation of their gains in the name of an incorporative politics.

Resisting Racisms, Eliminating Exclusions

Resistance to racisms consists in vigorously contending and disputing exclusionary values, norms, institutions, and practices, as well as assertively articulating open-ended specifications and means for an incorporative politics. Where racisms are openly and volubly expressed, it is likely a matter of time before a more or less organized resistance by its objects,[36] often in alliance with other antiracists, will be promoted in response: witness the emergence of resistance to slavery in the United States, to the destruction of indigenous people on all continents, to the Holocaust in Central Europe or *apartheid* in South Africa, to the political persistence of David Duke in Louisiana, Le Pen in France, Gottfried Küssel and the neo-Nazi right in Germany and Austria, or to Vladimir Zhrinovsky, the extreme nationalist, in Russia. I am not claiming that resistance in such cases will be inevitable nor that it will be necessarily or fully effective. Where it occurs at all, the effects of resistance will depend on numerous factors. These include the vehemence of the racist expression (the 'Final Solution' is perhaps the limit case), its explicit or covert nature, the resources committed to sustaining the expression and to combatting it, as well as the sorts of technologies available on either side. It is evident, further, that where the drive to racist exclusions is silent rather than silenced, where it is insinuated without being explicated, where it is institutionally pervasive and publicly taken for granted, privately denied but silently sanctioned; then any move to organized resistance or open combat, to vocal confrontation or public counteraction, will be taken as so much paranoia, hypersensitivity, or lack of a sense of humor.[37]

Those declaring themselves against racism may be reluctant to change because of resistance to change in general; or they may be resistant to changes required in some case(s) of racism because of the perceived costs to themselves, or more generally to those considered to be in their (racial) group;[38] or they may not think racism in general, or the particular manifestation, so serious as to warrant the effort; or they may not recognize changing forms of racist exclusion as representing what they take themselves to be against. These considerations suggest that the less effort it requires of agents to express their disapprobation of racism, the more likely they will do so: signing a petition, attending a rock concert, voting against a racist candidate in an election. It also suggests that we view with some skepticism the perhaps widely held claim that those who have for the most part created and express racism(s) are in the best position to end them.[39] While they may literally be in the best position to end the expressions they were instrumental in creating, it is terribly naive to rely on the benefactors to resist, transform, or end their benefits.

In contrast to this impotent picture of responding to racisms, I want to stress that ultimately resisting racist exclusions in the wide array of their manifestations is akin to a guerilla war. It will involve, and often unpopularly, hit-and-run sorts of skirmishes against specific targets, identified practices, and their rhetoric of rationalization; against prejudices and institutional rules; and against pregnant silences and unforseen outbursts. It is a guerilla war that is often ceaseless, though there may be the equivalent of cease-fires. In this war, positional strategies and tactics of maneuver need to be as fluid as the content of the racialized discursive formation and exclusionary expressions they oppose. In these battles, resistance may be more or less global or local: One may recognize the broad identities across all racist expressions however and wherever they manifest and the importance of standing against them, or one may immerse oneself in a particular struggle in a local community. Residents of the United States, for example, may protest *apartheid* in South Africa or they may organize to resist racist police brutality or the use of discriminatory profiles in their local precinct. German antiracists may simply join in a rally protesting the reemergence of neo-Nazism or they may more actively engage in promoting transformation of existing community structures through incorporation of (im)migrants. And South Africans may merely protest *apartheid* or they may engage in vigorously transforming the microstructures of long-standing racist institutions like universities in that country.

Resisting racisms requires also that we be sensitive to the distinction between cruelty and coercion. The harms of racialized coercion are often ignored, overshadowed by racist cruelty. Conservative liberal analysts often presume, on the basis that institutional cruelty of a racist kind has been outlawed, that the repugnant forms of racist expression are no longer. If temptations to racist exclusion are to be fully resisted, there is a need to confront racially motivated or effected coercion. The latter may assume the form of perpetuated impoverishment, social dismissal, maintenance of artificial and contrived differences, or institutional exclusivity. Acquiescence to and participation in coerced practices is no mark of their social acceptability or justifiability. The coerced by definition have few if any available alternatives to the practices with which they are confronted. Eliminating racist exclusions requires actively opposing practices coercive as much as cruel.[40]

Generally, both global and local struggles are committed to dissolving racist expression. Dissolving a racist discursive formation broadly requires struggles on three interrelated fronts, corresponding to the three broad constitutive elements of any discursive formation (see chapter 3). So discursive dissolution will necessitate transforming those sociomaterial conditions, in particular the political and legal economies, that promote, sustain, and extend racist exclusions and expression. It will require undermining the conceptual conditions and apparatus, the deep grammar, in terms of which the discourse is expressed. And it will involve taking apart the mechanisms by which social subjects come to identify themselves racially and discriminate against those deemed racially other.

Responding to discriminatory employment practices on the part of employment agencies, for example, involves a range of possibilities. Where there is evidence or a well-founded suspicion that an agency engages in discriminatory practices, a formal investigation could be required. The more widespread the practices at issue are evident throughout the industry, the stronger the need for an industrywide investigation. This might involve unannounced testing and auditing. Where discrimination is found, censure, fines, and license evaluation would be in order: the more severe the (pattern of) violation, the stronger need be the response of legal enforcement.[41]

Antiracist means may include confrontation, persuasion, punishment for racist expressions, or sometimes imaginatively rewarding anti- or even nonracist expression and racialized interaction, especially where racist exclusions are viable and, indeed, all too easy options.[42] Where a verbal racist expression or depiction—an epithet, joke, or story, for example—can be shown to be not just offensive but harmful, as it will be in a racially charged atmosphere or where the objects of the expression are group members who have long suffered more or less extreme forms of racialized exclusion, a range of personal and social alternatives seem available. Individually, all those witness to the expression should (be encouraged to) register their very vocal rejection of it, even at considerable personal risk. The response may be immediate, through letters to the local press (even if they are rejected), contributions to antiracist organizations in kind or cash, and so on. The point is to put those expressing themselves in racist fashions as well as those responsible for licensing racist expressions on the defensive. Socially, such expressions may be discouraged through disincentives, or alternatives may be encouraged through incentives. The more extreme and likely the harm, the more pressing becomes the case for some sort of formal restriction and penalty.

Censuring racist expressions may at the limit require censorship, which in any case may assume more or less acceptable form. In balancing the right to free expression and consumption with the social obligation to protect social members from harmful characterization and attack, I have little sympathy for the view that free expression should necessarily win out. The five or six volumes of 'truly offensive jokes' one now finds visibly displayed in almost every airport bookstore inevitably includes demeaning sections on various racial and ethnic groups, the longest and most virulent of which is always about black people. These characterizations, despite the title, are not simply offensive but perpetuate the historical image and tend to reproduce the disposition to exclude that black people, among others, have long suffered. We might tax such publications or penalize their publishers in a way that renders them uneconomical, though this seems regressive and suggests that the rich may 'enjoy' their racism exclusively.[43] If the society really is committed to eliminating racism, why not discourage racist expression in ways we discourage attacks on the national security or drunk driving?

I do not mean to deny that difficult cases will arise. These will be more likely to occur the less trivial the free expression and the less severe the harmful exclusion it promotes, or the less the particular expression is connected to a history of racialized exclusions. Proper response in such cases must be established circumstantially and with reasonable sensitivity to all the issues and principles at stake. The fact that they are difficult cases must not entail that the claim of those harmed by the expression be inevitably overridden by the competing principle at stake (say, free expression), as they so often have been. The difficulty of a particular case consists precisely in the dilemma that we be moved by more or less equally weighty yet inconsistent claims. Taking race seriously and attacking racist culture through the pragmatics of praxis require that we not so readily discount the claim of racialized harm and power, that we accord them their proper redressive due in the circumstantial and historical scheme of things.

An institution like a university in the United States or South Africa likewise has a range of options available to it in responding to racist expressions issued under its jurisdiction, more or less literally in its name. Racist arguments or arguments to racist conclusions by students, staff, or faculty should not be suppressed but vigorously challenged by individuals and the institutional community at large. Where it can be shown that the argument underpins a position of exclusionary power on the part of an administrator, instructor, or student in position of responsibility, more serious consideration should be given to curtailment of that power and where the exclusions are especially egregious possibly to dismissal. Where there is some doubt about individual intent, and perhaps about consequences, a caution or warning may suffice. Between counterargument and dismissal, widespread options are available, especially where a more or less vicious expression is made in the absence of argument: salary freezes or cuts, lack of promotion or other awards, denial of research resources, private or public censure.

The distinction generally at issue here is between the university as the site of a vigorous and open exchange of ideas, reflected in the construction and criticism of arguments, on one hand, and unargued expression that extends exclusion or harm, on the other. The point is not to 'legislate civility' but to prevent the conditions for perpetuating harmful exclusion.[44] Again, I am unmoved by the claim, popularized by Dinesh D'Souza in his diatribe against what has popularly come to be called 'political correctness', that a new regime of ideological terror has improperly restricted what university instructors can safely say in classrooms. D'Souza's anecdotal data, always partially described anyway, strike me almost invariably as cases of instructor insensitivity. I have never felt constrained to say what I think relevantly needs saying in a classroom, not because what I argue has the power of political correctness sustaining me, but because I use more or less sensitive modes of approach. In my classes on justice and ethics at an engineering school in the Northeast and at a large state-funded institution in the southwest, the generally conservative student bodies have always had full license to argue back against criticisms of their popular claims concerning reverse discrimination (this, after all, is the age of the Reagan revolution). In this atmosphere, political as much as academic charges of political correctness taste like sour grapes. All D'Souza has revealed is that teaching is tough now that some can no longer be racist or sexist with impunity.[45]

We should not, however, ignore or deny cases like those described to me by a colleague: A student charges racism of an instructor for using the word 'niggardly' in class, while another demands that a reproduction of a Klimt nude hanging in her instructor's office be removed because it is sexist. In both cases, the university administrator appealed to should engage not in placating the student conceived as consumer but in the practice for which the university in good part exists, namely, instruction. Charges of racism and sexism can be mistaken, a fact that victim-based determinations must tend to deny. The first student might be advised to consult an etymological dictionary to reveal that the roots of the two words at issue have nothing in common. The second student might be recommended to read up about art, perhaps to consult a good reader on censorship and pornography, or even encouraged to pursue a reading course in these issues with the instructor who stands accused. Is it too much to think that *both* might benefit from the exchange? Specific recommendations will circumstantially require a careful, nuanced, and reasoned response in terms of what I earlier referred to as the principles of equivalence rather than those of formal equality. If these examples are considered banal, it is only because the normality of racisms in everyday life manifests in the most ordinary of social relations and expressions.

Moral education and encounter groups seem to have little effect in eliminating racism for a variety of reasons. First, the effects are necessarily individualized in scope and so will not range over the population at large. The effects of the program, hardly cost effective in any case, will thus be undercut in a society that is institutionally or structurally racist. Moreover, the effects are likely to be short term at best and the desirable effects more probable where the education or group is responding to a specific issue or occurrence.[46] Moral education also tends to presuppose the conventional majority-minority model of racially defined demographics and reifies racialized social formations in terms of the model of 'race relations'. It seems to presuppose that only race awareness education will likely transform a racist into a nonracial society, and it fails to recognize and so adapt to changing conceptions of race and changing forms of exclusionary expression. In short, the moral education response to racisms is concerned primarily and first with changing individual attitudes, from which behavioral (and perhaps institutional) changes are thought to follow.

Nevertheless, there is no causal relation between attitudinal change and institutional alteration. The more direct undertaking is first to attack the manifestations and expressions (the acts, rules, procedures, and organizations), and attitudes may eventually follow. The primary concern is to get at the points of power that enable the articulation of racist expression and exclusion and that promote their persistence. Contrary to the pervasive liberal presupposition, making individuals the exclusive focus of reform is likely to have little enduring socioinstitutional effect in combating racisms.[47]

In general, we may emulate Bhikhu Parekh's insistence that no retreat in racist culture has been fully secured without the central, vigorous, and ongoing participation of those who have been the objects of racist expression. Moreover, no such restriction is secure unless those once excluded actively protect, consolidate, and extend their incorporative gains. If defining the adequacy of response is left to those who have never suffered the condition, and by extension to those who have created and perpetuated it, indeed, if left to a State that is historically racist, the objects of racisms are unlikely fully to have the complete range of their exclusionary experiences recognized. Gains are unlikely to be effective unless they are made part of a coherent set of incorporative strategies that are nevertheless revisable on the basis of experience.[48]

The pragmatics of social signification and the implications of it for subjection, for the making, marking, and demeaning of social subjects, suggest one important way of taking apart—or what I earlier called 'anatomizing'—the processes of racial othering. In the war of maneuver against and around the material rhetorics of racialized power, the strategy of 'standing inside the categories' of racial othering provides an effective means of redirecting racial orders, of altering their significance and effects, of making them work against the practices of exclusion they were supposed to further. There are at least two possibilities available here. One is to take advantage of the ambivalences and ambiguities in racist categories, to press and stress them so they collapse under their own connotative weight. The other is to turn the significance of the categories around, to appropriate them, to invest them with contested significance so as to confront, subvert, or redirect their racially exclusionary connotations. These are inherently dangerous undertakings, for they magnify the weaknesses and incompleteness of social identities at the same time that they invest in them. Looming at the edge of any such project is the ever-present possibility of totalized reemergences, of fascist regroupings, of the resort to race as massive identities, a fugitive fleeing from the nervousness of ambivalence and ambiguity, from fracturing selves and social subjectivities. And in this flight lurk reordered racial communities, newly imposed subjections, and extended exclusions.

The danger lies in proceeding with, in exacerbating the ambiguities at hand. On one hand, contestation is promoted in ambiguation, in multiplying the possible meanings. On the other, unleashed ambiguity enables one to emphasize (or to continue to emphasize) the racist content. Consider Paul de Man's wartime journalism in which he criticizes 'vulgar anti-Semitism' for overestimating the contribution of Jewish writers to European literature. De Man can clearly be read here as engaging in anti-Semitic expression, for he appears to identify Jews, in Geoffrey Hartman's description, 'as an alien and unhealthy presence in Western civilization'. Derrida, by contrast, takes De Man as subtly registering a resistant disagreement with prevailing anti-Semitic sentiment, for 'to condemn vulgar anti-Semitism, *especially if one makes no mention of the other kind,* is to condemn anti-Semitism itself inasmuch as it is vulgar, always and essentially vulgar'.[49]

Though Derrida perhaps fails to acknowledge the force of rational forms of racist expression, his reading of De Man does exemplify one possible way of, and the danger in, standing inside the problematic categories to subvert them.

Different examples may seem more appealing. A black South African friend heading a university department in Cape Town was interested in moving his family into a house in an area defined as 'white' by the then still-to-be repealed Group Areas Act. This act nevertheless made provision for servants to live on the premises of their employers. My friend made an arrangement with the institution for which he worked, a government university as all in South Africa are, to purchase the house and lease it to him. The act was repealed without his formerly having to test the argument in the South African courts. Tactics of resistance employed by plantation slaves offer further examples of the dangers inherent in standing inside racist categories: Slow work and malingering undermined the plantation economy but reinforced the stereotype of laziness; slave destruction of property fueled the stereotype of incompetence; self-mutilation increased labor costs but steeled the stereotype of barbarianism.[50] Rap songs about ghétto violence, gangs, and cop killing empower the (un)censored rage of racially marginalized youth as they reinforce status quo stereotypes of a vulgar and undisciplined underclass. Black-only dormitories or student clubs, situationally necessitated by principles of pragmatic antiracism as forms of redress or promotion of long denied autonomy, may fuel the countercharge of reverse discrimination and segregation.

The self-assumption in the 1960s of the category 'black' to replace the imposition of 'Negro' provides another historical instance of the same general phenomenon. Investing positive content in a category so long carrying racist connotation was especially subversive, emphasizing self-assertion and self-representation, the power to name and to do. But it was also dangerous, for the term still bore with it more or less explicitly the sedimented significations of its racist history. One finds this latter legacy now subtly reproduced in the widespread use of '*the* blacks', a use of the emphatic indexical that tends surreptitiously to affirm, to insist upon, to exaggerate difference, and to do so by fixing an imposed identity that at once denies intragroup distinction and intergroup diversity. The indexical here establishes, extends, and magnifies apartness; it reveals the user's predisposition to othering that underlies the variety of projects to separate out, to exclude.

To make some of this a little more concrete, consider the general case of academics who use their professional positions and the tools and status of their respective disciplines to perpetuate racist views. They use the channels of the academy and the more public institutions of their professional bodies—national newsletters, speakers' programs, op-ed pages, grants, and so on—to perpetuate long-discredited claims about intelligence levels of black people, of their capabilities and dispositions to crime, or to deny the occurrence of well-established events like the Holocaust.[51] It is perhaps not to be passed over silently that those committed to such brazenly anti-Semitic claims are readily dismissed within their professions in a way in which those committed to equally false claims about black persons tend not to be.

Antiracist resistance to those expressing either sort of view must assume various forms. First, antiracists within the academy, in general, and the discipline at issue, in particular, are bound to furnish vigorous counterarguments to the racist expressions, to challenge the questionable premises and empirical claims upon which the expressions rest, to indicate the politics of exclusionary implications that are almost invariably the issue. Letters to editors expressing racist claims, or articles laying out racist arguments or with racist implications, necessitate strong professional response, especially by prominent figures. Grant proposals with racist agendas ought to be rejected, and the reasons made public. Here, I take it that given my arguments about the social creation of racial groups (see chapter 4), any proposal that undertakes to examine whether members of one group are inferior or less capable in some racialized sense than members of another is motivated by exclusionary purposes and counts prima facie as racist. This raises a second mode of resistance. Failing a compelling overriding reason, professional fora—public lectures, colloquia invitations, panels, and seminars—should not be open for expressing such views. The right to free expression does not entail extending the right to be granted a forum to express whatever views one wants. Finally, and perhaps what will be most difficult because it requires substantial commitment and material resources, the professional body at issue should make every effort to remove professional conditions that enable or encourage the exclusionary views to thrive. In the context of the academy in the United States, this means that the discipline, where at all relevant and possible, must be prepared to open itself to taking seriously the sorts of disciplinary issues and concerns raised by those traditionally excluded as they incorporate into the profession. This clearly also implies that we take seriously preferential treatment programs.

Whatever side of the preferential treatment debate one may come down on, one is likely to accept the importance of equal opportunity as a political principle. Equal opportunity is appealed to by those claiming that preferential treatment policies are reverse discrimination, particularly against white males, as it is by those who claim such policies are currently necessary in the United States for reversing discrimination. It seems likely, though, that the antagonists have different readings of the principle. Steven Lukes usefully distinguishes between the equality of opportunity to achieve scarce social rewards, to widen the competition for them, on one hand, and equalizing opportunities to develop individual powers and talents, on the other.[52] Those opposed to preferential treatment programs tend to accept the former, narrower reading of equal opportunity, concerning themselves only with removing past institutional barriers to maximizing competition. This commitment has both ideological and economic underpinnings: Fairness is taken to consist in being rewarded on individual merit and in the absence of privileged preferences, while maximizing competition is supposed to drive down the costs of labor and advance excellence. By contrast, those supporting preferential treatment programs tend to presuppose that fairness will be achieved once we more or less equalize—or render equivalent—the availability of a whole range of material resources that would equally enable persons to maximize their potentials: from neo- and postnatal treatment to nutrition, education, and health care.

Racist exclusions have tended severely to restrict the opportunities of the excluded from developing their potentials fully. Accordingly, pragmatic antiracism would more likely be committed to the fuller conception of equal (or equivalent) opportunities. Indeed, given the widespread political commitment to the narrower conception among those considered white in the United States, one insurgent possibility available to antiracists is to take on the mantle of equal opportunity more vigorously. The undertaking would be to show holders of the narrower conception that their commitment necessarily entails far greater investment in the social resources, particularly educational resources, available to the poor and marginalized. The emerging concern about property tax funding of public schools is a case in point.[53]

In the ongoing absence of available opportunities, preferential treatment programs for college admissions or job hiring and promotion seem a modest means, one among many necessary not simply to integration but to advancing an incorporative politics. Such programs have served to draw those voices into academic and professional positions that have tended to be silenced by their exclusion, voices that have mostly proved resistant to mainstream appropriation. Perhaps this is why the programs have become so controversial in the United States. We should take care not to generalize any local experience, either to assume that the failure of a racial preference program elsewhere inevitably entails doubts about such programs locally[54] or to encourage the assumption of locally successful programs in those societies where conditions may be quite different. Suggestions have been made recently, for instance, concerning their adoption in South Africa. This seems inadequate for a number of reasons. First, the eventuality of a majority government in South Africa will naturally lead to appointment of its supporters in civil jobs, and appointments are likely to be overwhelmingly of black persons. Second, some positions are desperately needed—rural doctors, for example—and preferential policies will do nothing alone to meet the need. Third, emphasis on preferential treatment programs in the private or public sectors presupposes the status quo, namely, continued economic and political control by whites, and this hardly seems acceptable though continued white economic domination may yet be the outcome of current political negotiations. In general, my point is that the acceptability, if not the necessity, of preferential treatment programs will depend upon the sociohistorical conditions present in a society at a specific conjuncture.

Consider the current concerns about such programs in the United States. Preferential programs this past decade have come under increasing political and politically motivated jurisprudential attack. It is not my concern here to rehearse the historical debate, which is now generally well-known.[55] I wish only to respond to the prevailing criticisms that have recently emerged and to offer in conclusion an argument in support of preferential programs in terms of current conditions as one rather modest practical means, among others, for facilitating the emergence of incorporative politics.

One current argument against preferential treatment is that 'race' is being used to address the problems of race. Underlying this is the liberal presupposition that race is a morally irrelevant category, one that is necessarily arbitrary and irrational. Any appeal to or use of the category to end its use seems inconsistent: Continued use extends rather than ends categorical employment and so seemingly its discriminatory modes. Nevertheless, race is being employed in relation to preferential programs not to end the use of or appeals to race but to end racisms, namely, to eliminate racist exclusions. Race, accordingly, is used here as a marker for past and continuing exclusions in order to promote integration of professional and corporate work forces and incorporation in the academy and society. It is being used as a means, a small bridge, to more equal opportunity, both to rectify for past discriminatory inequalities affecting present beneficiaries and to facilitate more equal opportunities for future generations.[56]

Critical questions about preferential treatment programs are not misplaced. What we should find disturbing is how and why such questions are now being raised and criticisms advanced, as well as what sorts of criticisms are leveled. Affirmative action principles are not all so easily open to question. As I argued in chapter 5, for example, a principle of fairness seems straightforwardly to justify the insistence upon impartial rules and procedures in conducting interviews irrespective of a person's racial or gender identity. In attacking preferential treatment policies in the name of affirmative action without giving due care to the distinctions at issue, all of the advances in fair treatment that general affirmative action policies have helped to promote are similarly placed in question.

The more fashionable attack on affirmative action programs reflects the degree to which racist culture lingers. Beneficiaries of affirmative action policies like Stephen Carter are fully justified in their frustration, resentment, and ambivalence concerning the sorts of skepticisms about their abilities and the sorts of characterizations about 'minorities' in general that have increasingly tended to accompany preferential treatment benefits. Nevertheless, their criticisms of the policies seem to me tellingly misplaced. The proper objects of such criticism are not the policies that generally go under the name of preferential treatment. This is not to deny that there have been excesses, failures, and misapplications. Yet, every program suffers these, and we have heard little by comparison of educational drop outs from the GI Bill, or of the failures of white men who were accepted into college earlier this century only because their potential competitors were politically restricted, or about the white men who fail to advance from the remedial college programs at state institutions.[57] To attribute the innuendoes about inability, the barbs about lack of qualifications, and the stereotypes about 'minority' needs to the policies that promoted them is to misconstrue their causal determination. Continued racial belittlement is not built into the policies per se. Rather, they are largely the lingering prejudices of administrators who implement the policies and administer the students and employees whom the policies are supposed to affect. Indeed, the ambivalence of such administrators in implementing and defending the programs, the energy with which they guard the secrecy of administrative procedures, the linguistic insensitivities in addressing the concerns of the programs' beneficiaries ('minorities' is a case in point), and the insistent lumping of all black persons, women, and anyone else so admitted, hired, or promoted into the category of the preferentially treated attests to the pervasiveness of a lingering, or perhaps a reordered, racist and sexist culture.[58]

The basic shortcoming of preferential policies, then, is not that preferential treatment programs are divisive, as Dinesh D'Souza and Stephen Carter would have it.[59] They are only as divisive as powerful people want and direct them to be. The fundamental difficulty is deeper, more difficult to make out. In a social order that is deeply racialized, any policy that invokes race as a sign, a mark of, rather than as grounds for preferential treatment, even where justified, is likely *to be used* to exacerbate racial tensions and divides, to magnify whatever racially characterized tensions and ambivalences there are. I have stressed that race is an inherently political category. Public policies that are racially characterized, that have a racial component, will hardly escape the political push and pull. Where race bashing gets votes, in the name of fairness, watch out. The domestication of David Duke, the racializing of Patrick Buchanan's presidential campaigning, and President Bush's racial puppeteering provide more than enough evidence. If we are to replace affirmative action policies, it cannot be just with nonracial poverty- or need-based programs, though we may want to prioritize the available degree of preferential treatment in terms of need. It is undeniable that the major beneficiaries of racial preferences in the United States have been the sons and daughters of the black middle class. They were especially well-placed to take advantage of the programs offered. However, the plight of the racially marginalized has been simultaneously erased. The message: If you cannot get a boot up with discriminatory programs, there's nothing we can do for you. The weight of William Julius Wilson notwithstanding, universal poverty- or need-based programs have been historically ineffectual in getting to the needs of the racially marginalized. This simply underlines the call to go much further in implementing the effective grounds of equivalent opportunities for all.

How different might attitudes now be if for the last decade or so politicians and politically minded bureaucrats had spent as much breath stressing the importance and general fair-mindedness of preferential programs as they have scuttling them. Philosophers have plenty of good arguments available to support the general justifiability of preferential policies, though politicians seem to have been less than active in noticing them. This is perhaps partly the fault of philosophers who tend to bury their arguments in technical abstraction and perhaps shy away from political engagement.[60] Carter, I think, does get something basically right in insisting that the strongest argument supporting preferential treatment programs rests upon their making opportunities available for developing talents to those who for sociostructural reasons would otherwise find it far more difficult to do so. This rubs up against a needs-based qualification test, a factor that simply exacerbates the political nature of the issues at hand. It is in the spirit of providing a pragmatic argument along these lines for preferential policies under contemporary sociopolitical conditions in the United States that I offer the following general justification.

Assume that over his lifetime and in the absence of preferential treatment programs, the average white educated male may in principle be capable of competing for approximately seventy-five jobs. From these, the person may receive, say, three actual offers for jobs for which he in fact competes. A black person, equally qualified and without the benefit of preferential treatment programs and in the sort of racially charged world we have been used to, may effectively compete, say, for twenty-five positions and be lucky to land one. These ratios seem fair, given the recent findings in Washington, D.C., and Chicago that black jobseekers will find it three times as difficult to get job interviews and employment offers as a more or less identically qualified white person. With preferential treatment programs in place, it seems reasonable to assume, for the sake of argument, that the black candidate's competitive pool will be stretched by about half and the white candidate's reduced by about the same amount the black person's is increased. The black candidate will now have a crack at something like forty positions, the white candidate close to sixty. Both can expect something like two offers. The difference between the number of positions each can expect to compete for is reflective of the fact that there will be more competitors in the nonpreferential category, and so the greater number of competitive possibilities will more or less equalize the competitive chances of whites. The playing field has thus been relatively leveled, and the white candidate can hardly claim to be wronged. Of course, he no longer has the competitive edge white men might once have enjoyed, but this original wealth of possibilities turned on wrongful exclusion and the dearth of possibilities facing the black person. So past privilege can hardly claim justification.

This argument flies in the face of the basic liberal assumption that any invocation of race is irrelevant and arbitrary, that it therefore necessarily and problematically undermines application of the proper standards of merit and worth. These presuppositions imply that race-based preferences necessarily discriminate against whites; and if this 'compensatory racism' is to be permissible in some case, it requires special justification.[61] We should realize, nevertheless, that merit and worth, defined as they are by certain tests and qualifications, are the products of social choice, expressing 'structured preferences'.[62] They are thus imbued with contingent value paraded as given and natural, objective, universal, and above all necessary. They are necessary only to preserve privilege, veiling as they valorize the expression of exclusive power exerted in their name. The invocation of merit accordingly presupposes, though silently, that blacks—all blacks because they must be beneficiaries of preferential treatment to have gotten ahead—are inevitably unworthy, and they must be unworthy because inferior. By extension, any nonaffirmative action admission or appointment—most often white—is deemed meritorious no matter the grounds on which it was effected, and so no matter the exclusions it presupposes or perpetuates.[63] Merit and worth, in short, are silently racialized, and where convenient they are racially discounted.

Despite common contemporary rhetoric, proportional representation of racially defined representatives in educational and employment settings, in positions of privilege and power, is not an end in itself. Proportional representation serves only as a rough-and-ready marker, perhaps the best currently available, that those traditionally excluded on racialized grounds in the historical experience of the United States are in the process of incorporating themselves into the social fabric. This should not be taken as a guarantee of racisms' total elimination; it simply furnishes a rough indication that some of the more insidious forms of institutional exclusion, subjection, and undue burden are in the process of being delimited, if not fully redressed.[64] It is in this sense, and despite the self-serving and class-conscious cries of affirmative action babies and their political projection, that preferential policies remain one modest pragmatic means, among others, for achieving incorporative justice.

In giving theoretical voice to the radically antiessentialist fluidity of racialized expressions, I have undertaken to identify and interrogate the ambiguities of racialized identities and the effects of exclusionary practices and institutions, the flux and flows of racialized subjectivities and racist subjections, the disciplinary definitions and discriminations of and sustained by the discourse of race. Racisms are tied up in various ways with other discursive formations and social conditions, with economic, political, legal, and cultural terms. Racisms are exacerbated by the multiplier effects of these intersecting formations, expressions, and conditions, just as they intensify any wrongs effected by the latter. Racisms are like weeds. To weed them out will often require also getting at other invidious and exclusionary social expressions and entrenched conditions. The stance of antiracisms, then, encourage principled, pragmatic alliances between the objects of the various exclusionary conditions and experiences to resist the discursive practices underpinning their respective exclusions in the name of countertheoretical discourses. So pragmatic antiracists must be concerned to articulate views of persons and of the political, of selves and the social, that are not just nonexclusionary but antiexclusionary, not just integrative but incorporative, not merely neutral but committed.

Racists have been very effective in recognizing the commonality of their culture across social formations. The most persistent image from the notorious Howard Beach event in New York City is that of a white, bare-chested bystander heckling an antiracist street demonstration through the neighborhood shortly after the horrifying death of a young black man at the hands of a gang of local white youths. The heckler, screaming 'Niggers go home', held a placard high above his head. The placard read 'Keep South Africa White'.

Antiracism, accordingly, has in many senses to be an all-or-nothing commitment, a renewable undertaking to resist all racisms' expressions, to strike at their conditions of emergence and existence, to promote 'the internal decomposition of the community created by racism'.[65] It involves nothing short of assuming power: the power of the racialized, of the racially excluded and marginalized, to articulate for themselves and to represent for others who they are and what they want, where they come from, how they see themselves incorporated into the body politic, and how they see the social body reflecting them. Consequently, if freedom is to ring true for all, antiracism must be committed in the final analysis to dissolving in theories and in practice both the institutions of exclusionary power and the powers of exclusionary institutions. These commitments face the future rather than the past.

Notes

1 Introduction

1 J.-J. Rousseau (1978), p. 99.
2 Gellner (1983), p. 79; Koyre (1958).
3 Cf. Foucault (1977).
4 See the classic and stimulating analysis by Lovejoy (1960).
5 On 'race' as a chameleonic concept, see Wasserstrom (1978).
6 Cf. Bauman (1991), pp. 3–11.
7 Poole illuminates the related condition with which nationalism confronts modernity. Cf. Poole (1991), pp. 1–8, and esp. 90–109.
8 Cf. Gray (1986), esp. pp. ix–xi, 45–57.
9 Feinberg (1973), p. 103.
10 Rawls (1971), p. 19.
11 Mendus (1989), pp. 149–50.
12 Bauman (1991), p. 8.
13 The claim to finality is reflected in the title of an essay by Derrida (1985). Derrida characteristically plays upon the ambiguity of the word 'last', most notably, that between *apartheid* as the final expression of racism and as merely the latest one. At the time of his writing, Derrida seems mistaken about *apartheid* in both the senses at issue. It is possible to interpret Derrida's title more generously as a commitment to making what he takes to be the latest expression racism's last. For reasons that will be obviated as we proceed, this strikes me as a case of too little too late.
14 Cf. Wagner (1975); R. Williams (1983), pp. 87–93; Nelson, Treichler, and Grossberg (1992), pp. 4–5; Ryan (1989), p. 11.
15 Geertz (1984), pp. 47–76.
16 Bourdieu and Passeron (1977), p. 4.
17 Cf. Grillo (1989), pp. 160–61, 179.
18 On the distinction between subject and agent, see P. Smith (1988).
19 On map and territory as the appropriate methodological analogues for racism, see the thoughtful remarks in P. Cohen (1988), esp. pp. 54–63.

2 Modernity, Race, and Morality

1 Cf. MacIntyre (1981), ch. 6.
2 See Aristotle, *Nicomachean Ethics,* books II–IV. Various translations and commentaries are helpful: Ackrill's (1973); Irwin's (1985); Apostle's (1980). Cf. MacIntyre (1981); R. Putnam (1988); Goldberg, ed. (1989), pp. 15–17.
3 Cf. MacIntyre (1981), pp. 141–7.

4 Aquinas (1948); cf. Goldberg, ed. (1989), 17–19; MacIntyre (1981), pp. 154–68.

5 Gellner (1983), pp. 14–15.

6 As MacIntyre critically notes, Hume and Diderot have been taken, as they largely took themselves, to be moral radicals in the sense that they were deeply skeptical about furnishing purely rational grounds for the force of the moral. Nevertheless, they were as traditional as Kant in terms of their commitments to particular moral principles like fidelity in marriage or promise keeping. MacIntyre (1981), pp. 35–48.

7 J.-J. Rousseau (1968); J.-J. Rousseau (1978); Kant (1959); cf. Goldberg, ed. (1989), pp. 98–103.

8 In response to criticisms of this, J. S. Mill distinguished between qualities of pleasures, that is, between the higher or generally intellectual pleasures and the lower or physical ones. But in doing this Mill was obviously moving away from the strictly empirical basis Bentham had claimed for the theory. Also, it has been commonly pointed out that the principle of utility is ambiguous between requiring that total utility be maximized ('aggregate utilitarianism') and requiring that the number of people enjoying maximal equal utility be maximized ('average utilitarianism'). Bentham tended to endorse the former, Mill the latter. Rightness or wrongness of an expression is (to be) determined by the balance of immediate and distant pleasure or pain that will tend thus to be produced for all the agents, taken equally, who would be affected. Pleasures and pains are to be measured in terms of their intensity, the span of time they last, their certainty of occurrence, nearness or remoteness, and their tendency to promote further pleasure- or pain-promoting expressions. Cf. Bentham (1907); J. S. Mill (1863); J. S. Mill (1859). All of these works are reprinted in Warnock, ed. (1974). Cf. Goldberg, ed. (1989), pp. 131–4.

9 See J. S. Mill, *On Liberty,* in Warnock, ed. (1974), pp. 135–6.

10 Cf. Mackie (1978); Goldberg (1988), pp. 181–2; Lomasky (1987), pp. 10–12; Feinberg (1973), p. 252. There are fundamental differences in scope as well as significance between various important contemporary rights theorists. At one end, Nozick's Lockean notion of rights as nothing more than noncoercive and uncoerced claims or entitlements entails that any state larger than the minimal one will violate individual rights. At the other end, Dworkin's commitment to the fundamental right of each individual to equal treatment and Rawls's to the primary principle that each should have the equal right to the maximum liberty compatible with a like liberty for all imply much larger and more robust forms of state regulation and oversight. Cf. Nozick (1974); Dworkin (1976); Rawls (1971).

11 See Hohfeld (1919).

12 For an argument similar in form but couched more generally against the moral tradition of modernity, see MacIntyre (1981), p. 66.

13 That we may more usually speak of having rights indicates the logical closeness of rights and duties as well as the historical closeness of their emergence as concepts defining the moral space of modernity.

14 See, for example, the translation of Aristotle's *Politics,* line 1252a27 in Aristotle (1946); Marco Polo's *Travels* (written in Latin in the early fourteenth century) speaks in the English translation (1958, p. 258) of 'a race of men'; and Sir John Mandeville's *Travels* (written in Latin around 1346) refers in the English translation (1983, p. 137) to both 'races' and 'peoples'. Despite the title of his book, Sherwin-White (1970) more or less admits that the prevailing form of discrimination by Romans against

those who were not amounts not to 'racial prejudice' but to ethnocentrism. J. B. Friedman's characterization in the title of his book (1981) of the medieval *monstra* as races has been widely influential. Thus, Mason (1990) refers indiscriminately in terms of race to characterizations of monstrous beings as early as those of Hellenistic Greeks and as late as those in the eighteenth century of 'Europeans' and 'non-Europeans' (particularly American Indians) alike. Indeed, there is a sense in which the term 'race' carries Mason's undertaking to establish an overarching structural identity for all such characterizations, to establish synchronic rules of ethnocentric reference. In each of these cases, the conception of race emerging with modernity is inappropriately being read back by contemporary scholars via translation and imposed interpretation into premodern texts.

15 Cf. Hall (1989), p. ix.

16 Ibid., ch. 3.

17 Aristotle, *Politics*, lines 1255a3–1255b15. MacIntyre (1988) fails to acknowledge this point and, actually, mistakenly denies it. See p. 149.

18 J. B. Friedman calls the figures so cataloged 'Plinian *races*' but this again imposes 'race' retrospectively upon a form of thinking for which the concept was not yet available. Cf. J. B. Friedman (1981), esp. ch. 1. Friedman's account has been influential not only in its phenomenology of medieval monstrous representations but in the unquestioned contemporary acceptance that the figures so characterized were at the time *racially* conceived. See, for example, Mason (1990), pp. 18, 32.

19 J. B. Friedman (1981), pp. 9–15.

20 Cf. J. B. Friedman (1981), pp. 178–92.

21 For accounts of the genealogy of the Wild Man, see Mason (1990), pp. 45 ff.; Taussig (1987); and Dudley and Novak (1972).

22 See Netton (1989), esp. p. 24.

23 Hanke (1959), p. 8.

24 For a fuller characterization of the exchange between Sepulveda and Las Casas along the lines developed here, see Todorov (1984), pp. 146–67. The year 1550 also marks the date of the remarkable exhibition in Rouen for the king of France of conditions of existence and war in a Brazilian Indian settlement. Approximately fifty Brazilian Indians were brought to France for the event and were assisted by five times as many French sailors dressed as Indians. Mason (1990), p. 23.

25 It may also be pointed out that Las Casas initially supported 'Negro' slavery, indeed, he owned a few African slaves, while consistently opposing American Indian enslavement. In all fairness, he rejected 'Negro' slavery after 1544, and on the same grounds as American Indian slavery, but he hardly raised his voice against the former as he did so energetically against the latter. As one might expect, there was little opposition to 'Negro' slavery throughout the sixteenth century. See Hanke (1959), p. 9.

26 Wolf (1981), pp. 380–1.

27 Locke (1960), I, #1, II, #22–24. See also the editor's footnote to II, #24, Gay (1969), II, pp. 409–10, and Higginbotham (1978), pp. 163–4. The percentage of people of African descent in the population of the Carolinas was greater than in any other of the North American colonies at the time.

28 Locke (1960), I, #58, II, #172. Locke's indictment of slavery in the *First Treatise* covers only natural slavery. Underlying his justification of enslavement as a result of

war lies Locke's labor theory of value, a forerunner of both Adam Smith's and Marx's, which distinguishes between those who improve what they mix their labor with, who are thereby rational, and those ('savages' in the 'state of nature') who simply collect, who thereby merely survive. Cf. Hulme (1990), pp. 29–30.

29 Locke (1964), III, vi, #6, IV, vii, #16.
30 Dabydeen (1985), pp. 30–2.
31 Chomsky (1977), pp. 92–3; Bracken (1978), p. 250.
32 Leibniz (1981), I, ii, #17; see also I, i, #76, 84.
33 Cf. Gay (1969), p. 8; G. S. Rousseau and Porter, eds. (1989), pp. 1–2.
34 Balibar and Wallerstein (1991) subtitle their book on race, nation, and class *Ambiguous Identities*. Of course, where these identities are assumed—consciously taken on—as modes of resistant self-identification, it may be for the sake of countering marginality, exploitation, or domination.
35 Cf. Mosse (1979), pp. 10–11, 21–2; West (1982), pp. 53–4, 58–9.
36 Locke (1960), *Second Treatise,* #25–51.
37 Mosse and others have documented in detail this aesthetic tendency by Enlightenment theorists of race such as Buffon, Camper, and Lavater and the influence upon their work by art historian J. J. Winckelmann. Cf. Mosse (1979), pp. 1–29; West (1982), pp. 53–9; Gossett (1965), pp. 32–9; Jordan (1969), 3–95.
38 For a fuller analysis of this tendency, see Dabydeen (1985), pp. 17–40, and esp. pp. 32–3.
39 Hume (1964), pp. 244–58.
40 See section IV, 'Of National Characteristics' of Kant (1960), pp. 97–116.
41 Kant (1950), p. 18.
42 In 1794 William Robertson listed Indians with most Europeans as 'commercial peoples'. See Marshal (1989), pp. 54–5.
43 J.-J. Rousseau's view, by contrast, is notable for the absence of a catalog of national characters and pernicious characterization of racial others. Indeed, Rousseau's 'noble savage' and 'primitive man' are positively portrayed as having desirable, uncorrupted characteristics. But these concepts are exemplified for Rousseau by American and African indigenes, and they form part of the Enlightenment discourse of exoticism. The precivilized and primitive lack reason and autonomy, and so they cannot be party to the general will and civil society.
44 Kant (1960), p. 111.
45 Ibid., p. 113. My emphasis. Some may object that this is an early, pre-Critical and so immature work, and that this sort of reasoning does not appear in the Critical and especially moral writings with which it is inconsistent. It need only be pointed out in response that similar sentiments are expressed by Kant in his essay on race in 1775 and repeated again in his philosophical anthropology of 1791. The latter are hardly products of an immature mind.
46 See, for example, Higginbotham (1978), pp. 377 ff.; Gates (1990), pp. 320–3; Dabydeen (1985), pp. 46–7.
47 Brock (1982), p. 227.
48 Voltaire, *Traite de Metaphysique* (1734), and *Essai sur les Moeurs L'Esprit des Nations* (1754), both quoted in Poliakov (1974), p. 176.
49 Bentham (1907), pp. 310–11, n. 1; and 62–3.
50 W. Williams (1982), pp. 86–7; cf. MacIntyre (1974), pp. 237–8.

51 J. S. Mill (1848), p. 233; cf. A. Ryan (1984), p. 190.

52 J. Mill (1820), vol. 2, pp. 135, 166–7; cf. Stokes (1959), pp. 48, 53–4.

53 Stokes (1959), pp. 48, 298–9.

54 Taylor (1989), p. 83.

55 Quoted in Stember (1976), p. 38.

56 The degree to which racial others were perceived inhuman rendered them outside the scope both of the Bill of Rights (the first ten Amendments to the U.S. Constitution ratified by the end of 1791) and the Declaration of the Rights of Man in France (1789). The U.S. Constitution made the principle of exclusion explicit: A slave was declared to be but three-fifths a person. While some constitutional commentators are quick to point out that this clause was explicitly (and so only) for the sake of taxation and representation, this reading rubs up against the opening constitutional claim that declares all human beings to be born equal. Reading the three-fifths clause as presupposing a principle of *de*humanization renders it consistent with claims of inherent human equality.

57 Mackie (1977), p. 174; cf. MacIntyre (1981), p. 65.

58 MacIntyre (1981), p. 68.

59 Cf. Taylor (1989), p. 413.

60 P. J. Williams (1987), p. 424.

61 Ibid., p. 417.

62 MacIntyre (1981), p. 68.

63 I have chosen to use the term 'postmodern' for two related reasons: First, I wish to reflect the broad contrast with the moral discourse of modernity; and second, I want to contrast the distinctions between premodernity, modernity, and postmodernity which concern me here with the much narrower one between modernism and postmodernism, which does not—at least not directly or explicitly. By postmodernity I mean the period that begins to emerge roughly in the mid-1970s with the shift from the Fordist mode of accumulation to what Harvey (1989) characterizes as 'flexible accumulation' together with deeply related transformations in political economy, culture, and sociodiscursive orders. Bauman characterizes postmodernity definitively in terms of incoherence and as the privatizing of political and moral choice in the face of the splintering, the radical multiplicity, of possibilities. For extended analyses, see Harvey (1989) and Bauman (1992), esp. pp. xvii–xxiv and 40–2. For an analysis of what he characterizes as 'the age of high modernity', see Giddens (1991). For an account, by contrast, of social theory in the light of postmodernism, see Woodiwiss (1990).

64 MacIntyre (1981), pp. 173–4. There runs through MacIntyre's account a strong nostalgia for a simpler order, one that is reflected in his Christianizing of Aristotle's virtues and his explicit embracing in a later work of 'Augustinian Christianity'. MacIntyre (1988).

65 MacIntyre (1981), p. 175.

66 Grillo (1989), p. 6.

67 Taylor (1989), pp. 76–7; B. Williams (1985), pp. 116–7; Foucault (1988), pp. 146, 150–1.

68 Geertz (1973).

3 Racialized Discourse

1 Gilroy (1990), pp. 264–5. My emphasis.
2 See Goldberg (1990a), esp. pp. 296–8.
3 B. Anderson (1983), esp. ch. 2; Gellner (1983), esp. chs. 2 and 3.
4 For the best representative of this position, see Hegel (1952), pp. 241–7. Hegel's text was originally published in 1821.
5 Cf. Aronowitz (1981), pp. 89–100. For a good example of this in the 1880s, consider the moral panics that led to the reading of the figure of Jack the Ripper in London's East End as an East European Jewish proletarian. See Gilman (1990), pp. 146–70.
6 Plato (1972), 59b–69d ; Plato (1975), 2120a–2212a.
7 This is a fact to which Smith's 'invisible hand of reason' bears witness. See A. Smith (1978), p. 158. *The Wealth of Nations* was first published in 1776. It should be pointed out that Smith does not use the concept of 'equilibrium', a later invention, but rather that of 'natural price'.
8 Hauser (1952), p. 82; Marshall (1890), pp. 323–50.
9 Rorty (1980), pp. 129–312; cf. West (1982), p. 53. I am aware that this bald Rortyan characterization fails to capture some of the complexities of modernist epistemology, but these are beyond my concern here. Cf. MacKeen (1991).
10 B. Anderson (1983), p. 40.
11 Fields (1990), p. 106. My emphasis: one would think that material determination requires actual oppression, not simply the perception of it.
12 Fields (1990), pp. 109–110.
13 Said (1978), pp. 21–2.
14 The former is taken from Baldwin (1853), p. 300. For the latter representation in antebellum Southern literature, see A. Rose (1976), pp. 46 ff. In general, cf. West (1982), esp. pp. 49–53.
15 See Chamberlain (1968), pp. 542 ff. Alfred Rosenberg, Hitler's court philosopher, made much of this notion. Rosenberg (1970), pp. 35 ff. For the depiction of Sambo in historical sources, see Boskin (1986).
16 '[Jewish elders] have the tenacity of a snake, the cunning of a fox, the look of a falcon, the memory of a dog, the diligence of an ant and the sociability of a beaver.' Hermann Goedsche (under the pen name of Sir John Radcliffe) in his novel *Biarritz*, 1868. Quoted in Mosse (1979), p. 117.
17 For a comprehensive collection of analyses, see Gates, ed., (1986); Gilman (1984); Todorov (1984). See also Stepan (1990), pp. 38–57.
18 Cf. Foucault (1972), p. 33.
19 An entry in Himmler's diary associates Jews with Reds. Examples abound in which Jews are identified as 'Red'. Mosse (1979), p. 178.
20 Cf. Foucault (1972), pp. 32–6.
21 Foucault (1972), p. 60.
22 Lovejoy (1960), pp. 7 ff. If introduction of words into the language is any guide, 'classification' appears only in the eighteenth century. Febvre (1975), p. 111.

23 'Every note should be a product of number, of form, of proportion, of situation.' Carolus Linnaeus, *Philosophie Botanique,* #299, quoted in Foucault (1970), p. 134. Foucault calls this ordered observation 'seeing systematically'.

24 P. Caws (1968), p. 106.

25 Lovejoy (1960), p. 8.

26 The assumptions and reasoning are uniform, whether those of Kant's hardheaded rationalism or of Buffon's and Lamarck's environmentalism. Though author of the principle that 'all men are (created) equal', Jefferson believed that nature condemned the 'Negro' to inferiority on the scale of being: 'Blacks, whether originally a distinct race or made distinct by time and circumstance, are inferior to the whites in the endowment both of body and mind.' Jefferson (1954), p. 143. These premises run clear through Darwinism, eugenicism, and the IQ movement. Cf. Gould (1981).

27 Lovejoy (1960), p. 317.

28 Ibid., p. 320.

29 Cf. Dumont (1970), pp. 66–7.

30 'The planters do not want to be told that their Negroes are human creatures ... they ... [are] no better than dogs or horses.' Long, (1972), II, pp. 270–1. Long appealed to his contemporary, David Hume, for justification of his racist views: 'Mr. Hume presumes, from his observations of native Africans, to conclude, that these are inferior to the rest of the species, and utterly incapable of all the higher attainments of the human mind.' Long (1972), p. 376. Cf. Hume (1964), esp. p. 252 n. 1.

31 Cf. Eckberg (1979), foreword by J. Garcia, pp. vii–viii.

32 This latter reasoning is quite widespread in popular thinking. It is implicit, philosophically, in Michael Levin's claim that the use of the term *racist,* like *sexist,* is scientifically and morally illegitimate. Levin, (1981b), p. 40 n. 12. Cf. Gilroy (1987), pp. 60 ff. and Gilroy (1990), pp. 263–82.

33 Foucault (1970), pp. 138 ff. Cf. Eagleton (1982), pp. 66–7.

34 'Belonging together' is Heidegger's term. Heidegger (1969), pp. 25–6. Identification may be motivated by a variety of factors: economic, political, legal, cultural, linguistic, historical, psychological, or psychoanalytic. It may be more or less rational.

35 Foucault (1980b), p. 131.

36 Foucault (1980a), pp. 57–8. Cf. Said (1980), p. 120; and Said (1978), pp. 19–20.

37 Cf. W. Reich (1970), pp. 46–7. Cf. Erikson (1965) pp. 227–53; Althusser (1971a), pp. 170–1. Where authority assumed institutional form, it may have been as abstract as *'the nation'.* See Gilroy (1990), pp. 262–83; and Balibar (1990), pp. 283–94.

38 Foucault (1977), pp. 135–69. The coherence drawn by racism from the general discourse of the body may be gleaned from the fact that racist metaphors often turn around corporeal references. This may function directly or indirectly. For the former, consider Hume's likening of 'negroes' to parrots, or then U.S. Secretary of the Interior James Watt's equations, in a speech on September 27, 1983, of Jews and blacks with 'cripples'. For the latter, consider the common attribution of the symbolism of dirt to blacks and Arabs. Cf. Kristeva (1990), pp. 171–82.

39 Foucault (1977), p. 138.

40 I have been influenced in this symbolic construction of the body by two provocative analyses: Douglas (1966), p. 115; and Nedelsky (1990), pp. 162–189.

41 Douglas (1966), pp. 125, 2–4, 103–4, 162. Cf. Dumont (1970), pp. 47–8, 60. Some eugenicists bemoan the biological vices of racial miscegenation and hybridization between 'inharmonious stocks'. See Stepan (1982), p. 130.

42 See Goldberg (1992).

43 Karl Pearson, a leading eugenicist in Britain, suggested that only those immigrants be admitted who displayed physical and mental abilities 25 percent higher than the native British mean. Pearson (1925), pp. 1–127. Cf. Mudge (1920), pp. 202–12. See Stepan (1982), p. 130.

44 This bill was advocated by Albert Johnson, Republican chair of the House Committee on Immigration. In 1923, Johnson was elected president of the Eugenics Research Association. Eugenic presuppositions had wide influence. In 1922, U.S. vice president Coolidge claimed in a popular essay that biological laws reveal the deterioration of Nordics when mixed with other races. Gossett (1965), p. 466.

45 For a discussion of recent immigration policy of both Tory and Labour parties in Britain, see M. Barker (1981), pp. 12–29; cf. Gilroy (1987); Solomos (1989), pp. 40–67; and Miles and Phizacklea (1984). On Europe, see Sivanandan , ed. (1991); Balibar (1991); and Baubock (1992). On the United States, see Karst (1989).

46 These presumptions militate against insistence upon moral responsibility of racists. See chapter 6.

47 Benveniste (1971); cf. Althusser (1971), pp. 179 ff. Cf. W. Reich (1970), pp. 46–7; Erikson (1965), pp. 227–53.

48 I do not mean to imply that the individual, theoretically or historically prior to this discursive intersection, is just a blank tablet, an empty receptacle. One may have an immediate intuition of one's individuality, which nevertheless may be actualized and expressed only in and by means of language. Nor need this commit us to untenable forms of relativism. Some physical states and psychological dispositions (e.g., emotions) may be innate though incapable of recognizable expression in a discursive vacuum. Expressions (including acts) are mediated largely by the discourses definitive of the agent's subjectivity. Cf. Hegel (1967), pp. 529 ff.; Lemaire (1977), p. 53.

49 The 'practico-inert' is the 'material product of past *praxis*'. Sartre (1976), pp. 318–20.

50 Cf. Lacan (1977), pp. 1–7; Althusser (1971), p. 181; Hirst (1979), pp. 64 ff.; Shapiro (1981), p. 130.

51 Kant's deep insight reads thus: 'Without sensibility no object would be given to us, without understanding no object would be thought. Thoughts without content are empty, intuitions without content are blind.' Kant (1965), p. 93.

52 For the distinction between conscious and unconscious factors in the determination of the text, see P. Caws (1974), pp. 274 ff.

53 For remarks on fear, see Therborn (1980), pp. 94 ff. For an account of conformism in Heidegger's work, see Haugeland (1982), pp. 15–25.

54 Cf. Fanon's 'fact of blackness' in Fanon (1970a), esp. pp. 98–9.

55 Sartre (1976), p. 720. On the violence of racializing reduction, see Mason (1990), p. 25.

56 Cf. Hegel (1967), pp. 229–40.

57 For Fanon's suggestive remarks on racial self-hatred, see Fanon (1970a), pp. 82–3. On Jewish self-hatred, see Gilman (1986).

4 The Masks of Race

1 Director of the Performing Arts Council of the Orange Free State, one of the four provinces of South Africa, July 1991.

2 For a somewhat different conception of the reproducibility of a racist social formation, see Brown (1986a), pp. 394–5. On the notion of 'transformation', see S. Hall (1988), pp. 35–58; and on the notion of 'articulation', see S. Hall (1980), pp. 305–46.

3 On the relation between 'Eye' and 'I' in the articulation of the colonial project, see Pratt (1985), pp. 119–143.

4 *Oxford English Dictionary.*

5 Contra Guillaumin (1980), pp. 37–68. The view expressed by Guillaumin is nevertheless widespread. Mason makes a similar point to mine, though in a slightly different context. P. Mason (1990), pp. 23–4, 35.

6 The Shakesperian quote is from *The Tempest* I, ii, 358–60. I am grateful to Peter Fitzpatrick for the initial reference. Half a century earlier, Captain John Lok wrote of 'Moores ... or Negroes, a people of beastly living, without a God, lawe, religion, or commonwealth.' 'The second voyage to Guinea..., in the year 1554.' Quoted in Hakluyt (1962), vol. 4, p. 57.

7 Banton (1988), pp. ix, 11.

8 'They are so scorched and vexed with the heat of the sunne' wrote John Lok in 1554. Quoted in Hakluyt (1962), vol. 5, p. 57. And an Italian explorer to India declared: 'His complexion is of a brown weasel color inclining to blacke, as are most of the native Indians, being scorched by the heat of the sun.' Quoted in Cole (1972), p. 65. See also Hay (1957). Descartes and Hobbes furnished the philosophical expression underlying this view: The Cartesian 'universal subject' was reflected in the Hobbesian identification of the natural state of 'man'—of European 'man'— with 'the savage people in many places of *America*'. Hobbes (1651), #63, p. 187. Cf. Hulme (1990), pp. 20, 24–5, 33.

9 Cf. Popkin (1978), pp. 208, 214–5; Poliakov (1974), p. 132.

10 Banton (1988), pp. 38–42.

11 Gliddon and Nott (1988), p. 41.

12 'The Niger Expedition' by Charles Dickens as quoted in Brantlinger (1985), p. 174.

13 See especially Gould (1981).

14 Cf. Banton (1988), pp. xi–xii, 167–9.

15 John Baker defines a species as a group whose members *do* interbreed only with their own kind, but this is obviously too strong, perhaps for ideological reasons. Shifting the criterion to *capability* decreases the number of different species. Whether it increases the number of subspecies depends on whether the species properly speaking has any. As will become clear, this is a point of contention in the case of Homo sapiens. Cf. J. Baker (1974), p. 4.

16 J. Baker (1974), p. 66.

17 Abercrombie et al., eds. (1978), pp. 268, 276.

18 '[T]wo groups..., so different as to be incapable of fusion by generation, do not belong to the same species. This is an incontestable and uncontested truth.' Broca (1950), p. 70.

19 Banton (1988), pp. 65–71, 167–9.
20 Appiah (1986), pp. 21–2, 31.
21 On the notion of 'common sense', see S. Hall (1988), p. 44.
22 Gobineau (1967), p. 193. On race and blood type, see Reed (1969), pp. 762–8; Boyd (1963), pp. 1057–64.
23 For an early warning in this respect, see Fleure (1950), pp. 546–8.
24 Sometimes explanations will conflate the social and biological, for example, in reducing racial phenomena to psychosexual drives. See Stember (1976).
25 Cf. R. Williams (1983), pp. 299–301; and Lal (1986), p. 286.
26 R. Williams (1983), p. 61.
27 Cf. Sollors (1990), p. 289. I am grateful to Anthony Appiah for calling my attention to this article.
28 Müller (1895), p. 45. Though published at the end of the century, the work of Müller (1823–1900), an Oxford philologist, was already well known earlier in the century.
29 O. Smith (1984), p. 3; cf. Grillo (1989), p. 175. Interestingly enough, Ernest Renan explicitly denied this capacity of language to unite people in a common social body, whether race or nation. Cf. Renan (1990), pp. 16–17.
30 See, for example, Miles (1989), p. 70–71; 74–6.
31 See Appiah (1990a), pp. 276–7, 280.
32 In this sense, Hersch's analysis for instance is simply outdated. Hersch (1967), pp. 116.
33 See Appiah (1990b), pp. 3–17.
34 Actually, I doubt I share much of anything nonbiologically with the names cited here.
35 Appiah (1986), esp. p. 27.
36 See Barker (1981).
37 S. Hall (1990), pp. 222–237. On defining Jewishness, see Goldberg and Krausz, eds. (1993).
38 Appiah (1989), p. 48.
39 Van den Berghe (1967), p. 9; Brown (1986b): 177–8; Cf. Eipper (1983), pp. 428, 440. Appiah, interestingly, has made a similar point in claiming that 'biological "inheritance" is a metaphor from social relations and not the other way about.' Appiah (1986), p. 21.
40 Sollors (1986).
41 Ibid., pp. 38–9.
42 See, for example, the popular writings of Masami Uno. Wetherall (1987): 52–4. Uno is well-known for translating books denying the occurrence of the Holocaust. There is an expanding market for popular anti-Semitic literature in Japan. On the politics of the designation 'Hispanic' in the context of race, see Haynes-Bautista (1980), pp. 353–6.
43 Barth (1969), p. 15; Sollors (1986), pp. 27–8.
44 Cf. Sollors 1986, pp. 165 ff., 236.
45 Cf. Jenkins (1986), p. 178.
46 De Lepervanche pushes this intersection between race and ethnicity still further by suggesting that ethnicity, like race, may now be about proletarianizing labor. This may be overstated, on both sides of the race/ethnicity correlation, but it is possible that ethnicity, like race, has at times and in part served this function. De Lepervanche (1980), p. 34.

47 Margalit (1991), p. 23. Margalit reveals that in referring to Sephardic Jews, 'Asiatic' signifies dirt, lack of culture and hygiene, and public loudness.

48 Contra Appiah (1990a), pp. 275–6.

49 Omi and Winant (1987), pp. 14–24; cf. Jenkins (1986), pp. 176–7.

50 Cf. R. Williams (1983), pp. 213–6.

51 '[T]he unassimilable phenomena linked to nationalism and its many derivatives (racism, anti-Semitism, etc).' Nairn (1980), p. 337.

52 B. Anderson (1983), pp. 135–6. The more extreme version of this misconception is to equate race and nation conceptually and, by extension, nationalism with racism: 'Thinking in terms of race is racism. Thinking in terms of nation is nationalism, and also a form of racism.... [D]efensive nationalism, ... as nationalism, is already a form of racism.' Weinroth (1979), pp. 67–86.

53 Bauman (1989), p. 52; Balibar (1990), pp. 283–94. My formulation may be thought straightforwardly to contradict Ernest Renan's classic conceptualization of the nation (1882). The principles at issue are more complex than this conclusion would suggest. Renan flatly denies that contemporary nations in any way map isomorphically onto races. In this, Renan was clearly at odds with prevailing opinion in his day. Yet, he wasn't that far removed from nineteenth century thought, for he accepted—indeed, insisted on—the ontological reality of both nations and races. I am not arguing that these entities have ontological standing, but rather that race and nation may and sometimes do intersect conceptually, that is, in the ideological and political usage by social subjects of these terms and the values they represent. Cf. Renan (1990), esp. pp. 13–16.

54 Banton (1988), pp. xi, 63.

55 Cf. S. Hall (1988), p. 44.

56 Cf. Guillaumin (1980), pp. 38, 51. In Guillaumin's view, however, racial determinism is always somatic. What alters historically are the claims concerning where, somatically speaking, the determining cause is located: blood, brain, or genes. This way of putting it fails to acknowledge that the conception of race itself alters over time and so subtly alters social subjects' sense of self and other, even though the abstract processes of racial constitution generally have a similar social dynamic.

57 Cf. B. Anderson (1983), ch. 8, 'Patriotism and Racism'.

58 For the distinction between illocutionary, perlocutionary, and locutionary acts in linguistic theory, see Austin (1962).

59 Cf. S. J. Smith (1989), p. 5.

60 Contra Miles (1989), p. 61. Miles no doubt would deem this conceivable identity of racism with sexism a case of conceptual inflation, stretching the concept of *racism* to the point of vacuity. However, the historical analogizing of women and blacks suggests otherwise. Miles tries to make the same point concerning Jews and the Irish, namely, that to deem their exclusion racist is conceptual inflation. As I have argued above, he is just historically mistaken here. Earlier and elsewhere, Miles acknowledges that the Irish have been characterized as a race. One would think that exclusion in terms of this characterization would accordingly count as a case of racism. Miles (1989), p. 58 and Miles (1988), p. 246. Cf. Stepan (1990), pp. 38–57 and Gilman (1990), pp. 146–170; on Irish racism, McVeigh (1992). Indeed, the intersection, the conflation of race and gender, is as old as racialized discourse itself. The christening of 'America' as such literally involves the femininizing by Amerigo

Vespucci of his 'Christian' name, so that the continent is engendered at the very
inception of its racialized construction. Europe and Asia, whose identities likewise
figure large in racializing representation, similarly acquire their designations from
the names of women. Mason (1990), pp. 27, 37 n. 26.

61 Eipper (1983), p. 442.
62 Balibar (1991c), p. 39. Balibar's emphasis.
63 The concept *to be racialized* can be traced to Fanon (1970a), p. 86. Fanon contrasts
    this with *to be humanized*. Following Taguieff, Balibar uses the even more awkward
    'racization'. Balibar (1991b), pp. 20, 27, n. 5.
64 Race, in this view, is an 'unstable and *decentred* complex of social meanings
    constantly being transformed by political struggle'. Omi and Winant (1987), pp. 68,
    64, 66–7; Winant (1990); cf. Miles (1989).
65 This is an extension of the point made by Prager (1987a) concerning the United States.
66 Michael Levin advances the latter argument. I want to suggest that he has been able
    to impute credibility to this position, at least to the degree he has, in large part because
    the prevailing condemnation of racism in moral philosophizing in the past twenty
    years has been in terms of arbitrariness. This has created, by omission rather than by
    commission, a general disposition to evade the more distressing features of racialized
    social structure. Weinroth, for example, is simply representing the standard view when
    he writes that ' "Nation" and "race" are arbitrary ... ludicrously pseudoscientific, and
    thus lead to oppression and crimes against humanity.' Weinroth (1979), pp. 84, 76.
    Levin (1981a), pp. 225–34. Cf. the ambiguous account of Kant offered by D. Lloyd
    (1991).
67 Guillaumin (1980), p. 39.
68 For example, cf. Baker (1974), p. 65.
69 We might call this racial imputation from phenotypical variation the 'ontological
    fallacy of phenotypes'. Those who in various ways commit the fallacy include Baker
    (1974), pp. 421 ff., 99–117; Coon (1982), p. 144; and M. G. Smith (1986), pp. 189–93.
70 Van den Berghe (1981), pp. 27, 29–30, 35.
71 Van den Berghe (1986), p. 256.
72 'Human culture is necessarily "carried" by biological organisms *who* (sic!)
    reproduce.' Van den Berghe (1986), p. 255. If it needs acknowledging, the emphasis
    here is mine. For an elaboration of the distinction between genetic being and person,
    see Warren (1973).
73 Van den Berghe (1986), pp. 255–6, 258.
74 This is only a disposition and, as such, a necessary truth simply of reproductive
    features of human beings. I am not thus committed to the metaphysical claim and its
    attendant moralizing, as sociobiologists tend to be, that the reproductive drive is a
    necessary feature of human nature, physically unavoidable and morally imperative.
75 Cf. D. Mason (1986), pp. 6–8.
76 Smith, for example, lists 'Negroes, Asiatic Mongols, Whites (including Arabs,
    Australian Aborigines, Amerindians, Pygmies, and Bushmen' and some pages later
    a set of only five races, namely, 'Blacks, Whites, Indians, Pygmies, and hybrids'. M.
    G. Smith (1986), pp. 189, 192.
77 Houston Baker's more rhetorical outbursts notwithstanding, I take it that he has
    something like 'civilization' in mind in speaking of 'black', 'white',
    'Afro-American', 'racial poetry', and, metaphorically, of 'Caliban' and 'Prospero'.

These are racial references culturally conceived. Indeed, if I am right, then Baker's racialized rhetorical outbursts are testament to my latter point. H. A. Baker, Jr. (1986), pp. 182–96; Appiah (1989), p. 48; Montagu (1974), pp. 24 ff.; R. Miles (1989), pp. 69–73. Also, 'civilization' has often been used in an exclusionary way.

78 Omi and Winant (1987), p. 68.

79 Cf. Guillaumin (1980), pp. 47–8.

80 The old rule was replaced in Louisiana only in 1983. This example offers a clear instance of state implication in racial definition. The rule was altered as a result of litigation brought by Susan Guillory Phipps to alter her birth certificate designation from 'Negro' to 'white'. Acknowledging the change in the Louisiana law to self-definition, the lower court in Louisiana nevertheless denied Phipps's application on grounds that history cannot be altered. Both the Louisiana and U.S. supreme courts refused to hear the case, the former concurring with the lower court and the latter on grounds that 'a substantial federal question' was lacking. On the management of racial identity and the recent politics of this legal principle in Louisiana, see *Doe v. State of Louisiana,* CA 1120 (1985); Davis (1989), pp. 9–11; Diamond and Cottrol (1983), pp. 255–85; and Trillin (1986), pp. 62–78.

81 'The Negro is an animal ... the little boy throws himself into his mother's arms: Mama, the nigger's going to eat me up.' To which Fanon responds, 'I had incisors to test. I was sure they were strong.' Fanon (1970a), pp. 80–1.

82 As I argue in the following chapter, this is a necessary implication of the definition Omi and Winant offer for 'racism'.

83 Lucius Outlaw offers an affirmative response to this question by investing positive value in the racial category 'black'. This way of proceeding strikes me as assuming the very issue I've placed in question here. Outlaw (1988) and Outlaw (1990), pp. 58–82. For an illuminating analysis of oppression of Jews in the Holocaust and of blacks under slavery in the United States, see Thomas (1993).

5   Racist Exclusions

1 Cf. West (1990), p. 28.

2 Gramsci (1952), p. 185. See N. Cheboksarov (1980), p. 363.

3 Bauman (1989), p. 33.

4 Witness John Rex on assuming directorship of Britain's Home Office Research Unit in 1979:

> While the Home Office is interested in policy-oriented research, it is ... far from being the principal executant or initiator of such research. The largest single body of recent published academic research on ethnic relations which bears on issues of social policy is that undertaken by the SSRC ethnic relations unit, the directorship of which has just passed from ... Michael Banton ... to ... John Rex.

Rex goes on to declare that research in the unit under his directorship 'will also form an essential and complementary background to the work carried on for more immediate policy and political purposes by the Home Office'. (Home Office Research

Bulletin No. 8, 1979). See Gilroy (1980), pp. 58–9. On defining 'race relations situations', see Rex (1986), pp. 71–2. For one example among many of racism as 'infection', see Rex and Tomlinson (1979), p. 294.

5 Banton (1986), p. 50.

6 Ibid., p. 56. It is curious to note how readily Banton himself has engaged in a wider sort of historical and conceptual analysis over the years, his skepticism notwithstanding. Cf. Banton (1988).

7 Miles (1989), pp. 77–84.

8 For the general definition, see for example Banton (1970), p. 18; Barrett (1987), p. 5; Dominguez (1977), pp. 262–3. On the point of biological insistence, see Miles (1989), p. 76; Barker (1981), p. 4; S. J. Smith (1989), p. 5; and Appiah's definition of 'racialism' spelled out in Appiah (1990b), pp. 4–5. For two examples among many, on the point of superiority and inferiority, see Richter (1986), pp. 785–94; and Essed (1990), p. 11. On the point of ideological insistence, see Miles and Phizacklea (1982), p. 78; Miles (1989), pp. 42–50, 87; and Barrett (1987), p. 5. On the claim to the necessity of domination, see Miles (1989), p. 66; Hodge (1975), pp. 10–11; Carmichael and Hamilton (1967), p. 3; Dominguez (1977), p. 262; and Weinroth (1979), p. 68. This disjunction between an ideology of racial inferiority and discriminatory practices for the sake of domination is sometimes signified by the use of different terms. So some analysts may distinguish between racism and racialism (sometimes the former is made to signify the theory, at other times it refers to the practice), or between racialist beliefs or prejudices and racist or discriminatory practices.

9 Clark's claim is quoted in Fikes (1988), p. 142. Clark may seem to suppose that the value of American life is greater than that of Chinese life, and so superior. However, the grounds of his claim lie explicitly in the appeal to preferential difference. Page is quoted in Barker (1981), p. 20.

10 Reeves (1983), pp. 12–13. It should be noted that if Reeves's categories are assumed, 'strong racism' seems possible without the evaluative ordering into superior and inferior races. It may be recommended that members of some races deserve privileges others are denied simply because of a pertinent difference, say, in historical or cultural experience. Reeves fails to acknowledge this.

11 Bauman (1989), pp. 65–6. This is a point Richards insists on more generally in defining 'discrimination' as 'a rule that treats two groups differently as an end in itself'. Richards (1985), pp. 53–82.

12 Omi and Winant (1987), p. 145, and again on p. 172.

13 Disjuncts are intended inclusively here, as elsewhere.

14 Harry Lesser helpfully develops this point at some length. Lesser (1984), pp. 253–61. Unfortunately, given the insightfulness of his theoretical analysis, the account of the tenure example at the end of his paper is less than convincing. Michael Philips contrasts two theories for attributing racism: the standard 'agent-centered' and the 'act-centered' theories, respectively. The former attributes racism in terms only of the presence of appropriate beliefs, feelings, and intentions of agents. By contrast, Philips defends the latter, which judges acts racist in terms of 'the meaning of the act for the victims', that is, in terms of (racialized) objects' judgments of their 'mistreatment'. Nevertheless, it does seem that an act may turn out racist no matter the object's consideration, which after all may be mistaken. This suggests that a more

comprehensive account needs to be offered than either the 'agent-' or 'act-centered' theories alone can offer. Philips (1984), pp. 78–9.

15 Baier (1978), p. 129.

16 Ibid. Even if not racist, the officers may be guilty of (extra-economic) class discrimination. Robert Miles may be right, to take another case, that the disproportionate laying off of black workers in recessionary conditions may be a function not of a racist institutional aim but of the hard-fought union principle of seniority. Hired last, blacks will be fired first. But if the union and employer do little to alter the discriminatory effects of the principle over time, the suspicion must arise of racist collusion. Miles (1989), pp. 84–5. The Supreme Court of the United States, while stressing a state's intentionality, has permitted racially discriminatory impact of a statute as a standard for unconstitutionality. 'Sometimes a clear pattern, unexplainable on grounds other than race, emerges from the effect of state action.' *Village of Arlington Heights v. Metropolitan Development Housing Corp.*, 429 U.S., pp. 266, 267 (1977). See Diamond and Cottrol (1983), pp. 274–5.

17 Contra Baier (1978), p. 129, and Richards (1985), p. 71. The obligations of the institutional officer here can be likened to those of a knowing employee whose employer is engaged in committing egregious social harms. For more on whistle blowing, see Goldberg (1990c).

18 Examples of institutional racism can easily be multiplied. A recent study of mortgage practices by banks in the United States showed that blacks are more than twice as likely to be denied home loans even after disaggregating for obvious causal factors like class and home location differences. The kind of analysis pursued in the student newspaper case should be followed to establish whether cases like these exhibit institutional racism.

19 Cf. D. Baker (1978), pp. 316–21.

20 For the analysis of exploitation, see Wright (1989), p. 8; Reeve, ed. (1987); and Young (1988), p. 278.

21 The sometime appeal of racial separatism to the racially subjugated may be characterized as a resistant attempt to avoid racially defined political oppression and economic exploitation. It should be noticed, however, that the very terms that this form of resistance entails remain inevitably under the control of the racially dominant.

22 For enlightening analyses of exploitation, see Feinberg(1988), pp. 176 ff.; and Goodin (1987), pp. 167–200.

23 For a popular expression of this sort of claim, see Powell (1988). For critical analysis, see Barker (1981), pp. 16–20; A. Dummett and M. Dummett (1982), pp. 58–92.

24 Cf. *Batson v. Kentucky*, 476 U.S., pp. 79, 92–93 (1986).

25 'Sexual racism' involves the claim that racism is really the veiled concern about sexual deprivation. Stember (1976). 'Symbolic racism' is defined as 'the expression in terms of abstract ideological symbols and symbolic behaviors of the feeling that blacks are violating cherished values and making illegitimate demands for changes in the racial status quo'. McConahay and Hough (1976), p. 38. 'Visceral racism' is defined as 'a set of unacknowledged attitudes: dispositions to perceive and describe social events involving blacks and whites'. Thalberg (1972), p. 45.

26 Balibar and Wallerstein (1991), p. 39. Balibar misleadingly characterizes the former as an 'exclusive racism' due to its concern with elimination and the latter as an 'inclusive racism' because of its exploitative design.

27 Cf. Field (1977).
28 Comaroff (1987), pp. 302–3.
29 Kovel (1970), pp. 5, 13, 14.
30 Cf. Allport (1954), pp. 6–9; Jones (1972), pp. 2 ff. and 60 ff.; Newman (1979), pp.
    47–57; Klineberg (1953); Saenger (1953), pp. 3, 153; Simpson and Yinger (1953),
    pp. 13–16; Zubaida, ed. (1970), pp. 18–19.
31 Taguieff (1988); cf. Bauman (1989), pp. 62–5.
32 Taguieff, it should be noted, implausibly denies any such difference. Taguieff (1988),
    p. 91.
33 Boxill (1983), p. 109.
34 Rex (1986), p. 71. Thus, Wallerstein's reduction is too restrictive in suggesting that
    racism is only post hoc ideological rationalization. Wallerstein (1983), pp. 78–9.
35 Rex (1986), p. 76; Wolpe (1986), pp. 110–130; Solomos (1986), p. 103; Wallerstein
    (1988), pp. 7–8; Gimenez (1988), pp. 42–3; Cheboksarov (1980), p. 352; Callinicos
    (1992).
36 Hill (1989), pp. 496–500.
37 Szymanski (1985), p. 118. Similarly, 'if a race really represents a class in a society
    (which it does), then the elimination of a class society would eliminate racism'.
    Bruening (1974), p. 16.
38 For an account of Las Casas's position, see chapter 2 above.
39 On the 'chameleonic' character of race, cf. Wasserstrom (1978), pp. 1–28.
40 Cf. Foucault (1977), pp. 63–108
41 Chametzky (1984), pp. 435–6. Cf. Febvre and Martin (1976).
42 My emphasis. The televised version of the advertisement emphasizes 'all'.
43 Bauman (1989), pp. 61–2.
44 Ibid., p. 45.
45 Brown (1986a), p. 388.
46 Bauman (1989), pp. 80–1.
47 Ibid., (1989), p. 189. My emphasis.
48 Problematically, because as my good friend Nahum Chandler has pointed out to me
    most forcefully, the concept of natal alienation tends to connote, in the hands of
    Patterson and his followers, that black culture in the United States has been reduced
    because of the historical context to pathological expression. That the dominant and
    hegemonic political economy and culture has sought to repress, constrain,
    circumscribe, and marginalize the cultural expression of African-Americans does not
    entail that it has succeeded. The wealth of black culture has flourished both in spite
    and perhaps at times because of this repressive focus. Indeed, Simone's remark that
    'instead of picking cotton for us, blacks will make our culture for us' rings hauntingly
    true. Patterson (1983); West (1990), pp. 26–7; Thomas (1993); Simone (1989), p. 93.
    Patterson's general point is advanced concerning American Indians by Monture
    (1991).
49 Cf. Appiah (1984), p. 128. Goldberg (1986), pp. 77–8.
50 Bauman (1989), p. 18.
51 Appiah (1990b), pp. 10–12.
52 See Seidel (1986); and Barret (1987), pp. 156–65.
53 Levin (1981a), pp. 225–34.

54 Claims about racial differentiation in IQ are almost as old as IQ testing itself. The racialized IQ controversy peaked in the late 1960s with publication of Audrey Shuey's mammoth study and Jensen's polemic. Shuey (1965); Jensen (1969). The most recent resurrection of these claims has been by Levin and Gottfredson, both of whom rely on the now firmly falsified 'evidence' of Shuey and the like. Levin has recently argued that it is unsurprising that blacks comprise no more than 2 percent of professional philosophers in the United States, given the claimed difference of one standard deviation in intelligence (ten to fifteen points) between whites and blacks. Michael Levin, letter to *Proceedings and Addresses of the American Philosophical Association* (January 1990). For responses to this claim, see letters to *Proceedings and Addresses of the American Philosophical Association* (June 1991). Gottfredson (1986) rationalizes in much the same fashion the more general absence of blacks from positions in higher education. Both are primarily concerned with attacking affirmative action policies. For a critique of the IQ literature, see Gould (1981); Kamin (1974), Block and Dworkin (1974a) and (1974b).

55 For the most recent example of this view, see Steele (1990). Earlier versions of this view were articulated by economists Sowell, Williams, and Loury. Sowell's formal (as opposed to his popular) work is perhaps to be taken most seriously: By far the most complex and subtle, it has the virtue at least of a certain social scientific rigor. Sowell (1975) and (1981) and (1984); W. Williams (1982); Carter (1991b). It is interesting to note that Russell Lewis makes just this attack on blacks in Britain, and in doing so analogizes what he predicts to be the future of overpoliticized black Britains with what he perceives to be the recent political experience of American Indians. Lewis (1988), esp. pp. 120 ff.

56 For a critique of this 'tradition' of rationalization, see Boston (1988) and the provocative review of Steele's book by A. Reed (1991). See also A. Reed (1979).

57 See Lewis (1988), pp. 47 ff.; Flew (1984).

58 Baier (1978), p. 127. Of course, if some forms of racism may turn out to be morally acceptable, racism can only be 'prima facie wrong'. See Philips (1984).

59 Under different conditions there may be other discursively defined distancing technologies at work. Southern slavery, for example, may have relied upon anonymity only to initiate enslavement. Once enslaved, other modes of objectification took over.

60 Cf. Bauman (1989), pp. 21, 190–1.

6 Racisms and Rationalities

1 Baier (1978), p. 126; Singer (1978), p. 176.

2 Bauman (1989), p. 84.

3 MacIntyre (1988), p. 4.

4 Ruddick (1987), p. 238.

5 Lloyd (1984), p. ix.

6 Cf. Harding (1987), pp. 296–316.

7 Lloyd (1984), p. ix. Consider: '[O]ne would have to be as brutish as the American savages to approve their customs which are more cruel than those of wild animals.' Leibniz (1981), vol. 1, ii, #17. And: 'The Negro race is a species of men as different from ours as the breed of spaniels is from that of greyhounds.... If their understanding

is not of a different nature from ours, it is at least greatly inferior. They are not capable of any great application or association of ideas, and seemed formed neither for the advantages or the abuses of philosophy.' Voltaire (1901), vol. 34, pp. 240–1. And: 'Comparing [blacks] by their faculties of memory, reason, and imagination, it appears to me, that in memory they are equal to the whites; in reason much inferior; and in imagination they are dull, tasteless, and anomalous'. Jefferson (1954), pp. 139–40.

8 Cf. Lukes (1970), pp. 194–213. It should be pointed out that some theorists of deviant logics now deny even the minimal claim that noncontradiction is logically necessary.

9 MacIntyre (1988), p. 7.

10 I borrow the term 'whitemale' from H. Baker(1986), p. 183.

11 Jarvie and Agassi (1970), pp. 172–3. See also Agassi (1987), pp. 260–3; and Agassi and Jarvie (1987a), p. 432.

12 Kekes (1987), pp. 266–7.

13 Agassi and Jarvie (1987a), pp. 446–7.

14 That individual psychology and intersubjective social relations are so readily taken to be different domains of existence or analysis may in the wider scheme of things be part of the problem, but pursuit of this point must be left to another occasion.

15 Coetzee (1986).

16 Cf. A. G. Miller, ed. (1982), p. 31; Tajfel (1973); and Stroebe and Insko (1989), pp. 4, 28.

17 Newcomb and Charters (1950), p. 214.

18 Fishman (1956), p. 35 ff.; Tajfel (1973), p. 84.

19 Here I have followed Stroebe and Insko (1989), pp. 4, 8, 15.

20 Wuthnow (1982), pp. 181–2.

21 Allport, (1954), p. 109.

22 For similar examples, see P. Singer (1978), p. 188; M. Jones (1985), p. 223.

23 For a more formal expression of Piper's view, see Piper (1991).

24 Some hypotheticals from contemporary popular culture highlight this point. Vanilla Ice, a white rap artist engaging in a form of expression generally identified with black urban culture, may be convincing in the role of Ice T, a black rap artist, in a film about ghetto rapping. Yet the fact that *race* has now come to reflect the nuanced specificity of cultural reference suggests that one does not have to resort to anything like a fixed 'racial nature' biologically conceived to hold that the film would ring truer were Ice T himself to play the role. There is no necessity about this; a person considered white but steeped in black culture may do well at the part, may very well be (deemed) black. But which white actors could convincingly rather than parodically play the members of popular black rap groups like Niggers With Attitude (NWA), Public Enemy, Bitches With Problems, or The Fat Boys?

25 On illusory correlations, see Hamilton and Sherman (1989), pp. 59, 75.

26 Allport (1954), p. 103–4.

27 The claims in this paragraph may be found respectively in Tajfel (1973), pp. 80–5; Campbell (1967), pp. 823–35; Allport (1954), pp. 176, 166; Stephan and Rosenfield (1982), p. 119; Stephan (1989), pp. 48, 47.

28 I am grateful to Alena Goldberg and Pat Lauderdale for the former example and to Laurence Thomas for the latter.

29 Stroebe and Insko (1989), p. 16. Bauer and Bauer (1970), p. 38.

30 R. A. Jones (1982), p. 41. On Aristotle's distinction, see the *Nicomachean Ethics* in Aristotle (1946), III.1, 1110b15 ff. On the reliability of methods, see Clarke (1984).

31 For a similar analysis using Bayes, see Stephan (1989), pp. 48, 47.

32 A 'pandiacritic race' is defined as one for which every member is easily identifiable; a 'macrodiacritic race' is signified by an identification rate of over 80 percent; 'mesodiacritic' between 30 and 80 percent; and a 'microdiacritic race' is one in which members are less than 30 percent recognizable. Cf. Keith, (1928); Allport (1954), pp. 132–3.

33 Carleton Putnam, founding president of Delta Airlines, exemplifies this reasoning. Putnam resigned from Delta to lobby publicly against desegregation, which he thought would be disastrous for both blacks and whites. See Putnam (1961), pp. 6–7. We should also remember that the history of science (and not just the history of racial science) would be distorted if we restrict rationality only to true beliefs. Here, rationality requires simply that the evidence be the best available. Jarvie and Agassi (1970), p. 188.

34 See Fiske and Neuberg (1989), pp. 83–104.

35 Cf. Liska (1975), p. 19 and Stroebe and Insko (1989), p. 11. Whether there is evidence of a similar sort of inconsistency concerning other issues in fields like anthropology is a question beyond my present scope.

36 Cf. Hare (1980). Cf. MacIntyre on Hume, in MacIntyre (1988), pp. 301–5.

37 The object of my criticism is much more modest than the widely held belief-desire theory of action as such. Rather, it is the unsophisticated application of this model in social psychology to corroborate the presumption of racism's irrationality.

38 Stephan (1989), p. 52.

39 Liska, ed. (1975), pp. 15, 245–59.

40 Allport (1954), pp. 194–8; Adorno et al. (1950), pp. 605–53.

41 Kelman has suggested that it may not even be inconsistent for a person to exhibit some personal racial prejudice while supporting antidiscrimination legislation: Different ends and considerations are at issue. Kelman (1981). This point also bears upon the 'attitude-behavior inconsistency' discussed above.

42 Cf. Graumann and Wintermantel (1989), pp. 188–204.

43 Stephan and Rosenfeld (1982), p. 96. My emphasis.

44 For the first claim, see Becker (1957), p. 6; cf. Prager (1972), pp. 118–9, 121. For the latter two claims, see Becker (1957), p. 109; cf. Prager (1972), p. 125; and Godelier (1972), pp. 30–5.

45 Sowell (1975), p. 167.

46 For the former claim, see Thurow (1969), p. 135; and Prager (1972), p. 143; and for the latter, see Greenberg (1987), pp. 123–76; Innes (1984); Wolpe (1972); Goldberg (1986b); and Cell (1982).

47 Jencks (1983), pp. 37–8; cf. Banton (1983).

48 Reich (1977), p. 110; cf. Prager (1972), p. 126.

49 Cf. P. Singer (1978), pp. 88–91.

50 Carter (1991b), pp. 166–7.

51 See Dex (1985); Chivers (1985a); Elster (1985); Mason (1984), p. 1042. Sen (1985), however, is critical of the approach, arguing that rationality should be analyzed less mechanistically. Banton (1983) and Hechter et al. (1982) attempt to extend the model to an analysis of group relations.

52 See Mason (1984); Lyon (1985); McClendon (1983).
53 Cf. Shapiro (1989); Agassi and Jarvie (1987b), p. 445; Ben-Tovim et al. (1986), p. 137.
54 Cf. Boggs (1970), p. 155; Prager (1972), pp. 137–8; Boston (1988); Wolpe (1972).
55 Prager (1972), pp. 130, 133, 137; cf. Prager (1987a) and (1987b) and Banton (1987); Gabriel and Ben-Tovim (1977). Banton assumes that individuals are basically rational in calculating the effects of alternative courses of action for achieving their subjective goals and that values of differences in skin color enter the utility function as one among other variables. Macrolevel determinations for Banton are simply accumulations of individual, microlevel ones. For Prager, by contrast, irrational assumptions about racial difference are basic to macrolevel collective representations about the other. These irrational racist assumptions then serve to determine microlevel choices of individuals. Prager (1987b), p. 469. While I am sympathetic to Prager's suggestions concerning the irreducibility of racial determinations, I argue later that the racial assumptions need not be irrational.
56 R. Miller (1984), pp. 45–6; cf. Prager (1972), p. 138.
57 On the claim about rationality, see R. Miller (1987), p. 97. On the claim of intellectual defects, see Miles (1989), p. 42; and Reich (1981).
58 Cf. R. Miller (1987), pp. 97–8; Prager (1987a) and (1987b).
59 Cf. Miles (1989); Gilroy, (1987); Goldberg (1987); Jordan (1969); Cox (1948); cf. R. Miller (1987), pp. 97–8; Prager (1987a) and (1987b).
60 Goldberg (1990a); cf. Prager (1987a) and (1987b); and Banton (1987).
61 Cf. Goldberg (1991b); Gates (1990).
62 This captures the sense of Mill's argument about 'nations in their nonage'. J. S. Mill (1859). Carleton Putnam's comments about blacks in the United States furnishes another example. Putnam (1961). Beliefs of this kind will turn out largely to be false. But to rule out the argument at hand, utilitarianism would have to establish that they are *inherently* false.
63 In general, see Cavell (1976), pp. 254 ff. On the rationality of science, see Jarvie and Agassi (1970), p. 178.
64 For the dispute at issue here, cf. Goldberg (1986b).
65 Urbach (1974), pp. 115–25, 133–5; Kamin (1974); Gould (1981); Lewontin, Rose, and Kamin (1984), ch. 5.
66 Rawls (1971), pp. 149–50; Cohen (1979); Wasserstrom (1978), pp. 84 ff.; M. Jones (1985), p. 223.
67 Gewirth (1983), p. 226.
68 Cf. Foot (1978), pp. 181–8.
69 Baier (1984), p. 194; cf. Baier (1982). Concerning Rawls's early work, see Rawls (1951), p. 179; cf. Scanlon (1984), pp. 110 ff.
70 Gewirth (1983), esp. pp. 225–33.
71 I am aware that Kant took respect and autonomy to be in some sense morally (and perhaps conceptually) equivalent. One can still argue that the autonomy or respect denied in the one case at hand differs from that in the other case. The constraints on autonomy that are the product of the attack on self-respect seem to me to differ, at least in degree if not in kind, from the lack of autonomy in denying one the capacity to determine self-identity.
72 Abelson (1976).

73 Van den Berghe (1981), pp. xii, 29–35; Wilson (1975), pp. 562 ff.
74 Prager (1987b), p. 471.
75 Cf. Dummett (1986), p. 14; M. Jones (1985), p. 226.
76 Cf. Brandt and Muir (1986), p. 64; Goldberg (1986a); cf. Sivanandan (1990), ch. 4 for a critique of Race Awareness Training programs in Britain.

7 Racial Knowledge

1 See Joseph, Reddy, and Searle-Chatterjee (1990); Joseph (1987); Amin (1989); Sahlins (1985); Young (1990); Derrida (1992); Rorty (1982b), pp. 191–210.
2 Perhaps for postmodernity the primacy of the printed word in fashioning cultural identity has been replaced by the signifying power of electronic media. The importance of television for the constitution of racialized identity has often been highlighted. We should also note here the potentialities for computer software to be used to these ends. Protofascist parties in Germany have begun distributing crude video games, the theme of which is extermination of various racialized groups, including Jews, blacks, and Arabs.
3 Cf. Habermas's characterization of Foucault's thesis on knowledge and power. Habermas (1988), p. 272.
4 Foucault (1970), p. 346.
5 I have adapted loosely and liberally from Said's stimulating analysis of Orientalism. Said (1979a), pp. 31–49. Cf. Wolf (1981), p. 388; Mudimbe (1988), pp. 1–43; and on art, Nettleton and Hammond-Tooke, eds. (1989).
6 This expresses philosophically what anthropological ethnography has long practiced: 'given the dominant rhetoric of anthropological discourse, the Other's ethnographic presence goes together with his theoretical absence. In ethnography, as we know it, the Other is displayed, and therefore contained, as an object of representation; the Other's voice, demands, teachings are usually absent from our theorizing.' Fabian (1990), p. 771.
7 Foucault (1970), p. 351; more generally, see Bauman (1989), pp. 179–80. And on the epistemological politics of the social sciences in historical context, see Mafeje (1976).
8 Balibar (1991), p. 15.
9 Human Sciences Research Council (HSRC of South Africa) (1987), p. 6. This may seem an extreme case. But substituting various other states for South Africa in the quotations—the United States, Israel, Britain, to name only the more obvious—will hardly change their significance. In the case of the United States, there may be more self-consciousness and skepticism about the designations, a greater personal and institutional wrestling with the identifications than may have once been the case in South Africa, though even in this respect the latter may now be in the process of emulating the former. I have learned, not without cost and whether one intends it or not, that claims about South Africa, however generally stated, are dated: This is written in June 1991.
10 HSRC (1987), p. 157. It should be pointed out that leading South African ideologues are no longer committed to this claim, which is not the same as saying that they are no longer committed to some more or less formal racialized dispensation. I will be analyzing this document in greater detail later in the chapter.

11 A booklet published by the South African state in 1969, *Progress through Separate Development,* makes just this claim. However, the South African Museum, a state-sponsored national institution, for example, now acknowledges the arrival of blacks in South Africa two thousand years ago.

12 For evidence of the collaboration between anthropological study and colonial administration: 'It has been said that modern anthropology is destined to be of great assistance to colonial governments in providing the knowledge of the social structure of native groups upon which a sound and harmonious Native Administration, as envisaged in indirect Rule, should be built. Let me say that I for one firmly believe in the possibility of such cooperation between anthropologists and administrators.' S. F. Nadel, A black Byzantium (1942), quoted in Frank (1979), p. 206. Cf. Foucault (1988), p. 162. Anthropologists have become much more self-conscious about the processes of what Johannes Fabian calls 'othering'. They no longer assume 'the givenness of the Other as the object of their discipline'. Fabian (1990), p. 755. In the first draft, I used 'peoples' in referring to the colonized. Alena Goldberg reminded me most forcefully that this, too, was to invoke, perhaps euphemistically, a category of the sort I am engaged in critiquing.

13 Theorization of 'development' in terms of stages can be traced to the Enlightenment. The four-stage theory of human development proposed by the Russian Semyon Efimovich Desnitsky, a student of Adam Smith's, is typical: The earliest mode of human development consists of 'peoples' living by hunting-gathering. The second stage consists of 'peoples' engaged in the pastoral lives of shepherds. The third stage is agricultural. And the fourth consists of 'peoples' living by commerce. ('Peoples' is the term used by Desnitsky in the eighteenth century.) See Meek (1976), p. 5. W. W. Rostow's five-stage theory of economic development has been the major influence in mainstream developmental economics in the past three decades.

14 See Mafeje (1976); and Mudimbe (1988), p. 44. The contemporary experience of South Africa in relation to the World Bank and the IMF is revealing. With the lifting of sanctions, the South African government is voluntarily subjecting itself to the 'advice' of these funding bodies without expecting further loans in the short term. Thus, they are using the economic expertise now being exported in the name of the G7 to rationalize greater privatization of nationalized industries, reduction in the tax rates, and introduction of an increasingly regressive tax structure in the form of a comprehensive value added tax, reduced government social service expenditures, and diminished welfare commitments.

15 Cf. Kuper (1988), pp. 1–4; Torgovnick (1990), pp. 18–19; Rubin (1984), p. 2.

16 Kuper thinks that *transformations* in the significations of theoretical concepts have played a major role in science, at least as significant as the role advocated by Kuhn's 'paradigms'. Kuper (1988), pp. 10–14. For the role of transformations in my theory of racialized discourse, see chapter 3 above.

17 On the formal qualities of the Primitive, see Kuper (1988), p. 5; on the popular conception, see Torgovnick (1990), pp. 8, 99, 192. Torgovnick points out that the concept was also used to rationalize control of 'lower classes, minorities, and women … the primitives at home' (p. 192). This rationalization was sustained by the economy of conceptual identification in the late nineteenth century between racial Others, mainly blacks and Jews, women, and the working class. Torgovnick also points out that primitive society became the 'testing ground' for early twentieth-century

psychoanalytic hypotheses about human sexuality (p. 7). She is only partially correct in ascribing this to the anthropological constitution of the Other and its corollary assumption that the Primitive was the Other in us, the precivilized form through which, in the form of our ancestry, we passed. The rush of sex theorists into the field of anthropological study also had to do with prevailing Victorianism in sexual matters, the veil of taboos prohibiting frank, open, unbiased study of sex in civilized society. If Victorianism proved to be the push, the lure of the Savage was the invitation behind the veil of taboos, the pull of an object pristine and pure, unself-conscious, and so perhaps a view into the unconscious.

18 Levi-Strauss, perhaps a little gingerly, refers to these (non)histories as 'cold'. Wolf (1981), p. 385.

19 Kuper (1988), pp. 13–14. Compare Leni Riefenstahl's popular photographic collection of African bodies with Lawrence and Lorne Blair's *Ring of Fire,* an account of their journeys through Indonesia. For more on the latter, see Torgovnick (1990), pp. 177–82.

20 Torgovnick (1990), p. 38; Kuper (1988), pp. 7–9.

21 Three brief quotes should suffice: '[The Asmat of New Guinea] is a good example of how rare an untouched example of a primitive culture really is'. 'The tropes and categories through which we view primitive societies establish relations of power between them and us.' And '[these are] some of our greatest thinking and thinkers about the primitive'. Torgovnick (1990), p. 280 n. 3, pp. 11 and 190.

22 Torgovnick (1990), ch. 2. Torgovnick (p. 186) badly misrepresents the history of racial theorizing in claiming that post-Darwinist views on race were a return to the monogenist conception that predated polygenism, and that monogenism 'became the antiracist position' while polygenism 'became the assumption of the racist position'. That Gould, in another context, calls this a common misreading of the debate does not mitigate her mistake. Gould (1991), p. 13.

23 Torgovnick (1990), pp. 69–70. My emphases.

24 On realism as the dominant mode of ethnographical writing, see Fabian (1990).

25 Torgovnick (1990), p. 71. Similarly, she approves largely of the 1980s film *Greystoke: The Story of Tarzan,* failing to question why this film at that time.

26 Ibid., p. 185.

27 Ibid., pp. 40–1. This reduction strikes me as consistent with what Patricia Williams in a different context has convincingly called the contemporary 'rhetoric of increased privatization'. P. J. Williams (1991), p. 47.

28 See, in general, Stocking, ed. (1985), esp. E. A. Williams (1985), pp. 146–66. For the experience of American Indians in this respect, see Wade (1985), p. 187.

29 Torgovnick (1990), p. 12. My emphasis.

30 Anthony Appiah has an interesting discussion of the conceptual and political relations and differences between postmodernism and postcolonialism. Cf. Appiah (1991).

31 Rubin (1984), pp. 5–6; Varnedoe (1984b), pp. 180–1. Elsewhere, in a less guarded moment towards the close of the two volumes, Varnedoe speaks of 'the Primitive mind' (capitalized), and of 'Primitive thought and belief'. Contrary to Rubin's claim that only 'Primitivism' will be capitalized, 'the Primitive' is objectified as inalienably Other. Varnedoe (1984a), vol. 2, p. 661. Moreover, Rubin has no reference at all either to Rousseau's own work or, more significantly, to any of the primary interpretive literature about Rousseau on the role of the 'noble savage'. Varnedoe references

Rousseau's *Discourse on Inequality* only in passing, and his references to the interpretive literature are outdated and superficial. It seems clear, also, that they are references his research assistants have uncovered. This goes also for his references to anthropological literature, in particular to work on the conceptual history of *race*. These absences and lacks contrast starkly with the otherwise voluminous references to the art historical data. This is a point noted in a slightly different context by Clifford (1988), pp. 189–214.

32 On a similar point concerning the later exhibition, 'Perspectives: Angles on African Art' at the Center for African Art in New York, 1987, see Appiah (1991). Here, as elsewhere, I do not mean to be endorsing a simplistic form of 'experientialism', or that the content of self-representation is necessarily convincing. Whether its products are convincing or not, self-representation seems integral to autonomy and valuable for that reason at least.

33 Jenkins (1986), p. 173; cf. Fried (1975)

34 My characterization of the three worlds has been informed by Pletsch (1981), pp. 569–74; and Worsley (1984), ch. 1, and p. 308. See also Tipps (1973), esp. pp. 204, 208.

35 Pletsch (1981), p. 565.

36 Ibid., p. 581.

37 Gorra suggests that the characterization can be generalized in the colonial context to Africa as (being) Europe's, as belonging to Europe. Gorra (1991), p. 87. This spatial appropriation of Africa is accompanied, as Patricia Williams so forcefully argues, by an eviction of the cultural legacy of Africa from and the denial of black contributors to the canon of 'Western civilization'. P. J. Williams (1991), pp. 113–4.

38 As I was composing this, an article appeared in *The New York Sunday Times,* June 23, 1991, on the expressed commitment of the Congress Party in India (newly returned to power after Rajiv Ghandi's assassination) to a 'free market' economy. The article referred to the encouragement of this newfound capitalism as expressed by 'a senior *Western* diplomat'. Whose interests, one wonders, does this diplomat represent? The cementing of 'the West' in the aftermath of the Gulf War seems at once and paradoxically impenetrable and transparent. By contrast, adding a 'Fourth World' to distinguish between different sorts of non-Western states simply reiterates the restrictions of the three-world system.

39 See Ridgeway (1990), p. 21; Varnedoe (1984a), p. 679. Chafets (1990), pp. 20–6.

40 Balibar (1991a), p. 14; cf. Balibar (1990), pp. 283–94. Two points attest to this growing phenomenon: In Germany, those initially deemed *Gastarbeiter* were later referred to as 'foreign workers' and now just as 'the foreigners'. There is no immigration law, only *Auslandergesetz*, or 'foreigner's law', dating back to 1965 and evocative of 1938 Nazi legislation, which it appears to emulate. Nonalien residents of European Community countries have the right of entry, employment, and self-employment. Rathzel (1990), pp. 32 ff.

41 Worsley (1984), pp. 238, 236.

42 Torgovnick, arguing for use of *primitive,* offers a somewhat different, and inconclusive set of substitutes. Cf. Torgovnick (1990), pp. 21–2, 257 n. 45.

43 Myrdal (1962).

44 Gans (1990), p. 271; Jencks (1988), p. 23; Innis and Feagin (1989), p. 14.

45 Magnet (1989), p. 130.

46 Jencks (1988), p. 23; Reed (1988). An article in the *Chronicle of Higher Education* in 1988 described the 'social pathologies' as including 'teenage pregnancies, out of wedlock births, single parent families, poor educational achievement, chronic unemployment, welfare dependency, drug abuse, and crime'. Coughlin (1988).

47 This is Boxill's critical characterization of the 'poverty of culture' thesis. Boxill (1991), p. 588.

48 For an explicit expression of the Underclass in terms of idleness, see Jencks (1988), p. 24. Cf. Coetzee (1989), pp. 12–35. Another indication of the racialized character of the Underclass is revealed in its popular use to characterize animal pecking orders. Gans reports finding a news story referring to 'underclass Mexican iguanas'. Gans (1990), p. 272.

49 Wilson (1987), p. 126. In a more recent paper, Wilson seeks to develop a 'broader theoretical ... framework that integrates social structural and cultural arguments'. Wilson (1991b), p. 1.

50 Reed (1988), p. 168.

51 Wilson (1991a), p. 600.

52 Where they help blacks in any measure at all, these programs tend to assist the black middle class more than the black poor, for the former are in a better position to take advantage of them because of better knowledge, greater institutional access, and more available resources.

53 Hochschild (1991), p. 564. Contrast E. Anderson (1990), pp. 72, 112–3.

54 Hochschild (1991), pp. 575 ff.

55 Fainstein (1986), p. 440. See also pp. 418, 439. Duster notes that when inner city businesses relocate to areas where employment of black youth is less likely, the proportion of blacks in the community may be one of the decisive considerations. Duster (1988), p. 3. Jencks also addresses this point. Jencks (1988). Even in respect to welfare treatment, whites on welfare fare better than those who are not white. See Torres (1988), p. 1058.

56 Hochschild (1991), p. 563.

57 On this latter point, see Gans (1990), p. 274.

58 Wilson (1991a), pp. 600–602. Cf. Hochschild (1991), p. 561. In his presidential address to the American Sociological Association, Wilson pertinently substitutes for his use of 'the Underclass' the term 'the ghetto poor'. And he does this commendably 'to focus our attention less on controversy and more on research and theoretical issues'. He nevertheless emphasizes that he 'hop[es] that I would not lose any of the theoretical meaning that this concept *[the Underclass]* has had in my writing'. Wilson (1991b), p. 11.

59 Hughes (1989), pp. 191–2.

60 Defending the Bush administration's new 'violence initiative' to 'identify early in their lives people who may be prone to violent or antisocial behavior', the senior health official in the Health Department, Dr. Frederick Goodwin, argued that 'male monkeys, especially in the wild ... roughly half of them survive to adulthood. The other half die by violence. That is the natural way of it for males, to knock each other off ... the same hyperaggressive monkeys who kill each other are also hypersexual, so they copulate more.... Maybe it isn't just the careless use of the word when people call certain areas of certain cities jungles, that we may have gone back to what might be more natural, without all of the social controls that we have imposed upon ourselves

as a civilization over thousands of years in our own evolution.' *The New York Times,*
February 28, 1992, p. A:7. Torgovnick also insists on using the term the 'urban jungle'
in her analysis of contemporary primitivism discussed above. Theodore Lowi rightly
asks why we now need concepts like 'culture of poverty' and 'underclass' in relation
to black ghettoes but not formerly in relation to Jewish or Irish ones. Lowi (1988), p.
855. On 'the West', see Young (1990), Derrida (1992).
61 Surveys of racial attitudes of whites in the United States date at least to the 1950s.
The first major social science survey of the racial attitudes of blacks nationwide in
over twenty years only recently appeared. Sigelman and Welch (1991). The same is
largely true in South Africa. Blauner and Wellman discuss some of the political issues
involved in conducting attitude research among the black poor. Blauner and Wellman
(1973), pp. 310–30. The title of Ladner's well-known volume, *The Death of White
Sociology,* strikes one with the hindsight of nearly two decades and in spite of some
dramatic changes, as overly optimistic.
62 Blauner and Wellman (1973), p. 315.
63 Bauman (1989), p. 85.
64 See, for example, the book *Becoming More Civilized* by self-described liberal social
psychologist Leonard Doob. Published in 1960, Doob's study is concerned with the
psychological effects of Africans as they 'become more civilized'. 'Civilization is
intended as a description of the differences between the values of people who
'unwittingly live next to one another in the bush and those who wittingly live on top
of one another in modern apartment houses'. Though Doob does not intend the term
to designate or justify inferiority or superiority, the comparison of the irrational
necessity of bush life with the free choice of modernity reproduces a presumption
long considered to be well-established. See Doob (1960), pp. ix–x.
65 Ranger (1989), pp. 1–3.
66 Ibid., pp. 1–13, 18. My emphasis. Religious animism is converted into referential
animalism—again!
67 Ibid., p. 19.
68 Ibid., p. 21.
69 Ibid., p. 22. My emphasis.
70 Ibid., p. 24.
71 Said (1990), pp. 210–22.
72 HSRC (1970).
73 HSRC (1985), pp. 164 ff.
74 'Research ... shows that *these people* at present accept their lot, but that *their* attitude
can in no way be interpreted as implying loyalty or satisfaction.' HSRC (1985), p.
106. My emphases.
75 It should be noted that the Population Registration Act, first introduced in 1950, which
legally required race classification and defined the categories, was repealed by
President de Klerk on June 17, 1991, as I wrote this.
76 'It was considered ... that it would be more meaningful to present from the research
undertaken those principles and guidelines for the improvement of intergroup
relations that could be considered as essential conditions for the accommodation of
conflict.' HSRC (1985), p. 5. For the discussion of the law report, see pp. 64, 129 ff.
77 'South African society ... includes population categories that have been entrenched
in the juridical and political systems. For example ... in all aspects of public life the

following main population categories apply: blacks, whites, coloureds and Indians.' And further: '[A]t the school level history *must* be presented from the point of view and orientation of the pupil's own community.... [I]f the principle of an own approach to history is underrated, the teaching of history can hardly assist in creating loyalty towards and identification with the pupil's own past, *which remains an aspect of constructive intergroup relations.'* HSRC (1985), pp. 6, 74. My emphases.

78 Ibid., pp. 150, 156.

79 Ibid., pp. 59, 111. By the same token, the report accepts the euphemistic state definition of education as the '"own affair" ... of each population category' according to which 'formal education management structures ... function independently of one another'. And it concludes that 'education for Africans cannot be improved qualitatively unless [their] use of either of the two official languages [English and Afrikaans] is improved'. Ibid., pp. 34, 169. South Africa's severe shortage of skilled technical manpower is blamed on the British colonial insistence upon *academically* oriented education' and on blacks' 'unrealistic educational expectations' rather than on the history of institutional job color bars. Ibid., pp. 114–15. These examples strike me as classic cases of blaming the objects of racialized discourse, those subjected to racist exclusion.

80 Ibid., pp. 42, 83, 154, 62–3. Cf. Bergesen (1980), pp. 138–74.

81 HSRC (1985), p. 134. No account of the research is furnished.

82 Ibid., pp. 3, 15, 76.

83 Gould (1981), p. 74.

84 In Roland Barthes's terms, 'whites' is a 'massive plural'. See Barthes (1990), pp. 130–4.

85 Again, this is Barthes's terminology. It should also be noted here that it is notoriously difficult to talk about race in the context of South Africa without *using* the racialized categories of *apartheid.*

86 HSRC (1985), pp. 22, 30. More ludicrously still, we are told that 'unemployment is overestimated' because 'unemployed persons are always looking for work'. P. 48. Again, the South African Museum now acknowledges the need to replace 'outdated' group designations like 'Hottentot' and 'Bushmen' with more anthropologically acceptable terms like 'Khoi-Khoi' and 'San'. The museum then proceeds in its displays to use the old nomenclature liberally.

87 Ibid., pp. 39–40.

88 Ibid., pp. 4–5, 72–3, 125, 139, 162, 163.

89 'Reaction of the Government to HSRC Report on Intergroup Relations', postscript to HSRC (1985), pp. 192–202. My emphasis.

90 Cf. Foucault (1980c), pp. 63–108; and the analysis of science and ideology in Foucault (1972), pp. 184–6.

8 'Polluting the Body Politic': Race and Urban Location

1 B. J. Vorster, former prime minister of South Africa, *The Star* (Johannesburg), April 3, 1973.

2 Foucault (1982); Dear (1986), p. 375; Harvey (1989), p. 245.

3 Cf. Bachelard (1964), pp. 211–231; Sennett (1990), pp. xii, 8–9, 18.

4 Krieger (1986), pp. 385–6.

5 As specified in chapter 7, the concept of the *racially marginalized* is used to identify the peculiar intersection of race and class by referring to those social groups or *fractions* of social groups that are, or traditionally have been, deeply excluded from social powers, rights, goods, or services in racial terms or on racial grounds.

6 In South Africa, for example, rural space was divided by the various Land Acts from 1913 on. As Dhiru Sony reminded me, the Group Areas Act of 1950 was designed to segregate *urban* space. On this count, the South African experience may for the most part be differentiated from the racial experience elsewhere in terms of extremity, severity, and lateness, not in terms of kind. This, at least, is what I shall argue. Cf. Cell (1982); Swanson (1968); Swanson (1977); Stren (1972). On the emergence of racial segregation domestically in Britain, see S. J. Smith (1989), pp. 14–21, 105–45.

7 By 1949 the largest urban concentrations of blacks were in New York, Chicago, Philadelphia, Washington D.C., and Sao Paulo. Cell (1982), p. 248. These remarks apply well enough, with the appropriate qualifications, for the relations between North and South, to the internal experience of the United States. However, I do not intend by this to characterize the history of black experience in the United States in terms of the colonial model. Cf. Blauner (1972), chs. 2 and 3; Prager (1972), pp. 130–46. Nor do I mean to claim that there is anything like a radical momentary break either in the mode of production or in the aesthetic between modern and postmodern social formations. I tend to think of such historical transformations in the image of long cinematic dissolves rather than as jump-cuts, as emergent rather than as explosions. Cf. Harvey (1989).

8 Cf. Western (1981), p. 42. From the early 1950s to the mid-1970s, the suburban United States saw more than fifteen thousand shopping malls built. In some cases, malls built at the rural limits of cities encouraged housing developments close at hand; in others, malls inevitably followed demand. At more or less the same time, Chicago and New York each lost in the order of a half-million predominantly blue collar jobs. These were the jobs that traditionally offered blacks employment opportunities. See Duster (1988). Hughes's remark, formulated in the context of the debate over whether explanations in terms of 'race' or 'space' account for the mismatch between location of racialized populations and jobs, has wider relevance: *'Residence next to jobs* is not a test of *access to jobs;* and *access to jobs* does not require *residence next to jobs'.* Hughes (1989), p. 199 n. 12. Italics in original. The interposed fact of race looms large in any adequate explanation of the marginalized condition of ghetto dwellers in the United States.

9 On the promotion and cementing of racialized segregation by federal and state tax structure in the United States, see Kushner (1980), pp. 56–63. In general, cf. Harvey (1989), p. 77; E. Anderson (1990), pp. 46 ff.; Rose (1984); McCarthy and Smit (1984), pp. 76 ff. This renewed pull of the central business district, and the inner city in general, as appealing residential space may also reflect an emergent postmodern political economy of privatization and an accompanying aesthetic of cultural commodification. Cf. P. J. Williams (1991), esp. chs. 3 and 4; Jameson (1984). Moreover, as large landowners and landlords, the corporatist commitments of some major urban universities in the United States have helped to reproduce racial marginality, for they have often pioneered gentrification in their cities. Elijah Anderson's urban ethnography, for example, describes in some detail, though in

veiled terms, the roles of Drexel University and the University of Pennsylvania in the gentrification of Powelton Village in Philadelphia, indicating the processes by which the majority of its black population to the north and west have become increasingly marginalized. E. Anderson (1990), esp. ch. 1.

10 For example, blacks in the United States are twice as likely as whites to have their applications for home loans rejected by loan institutions—even after allowing for class differentiations. See *The New York Times,* October 22, 1991, pp. C1, C2. On the promotion of racialized segregation by the banking and real estate industries in the United States, see Kushner (1980), pp. 52–6.

11 Dear (1986), pp. 376–80; cf. McCarthy and Smit (1984), pp. 7, 62.

12 Kushner (1980), pp. 44–52.

13 Quoted in Swanson (1977), p. 388.

14 Ibid., pp. 387–9. See also Fanon (1970b), p. 37. I am grateful to Ben Magubane for reminding me of Fanon's distinction between the 'native' and 'European cities'. A corollary concern with immigration, spurred by the influence of eugenics, began to emerge at about this time. For example, Sir Ralph Cilento, a medical doctor in Australia, argued that the greatest urban danger to Australia stemmed not from invasion by foreign forces, but 'by foreign germs introduced by indiscriminate Asian immigration'. De Lepervanche (1980), p. 28.

15 Under the act, urban renewal agencies were also empowered to condemn substandard private property and to promote its resale to private contractors undertaking to develop the agency's housing plan. Glazer (1965), p. 195.

16 Nationwide, blacks constituted two-thirds of those removed from sites designated for urban renewal. Glazer (1965), p. 198–200; Kushner (1980), pp. 37–8; on Philadelphia, see Baumann (1987), esp. p. 176. The generality of the postcolonial experience, the structural similarity of (discriminatory) immigration laws, and the transspatial 'universality' of racialized discourse (keeping in mind its space-time specificities) suggest that the principles of my argument are not unique to the United States, local variations notwithstanding. Conditions of racialized housing in Britain, France, Germany, and the Netherlands are not that dissimilar. One significant difference, especially in France, is that the primary form of racialized housing—high-rise apartments or hostels for immigrants and migrants—tends to be located in the suburbs and not in the inner cities which remain 'European'. On the racial structuring of urban space in Britain, see S. J. Smith (1992), pp. 128–43; Harvey (1989), pp. 69–70; S. J. Smith (1989), esp. chs. 2–4; Phillips (1987); and Gregory and Urry, eds. (1985). See Sivanandan, ed. (1991); Essed (1990). Cf. Balibar (1991); Balibar (1988).

17 Cf. Abrams (1966); Grier and Grier (1966); Friedman (1967); Foucault (1986).

18 Approximately 50 percent of the city of Durban's population was forced to move from the 1950s to the 1970s to accommodate imposition of the Group Areas Act. Nine-tenths of this movement consisted of black removal to peripheral township locations, dumping grounds, or 'homelands'; the rest consisted largely of rehousing poor whites. McCarthy and Smit (1984), p. 57. Durban is not atypical of the urban experience of *apartheid* South Africa. This imposed spatial segregation, more than anything else, will serve to slow and circumscribe emergence of what the state is now heralding as 'the new South Africa'. Durban is identified as the fastest growing city in the world. Its formal population is listed at one million people, half Indian, the rest

a mix of white and African. The informal—and unrecognized—population adds another three million people, living with no running water or sewage in endless shantytown squatter camps around the urban periphery, though spilling over into residential areas. It is estimated that two hundred African families *per week* are migrating from rural areas into the extended urban space. A modest projection suggests that this amounts to an annual increase of a half million people. City and state are clearly unprepared to face up to, let alone accommodate this.

19 Though informal, this effect is not accidental: witness bank 'red-lining' and real estate 'directing' practices, less efficient services tied to affordability, and lower real estate yields. While yielding lower collected amounts, higher real estate tax rates are strongly regressive, placing a relatively far heavier burden on homeowners in poor—and racialized— neighborhoods.

20 'The literature is replete with case studies of highways built over ghettoes to facilitate the affluent suburbanite's trip to shopping centres.' McCarthy and Smit (1984), p. 56. Cf. Kushner (1980), pp. 38–9.

21 Foucault (1982).

22 Residential Environment Bill, Republic of South Africa [B 93–91 (GA)] pending. See Davis and Marcus (1991). I am grateful to Dhiru Sony for bringing my attention to this bill, as well as for much of the contemporary detail of Durban's urban experience.

23 Kushner (1980), pp. 18–20; P. J. Williams (1991), pp. 116–7.

24 'Surveys of state economic development agencies in the [U.S.] South reveal a significant pattern of desire of firms to avoid areas of large black populations'. Creigs and Stanback (1986), p. 27. Cf. Duncan and Mindlin (1964); Harvey (1973), p. 63; Hughes (1989). A 'Primetime' report by Diane Sawyer on ABC, September 26, 1991, gave some indication of the depth of the relative difficulties and increased expense experienced by black people in urban settings in the United States in finding equal employment, buying used cars, renting an apartment, and generally shopping or window shopping. To this must be added the fact that state-mandated auto insurance is invariably much higher in inner cities, particularly in ghetto areas where auto crime rates are high, than in the suburbs.

25 For example, until recently, the black townships on the Cape Flats outside Cape Town completely lacked competitively priced shopping areas, for white businesses in the city would have been adversely affected by commuting black consumers. Cf. Western (1981), p. 232. Economic rationalization in the era of sanctions ironically had an impact on transforming this. With the changes in South Africa's political economy at the opening of the 1990s, growth in consumer demand among working and middle-class blacks has been most dramatic. The state is in the process of trying 'to harness' black consumption to the ends of informal and privatized means of control.

26 Deleuze (1988), p. 26.

27 Lowman (1986), pp. 85–6.

28 It is well-known that the racially marginalized make up the overwhelming majority of victims of crimes committed by the racially marginalized and that these crimes are a small proportion of the total number of crimes committed in the society. In the United States, whites are arrested for roughly 70 percent of crimes committed, while *all* others are arrested for the rest. As the Charles Stuart case in Boston so vividly dramatized, white offenders face a significantly lower probability of arrest than do blacks. P. J. Williams (1991), pp. 73–4. On producing, localizing, and thereby

containing black criminality in inner city Britain, see M. Keith (1992), pp. 193–209. Contrast this with Herrnstein (1990), p. 14; Wilson and Herrnstein (1985).

29 Baumann (1987), p. 130.

30 See Harvey (1989), pp. 89–95.

31 K. Anderson (1987); K. Anderson (1988).

32 The film is dated 1946. My emphasis. While the italicized words might be read to refer to 'man' generically, the film is exclusively about white America. I am grateful to my friend Michael O'Shea for bringing the quote in his Joycean way to my notice. On the racialized conditions of home ownership in Britain, see S. J. Smith (1989), pp. 52–3, 60–3, esp. 87–92.

33 'By removing Coloureds from District Six, whites are more than clearing slums or underpinning their exclusive claim to central Cape Town's sacred space. *They are also destroying one of the symbols of whatever Coloured identity may exist, a space in part at least seven generations deep with associations with slave emancipation.'* Western (1981), p. 150. Emphases in original. In general, see ibid., pp. 7, 46, 142–59; McCarthy and Smit (1984), pp. 82, 95–6.

34 For the Spencer quote, see Nye (1985), p. 58. In general, see Stuart Gilman (1985), pp. 165–98; Stepan (1985), pp. 97–120; Sander Gilman (1985), pp. 72–9; Jones (1971), pp. 127–31, 281–9.

35 All the quotes in this paragraph are taken from Baumann (1987), pp. 55, 183–4, and 164 respectively. My emphases. On race and space in Yonkers, see the *New York Times,* August 4,7, 9, and 27, 1988. Again, Enoch Powell's remarks in 1968 about 'rivers of blood', Margaret Thatcher's comments a decade later about 'swamping', general British concerns about cultural contamination, the phenomenal rise of Jean-Marie Le Pen, and the municipal reassertion of neofascism in Germany on a platform of antimigrants and nonimmigration lead me to suggest that my history is not simply local to the United States. Various members of the British House of Commons in the late 1950s and early 1960s observed that as a result of postcolonial immigration 'coloured people segregate themselves in certain areas', creating 'slums ... in hundreds or perhaps even in thousands where previously they could be measured in dozens', where there was now unprecedented 'filth and ... obscenity'. All quotes from S. J. Smith (1989), p. 119, esp. chs. 5 and 6; Barker (1981). Cf. Sivanandan, ed. (1991); Essed (1990).

36 Rose (1984), pp. 50–7; E. Anderson (1990); Palen and London, eds. (1984).

37 B. Anderson (1983); K. Anderson (1987), p. 594. Said (1979), p. 54, speaks of 'imaginative knowledge of geography and history'.

38 Shue (1988), p. 691. Shue is characterizing the standard view, modernist in the tradition of Kant and Bentham, and he goes on to offer a modest internal critique of it. On 'generative metaphors', see Stuart Gilman (1985), pp. 165–198.

39 Cf. Dear (1986), p. 380.

40 On the Detroit Expedition, see Bunge (1962).

41 Western (1981), p. 8.

42 R. Williams (1985), p. 373.

9 Taking Race Pragmatically

1 Rorty (1983). See also Rorty (1991b), pp. 279–302; Burrows (1991), pp. 322–38.
2 David Harvey contrasts the 'flexible accumulation' of 'the condition of postmodernity' to the rigidities of modernism's 'Fordist' mode of capital accumulation. The former is 'flexible with respect to labour processes, labour markets, products and patterns of consumption'. Harvey (1989), pp. 147–97.
3 Goldberg (1988).
4 Sowell (1984), p. 116; Carter (1991a), p. 82.
5 On the sorts of implications this can have in a material sense, on one kind of legal effect in the case of Indian land claims, see Torres and Milun (1990).
6 I am grateful to Laurence Thomas for this explication of my argument concerning the rationality and unreasonableness of racisms.
7 Much of Stephen Carter's argument is carried by the dubious first claim in respect to middle-class blacks in the United States. Carter (1991a). See Nakanishi (1988), p. 164. It is significant that ethno-Americanizing seems to require hyphenation, that hyphenation signifies ethno-American belonging, whereas racializing names erases hyphenation. The racializing absence of hyphenation thus seems to insinuate division and divisiveness.
8 Cf. Ramirez (1988), esp. pp. 150–3.
9 Connolly (1991), p. 39.
10 These are Connolly's suggestive words. Ibid., p. 28. On modernity and ambivalence, see Bauman (1991).
11 Foucault (1984), pp. 244–5.
12 For an example of the devastating effects of this delimitation in the case of Mashpee Indians, see Torres and Milun (1990).
13 On racist metaphors in science, see Stepan (1990), pp. 38–57. On resistance to racist science, see Stepan (1982); Stepan and Gilman (1991), pp. 72–103. Stepan and Gilman analyze the various strategies of resistance to the categories of racial science in the late nineteenth and early twentieth centuries employed by those—in particular blacks and Jews—marginalized by the discourse. These strategies ranged from internalization of the discursive categories to their explicit rejection. It should be pointed out that Stepan and Gilman (and LaCapra in editorially summarizing their contribution to the volume he edited) unquestioningly reiterate the racializing and infantilizing category of 'minorities' in referring to African-Americans and Jews.
14 Witness the debate within the African National Congress concerning whether 'the liberation struggle' precedes the struggle for women's emancipation or whether the two struggles are inextricable. McClintock (1990), pp. 104–23. Cf. Spelman (1988), pp. 114–132; Collins (1990); Hooks (1992).
15 See especially Torres (1991); Crenshaw (1988); Williams (1991). On pragmatism and social theory in general, see Brint and Weaver, eds. (1991); West (1989), esp. pp. 3–8, 211–42.
16 Crenshaw (1988), p. 1335, and generally, pp. 1384–7. For a very useful analysis of pragmatism in relation to feminism, see Radin (1990).
17 Rorty (1983) is committed in the first way; West (1989) in the second.

18 Rorty (1991c), p. 73. On the sense in which pragmatism is 'banal', see Rorty (1991a), pp. 89–98; Dworkin (1991), pp. 359–88.
19 Torres (1991), p. 1000.
20 I have purposely avoided talk of 'organic intellectuals' and 'prophetic pragmatism' for I find no pragmatic need to be tied to any ideological positionality implicit in both concepts, and principled pragmatists I would think should be especially troubled by the constraining religious connotations of the latter, notwithstanding West's assurances. In short, both notions suggest commitment to a foundation, or at least a founding vision, to which a critical pragmatism must in principle be opposed. Cf. West (1989); Gooding-Williams (1991). On the formulation of pragmatism I give here, it can equally characterize commitments of intellectuals, educators, community activists, politicians, or people generally in their everyday lives. Critical pragmatists and the formulation of pragmatism that reflects their practical commitments are not bound to privilege the perspective of any class.
21 See, for example, the declaration of intent by the Convention for a Democratic South Africa, the forum for entering into negotiations for a new constitution: 'South Africa will be a united, democratic, nonracial and nonsexist state'. The *New York Times,* December 22, 1991. Similar language can be found in The Freedom Charter of 1956, the document that best lays out the principles of ANC commitment.
22 Torres (1991), pp. 1001–2. Cf. Connolly (1991), p. 41; West (1989), p. 226.
23 Contra Allen (1991), pp. 173–95. See Finkielkraut (1988).
24 Cf. Simone (1989), pp. 216–17; Rorty (1991c), p. 72.
25 Simone unfortunately licenses the ambiguity here of 'occupying' the positions of others. Nevertheless, his point is not to take over, once again, those positions but to find out in person, so to speak, what it is like *to be* in those positions. Simone (1989), pp. 31–2, 19, 24, 212.
26 P. J. Williams (1991), pp. 129–30.
27 I am not suggesting that there was no resistance, especially by blacks, to segregation earlier in the century. However, the emergence of effective civil rights challenges can be traced to *Sweatt v. Painter* in 1938, through the effective education, employment and housing cases of the 1940s, to the *Brown v. Board of Education* decisions in 1954–55. For an interesting account of this history in terms of a biography of Charles Hamilton Houston, arguably the leading litigator in virtually every case through this period, see McNeil (1983).
28 Cf. Parekh (1987), p. viii.
29 Torres (1991), pp. 995–6. Cf. Coffey (1987), p. 123; and Triandis (1988), p. 31.
30 Cf. Coffey (1987), p. 123; Bhabha (1990), pp. 207–8.
31 P. J. Williams (1991), p. 121.
32 Bhabha (1990), p. 211.
33 Connolly (1991), p. 211.
34 Ibid., p. 208.
35 Ibid., pp. 92, 159, and more generally pp. 35, 120, 160–1.
36 I use the term 'object' of racist expression here rather than the more popular usage of 'victim' for two reasons. First, 'victim' suggests the misleading connotation of helplessness. Second, in so far as there is a warranted insistence upon victimization, we might want to suggest that members of society at large are victimized by the violence of the expression, though some—those who are its objects—more directly

and damagingly than those who are not. 'Objects' is intended also to highlight the
objectification that occurs in being subjected to racist expression.
37 Cf. Simone (1989), p. 90.
38 Cf. Bobo (1988), pp. 85–114.
39 Cf. Parekh (1987), p. vii.
40 For an analysis of the distinction between cruelty and coercion with respect to slavery,
see Frederickson and Lasch (1970), p. 179.
41 Commission for Racial Equality in Britain generally proceeds in this manner.
42 Cf. Chesler and Delgado (1987), p. 195; Hunt (1987), p. 24.
43 Bell (1992b) demolishes the 'pay per discrimination' suggestion in his satirical
construction of a 'racial preference licensing scheme'. Cf. Bell (1992a).
44 See the generally thoughtful column by O'Neill (1991), p. A44.
45 See D'Souza (1991).
46 Cf. P. B. Smith (1987), p. 69.
47 For an example of a policy proposal embodying this individualist presupposition, see
'The Wrong Way to Reduce Campus Tensions: A Statement of the National
Association of Scholars', a political advertisement taken out in the *New York Review
of Books,* December 5, 1991, p. 23.
48 Parekh (1987), pp. x–xi.
49 Hartman (1988), p. 28; and Derrida (1989), p. 206.
50 See Bauer and Bauer (1970), p. 38.
51 To name some names: Michael Levin, Linda Gottfredson, and her collaborator Robert
Gordon have been arguing over the last decade that black people are one standard
deviation less intelligent than whites. The evidence they continue to rely upon is
traceable to the long-discredited intelligence testing by Audrey Shuey in the 1960s.
Levin has also publicly argued that the New York City subway system should reserve
one coach on each train exclusively for black youth so as to restrict subway crime.
Cf. Levin (1992). Gottfredson received a grant from the Pioneer Foundation, long
committed to perpetuating white supremacy, which she used not for research but to
send materials, in the name of both the foundation and her university, to medical
school registrars to discourage them from pursuing preferential admissions policies.
Leonard Jeffries has received considerable press, not to mention rightful wrath, for
the anti-Semitic remarks he has made in public. Recent academically related denials
that the Holocaust occurred have been made by Arthur Butz, a professor of
engineering at Northwestern University, and David Irving in Britain. Bradley Smith,
a California amateur academic, has recently attempted, with mixed success, to buy
advertizing space in student campus newspapers for a view that claims Hitler's gas
chambers were used only to fumigate clothes. It strikes me that challenging the
historical facticity of the experience of European Jews in World War II is akin to
challenging the occurrence of the Pearl Harbor bombing or the blitz on London. Why
does there seem to be greater tolerance of the former than there would be for the latter?
52 Lukes (1980), pp. 218–9.
53 Kozol (1992).
54 Contra Sowell (1990).
55 Ezorsky (1991); Rosenfeld (1991); Carter (1991a); Lynch (1989).
56 For one representative of the argument, see Allen (1991), 172–95; for a critique, see
Radin (1991), pp. 130–49.

57 I taught in a remedial program in a state-funded institution in New York City in the mid-1980s. Fifty percent of incoming students functionally could not read or write, a rough indication of the massive failure of the public school system. Students in my classes were men and women, blacks, Latino and Latina, and whites of every ethnic description.

58 See Peller (1991), p. B2. See also Radin (1991), pp. 130–49.

59 D'Souza (1991); Carter (1991a). D'Souza's and Carter's books are united in attacking preferential policies from similar assumptions, in common terms, and on the basis of a largely anecdotal style. D'Souza's book is more journalistic, more fabricated. Like his public appearances, critical arguments in the book are underpinned only by the depthless mirror of argument from anecdote. Carter's book is better argued and so to be taken more seriously. But Carter is disingenuous in protesting his critical characterization as neoconservative: Why, after all, does he commit so much ink to advising the Republican party on how to approach blacks while he levels only repetitive criticism at what he refers to repeatedly and in totalizing terms as the 'civil rights establishment'? Moreover, the book rests upon some deep-seated and unquestioned assumptions: Carter's basic standard of policy evaluation is efficiency. This in turn is tied to free market and individualistic assumptions about labor. The point, he clearly thinks, is to get ahead individually in the competition, and efficiency requires alleviating monopolistic constraints on the market. This seems to also apply to ideas, which are repeatedly characterized in terms of a marketplace. Yet, if he is committed to the marketplace of ideas, how can Carter complain when positions he supports—whether expressed by himself or others—are rejected. They simply have no market. Carter's response seems to extend the economic model: the monopoly exerted by the civil rights status quo is taken to squash dissent. But, again, the civil rights establishment, such as it is, is far from hegemonic; and black neoconservative intellectuals have hardly had difficulty getting work published or speaking engagements. Actually, one could refer to neoconservativism as running a private preferential treatment program. In any case, if—as Carter believes with liberals—race is supposed to make no difference, if it is an irrelevant category, on what grounds can he complain that his most ardent critics are black like himself?

60 But see the useful little book by Ezorsky (1991).

61 Carter (1991a), p. 211; Baier (1978).

62 P. J. Williams (1991), p. 103, and in general p. 92. Cf. Peller (1991) and Radin (1991).

63 Peller (1991), p. B2.

64 Contra D'Souza (1991), pp. 54–5.

65 Balibar (1991b), p. 18.

Bibliography

Abelson, R. P. (1976) 'Social Psychology's Rational Man'. In S. I. Benn and G. Mortimer, eds. *Rationality and the Social Sciences,* (London: Routledge and Kegan Paul)

Abercrombie, A., Hickman, C. J., and Johnson, M. L., eds. (1978) *A Dictionary of Biology* (Harmondsworth: Penguin)

Abrams, C. (1966) 'The Housing Problem and the Negro', *Daedalus* 95, 1 (Winter): 64–75

Adorno, T. W., Frenkel–Breunswik, E., Levinson, D. and Sanford, R. N. (1950) *The Authoritarian Personality* (New York: Harper and Row)

Agassi, J. (1987) 'Theories of Rationality'. In J. Agassi and I. C. Jarvie, eds. *Rationality: The Critical View* (Dordrecht: Martinus Nijhoff)

Agassi, J. and Jarvie, I. C. (1987a) 'The Rationality of Dogmatism'. In J. Agassi and I. C. Jarvie, eds. *Rationality: The Critical View* (Dordrecht: Martinus Nijhoff)

Agassi, J. and Jarvie, I. C. (1987b) 'The Rationality of Irrationalism'. In J. Agassi and I. C. Jarvie, eds. *Rationality: The Critical View* (Dordrecht: Martinus Nijhoff)

Agassi, J. and Jarvie, I. C., eds. (1987) *Rationality: The Critical View* (Dordrecht: Martinus Nijhoff)

Allen, W. B. (1991) 'Black and White Together: A Reconsideration'. In E. F. Paul, J. Paul, and F. D. Miller, eds., *Reassessing Civil Rights (Oxford: Basil Blackwell)*

Allport, G. (1954) The Nature of Prejudice (Boston: Beacon Press)

Althusser, L. (1971a) 'Ideology and Ideological State Apparatuses'. In L. Althusser *Lenin and Philosophy.* Trans. Ben Brewster (London: New Left Books)

Althusser, L. (1971b) *Lenin and Philosophy.* Trans. Ben Brewster (London: New Left Books)

Amin, S. (1990) *Eurocentrism* (London: Verso)

Anderson, B. (1983) *Imagined Communities* (London: Verso)

Anderson, E. (1990) *Streetwise: Race, Class, and Change in an Urban Community* (Chicago: University of Chicago Press)

Anderson, K. J. (1988) 'Cultural Hegemony and the Race–Definition Process in Chinatown, Vancouver: 1880–1980', *Society and Space* 6, 2: 127–49

Anderson, K. J. (1987) 'The Idea of Chinatown: The Power of Place and Institutional Practice in the Making of a Racial Category', *Annals of the Association of American Geographers* 77, 4: 58–598

Appiah, K. A. (1991) 'Is the Post- in Postmodernism the Post- in Postcolonial?', *Critical Inquiry* 17 (Winter): 336–57

Appiah, K. A. (1990a) 'Race'. In F. Lentricchia and T. McLaughlin, eds., *Critical Terms for Literary Study* (Chicago: Chicago University Press)

Appiah, K. A. (1990b) 'Racisms' In D. T. Goldberg, ed., *Anatomy of Racism,* (Minneapolis: University of Minnesota Press)

Appiah, K. A. (1989) 'The Conservation of Race', *Black American Literature Forum* 23, 1 (Spring): 37–60

Appiah, K. A. (1986) '"Are We Ethnic? The Theory and Practice of American Pluralism." Rev. of *Beyond Ethnicity*, by Werner Sollors', *Black American Literature Forum* 20: 209–223

Appiah, K. A. (1985) 'The Uncompleted Argument: Du Bois and the Illusion of Race', *Critical Inquiry* 12, 1 (Autumn): 21–37

Appiah, K. A. (1984) 'Strictures on Structures: The Prospects for a Structuralist Poetics of Fiction'. In H. L. Gates Jr., ed., *Black Literature and Literary Criticism* (New York: Methuen)

Aquinas, T. (1948) *Basic Writings of St. Thomas Aquinas,* A. Pegis, ed. (New York: Random House)

Aristotle (1985) *Aristotle, Nicomachean Ethics.* Trans. T. E. Irwin. (Indianapolis: Hackett)

Aristotle (1980) *Aristotle's Nicomachean Ethics.* Trans. H. G. Apostle. (Dordrecht, Netherlands: D. Reidel)

Aristotle (1973) *Aristotle's Ethics.* Trans. J. L. Ackrill. (New York: Humanities Press)

Aristotle (1946) *The Basic Works of Aristotle,* R. McKeon, ed. (New York: Random House)

Aronowitz, S. (1981) *The Crisis in Historical Materialism* (New York: Praeger)

Austin, J. H. (1962) *How To Do Things with Words* (Cambridge, Mass.: Harvard University Press)

Bachelard, G. (1964) *The Poetics of Space.* Trans. M. Jolas. (Boston: Beacon Press)

Baier, K. (1984) 'Rationality, Reason and the Good'. In D. Copp and D. Zimmerman, eds. *Morality, Reason and Truth* (Totowa, NJ: Rowman and Alanheld)

Baier, K. (1982) 'The Conceptual Link Between Morality and Rationality', *Nous* 1, 16 (March): 78–88

Baier, K. (1978) 'Merit and Race', *Philosophia* 8, 2–3: 121–151

Baker, D. (1983) *Race, Ethnicity, and Power* (London: Routledge and Kegan Paul)

Baker, D. (1978) 'Race and Power: Comparative Approaches to the Analysis of Race Relations', *Ethnic and Racial Studies* 1, 3: 316–35

Baker, H. A., Jr. (1986) 'Caliban's Triple Play', *Critical Inquiry* 13, 1 (Autumn): 182–96

Baker, J. (1974) *Race* (Oxford: Oxford University Press)

Baldwin, J. (1853) *The Flush Times of Alabama and Mississippi* (New York: D. Appleton)

Balibar, E. (1991a) *'Es Gibt Keinen Staat in Europa*: Racism and Politics in Europe Today', *New Left Review* 187 (May–June): 5–19

Balibar, E. (1991b) 'Is There a Neo-Racism?'. In E. Balibar and I. Wallerstein, *Race, Nation, Class: Ambiguous Identities* (London: Verso)

Balibar, E. (1991c) 'Racism and Nationalism'. In E. Balibar and I. Wallerstein, *Race, Nation, Class: Ambiguous Identities* (London: Verso)

Balibar, E. (1990) 'Paradoxes of Universality'. In D. T. Goldberg, ed., *Anatomy of Racism* (Minneapolis: University of Minnesota Press)

Balibar, E. (1988) 'Propositions on Citizenship', *Ethics* 98 (July): 723

Balibar, E. and Wallerstein, I. (1991) *Race, Nation, Class: Ambiguous Identities* (London: Verso)

Banton, M. (1988) *Racial Theories* (Cambridge: Cambridge University Press)

Banton, M. (1987) 'United States Ideology as Collective Representation', *Ethnic and Racial Studies* 10: 466–8

Banton, M. (1986) 'Epistemological Assumptions in the Study of Racial Differentiation'. In J. Rex and D. Mason, eds., *Theories of Race and Ethnic Relations* (Cambridge: Cambridge University Press)

Banton, M. (1983) *Ethnic and Racial Competition* (Cambridge: Cambridge University Press)

Banton, M. (1970) 'The Concept of Racism'. In S. Zubaida, ed., *Race and Racialism* (London: Tavistock)

Barker, F., Hulme, P., Iversen, M., and Loxley, D., eds. (1985) *Europe and Its Others* (Colchester: University of Essex Press)

Barker, M. (1981) *The New Racism* (London: Junction Books)

Barrett, S. (1987) *Is God a Racist? The Right Wing in Canada* (Toronto: University of Toronto Press)

Bar-Tal, D., Grauman, C. F., Kruglanski, A. W., and Stroebe, W., eds. (1989) *Stereotyping and Prejudice: Changing Conceptions* (New York: Springer-Verlag)

Barth, F. (1969) *Ethnic Groups and Boundaries: The Social Organization of Cultural Difference* (Boston: Little, Brown)

Barthes, R. (1990) 'African Grammar'. In D. T. Goldberg, ed., *Anatomy of Racism* (Minneapolis: University of Minnesota Press)

Baubock, R. (1992) *Immigration and the Boundaries of Citizenship*, Monograph on Ethnic Relations No. 4 (Warwick: Warwick Centre for Research in Ethnic Relations)

Bauer, R. A. and Bauer, A. H. (1970) 'Day to Day Resistance to Slavery'. In J. Bracey, A. Meier, and E. Rudwick, eds., *American Slavery: The Question of Resistance* (Belmont: Wadsworth)

Bauman, Z. (1992) *Intimations of Postmodernity* (London: Routledge)

Bauman, Z. (1991) *Modernity and Ambivalence* (Ithaca: Cornell University Press)

Bauman, Z. (1989) *Modernity and the Holocaust* (Oxford: Polity Press)

Baumann, J. (1987) *Public Housing, Race, and Renewal: Urban Planning in Philadelphia, 1920–1974* (Philadelphia: Temple University Press)

Becker, G. (1957) *The Economics of Discrimination* (Chicago: University of Chicago Press)

Bell, D. (1992a) *Faces at the Bottom of the Well: The Permanence of Racism* (New York: Basic Books)

Bell, D. (1992b) 'The Racial Preference Licensing Act: A Fable About the Politics of Hate', *ABA Journal* (September): 50–5.

Bentham, J. (1907) *An Introduction to the Principles of Morals and Legislation* (Oxford: Clarendon Press)

Ben-Tovim, G., Gabriel, J., Law, I., and Stredder, K. (1986) 'A Political Analysis of Local Struggles for Racial Equality'. In J. Rex and D. Mason, eds., *Theories of Race and Ethnic Relations* (Cambridge: Cambridge University Press)

Benveniste, E. (1971) *Problems of General Linguistics* (Miami: University of Miami Press)

Bergesen, A. (1980) 'Official Violence During the Watts, Newark, and Detroit Race Riots of the 1960s'. In P. Lauderdale, ed., *A Political Analysis of Deviance* (Minneapolis: University of Minnesota Press)

Bhabha, H. (1990) 'The Third Space: Interview'. In J. Rutherford, ed., *Identity: Community, Culture, Difference* (London: Lawrence and Wishart)

Bhabha, H., ed., (1990) *Nation and Narration* (London: Routledge)

Blauner, R. (1972) *Racial Oppression in America: Essays in Search of a Theory* (New York: Harper and Row).

Blauner, R. and Wellman, D. (1973) 'Toward the Decolonization of Social Research'. In J. Ladner, ed., *The Death of White Sociology* (New York: Random House)

Block, N. J. and Dworkin, G. (1974a) 'IQ Heritability and Inequality. Part I', *Philosophy and Public Affairs* 3, 4 (Summer): 331–409

Block, N. J. and Dworkin, G. (1974b) 'IQ Heritability and Inequality. Part II', *Philosophy and Public Affairs* 4, 1 (Fall): 40–99

Bobo, L. (1988) 'Group Conflict, Prejudice, and the Paradox of Contemporary Racial Attitudes'. In P. A. Katz and D. A. Taylor, eds., *Eliminating Racism: Profiles in Controversy* (New York: Plenum Press)

Boggs, J. (1970) *Racism and the Class Struggle: Further Pages from a Black Worker's Notebook* (New York: Monthly Review Press)

Boime, A. (1990) *The Art of Exclusion: Representing Blacks in the Nineteenth Century* (Washington, DC: Smithsonian Institute Press)

Bosch, H. (1500) *Garden of Earthly Delights* (Madrid: Prado Museum)

Boskin, J. (1986) *Sambo* (Oxford: Oxford University Press)

Boston, T. (1988) *Race, Class, and Conservativism* (Boston: Unwin Hyman)

Bourdieu, P. and Passeron, J.-C. (1977) *Reproduction in Education, Society, and Culture* (London: Sage Publications)

Boxill, B. (1991) 'Wilson on the Truly Disadvantaged', *Ethics* 101 (April): 579–92

Boxill, B. (1983) 'The Race-Class Questions'. In L. Harris, ed., *Philosophy Born of Struggle: Anthology of Afro-American Philosophy Since 1917* (Dubuque: Kendall/Hunt)

Boyd, William (1963) 'Genetics and the Human Race', *Science* 140 (June 7): 1057–64

Bracey, J., Meier, A. and Rudwick, E., eds. (1970) *American Slavery: The Question of Resistance* (Belmont, CA: Wadsworth)

Bracken, H. (1978) 'Racism and Philosophy', *Philosophia* 8, 2–3: 241–60

Bracken, H. (1973) 'Essence, Accident and Race', *Hermathena* CXVI (Winter): 81–96

Brandt, G. and Muir, D. (1986) 'Schooling, Morality and Race', *Journal of Moral Education* 15:58–67.

Brantlinger, P. (1985) 'Victorians and Africans: The Genealogy of the Myth of the Dark Continent', *Critical Inquiry* 12, 1 (Autumn): 166–203

Brint, M. and Weaver, W., eds. (1991) *Pragmatism in Law and Society* (Boulder, CO: Westview Press)

Broca, P. (1950) 'On the Phenomena of Hybridity in the Genus Homo'. In E. Count, ed., *This is Race* (New York: Henry Schuman)

Brock, D. (1982) 'Utilitarianism and Aiding Others'. In H. B. Miller and W. H. Williams, eds., *The Limits of Utilitarianism,* (Minneapolis: University of Minnesota Press)

Brown, K. M. (1986a) 'Keeping their Distance: The Cultural Production and Reproduction of Racist Non-Racism', *Australian and New Zealand Journal of Sociology* 22, 3 (November): 394–5

Brown, K. M. (1986b) 'Establishing Difference: Culture, "Race", Ethnicity and the Production of Ideology', *Australian and New Zealand Journal of Sociology* 22, 2 (July): 175–86

Bruening, W. (1974) 'Racism: A Philosophical Analysis of a Concept', *Journal of Black Studies* 5, 1 (September): 3–17

Bunge, W. (1962) *Theoretical Geography* (Gleerup, Sweden: University of Lund)

Burrows, J. (1991) 'Conversational Politics: Richard Rorty's Pragmatist Apology for Liberalism'. In A. Malachowski, ed., *Reading Rorty* (Oxford: Basil Blackwell)

Callinicos, A. (1992) 'Race and Class', *International Socialism* 35 (Summer): 3–39

Campbell, D. (1967) 'Stereotypes and the Perception of Group Differences', *American Psychology* 22: 823–35

Carmichael, S. and Hamilton, C. V. (1967) *Black Power: The Politics of Liberation in America* (New York: Random House)

Carter, S. L. (1991a) *Reflections of an Affirmative Action Baby* (New York: Basic Books)

Carter, S. L. (1991b) 'The Logic of Racial Preferences', *Transition: An International Review* 51: 158–82.

Cashmore, E. E. (1988) *Dictionary of Race and Ethnic Relations* (London: Routledge)

Caws, M. A., ed. (1974) *About French Poetry from Dada to 'Tel Quel'* (Detroit: Wayne State University Press)

Caws, P. (1974) 'On the Determination of the Text'. In M. A. Caws, ed., *About French Poetry from Dada to 'Tel Quel'* (Detroit: Wayne State University Press)

Caws, P. (1968) 'Order and Value in the Sciences'. In P. Kuntz, ed. *The Concept of Order* (Seattle: University of Washington Press)

Cavell, S. (1976) *The Claim of Reason* (Oxford: Oxford University Press)

Cell, J. (1982) *The Highest Stage of White Supremacy: The Origins of Segregation in South Africa and the American South* (Cambridge: Cambridge University Press)

Chafets, Z. (1990) 'The Tragedy of Detroit', *New York Sunday Times Magazine* (July 29): 20–6, 38, 42, 50–1

Chamberlain, H. S. (1968) *The Foundations of the Nineteenth Century,* G. Mosse, ed. (New York: Howard Fertig)

Chamberlin, J. E. and Gilman, S. L., eds. (1985) *Degeneration: The Dark Side of Progress* (New York: Columbia University Press)

Chametzky, J. (1984) 'Styron's *Sophie's Choice,* Jews and Other Marginals, and the Mainstream', *Prospects* 9: 430–8

Cheboksarov, N. (1980) 'Critical Analysis of Racism and Colonialism'. In UNESCO, ed., *Sociological Theories: Race and Colonialism* (Paris: UNESCO)

Cherry, R. (1977) 'The Economics of Racism'. In D. Gordon, ed., *Problems in Political Economy,* 2nd ed. (Lexington, MA: D. C. Heath and Co.)

Chesler, M. and Delgado, H. (1987) 'Race Relations Training and Organizational Change'. In J. W. Shaw, P. G., Nordlie, and R. M. Shapiro, eds., *Strategies for Improving Race Relations: The Anglo-American Experience* (Manchester: Manchester University Press)

Chivers, T. S. (1985a) 'Introduction: Rationalizing Racial and Ethnic Competition', *Ethnic and Racial Studies* 8, 4 (October): 465–69

Chivers, T. S. (1985b) 'Is Expulsion Rational? Dealing with Unwanted Minorities as Issues of Morality', *Ethnic and Racial Studies* 8, 4 (October): 465–69

Chomsky, N. (1977) *Language and Responsibility* (New York: Pantheon Books)

Clarke, D. S., Jr. (1984) 'Ignoring Available Evidence', *Southern Journal of Philosophy* 22, 4 (Winter): 453–467

Clifford, J. (1988) 'Histories of the Tribal and the Modern'. In J. Clifford, *The Predicament of Culture: Twentieth Century Ethnography, Literature, and Art* (Cambridge, MA: Harvard University Press)

Coetzee, J. M. (1989) *White Writing* (New Haven: Yale University Press)

Coetzee, J. M. (1986) 'Tales of Afrikaners', *New York Sunday Times Magazine* (March 9): 19–22, 74–5

Coffey, J. F. (1987) 'Race Training in the United States: An Overview'. In J. W. Shaw, P. G., Nordlie, and R. M. Shapiro, eds., *Strategies for Improving Race Relations: The Anglo-American Experience* (Manchester: Manchester University Press)

Cohen, C. (1979) 'Why Racial Preference is Illegal and Immoral', *Commentary* 68, 3: 43–53

Cohen, P. (1988) 'The Perversions of Inheritance: Studies in the Making of Multi-Racist Britain'. In P. Cohen and H. S. Bains, eds., *Multi-Racist Britain* (London: Macmillan)

Cohen, P. and Bains, H. S., eds. (1988) *Multi-Racist Britain* (London: Macmillan)

Cole, R. (1972) 'Sixteenth Century Travel Books as a Source of European Attitudes Toward Non-White and Non-Western Culture', *Proceedings of the American Philosophical Society* 116, 1 (February): 59–67

Collins, P. H. (1990) *Black Feminist Thought: Knowledge, Consciousness, and the Politics of Empowerment* (London: Harper Collins)

Comaroff, J. (1987) 'Of Totemism and Ethnicity: Consciousness, Practice and the Signs of Inequality', *Ethnos* 52, 3–4: 301–323

Connolly, W. (1991) *Identity/Difference: Democratic Negotiations of Political Paradox* (Ithaca: Cornell University Press)

Coon, C. (1982) *Racial Adaptations* (New York: Nelson Hall)

Coughlin, E. K. (1988) 'Worsening Plight of the Underclass Catches Attention', *The Chronicle of Higher Education* (March): A5

Count, E., ed. (1950) *This is Race* (New York: Henry Schuman)

Cox, O. C. (1948) *Caste, Class and Race* (New York: Modern Reader)

Creigs, B. C. and Stanback, H. J. (1986) 'The Black Underclass: Theory and Reality', *The Black Scholar* (September): 24–32

Crenshaw, K. (1988) 'Race, Reform, and Retrenchment: Transformation and Legitimation in Antidiscrimination Law', *Harvard Law Review* 101, 7 (May): 1331–87

Cross, M. and Keith, M., eds. (1992) *Racism, the City, and the State* (London: Routledge)

Crush, J., Reitsma, H., and Rogerson, C., eds. (1982) 'Decolonizing the Human Geography of Southern Africa', *Tijdschrift voor Economische en Sociale Geografie* 73: 197–270

Dabydeen, D. (1985) *Hogarth's Blacks: Images of Blacks in Eighteenth Century English Art* (Copenhagen: Dangaroo Press)

Davis, D. and Marcus, G. (1991) 'Memorandum on the Residential Environment Bill', Mimeo (South Africa: Centre for Applied Legal Studies, University of Witwatersrand

Davis, F. J. (1989) *Who Is Black? One Nation's Definition* (University Park, PA: Penn State University Press)

Dear, M. J. (1986) 'Postmodernism and Planning', *Society and Space* 4: 367–84

DeLepervanche, M. (1980) 'From Race to Ethnicity', *Australian and New Zealand Journal of Sociology* 16 (March): 24–37

Deleuze, G. (1988) *Foucault.* Trans. S. Hand. (Minneapolis: University of Minnesota Press)

Derrida, J. (1992) *The Other Heading* (Bloomington: Indiana University Press)

Derrida, J. (1989) *Memoires: for Paul de Man,* Rev. ed. (New York: Columbia University Press)

Derrida, J. (1985) 'Racism's Last Word', *Critical Inquiry* 12, 1 (Autumn): 290–9

Devlin, R., ed. (1991) *Canadian Perspectives on Legal Theory* (Toronto: Emond–Montgomery Publishers)

Dex, S. (1985) 'The Use of Economist's Models in Sociology', *Ethnic and Racial Studies* 8, 4 (October): 516–33

Diamond, C. (1988) 'Losing Your Concepts', *Ethics* 98, 2 (January): 255–277

Diamond, R. and Cottrol, R. (1983) 'Codifying Caste: Louisiana's Racial Classification Scheme and the Fourteenth Amendment', *Loyola Law Review* 29, 2: 255–85

Dominguez, M. (1977) 'The Ideologies of Racism and Sexism: A Comparison', *Review Journal of the Philosophy of Social Science* 1: 261–71

Doob, L. (1960) *Becoming More Civilized* (New Haven: Yale University Press)

Douglas, M. (1966) *Purity and Danger: An Analysis of the Concepts of Pollution and Taboo* (London: Routledge and Kegan Paul)

Driver, F. (1985) 'Power, Space, and the Body: A Critical Assessment of Foucault's *Discipline and Punish'*, *Society and Space* 3: 425–46

D'Souza, D. (1991) *Illiberal Education: The Politics of Race and Sex on Campus* (New York: The Free Press)

Dudley, E. and Novak, M. E., eds. (1972) *The Wild Man Within: An Image from the Renaissance to Romanticism* (Pittsburgh: University of Pittsburgh Press)

Dummett, A. (1986) 'Race, Culture and Moral Education', *Journal of Moral Education* 15, 1 (January): 10–15

Dummett, A. and Dummett, M. (1982) 'The Role of Government in Britain's Racial Crisis'. In C. Husband, ed., *Race in Britain* (London: Open University Press)

Dumont, L. (1970) *Homo Hierarchus* (Chicago: University of Chicago Press)

Duncan, J. and Mindlin, A. (1964) 'Municipal Fair Housing Legislation: Community Beliefs and Facts', *Phylon* 25, 3 (Fall): 217–37

Duster, T. (1988) 'Social Implications of the "New" Black Underclass', *The Black Scholar* (May/June): 2–9

Dworkin, R. (1991) 'Pragmatism, Right Answers, and True Banality'. In M. Brint and W. Weaver, eds., *Pragmatism in Law and Society* (Boulder, CO: Westview Press)

Dworkin, R. (1976) *Taking Rights Seriously* (Cambridge: Harvard University Press)

Eagleton, T. (1982) 'Wittgenstein's Friends', *New Left Review* 135: 64–90

Eckberg, D. (1979) *Intelligence and Race* (New York: Praeger)

Eipper, C. (1983) 'The Magician's Hat: A Critique of the Concept of Ethnicity', *Australian and New Zealand Journal of Sociology* 19, 3: 427–46

Elster, J. (1985) 'Rationality, Morality, and Collective Action', *Ethics* 96 (October): 136–55

England, P. (1989) 'A Feminist Critique of Rational Choice Theories: Implications for Sociology', *The American Sociologist* (Spring): 14–28

Erikson, E. (1965) 'The Concept of Identity in Race Relations'. In T. Parsons and K. Clark, eds., *The Negro American* (Boston: Riverside Press)

Essed, P. (1990) *Everyday Racism: Reports from Women of Two Cultures* (Claremont, CA: Hunter House)

Ezorsky, G. (1991) *Justice and Affirmative Action* (Ithaca: Cornell University Press)

Fabian, J. (1990) 'Presence and Representation: The Other and Anthropological Writing', *Critical Inquiry* 16 (Summer): 753–72

Fabian, J. (1983) *Time and the Other: How Anthropology Makes Its Object* (New York: Columbia University Press)

Fainstein, N. (1986) 'The Underclass/Mismatch Hypothesis as an Explanation for Black Economic Deprivation', *Politics and Society* 15, 4: 403–51

Fanon, F. (1970a) *Black Skin White Masks.* Trans. C. L. Markmann (London: Paladin)

Fanon, F. (1970b) *A Dying Colonialism.* Trans. by H. Chevalier (London: Pelican Books)

Febvre, L. (1975) 'The Problem of Unbelief in the Sixteenth Century' in *Historians at Work,* P. Gay and G. Cavanaugh, eds. (New York: Harper and Row)

Febvre, L. and Martin, H.-J. (1976) *The Coming of the Book: The Impact of Printing 1450–1800* (London: New Left Books)

Feinberg, J. (1988) *Harmless Wrongdoings* (Oxford: Oxford University Press)

Feinberg, J. (1973) *Social Philosophy* (Englewood Cliffs: Prentice-Hall)

Feinberg, J. (1970) 'The Nature and Value of Rights', *Journal of Value Inquiry* 4: 263–7

Ferguson, R., Gever, G., Minh-ha, T. T., and West, C., eds. (1990) *Out There: Marginalization and Contemporary Cultures* (Cambridge: MIT Press)

Field, G. (1977) 'Nordic Racism', *Journal of the History of Ideas* 38 (July–Sept.): 523–40

Fields, B. (1990) 'Slavery, Race, and Ideology in the United States of America', *New Left Review* 181 (May/June): 95–118

Fikes, R. (1988) 'Racist Quotes from Persons of Note, Part I', *Journal of Ethnic Studies* 15, 4 (Winter): 138–42

Finkielkraut, A. (1988) *The Undoing of Thought* (London: The Claridge Press)

Fishman, J. (1956) 'Examination of the Process and Functions of Social Stereotyping', *Journal of Social Psychology* 43: 27–64

Fiske, S. T. and Neuberg, S. L. (1989) 'Category-Based and Individuating Processes'. In Bar-Tal et al., eds., *Stereotyping and Prejudice: Changing Conceptions* (New York: Springer-Verlag)

Fleure, H. J. (1950) 'Racial Theory and Genetic Ideas'. In E. Count, ed., *This is Race* (New York: Henry Schuman)

Flew, A. (1984) 'The Race Relations Industry', *The Salisbury Review* (Winter): 24–7

Foot, P. (1978) 'Are Moral Considerations Overriding'. In P. Foot, *Virtues and Vices* (Berkeley: University of California Press)

Foucault, M. (1988) 'The Political Technologies of Individuals'. In L. H. Martin, H. Gutman, and P. Hutton, eds., *Technologies of the Self,* (Minneapolis: University of Minnesota Press)

Foucault, M. (1986) 'Of Other Spaces', *Diacritics* (Spring): 22–7

Foucault, M. (1984) 'Space, Knowledge, and Power'. In P. Rabinow, ed., *The Foucault Reader* (New York: Random House)

Foucault, M. (1982) 'Space, Knowledge and Power: Interview with Paul Rabinow', *Skyline* (March): 16–20

Foucault, M. (1980a) 'Body/Power'. In C. Gordon, ed., *Power/Knowledge* (New York: Pantheon Books)

Foucault, M. (1980b) 'Truth/Power'. In C. Gordon, ed., *Power/Knowledge* (New York: Pantheon Books)

Foucault, M. (1980c) 'Two Lectures'. In C. Gordon, ed., *Power/Knowledge* (New York: Pantheon Books)

Foucault, M. (1978) *The History of Sexuality, Volume I* (New York: Random House)

Foucault, M. (1977) *Discipline and Punish* (New York: Pantheon)

Foucault, M. (1972) *The Archaeology of Knowledge.* Trans. A. Sheridan-Smith (London: Tavistock)

Foucault, M. (1970) *The Order of Things* (New York: Random House)

Frank, A. G. (1979) 'Anthropology=Ideology, Applied Anthropology=Politics'. In G. Huizer and B. Mannheim, eds., *The Politics of Anthropology* (The Hague: Mouton)

Frederickson, G. and Lasch, C. (1970) 'Resistance to Slavery'. In J. Bracey, A. Meier, and E. Rudwick, eds., *American Slavery: The Question of Resistance* (Belmont, CA: Wadsworth)

Frey, R. G., ed. (1984) *Utility and Rights* (Minneapolis: University of Minnesota Press)

Fried, M. (1975) *The Notion of Tribe* (Menlo Park, CA: Cummings Publishing)

Friedman, J. B. (1981) *The Monstrous Races in Medieval Art and Thought* (Cambridge: Harvard University Press)

Friedman, L. (1967) 'Government and Slum Housing: Some General Considerations', *Law and Contemporary Problems* 32, 2 (Spring): 357–70.

Gabriel, J. and Ben-Tovim, G. (1977) 'Marxism and the Concept of Racism', *Economy and Society* 7, 2: 118–42

Gans, H. (1990) 'Reconstructing the Underclass: The Term's Dangers as a Planning Concept', *APA Journal* 271 (Summer): 271–77

Gates, H. L., Jr. (1990) 'Critical Remarks'. In D. T. Goldberg, ed., *Anatomy of Racism,* (Minneapolis: University of Minnesota Press)

Gates, H. L., Jr., ed. (1986) *Race, Writing and Difference* (Chicago: University of Chicago Press)

Gates, H. L., Jr., ed. (1984) *Black Literature and Literary Criticism* (New York: Methuen)

Gay, P. (1969) *The Enlightenment: An Interpretation.* 2 vols. (New York: A. Knopf)

Gay, P. and Cavanaugh, G., eds. (1975) *Historians at Work* (New York: Harper and Row)

Geertz, C. (1984) 'Ideology as a Cultural System'. In D. Apter, ed., *Ideology and Discontent,* (New York: Free Press)

Geertz, C. (1973) *The Interpretation of Culture* (New York: Basic Books)

Gellner, E. (1983) *Nations and Nationalism* (Oxford: Basil Blackwell)

Gewirth, A. (1983) 'The Rationality of Reasonableness', *Synthese* 57: 225–47

Giddens, A. (1991) *Modernity and Self-Identity: Self and Society in the Late Modern Age* (Oxford: Polity Press)

Gilman, S. C. (1985) 'Political Theory and Degeneration: From Left to Right, from Up to Down'. In J. E. Chamberlin and S. L. Gilman, eds., *Degeneration: The Dark Side of Progress* (New York: Columbia University Press)

Gilman, S. L. (1990) '"I'm Down on Whores": Race and Gender in Victorian London'. In D. T. Goldberg, ed., *Anatomy of Racism* (Minneapolis: University of Minnesota Press)

Gilman, S. L. (1986) *Jewish Self-Hatred* (Baltimore: Johns Hopkins University Press)

Gilman, S. L. (1985) 'Sexology, Psychoanalysis, and Degeneration: From a Theory of Race to a Race to Theory'. In J. E. Chamberlin and S. L. Gilman, eds., *Degeneration: The Dark Side of Progress* (New York: Columbia University Press)

Gilman, S. L. (1984) *Pathology and Difference* (Ithaca: Cornell University Press)

Gilman, S. L. (1976) *Seeing the Insane* (Secaucus, NJ: The Citadel Press)

Gilroy, P. (1990) 'One Nation Under a Groove: The Politics of "Race" and Racism in Britain'. In D. T. Goldberg, ed., *Anatomy of Racism* (Minneapolis: University of Minnesota Press)

Gilroy, P. (1987) *There Ain't No Black in the Union Jack* (London: Hutchinson)

Gilroy, P. (1980) 'Managing the Underclass: A Further Note on the Sociology of Race Relations in Britain', *Race and Class* XXII, 1: 47–62

Gimenez, M. E. (1988) 'Minorities and the World System: Theoretical and Political Implications of the Internationalization of Minorities'. In J. Smith et al., eds., *Racism, Sexism and the World System* (New York: Greenwood Press)

Glazer, N. (1965) 'The Renewal of Cities', *Scientific American* 213, 3: 192–203

Gliddon, G. and Nott, J. (1988) *Types of Mankind.* Quoted in M. Banton, *Racial Theories* (Cambridge: Cambridge University Press)

Gobineau, A. de (1967) *Essay on the Inequality of Human Races.* Trans. A. Collins (New York: Howard Fertig)

Godelier, M. (1972) *Rationality and Irrationality in Economics* (New York: Monthly Review Press)

Goldberg, D. T. (1992) 'Polluting the Body Politic: Racist Discourse and Urban Location'. In M. Cross and M. Keith, eds., *Racism, the City, and the State* (London: Routledge)

Goldberg, D. T. (1991a) 'Racist Discourse'. In A. Zegeye, L. Harris, and J. Maxted, eds., *Exploitation and Exclusion: Race and Class in Contemporary US Society* (Oxford: Hans Zell)

Goldberg, D. T. (1991b) 'Democracy Inc. (The Return of the Repressed: Race and the Rise of David Duke)', *ArtForum* (January): 23–5

Goldberg, D. T. (1990a) 'The Social Formation of Racist Discourse'. In D. T. Goldberg, ed., *Anatomy of Racism,* (Minneapolis: University of Minnesota Press)

Goldberg, D. T. (1990b) 'Racism and Rationality: The Need for a New Critique', *Philosophy of the Social Sciences* 20, 3 (September): 317–50

Goldberg, D. T. (1990c) 'Tuning in to Whistle Blowing', *Business and Professional Ethics Journal* 7, 2: 85–94

Goldberg, D. T. (1988) 'Cultural Regulation and Censorship: The Case of Blacks Britannica'. In C. Schneider and B. Wallis, eds., *Global Television,* (New York: Wedge Books, MIT Press)

Goldberg, D. T. (1987) 'Raking the Field of the Discourse of Racism', *Journal of Black Studies* 18, 1: 58–71

Goldberg, D. T. (1986a) 'A Grim Dilemma About Racist Referring Expressions', *Metaphilosophy* 17, 4 (October): 224–9

Goldberg, D. T. (1986b) 'Reading the Signs: The Force of Language', *The Philosophical Forum* XVIII 2, 3 (Winter–Spring): 71–93

Goldberg, D. T., ed. (1990) *Anatomy of Racism* (Minneapolis: University of Minnesota Press)

Goldberg, D. T., ed. (1989) *Ethical Theory and Social Issues* (New York: Holt, Rinehart and Winston)

Goldberg, D. T. and Krausz, M., eds. (1993) *Culture and Jewish Identity* (Philadelphia: Temple University Press)

Goodin, R. (1987) 'Exploiting a Situation and Exploiting a Person'. In A. Reeve, ed., *Modern Theories of Exploitation* (London: Sage)

Gooding-Williams, R. (1991) 'Evading Narrative Myth, Evading Prophetic Pragmatism: A Review of Cornel West's *The American Evasion of Philosophy*', *APA Newsletter on Philosophy and the Black Experience* 90:3 (Fall): 12–16

Gordon, C., ed. (1980) *Power/Knowledge* (New York: Pantheon Books)

Gordon, D.,·ed. (1977) *Problems in Political Economy*, 2nd ed. (Lexington, MA: D. C. Heath and Co.)

Gorra, M. (1991) 'Tact and Tarzan', *Transition* 52: 80–91

Gossett, T. (1965) *Race: The History of an Idea in America* (New York: Schocken Books)

Gottfredson, L. (1986) 'Societal Consequences of the g Factor in Employment', *Journal of Vocational Behavior* 29: 379–410

Gould, S. J. (1991) 'The Birth of the Two-Sex World', *New York Review of Books* XXXVIII, 11 (June 13): 11–13

Gould, S. J. (1981) *The Mismeasure of Man* (New York: W. W. Norton)

Gramsci, A. (1952) *Gli Intellectuali e l'Organizzazione della Culture* (Torino, Italy: Einaudi)

Graumann, C. F. and Wintermantel, M. (1989) 'Discriminatory Speech Acts: A Functional Approach'. In D. Bar-Tal et al., eds., *Stereotyping and Prejudice: Changing Conceptions* (New York: Springer-Verlag)

Gray, J. (1986) *Liberalism* (Minneapolis: University of Minnesota Press)

Greenberg, S. (1987) *Legitimating the Illegitimate: State, Markets and Resistance in South Africa* (Berkeley: University of California Press)

Gregory, D. and Urry, J., eds. (1985) *Social Relations and Spatial Structures* (London: Macmillan)

Grier, E. and Grier, G. (1966) 'Equality and Beyond: Housing Segregation in the Great Society', *Daedalus* 95, 1 (Winter): 77–103

Grillo, R. D. (1989) *Dominant Languages: Language and Hierarchy in Britain and France* (Cambridge: Cambridge University Press)

Guillaumin, C. C. (1980) 'The Idea of Race and its Elevation to Autonomous Scientific and Legal Status'. In UNESCO, ed., *Sociological Theories: Race and Colonialism* (Paris: UNESCO)

Habermas, J. (1988) *Philosophical Discourse on Modernity* (Cambridge: MIT Press)

Hacker, A. (1991) *Two Nations: Black and White, Separate, Hostile and Unequal* (New York: Scribner's)

Hakluyt, R. (1962) *Voyages* (New York: Dutton)

Hall, E. (1989) *Inventing the Barbarian* (Oxford: The Clarendon Press)

Hall, S. (1990) 'Cultural Identity and Diaspora'. In J. Rutherford, ed., *Identity: Community, Culture, Difference* (London: Lawrence and Wishart)

Hall, S. (1988) 'The Toad in the Garden: Thatcherism Among the Thatcherites'. In C. Nelson and L. Grossberg, eds., *Marxism and the Interpretation of Culture* (Chicago: University of Illinois Press)

Hall, S. (1980) 'Race, Articulation and Societies Structured in Dominance'. In UNESCO, ed., *Sociological Theories: Race and Colonialism* (Paris: UNESCO)

Hamilton, D. L. and Sherman, S. J. (1989) 'Illusory Correlations: Implications for Stereotype Theory and Research'. In D. Bar-Tal et al., eds., *Stereotyping and Prejudice: Changing Conceptions* (New York: Springer-Verlag)

Hanke, L. (1959) *Aristotle and the American Indians* (Chicago: Regnery Press)

Harding, S. (1987) 'The Curious Coincidence of Feminine and African Moralities: Challenges for Feminist Theory'. In E. Kittay and D. Meyers, eds., *Women and Moral Philosophy* (Totowa, NJ: Rowman and Littlefield)

Hare, R. M. (1980) 'Prediction and Moral Appraisal'. In P. French, T. Uehling, and H. Wettstein, eds., *Midwest Studies in Philosophy III* (Minneapolis: University of Minnesota Press)

Harris, L., ed. (1983) *Philosophy Born of Struggle: Anthology of Afro-American Philosophy Since 1917* (Dubuque, IA: Kendall/Hunt)

Hartman, G. (1988) 'Blindness and Insight', *The New Republic* (March 7): 26–31

Harvey, D. (1989) *The Condition of Postmodernity* (Oxford: Basil Blackwell)

Harvey, D. (1985) *The Urbanization of Capital* (Baltimore: Johns Hopkins University Press)

Harvey, D. (1973) *Social Justice and the City* (Baltimore: Johns Hopkins University Press)

Haugeland, J. (1982) 'Heidegger on Being a Person', *Nous* 16 (March): 15–25

Hauser, A. (1952) *Social History of Art* (New York: Vintage)

Hay, D. (1957) *Europe: The Emergence of an Idea* (Edinburgh: Edinburgh University Press)

Haynes-Bautista, D. (1980) 'Identifying "Hispanic" Populations: The Influence of Research Methodology Upon Public Policy', *American Journal of Public Health* 70, 4 (April): 353–6

Hechter, M., Friedman, D., and Appelbaum, M. (1982) 'A Theory of Ethnic Collective Action', *Migration Review* 16: 412–34

Hegel, W. G. F. (1967) *The Phenomenology of Mind*. Trans. J. B. Baillie (New York: Harper Torchbooks)

Hegel, W. G. F. (1952) *The Philosophy of Right*. Trans. T. R. Knox (Oxford: Oxford University Press)

Heidegger, M. (1969) *Identity and Difference*. Trans. J. Stambaugh (New York: Harper Torchbooks)

Herrnstein, R. (1990) 'Still an American Dilemma', *The Public Interest* 98 (Winter): 3–17

Hersch, J. (1967) 'The Concept of Race', *Diogenes* 59: 114–33

Higginbotham, A. L. (1978) *In the Matter of Color, Race and the American Legal Process: The Colonial Period* (Oxford: Oxford University Press)

Hill, N. (1989) 'Blacks and the Unions', *Dissent* (Fall): 496–500

Hirst, P. (1979) *On Law and Ideology* (London: Macmillan)

Hobbes, T. (1975) *Leviathan*, C. B. Macpherson, ed. (Harmondsworth: Pelican)

Hochschild, J. (1991) 'The Politics of the Estranged Poor', *Ethics* 101 (April): 560–78

Hodge, J. (1975) 'Domination and the Will in Western Thought and Culture'. In J. Hodge et al., *Cultural Bases of Racism and Group Oppression* (Berkeley: Two Riders Press)

Hodge, J., Struckmann, D., and Trost, L. (1975) *Cultural Bases of Racism and Group Oppression* (Berkeley: Two Riders Press)

Hohfeld, W. N. (1919) *Fundamental Legal Conceptions as Applied in Judicial Reasoning* (New Haven: Yale University Press)

Hooks, B. (1992) *Black Looks: Race and Representation* (Bloomington: Indiana University Press)

Hughes, M. A. (1989) 'Misspeaking Truth to Power: A Geographical Perspective on the "Underclass" Fallacy', *Economic Geography* 65, 3 (July): 187–207

Huizer, G. and Mannheim, B., eds. (1979) *The Politics of Anthropology* (The Hague: Mouton)

Hulme, P. (1990) 'The Spontaneous Hand of Nature: Savagery, Colonialism, and the Enlightenment.' In Hulme, P. and Jordanova, L. *The Enlightenment and its Shadows* (London: Routledge)

Hulme, P. and Jordanova, L. (1990) *The Enlightenment and its Shadows* (London: Routledge)

Human Sciences Research Council (HSRC) (1985) *The South African Society: Realities and Future Prospects* (New York: Greenwood Press)

Human Sciences Research Council (HSRC) (1970) *First Annual Report* (Pretoria, South Africa)

Hume, D. (1964) 'Of National Characters'. In T. H. Green and T. H. Grose III, eds., *The Philosophical Works,* (Aalen, Germany: Scientia Veralg)

Hunt, R. G. (1987) 'Coping with Racism: Lessons from Institutional Change in Police Departments'. In J. W. Shaw, P. G., Nordlie, and R. M. Shapiro, eds., *Strategies for Improving Race Relations: The Anglo-American Experience* (Manchester: Manchester University Press)

Husband, C., ed. (1982) *Race in Britain* (London: Open University Press)

Innes, D. (1984) *Anglo American and the Rise of Modern South Africa* (New York: Monthly Review Press)

Innis, L. and Feagin, J. (1989) 'The Black "Underclass" Ideology in Race Relations Analysis', *Social Justice* 16, 4 (Winter): 13–34

Jackson, P., ed. (1987) *Race and Racism: Essays in Social Geography* (London: Allen and Unwin)

Jameson, F. (1984) 'Postmodernism, or the Cultural Logic of Late Capitalism', *New Left Review* 146: 53–92.

Jarvie, I. C. and Agassi, J. (1970) 'The Problem of the Rationality of Magic'. In B. Wilson, ed., *Rationality* (Oxford: Basil Blackwell)

Jefferson, T. (1954) *Notes on the State of Virginia* (Chapel Hill: University of North Carolina Press)

Jencks, C. (1988) 'Deadly Neighborhoods', *The New Republic* (June 13): 23–32

Jencks, C. (1983) 'Thomas Sowell vs. Special Treatment for Blacks', *The New York Review of Books* XXX, 4 (March)

Jenkins, R. (1986) 'Social Anthropological Models of Inter-ethnic Relations'. In J. Rex and D. Mason, eds., *Theories of Race and Ethnic Relations* (Cambridge: Cambridge University Press)

Jensen, A. (1969) 'How Much Can We Boost IQ and Scholastic Achievement?', *Harvard Educational Review* 39 (Winter): 1–123

Jones, G. S. (1971) *Outcast London: A Study in the Relationship between Classes in Victorian Society* (Oxford: Clarendon Press)

Jones, J. M. (1972) *Prejudice and Racism* (Boston: Addison and Wellesley)

Jones, M. (1985) 'Education and Racism', *Journal of Philosophy of Education* 19, 2: 223–34

286   *Bibliography*

Jones, R. A. (1982) 'Perceiving the Other'. In A. G. Miller, ed., *In the Eye of the Beholder* (New York: Praeger Publications)

Jones, T. P. and McEvoy, D. (1978) 'Race and Space in Cloud-Cuckoo Land', *Area* 10: 162–6.

Jordan, W. (1969) *White Over Black* (Chapel Hill: University of North Carolina Press)

Joseph, G. G. (1987) 'Foundations of Eurocentrism in Mathematics', *Race and Class* 28: 13–28

Joseph, G. G., Reddy, V. and Searele-Chatterjee, M. (1990) 'Eurocentrism in the Social Sciences', *Race and Class* 31, 4: 1–26

Kamin, L. (1974) *The Science and Politics of IQ* (Potomac, MD: Erlbaum)

Kant, I. (1965) *Critique of Pure Reason.* Trans. N. Kemp-Smith (New York: St. Martin's Press)

Kant, I. (1960) *Observations on the Feeling of the Beautiful and the Sublime.* Trans. J. T. Goldthwait (Berkeley: University of California Press)

Kant, I. (1959) *Foundation of the Metaphysics of Morals.* Trans. L. W. Beck (Indianapolis: Bobbs–Merrill)

Kant, I. (1950) 'On the Different Races of Man'. In E. W. Count, ed., *This is Race,* (New York: Henry Schuman)

Karst, K. (1989) *Belonging to America: Equal Citizenship and the Constitution* (New Haven: Yale University Press)

Katz, P. A. and Taylor, D. A., eds. (1988) *Eliminating Racism: Profiles in Controversy* (New York: Plenum Press)

Keith, A. (1928) 'The Evolution of the Human Species', *Journal of the Royal Anthropological Society* 58: 305–21

Keith, M. (1992) 'From Punishment to Discipline? Racism, Racialization, and the Policing of Social Control'. In M. Cross and M. Keith, eds., *Racism, the City, and the State,* (London: Routledge)

Kekes, J. (1987) 'Rationality and Problem Solving'. In J. Agassi and I. C. Jarvie, eds., *Rationality: The Critical View* (Dordrecht: Martinus Nijhoff)

Kelman, S. (1981) 'Cost–Benefit Analysis: An Ethical Critique', *Regulation* (January–February): 33–40

Kittay, E. and Meyers, D., eds. (1987) *Women and Moral Philosophy* (Totowa, NJ: Rowman and Littlefield)

Klineberg, O. (1953) *Social Psychology* (New York: Holt, Rinehart and Winston)

Kovel, J. (1970) *White Racism: A Psychohistory* (New York: Pantheon Books)

Koyre, A. (1958) *From the Closed World to the Infinite Universe* (New York: Harper Torchbooks)

Kozol, J. (1992) *Those Young Lives: Still Separate, Still Unequal: Children in America's Schools* (Boston: Crown)

Krieger, M. H. (1986) 'Ethnicity and the Frontier in Los Angeles', *Society and Space* 4: 385–389

Kristeva, J. (1990) '"Ours to Jew or Die": Celine and the Categories of Anti-Semitism'. In D. T. Goldberg, ed., *Anatomy of Racism* (Minneapolis: University of Minnesota Press)

Kuntz, P., ed. (1968) *The Concept of Order* (Seattle: University of Washington Press)

Kuper, A. (1988) *The Invention of Primitive Society* (London: Routledge)

Kushner, J. (1980) *Apartheid in America: An Historical and Legal Analysis of Contemporary Racial Segregation in the United States* (Arlington, VA: Carrolton Press)

Lacan, J. (1977) *Ecrits.* Trans. A. Sheridan-Smith (New York: W. W. Norton)

LaCapra, D., ed. (1991) *The Bounds of Race: Perspectives on Hegemony and Resistance* (Ithaca: Cornell University Press)

Ladner, J., ed. (1973) *The Death of White Sociology* (New York: Random House)

Lal, B. (1986) 'The "Chicago School" of American Sociology, Symbolic Interactionism, and Race Relations Theory'. In J. Rex and D. Mason, eds., *Theories of Race and Ethnic Relations* (Cambridge: Cambridge University Press)

Lauderdale, P., ed. (1980) *A Political Analysis of Deviance* (Minneapolis: University of Minnesota Press)

Leibniz, G. (1981) *New Essays on Human Understanding.* Trans. P. Remnant and J. Bennett (Cambridge: Cambridge University Press)

Lemaire, A. (1977) *Jacques Lacan.* Trans. D. Macey (London: Routledge and Kegan Paul)

Lentricchia, F. and McLaughlin, T., eds. (1990) *Critical Terms for Literary Study* (Chicago: University of Chicago Press)

Lesser, H. (1984) 'Can Racial Discrimination be Proved?', *Journal of Applied Philosophy* 1, 2: 253–61

Levin, M. (1992) 'Responses to Race Differences in Crime', *Journal of Social Philosophy* XXIII, 1 (Spring): 5–29

Levin, M. (1981a) 'Is Racial Discrimination Special?', *Journal of Value Inquiry* 15, 3: 225–34

Levin, M. (1981b) 'Sexism is Meaningless', *St. John's Review* (Autumn): 35–40

Lewis, R. (1988) *Anti-Racism: A Mania Exposed* (London: Quartet Books)

Lewontin, R., Rose, S., and Kamin, L. (1984) *Not in Our Genes: Biology, Ideology, and Human Nature* (New York: Pantheon)

Liska, A., ed. (1975) *The Consistency Controversy* (New York: John Wiley and Sons)

Lloyd, D. (1991) 'Race under Representation', *The Oxford Literary Review* 13, 1–2: 62–94

Lloyd, G. (1984) *The Man of Reason: 'Male' and 'Female' in Western Philosophy* (Minneapolis: The University of Minnesota Press)

Locke, J. (1964) *An Essay Concerning Human Understanding,* A. D. Woozley, ed. (New York: Meridian Books)

Locke, J. (1960) *Two Treatises of Government,* Peter Laslett, ed.(New York: Mentor Books)

Lomasky, L. E. (1987) *Rights, Persons, and the Moral Community* (Oxford: Oxford University Press)

Long, E. (1972) *History of Jamaica* (New York: Arno Press)

Lovejoy, A. (1960) *The Great Chain of Being* (New York: Harper Torchbooks)

Lowi, T. (1988) 'The Theory of the Underclass: A Review of Wilson's *The Truly Disadvantaged', Policy Studies Review* 7, 4 (Summer): 852–8

Lowman, J. (1986) 'Conceptual Issues in the Geography of Crime: Toward a Geography of Social Control', *Annals of the Association of American Geographers* 76, 1: 81–94

Lukes, S. (1980) 'Socialism and Equality'. In J. Sterba, ed., *Justice: Alternative Political Perspectives* (Belmont, CA: Wadsworth)

Lukes, S. (1970) 'Some Problems About Rationality'. In B. Wilson, ed., *Rationality* (Oxford: Basil Blackwell)

Lynch, F. (1989) *Invisible Victims: White Males and the Crisis of Affirmative Action* (New York: Greenwood Press)

Lyon, M. (1985) 'Banton's Contribution to Racial Studies in Britain: An Overview', *Ethnic and Racial Studies* 8, 4 (October): 472–83

McCarthy, J. J. (1982) 'Radical Geography, Mainstream Geography and Southern Africa', *Social Dynamics* 8: 53–70

McCarthy, J. J. and Smit, D. (1984) *South African City: Theory in Analysis and Planning* (Cape Town: Juta)

McClendon, M. (1983) 'Racism, Rational Choice, and White Opposition to Racial Change: A Case Study of Busing', *Political Opinion Quarterly* 49: 214–33

McClintock, A. (1990) '"No Longer in a Future Heaven": Women and Nationalism in South Africa', *Transition* 51: 104–23

McConahay, J. and Hough, J. (1976) 'Symbolic Racism', *Journal of Social Issues* 32, 2: 23–45

MacIntyre, A. (1988) *Whose Justice? Which Rationality?* (South Bend: University of Notre Dame Press)

MacIntyre, A. (1981) *After Virtue* (South Bend: University of Notre Dame Press)

MacIntyre, A. (1974) *A Short History of Ethics* (London: Routledge and Kegan Paul)

MacKeen, A. (1991) 'Liberalism and Ethnocentricity: Redescribing Rorty', *The Oxford Literary Review* 13, 1–2: 252–65

Mackie, J. (1978) 'Can There Be a Right-Based Moral Theory?'. In P. French, T. Uehling, and H. Wettstein, eds., *Midwest Studies in Philosophy*, Vol. III (Minneapolis: University of Minnesota Press)

Mackie, J. (1977) *Ethics: Inventing Right and Wrong* (Harmondsworth: Penguin Books)

McNeil, G. (1983) *Groundwork: Charles Hamilton Houston and the Struggle for Civil Rights* (Philadelphia: University of Pennsylvania Press)

McVeigh, R. (1992) 'The Specificity of Irish Racism', *Race and Class* 33: 31–45

Mafeje, A. (1976) 'The Problem of Anthropology in Historical Perspective: An Inquiry into the Growth of the Social Sciences', *Canadian Journal of African Studies* X, 2: 307–33

Magnet, M. (1989) 'America's Underclass: What to Do?', *Fortune* 115 (May 11): 130

Malachowski, A., ed. (1991) *Reading Rorty* (Oxford: Basil Blackwell)

Mandeville, J. (1983) *The Travels of Sir John Mandeville*. Trans. C. W. R. D. Mosley (Harmondsworth: Penguin)

Margalit, A. (1991) 'Israel's White Hope', *New York Review of Books* XXXVIII, 12 (June 27): 19–25

Marris, P. (1974) *Loss and Change* (London: Routledge)

Marshall, A. (1890) *Principles of Economics* (London: Macmillan)

Marshal, P. J. (1989) 'Taming the Exotic: The British and India in the Seventeenth and Eighteenth Centuries'. In G. S. Rousseau and R. Porter, eds., *Exoticism in the Enlightenment,* (Manchester: Manchester University Press)

Mason, D. (1986) 'Introduction, Controversies and Continuities in Ethnic and Race Relations Theory'. In J. Rex and D. Mason, eds., *Theories of Race and Ethnic Relations* (Cambridge: Cambridge University Press)

Mason, P. (1990) *Deconstructing America: Representations of the Other* (London: Routledge)

Mason, T. D. (1984) 'Individual Participation in Collective Racial Violence: A Rational Choice Perspective', *American Political Science Review* 78: 1040–56

Meek, R. L. (1976) *Social Science and the Noble Savage* (Cambridge: Cambridge University Press)

Mendus, S. (1989) *Toleration and the Limits of Liberalism* (London: Macmillan)

Miles, R. (1989) *Racism* (London: Routledge)

Miles, R. (1988) 'Racialization'. In E. E. Cashmore, *Dictionary of Race and Ethnic Relations* (London: Routledge)

Miles, R. and Phizacklea, A. (1984) *White Man's Country: Racism in British Politics* (London: Pluto Press)

Miles, R. and Phizacklea, A. (1982) *Racism and Migrant Labour* (London: Routledge and Kegan Paul)

Mill, J. (1820) *History of British India.* 2nd ed. (London)

Mill, J. S. (1863) *Utilitarianism* (London)

Mill, J. S. (1859) *On Liberty* (London)

Mill, J. S. (1848) *Principles of Political Economy* (London)

Miller, A. G., ed. (1982) *In the Eye of the Beholder* (New York: Praeger Publications)

Miller, H. B. and Williams, W. H., eds. (1982) *The Limits of Utilitarianism* (Minneapolis: University of Minnesota Press)

Miller, R. (1987) *Fact and Method* (Princeton: Princeton University Press)

Miller, R. (1984) *Analyzing Marx* (Princeton: Princeton University Press)

Montagu, A. (1974) *Man's Most Dangerous Myth* (Oxford: Oxford University Press)

Monture, P. (1991) 'Reflecting on Flint Woman'. In R. Devlin, ed., *Canadian Perspectives on Legal Theory* (Toronto: Emond–Montgomery Publishers)

Mosse, G. (1979) *Toward the Final Solution* (New York: Howard Fertig)

Mudge, P. (1920) 'The Menace to the English Race and its Tradition of Present Day Immigration and Emigration', *Eugenics Review* II: 202–12

Mudimbe, V. (1988) *The Invention of Africa* (Bloomington, IN: Indiana University Press)

Müller, F. M. (1895) *Three Lectures on the Science of Language* (New York: Longman Green)

Myrdal, G. (1962) *The Challenge to Affluence* (New York: Vintage Books)

Myrdal, G. (1944) *The American Dilemma: The Negro Problem and Modern Democracy* (New York: Harper and Row)

Nairn, T. (1980) *The Break-up of Britain* (London: New Left Books)

Nakanishi, D. T. (1988) 'Seeking Convergence in Race Relations Research: Japanese-Americans and the Resurrection of the Internment'. In P. A. Katz and D. A. Taylor, eds., *Eliminating Racism: Profiles in Controversy* (New York: Plenum Press)

Nedelsky, J. (1990) 'Law, Boundaries, and the Bounded Self', *Representations* 30 (Spring): 162–89

Nelson, C. and Grossberg, L., eds. (1988) *Marxism and the Interpretation of Culture* (Chicago: University of Illinois Press)

Nelson, C., Treichler, P., and Grossberg, L. (1992) 'Cultural Studies: An Introduction'. In Nelson, Treichler, and Grossberg, eds., *Cultural Studies* (London: Routledge)

Nelson, C., Treichler, P., and Grossberg, L., eds. (1992) *Cultural Studies* (London: Routledge)

Nettleton, A. and Hammond–Tooke, D., eds. (1989) *African Art in Southern Africa: From Tradition to Township* (Johannesburg: Ad. Donker)

Netton, I. R. (1989) 'The Mysteries of Islam'. In G. S. Rousseau and R. Porter, eds., *Exoticism in the Enlightenment,* (Manchester: Manchester University Press)

Newcomb, T. and Charters, W. (1950) *Social Psychology* (New York: Dryden Press)

Newman, J. (1979) 'Prejudice as Prejudgment', *Ethics* 90 (October): 47–57

Nicholson, L., ed. (1990) *Feminism/Postmodernism* (London: Routledge)

Nozick, R. (1974) *Anarchy, State, and Utopia* (New York: Basic Books)

Nye, R. (1985) 'Sociology and Degeneration: The Irony of Progress'. In J. E. Chamberlin and S. L. Gilman, eds., *Degeneration: The Dark Side of Progress* (New York: Columbia University Press)

Omi, M. and Winant, H. (1987) *Racial Formation in the United States: From the Sixties to the Eighties* (London: Routledge)

O'Neill, R. M. (1991) 'Dealing with Intolerance for Intolerant Views', *Chronicle of Higher Education* (December 18): A44

Outlaw, L. (1990) 'Towards a Critical Theory of "Race"'. In D. T. Goldberg, ed., *Anatomy of Racism* (Minneapolis: University of Minnesota Press)

Outlaw, L. (1988) 'Philosophy, Ethnicity, and Race', Mimeo (Hamden, CT: The Alfred P. Stiernotte Lectures in Philosophy, Quinnipiac College)

Palen, J. J. and London, B., eds. (1984) *Gentrification, Displacement and Neighborhood Revitalization* (Albany: SUNY Press)

Parekh, B. (1987) 'Preface'. In J. W. Shaw, P. G., Nordlie, and R. M. Shapiro, eds., *Strategies for Improving Race Relations: The Anglo-American Experience* (Manchester: Manchester University Press)

Parsons, T. and Clark, K., eds. (1965) *The Negro American* (Boston: Riverside Press)

Patterson, O. (1983) *Slavery and Social Death* (Cambridge: Harvard University Press)

Paul, E. F., Paul, J., and Miller, F. D., eds. (1991) *Reassessing Civil Rights* (Oxford: Basil Blackwell)

Pearson, K. (1925) 'The Problem of Alien Immigration in Britain Illustrated by an Examination of Russian and Polish Jewish Children', *Annals of Eugenics* I: 1–127

Peller, G. (1991) 'Espousing a Positive Vision of Affirmative-Action Policies', *Chronicle of Higher Education* (December 18): B1–2

Philips, M. (1984) 'Racist Acts and Racist Humor', *Canadian Journal of Philosophy* XIV, 1 (March): 75–96

Philipson, M. and Gudel P., eds. (1980) *Aesthetics Today* (New York: Meridian Books)

Phillips, D. (1987) 'The Rhetoric of Antiracism in Public Housing'. In P. Jackson, ed., *Race and Racism: Essays in Social Geography* (London: Allen and Unwin)

Piper, A. M. S. (1991) 'Higher-Order Discrimination'. In O. Flanagan and A. O. Rorty, eds., *Identity, Character and Morality: Essays in Moral Psychology,* (Cambridge: MIT Press)

Plato (1975) *Symposium* (New York: Bobbs–Merrill)

Plato (1972) *Philebus* (Cambridge: Cambridge University Press)

Pletsch, C. (1981) 'The Three Worlds, or the Division of Labor in the Social Sciences, circa 1950–75', *Comparative Studies in Society and History* 23, 4 (October): 565–90

Poliakov, L. (1974) *The Aryan Myth* (New York: Basic Books)

Polo, M. (1958) *The Travels.* Trans. R. Latham (Harmondsworth: Penguin)

Poole, R. (1991) *Morality and Modernity* (London: Routledge)

Popkin, R. (1978) 'Pre-Adamism in Nineteenth Century American Thought: "Speculative Biology" and Racism', *Philosophia* 8, 2–3: 205–39

Powell, E. (1988) 'Introduction'. In R. Lewis, *Anti-Racism: A Mania Exposed* (London: Quartet Books)

Prager, J. (1987a) 'American Political Culture and the Shifting Meaning of Race', *Ethnic and Racial Studies* 10, 1 (January): 62–81

Prager, J. (1987b) 'The Meaning of Difference: A Response to Michael Banton', *Ethnic and Racial Studies* 10, 4 (October): 469–72

Prager, J. (1972) 'White Racial Privilege and Social Change: An Examination of Theories of Racism', *Berkeley Journal of Sociology* XVII: 117–50

Pratt, M. L. (1985) 'Scratches on the Face of the Country; or, What Mr. Barrow Saw in the Land of the Bushmen', *Critical Inquiry* 12, 1 (Autumn): 119–43

Prescott, J. R. V. (1987) *The Geography of Frontiers and Boundaries* (Chicago: Aldine Publishing)

Putnam, C. (1961) *Race and Reason* (Washington, DC: Public Affairs Press)

Putnam, R. (1988) 'Reciprocity and Virtue Ethics', *Ethics* 98, 2 (January): 379–89

Rabinow, P., ed. (1984) *The Foucault Reader* (New York: Random House)

Radin, M. J. (1991) 'Affirmative Action Rhetoric'. In E. F. Paul, J. Paul, and F. D. Miller, eds., *Reassessing Civil Rights* (Oxford: Basil Blackwell)

Radin, M. J. (1990) 'The Pragmatist and the Feminist', *Southern California Law Review* 63: 1699–726

Ramirez, A. (1988) 'Racism toward Hispanics: The Culturally Monolithic Society'. In P. A. Katz and D. A. Taylor, eds., *Eliminating Racism: Profiles in Controversy* (New York: Plenum Press)

Ranger, T. (1989) *Rhodes, Oxford, and the Study of Race Relations* (Oxford: Clarendon Press)

Rathzel, N. (1990) 'Germany: One Race, One Nation?', *Race and Class* 32, 3: 31–48

Rawls, J. (1971) *A Theory of Justice* (Cambridge: Harvard University Press)

Rawls, J. (1951) 'Outline of a Decision Procedure for Ethics', *The Philosophical Review* 60: 171–92

Reed, A. (1991) 'Steele Trap', *The Nation* (March 4): 274–81

Reed, A. (1988) 'The Liberal Technocrat', *The New Republic* (Feb. 6): 167–70

Reed, A. (1979) 'Black Particularity Revisited', *Telos* (Spring): 71–93

Reed, T. E. (1969) 'Caucasian Genes in American Negroes', *Science* 165 (August 22): 762–8

Reeve, A., ed. (1987) *Modern Theories of Exploitation* (London: Sage)

Reeves, F. (1983) *British Racial Discourse* (Cambridge: Cambridge University Press)

Reich, M. (1981) *Racial Inequality* (Princeton: Princeton University Press)

Reich, M. (1977) 'The Economics of Racism'. In D. Gordon, ed., *Problems in Political Economy,* 2nd ed. (Lexington, MA: D. C. Heath and Co.)

Reich, W. (1970) *The Mass Psychology of Fascism* (New York: Simon and Schuster)

Renan, E. (1990) 'What is a Nation?'. In H. Bhabha, ed., *Nation and Narration* (London: Routledge)

Rex, J. (1986) 'The Role of Class Analysis in the Study of Race Relations—A Weberian Approach'. In J. Rex and D. Mason, eds., *Theories of Race and Ethnic Relations* (Cambridge: Cambridge University Press)

Rex, J., ed. (1981) *Apartheid and Social Research* (New York: UNESCO Press)

Rex, J. and Mason, D., eds. (1986) *Theories of Race and Ethnic Relations* (Cambridge: Cambridge University Press)

Rex, J. and Tomlinson, S. (1979) *Colonial Immigrants in a British City* (London: Routledge and Kegan Paul)

Richards, J. R. (1985) 'Discrimination', *Proceedings of the Aristotelian Society: Supplement V* 59: 53–82

Richter, R. (1986) 'On Philips and Racism', *Canadian Journal of Philosophy* 16, 4 (December): 785–94

Ridgeway, J. (1990) 'Here He Comes, Mr. America', *The Village Voice* (October 9): 21

Rorty, R. (1991a) 'The Banality of Pragmatism and the Poetry of Justice'. In M. Brint and W. Weaver, eds., *Pragmatism in Law and Society* (Boulder, CO: Westview Press)

Rorty, R. (1991b) 'The Priority of Democracy to Philosophy'. In A. Malachowski, ed., *Reading Rorty* (Oxford: Basil Blackwell)

Rorty, R. (1991c) 'The Professor and the Prophet', *Transition* 52: 70–8

Rorty, R. (1983) 'Postmodernist Bourgeois Liberalism', *The Journal of Philosophy* 80 (October): 583–9

Rorty, R. (1982a) *Consequences of Pragmatism* (Minneapolis: University of Minnesota Press)

Rorty, R. (1982b) 'Method, Social Science, and Social Hope'. In R. Rorty, *Consequences of Pragmatism* (Minneapolis: University of Minnesota Press)

Rorty, R. (1980) *Philosophy and the Mirror of Nature* (Princeton: Princeton University Press)

Rose, A. (1976) *Demonic Vision* (Hamden, CT: Archon Books)

Rose, D. (1984) 'Rethinking Gentrification: Beyond the Uneven Development of Marxist Urban Theory', *Society and Space* 1: 47–74

Rosenberg, A. (1970) *Race and Race History,* R. Pois, ed. (New York: Harper and Row)

Rosenfeld, M. (1991) *Affirmative Action and Justice* (New Haven: Yale University Press)

Rousseau, G. S. and Porter, R., eds. (1989) *Exoticism in the Enlightenment* (Manchester: Manchester University Press)

Rousseau, J.-J. (1978) *Discourse on the Origin of Inequality* (New York: Pocket Books)

Rousseau, J.-J. (1968) *The Social Contract.* Trans. M. Cranston (London: Penguin Classics)

Rubin, W. (1984) 'Modernist Primitivism'. In W. Rubin, ed., *"Primitivism" in 20th Century Art: Affinity of the Tribal and the Modern* Vol. I (New York: Museum of Modern Art)

Rubin, W., ed. (1984) *"Primitivism" in 20th Century Art: Affinity of the Tribal and the Modern* Vols I and II (New York: Museum of Modern Art)

Ruddick, S. (1987) 'Remarks on the Sexual Politics of Reason'. In E. Kittay and D. Meyers, eds., *Women and Moral Philosophy* (Totowa, NJ: Rowman and Littlefield)

Rutherford, J., ed. (1990) *Identity: Community, Culture, Difference* (London: Lawrence and Wishart)

Ryan, A. (1984) 'Utility and Ownership'. In R. G. Frey, ed., *Utility and Rights* (Minneapolis: University of Minnesota Press)

Ryan, M. (1989) *Politics and Culture: Working Hypotheses for a Post-Revolutionary Society* (London: Macmillan)

Saenger, G. (1953) *The Social Psychology of Prejudice* (New York: Harper)

Sahlins, M. (1985) *Islands of History* (Chicago: University of Chicago Press)

Said, E. W. (1990) 'Zionism from the Standpoint of its Victims'. In D. T. Goldberg, ed., *Anatomy of Racism* (Minneapolis: University of Minnesota Press)

Said, E. W. (1980) 'The Problem of Textuality: Two Exemplary Positions' in *Aesthetics Today*, M. Philipson and P. Gudel, eds. (New York: Meridian Books)

Said, E. W. (1979a), 'Knowing the Oriental'. In E. W. Said, *Orientalism* (New York: Vintage Books)

Said, E. W. (1979b) *Orientalism* (New York: Vintage Books)

Sartre, J.-P. (1976) *Critique of Dialectical Reason.* Trans. A. Sheridan–Smith (London: New Left Books)

Scanlon, T. M. (1984) 'Contractualism and Utilitarianism'. In A. Sen and B. Williams, eds., *Utilitarianism and Beyond* (Cambridge: Cambridge University Press)

Seidel, G. (1986) *The Holocaust Denial: Anti-Semitism, Racism and the New Right* (Leeds: Beyond the Pale Collective)

Sen, A. (1985) 'Rationality and Uncertainty', *Theory and Decision* 18, 2: 109–27

Sennett, R. (1990) *The Conscience of the Eye* (New York: Alfred Knopf)

Shapiro, M. (1989) 'Politicizing Ulysses: Rationalistic, Critical, and Genealogical Commentaries', *Political Theory* 17, 1 (February): 9–32

Shapiro, M. (1981) *Language and Political Understanding* (New Haven: Yale University Press)

Shaw, J. W., Nordlie, P. G., and Shapiro, R. M., eds. (1987) *Strategies for Improving Race Relations: The Anglo-American Experience* (Manchester: Manchester University Press)

Sherwin-White, A. N. (1970) *Racial Prejudice in Imperial Rome* (Cambridge: Cambridge University Press)

Shue, H. (1988) 'Mediating Duties', *Ethics* 98 (July): 687–704

Shuey, A. (1965) *The Testing of Negro Intelligence* (New York: Social Science Press)

Sigelman, L. and Welch, S. (1991) *Black Americans' Views of Racial Inequality: The Dream Deferred* (Cambridge: Cambridge University Press)

Simone, T. M. (1989) *About Face: Race in Postmodern America* (New York: Autonomedia Press)

Simpson, G. and Yinger, J. (1953) *Racial and Cultural Minorities* (New York: Harper and Bros.)

Singer, M. (1978) 'Some Thoughts on Race and Racism', *Philosophia* 8, 2–3: 153–84

Singer, P.(1978) 'Is Racial Discrimination Arbitrary?' *Philosophia* 8, 2–3: 185–203

Singh, M. (1992) 'Transformation Time', *Transformation* 17: 48–60

Sivanandan, A. (1990) *Communities of Resistance* (London: Verso Books)

Sivanandan, A., ed. (1991) 'Europe: Variations on a Theme in Racism', *Race and Class* 32, 3: 1–158

Smith, A. (1978) *The Wealth of Nations* (London: Pelican)

Smith, J., Collins, J., Hopkins, T. K., and Muhammad, A., eds. (1988) *Racism, Sexism and the World System* (New York: Greenwood Press)

Smith, M. G. (1986) 'Pluralism, Race and Ethnicity in Selected African Countries'. In J. Rex and D. Mason, eds., *Theories of Race and Ethnic Relations* (Cambridge: Cambridge University Press)

Smith, O. (1984) *The Politics of Language, 1791–1804* (Oxford: The Clarendon Press)

Smith, P. (1988) *Discerning the Subject* (Minneapolis: University of Minnesota Press)

Smith, P. B. (1987) 'Group Process Methods of Intervention in Race Relations'. In J. W. Shaw, P. G., Nordlie, and R. M. Shapiro, eds., *Strategies for Improving Race Relations: The Anglo-American Experience* (Manchester: Manchester University Press)

Smith, S. J. (1992) 'Residential Segregation and the Politics of Racialization'. In M. Cross and M. Keith, eds., *Racism, the City, and the State,* (London: Routledge)

Smith, S. J. (1989) *The Politics of 'Race' and Residence: Citizenship, Segregation, and White Supremacy* (Oxford: Polity)

Smith, S. J. (1987) 'Residential Segregation: A Geography of English Racism?' In P. Jackson, ed., *Race and Racism: Essays in Social Geography* (London: Allen and Unwin)

Sollors, W. (1990) 'Ethnicity'. In F. Lentricchia and T. McLaughlin, eds., *Critical Terms for Literary Study* (Chicago: Chicago University Press)

Sollors, W. (1986) *Beyond Ethnicity: Consent and Descent in American Culture* (Oxford: Oxford University Press)

Solomos, J. (1989) *Race and Racism in Contemporary Britain* (London: Macmillan)

Solomos, J. (1986) 'Varieties of Marxist Conceptions of "Race," Class and the State: A Critical Analysis'. In J. Rex and D. Mason, eds., *Theories of Race and Ethnic Relations* (Cambridge: Cambridge University Press)

Sowell, T. (1990) *Preferential Policies: An International Perspective* (New York: William Morrow)

Sowell, T. (1984) *Civil Rights: Rhetoric or Reality?* (New York: William Morrow)

Sowell, T. (1981) *Markets and Minorities* (New York: Basic Books)

Sowell, T. (1975) *Race and Economics* (New York: David McKay)

Spelman, E. V. (1988) *Inessential Woman* (Boston: Beacon)

Steele, S. (1990) *The Content of Our Character: A New Vision of Race in America* (New York: St. Martin's Press)

Steinberg, S. (1989) 'The Underclass: A Case of Color Blindness', *New Politics* 2, 3 (Summer): 42–60

Stember, C. H. (1976) *Sexual Racism* (New York: Harper Colophon)

Stepan, N. L. (1990) 'Race and Gender: The Role of Analogy in Science'. In D. T. Goldberg, ed., *Anatomy of Racism* (Minneapolis: University of Minnesota Press)

Stepan, N. L. (1985) 'Biology and Degeneration: Races and Proper Places'. In J. E. Chamberlin and S. L. Gilman, eds., *Degeneration: The Dark Side of Progress* (New York: Columbia University Press)

Stepan, N. L. (1982) *The Idea of Race in Science: Great Britain, 1800–1960* (London: Macmillan)

Stepan, N. L. and Gilman, S. L. (1991) 'Appropriating the Idioms of Science: Rejecting Scientific Racism'. In D. LaCapra, ed., *The Bounds of Race: Perspectives on Hegemony and Resistance* (Ithaca: Cornell University Press)

Stephan, W. G. (1989) 'A Cognitive Approach to Stereotyping'. In D. Bar-Tal et al., eds., *Stereotyping and Prejudice: Changing Conceptions* (New York: Springer-Verlag)

Stephan, W. and Rosenfield, A. G. (1982) 'Racial and Ethnic Stereotypes'. In A. G. Miller, ed., *In the Eye of the Beholder* (New York: Praeger Publications)

Sterba, J., ed. (1980) *Justice: Alternative Political Perspectives* (Belmont, CA: Wadsworth)

Stocking, G., ed. (1985) *Objects and Others: Essays on Museums and Material Culture* (Madison: University of Wisconsin Press)

Stokes, E. (1959) *The English Utilitarians and India* (Oxford: The Clarendon Press)

Stren, R. (1972) 'Urban Policy in Africa: A Political Analysis', *African Studies Review* XV, 3 (December): 489–516

Stroebe, W. and. Insko, C. A. (1989) 'Stereotype, Prejudice, and Discrimination: Changing Conceptions in Theory and Research'. In D. Bar-Tal et al., eds., *Stereotyping and Prejudice: Changing Conceptions* (New York: Springer-Verlag)

Swanson, M. W. (1977) 'The Sanitation Syndrome: Bubonic Plague and Urban Native Policy in the Cape Colony, 1900–1909', *Journal of African History* XVIII, 3: 387–410

Swanson, M. W. (1968) 'Urban Origins of Separate Development', *Race* X: 31–40

Szymanski, A. (1985) 'The Structure of Race', *Review of Radical Political Economics* 17, 4: 106–20

Taguieff, P.-A. (1988) *La Force du Prejuge: Essai sur le Racism et ses Doubles* (Paris: La Decouverte)

Tajfel, H. (1973) 'The Roots of Prejudice: Cognitive Aspects'. In P. Watson, ed., *Psychology and Race* (Chicago: Aldine Press)

Taussig, M. (1987) *Shamanism, Colonialism and the Wild Man* (Chicago: University of Chicago Press)

Taylor, C. (1989) *Sources of the Self* (Cambridge: Harvard University Press)

Thalberg, I. (1972) 'Visceral Racism', *The Monist* 56 (January): 43–63

Therborn, G. (1980) *The Ideology of Power and the Power of Ideology* (London: Verso Books)

Thomas, L. (1993) 'Characterizing Evil: American Slavery and the Holocaust'. In D. T. Goldberg and M. Krausz, eds., *Culture and Jewish Identity* (Philadelphia: Temple University Press)

Thomas, L. (1983) 'Rationality and Moral Autonomy: An Essay in Moral Psychology', *Synthese* 57: 249–66

Thurow, L. (1969) *Poverty and Discrimination* (Washington, DC: Brookings Institute Press)

Tipps, D. (1973) 'Modernization Theory and the Comparative Study of Societies: A Critical Perspective', *Comparative Studies in Society and History* 15, 2: 119–226

Todorov, T. (1984) *The Conquest of America*. Trans. R. Howard (New York: Harper Colophon)

Torgovnick, M. (1990) *Gone Primitive: Savage Intellects, Modern Lives* (Chicago: University of Chicago Press)

Torres, G. (1991) 'Critical Race Theory: The Decline of the Universalist Ideal and the Hope of Plural Justice—Some Observations and Questions of an Emerging Phenomenon', *Minnesota Law Review* 75: 993–1007

Torres, G. (1988) 'Local Knowledge, Local Color: Critical Legal Studies and the Law of Race Relations', *San Diego Law Review* 25 (December): 1043–107

Torres, G. and Milun, K. (1990) 'Translating *Yonnondio* by Precedent and Evidence: The Mashpee Indian Case', *Duke Law Journal* 4 (September): 625–59

Triandis, H. C. (1988) 'The Future of Pluralism Revisited'. In P. A. Katz and D. A. Taylor, eds., *Eliminating Racism: Profiles in Controversy* (New York: Plenum Press)

Trillin, C. (1986) 'American Chronicles: Black or White', *New Yorker* (April 14): 62–78

UNESCO, ed. (1980) *Sociological Theories: Race and Colonialism* (Paris: UNESCO)

Urbach, P. (1974) 'Progress and Degeneration in the IQ Debate (1)', *British Journal of the Philosophy of Science* 25: 99–135

Van den Berghe, P. (1986) 'Ethnicity and the Sociobiology Debate'. In J. Rex and D. Mason, eds., *Theories of Race and Ethnic Relations* (Cambridge: Cambridge University Press)

Van den Berghe, P. (1981) *The Ethnic Phenomenon* (New York: Elsevier)

Van den Berghe, P. (1967) *Race and Racism: A Comparative Perspective* (New York: John Wiley)

Van Dyck, A. (1634) *Henrietta of Lorraine* (Paris: Museé de l'Ecole Superiéure des Beaux-Arts)

Varnedoe, K. (1984a) 'Contemporary Explorations'. In W. Rubin, ed., *"Primitivism" in 20th Century Art: Affinity of the Tribal and the Modern* Vol. II (New York: Museum of Modern Art)

Varnedoe, K. (1984b) 'Gauguin'. In W. Rubin, ed., *"Primitivism" in 20th Century Art: Affinity of the Tribal and the Modern* Vol. I (New York: Museum of Modern Art)

Voltaire, F. (1901) *The Works of Voltaire,* W. F. Fleming, ed. (New York)

Wade, E. L. (1985) 'The Ethnic Market in the American Southwest'. In G. Stocking, ed., *Objects and Others: Essays on Museums and Material Culture* (Madison: University of Wisconsin Press)

Wagner, R. (1975) *The Invention of Culture* (Englewood Cliffs, NJ: Prentice–Hall)

Wallerstein, I. (1988) 'The Ideological Tensions of Capitalism: Universalism versus Racism and Sexism'. In J. Smith et al., eds., *Racism, Sexism and the World System* (New York: Greenwood Press)

Wallerstein, I. (1983) *Historical Capitalism* (London: Verso)

Warnock, M., ed. (1974) *Utilitarianism* (New York: Fontana)

Warren, M. A. (1973) 'On the Moral and Legal Status of Abortion', *The Monist* 57, 1 (January): 43–61

Wasserstrom, R. (1978) 'On Racism and Sexism'. In R. Wasserstrom, ed., *Today's Moral Problems* (New York: Macmillan)

Weinreich, P. (1985) 'Rationality and Irrationality in Racial and Ethnic Relations: A Metatheoretical Framework', *Ethnic and Racial Studies* 8, 4 (October): 500–15

Weinroth, J. (1979) 'Nation and Race: Two Destructive Concepts', *Philosophy Forum* 16: 67–86

West, C. (1990) 'The New Cultural Political Of Difference'. In Ferguson et al., eds., *Out There: Marginalization and Contemporary Cultures* (Cambridge: MIT Press)

West, C. (1989) *The American Evasion of Philosophy: A Genealogy of Pragmatism* (Madison: University of Wisconsin Press)

West, C. (1982) *Prophesy Deliverance: An Afro-American Revolutionary Christianity* (Philadelphia: Westminster)

Western, J. (1981) *Outsider Cape Town* (Minneapolis: University of Minnesota Press)

Wetherall, W. (1987) 'Pride and Sometimes Prejudice in Japan', *Far Eastern Economic Review* 138 (October): 52–54

Williams, B. (1985) *Ethics and the Limits of Philosophy* (Cambridge: Harvard University Press)

Williams, E. A. (1985) 'Art and Artifact at the Trocadero: *Ars Americana* and the Primitivist Revolution'. In G. Stocking, ed., *Objects and Others: Essays on Museums and Material Culture* (Madison: University of Wisconsin Press)

Williams, P. J. (1991) *The Alchemy of Race and Rights: Diary of a Law Professor* (Cambridge: Harvard University Press)

Williams, P. J. (1987) 'Alchemical Notes: Reconstructed Ideals from Deconstructed Rights', *Harvard Civil Rights–Civil Liberties Review* 22, 2 (Spring): 401–34

Williams, R. (1985) 'Interview', *Society and Space* 2: 369–74

Williams, R. (1983) *Keywords* (London: Fontana)

Williams, W. (1982) *The State Against Blacks* (New York: McGraw–Hill)

Wilson, B., ed. (1970) *Rationality* (Oxford: Basil Blackwell)

Wilson, E. O. (1975) *Sociobiology* (Cambridge: Belknap Press)

Wilson, J. Q. and Herrnstein, R. (1985) *Crime and Human Nature* (New York: Simon and Schuster)

Wilson, W. J. (1991a) 'The Truly Disadvantaged Revisited: A Response to Hochschild and Boxill', *Ethics* 101 (April): 593–609

Wilson, W. J. (1991b) 'Studying Inner City Social Dislocations: The Challenge of Public Agenda Research', *American Sociological Review* 56 (February): 1–14

Wilson, W. J. (1987) *The Truly Disadvantaged: The Inner City, the Underclass, and Public Policy* (Chicago: Chicago University Press)

Winant, H. (1990) 'Postmodern Racial Politics in the United States: Difference and Inequality', *Socialist Review* 20, 1 (January–March): 121–47

Wolf, E. (1981) *Europe and the People Without History* (Berkeley: University of California Press)

Wolpe, H. (1986) 'Class Concepts, Class Struggle and Racism'. In J. Rex and D. Mason, eds., *Theories of Race and Ethnic Relations* (Cambridge: Cambridge University Press)

Wolpe, H. (1972) 'Capitalism and Cheap Labor Power in South Africa: From Segregation to Apartheid', *Economy and Society* I, 4: 425–56

Woodiwiss, A. (1990) *Social Theory after Postmodernism: Rethinking Production, Law and Class* (London: Pluto Press)

Worsley, P. (1984) *The Three Worlds* (London: Weidenfeld and Nicolson)

Wright, E. O. (1989) 'A General Framework for the Analysis of Class Structure'. In E. O. Wright et al., *The Debate on Classes* (New York: Verso)

Wright, E. O., et al. (1989) *The Debate on Classes* (New York: Verso)

Wuthnow, R. (1982) 'Anti-Semitism and Stereotyping'. In A. G. Miller, ed., *In the Eye of the Beholder* (New York: Praeger Publications)

Young, I. (1988) 'Five Faces of Oppression', *The Philosophical Forum* XIX, 4 (Summer): 270–90

Young, R. (1990) *White Mythologies: Writing History and the West* (London: Routledge)

Zegeye, A., Harris, L., and Maxted, J., eds. (1991) *Exploitation and Exclusion: Race and Class in Contemporary US Society* (Oxford: Hans Zell)

Zubaida, S., ed. (1970) *Race and Racialism* (London: Tavistock)

Index

Index